Sisters and Workers
in the Middle Ages

Sisters and Workers in the Middle Ages

EDITED BY
Judith M. Bennett, Elizabeth A. Clark,
Jean F. O'Barr, B. Anne Vilen,
and Sarah Westphal-Wihl

The University of Chicago Press
Chicago and London

On the cover: Silk women collecting cocoons and weaving cloth, MS
Royal 16GV fol. 542. By permission of the British Library.

The essays in this volume originally appeared in various issues of SIGNS:
JOURNAL OF WOMEN IN CULTURE AND
SOCIETY. Acknowledgment of the original publication date can be found on the
first page of each essay.

The University of Chicago Press, Chicago 60637
The University of Chicago Press, Ltd., London
© 1976, 1980, 1982, 1987, 1989 by The University of Chicago
All rights reserved. Published 1989
Printed in the United States of America
93 92 91 90 89 5 4 3 2 1

Library of Congress Cataloging-in-Publication Data

Sisters and workers in the Middle Ages / edited by Judith M. Bennett . . . [et al.].

p. cm.

Includes bibliographies and indexes.
ISBN 0-226-04247-2 (alk. paper) : $30.00 (est.). —ISBN
0-226-04248-0 (pbk. : alk. paper) : $15.00 (est.)
1. Women—History—Middle Ages, 500–1500. 2. Monastic and religious life
of women—History—Middle Ages, 600–1500. 3. Women—Employment—
Europe—History. 4. Sex role—Europe—History.
I. Bennett, Judith M.
HD1143.S55 1989
305.4'09'02—dc20

89-9137
CIP

The paper used in this publication meets the minimum
requirements of American National Standard for Information Sciences—
Permanence of Paper for Printed Library Materials, ANSI Z39.48-1984.♾

CONTENTS

1   **Introduction**

Maryanne Kowaleski   11   **Crafts, Gilds, and Women in the Middle Ages:**
and Judith M. Bennett   Fifty Years after Marian K. Dale

Monica Green   39   **Women's Medical Practice and Health Care in
Medieval Europe**

James A. Brundage   79   **Prostitution in the Medieval Canon Law**

Ruth Mazo Karras   100   **The Regulation of Brothels in Later Medieval
England**

Susan Groag Bell   135   **Medieval Women Book Owners:** Arbiters of Lay
Piety and Ambassadors of Culture

Sarah Westphal-Wihl   162   ***The Ladies' Tournament:*** Marriage, Sex, and Honor
in Thirteenth-Century Germany

Michael H. Shank   190   **A Female University Student in Late Medieval
Kraków**

Ross S. Kraemer   198   **The Conversion of Women to Ascetic Forms of
Christianity**

Jane Tibbetts   208   **Women's Monastic Communities, 500–1100:**
Schulenburg   Patterns of Expansion and Decline

Carol Neel   240   **The Origins of the Beguines**

Mary Martin   261   **Creating and Recreating Communities of
McLaughlin   Women:** The Case of Corpus Domini, Ferrara,
1406–1452

289   **About the Contributors**

293   **Index**

ACKNOWLEDGMENTS

Many people have contributed their efforts to this collection. We wish to thank in particular those who have diligently checked citations, assisted in proofreading, and gathered various and sundry other bits of information that have brought this book to fruition: Alice Poffinberger, Connie Pearcy, Leisy Thornton, and especially Jill Petty, who compiled the index. Finally, we greatly appreciate the kind and helpful consultations of Elaine Tuttle Hansen, Maryanne Kowaleski, and Susan Mosher Stuard.

As feminists we struggle daily to free ourselves from the limiting perspectives of our own experiences and cultures. Although we quite rightly tend to think about this struggle in contemporary terms, it also properly includes a chronological element, an awareness of the differences and uniquenesses imposed by the passage of time. After all, the history of women did not begin with the fight for suffrage or the emergence of industrial society. The articles in this collection discuss women who are far from our everyday experiences and thoughts—ordinary women who worked in urban crafts, prostitution, and medical care; elite women who collected books, sought higher education, and lived in feudal courts; and women religious who gathered together in ascetic communities, monasteries, and beguinages. Nevertheless, in revealing commonalities as well as contrasts to our own struggles and times, the experiences of these women document a rich history of women's historical agency within the constraints of patriarchy.

As commonly used, the term "Middle Ages" identifies the millennium of Western history that stretches from the decline of Rome (ca. 500 C.E.) to the development of modern nation states (ca. 1500 C.E.). The essays in this volume cover a slightly broader historical range, beginning with a study of women's conversions to Christianity in the late years of the Roman Empire and running to the threshold of the modern age. With great changes occurring over the centuries and great differences dividing regions, this medieval millennium was not a single homogeneous culture, and it certainly did not produce any single type of "medieval woman." Although we regret the absence in this collection of articles on such groups as peasant women, Jewish women, and single women, we hope that the variety of subjects examined in this volume will emphasize for readers the broad diversity of women's experiences in the Middle Ages. As sisters and workers, medieval women lived consecrated lives and productive lives, carving spaces for themselves within the defining structures of their families (monastic and residential as well as biological) and their economic opportunities.

In the late nineteenth century, some pioneering feminist scholars took up the challenge of studying medieval women. Their now
often-overlooked efforts are acknowledged in this collection by the
reprinting of Marian K. Dale's study of London silkworkers, originally published in 1932. The dominant question that guided this
early research on medieval women (and indeed much subsequent
research) focuses on the status of women: Was the Middle Ages a
golden age of rough-and-ready equality for women, as argued by
Eileen Power in 1926, or was it a dark age of patriarchal oppression
and restraint?[1] The more we study medieval women, the more
subtle and nuanced our answers become. For although people in
the Middle Ages did revere powerful political women (such as
Eleanor of Aquitaine), influential intellectual women (such as
Hildegard of Bingen), and women renowned for their religiosity
and sanctity (such as Catherine of Alexandria), many medieval
women were constrained by the male-dominated institutions of the
age.

For medievalists, then, the task of assessing women's status in
the Middle Ages is a complex and ongoing one. The various
methodologies and criteria used by scholars, including those who
contributed to this collection, to recover the experiences of medieval women have led to many different interpretations and conclusions. This diversity is both proper and exciting, for eventually it
will enable us to talk with sophistication and precision about the
multiplicity of women's experiences in the Middle Ages—about the
implications of differences in class, occupation, marital status,
ethnicity, and sexual preference, about changes over time, and
about the many conflicting images of and ideas about women that
circulated during the medieval millennium. The articles in this
particular volume reflect this diversity by examining, on the one
hand, the nature of the patriarchal structures that constrained the
lives of women, and on the other, the expression of women's agency
within these constraints, especially in the formation of sustained,
strong, autonomous communities.

One of the greatest constraints upon medieval women was
economic. For women engaged in a religious life, success often
depended not only upon access to economic resources (for the
endowment of the original community) but also upon the ability to
generate income (for ongoing expenses). As Jane Tibbetts Schulenburg shows in her study of women's monastic communities,

---

[1]Eileen Power, "The Position of Women," in *Legacy of the Middle Ages*, ed. C.
G. Crump and E. F. Jacob (1926; reprint, New York: Oxford University Press, 1943),
410.

changing patterns of patronage in the early Middle Ages slowly aggravated the imbalance between numbers of male and female monasteries. And, as Mary Martin McLaughlin suggests in her study of the slow institutionalization of the female community of Corpus Domini in the fifteenth century, when patronage for female communities was forthcoming, it often came with strings attached. Moreover, once a female monastery was established through patronage, its nuns often faced such severe restrictions that they were unable to manage their endowments successfully. Schulenburg demonstrates how the monastic reforms of the tenth and eleventh centuries, with their emphasis on strict enclosure for women, contributed further to the economic woes and dependency of female monasteries. Carol Neel's study of beguines illustrates one way in which women avoided this dependency: since beguines were not officially recognized or regulated by the Church, they were better able than were regular monastic women to support themselves and their charitable operations through productive labor.

The lives of secular women also were shaped profoundly by economic power and economic opportunity. Working women found that their efforts to support themselves were hedged about both by male denigration of women's occupations and by women's seeming inability to secure better working conditions. Prostitutes, as described by both James Brundage's study of canon law and Ruth Mazo Karras's study of English brothels, worked in a trade that they themselves did not control. Townswomen, as shown by Maryanne Kowaleski and Judith M. Bennett in their introduction to Dale's study of London silkworkers, faced very severe restrictions on their abilities to receive skilled training and, if trained, to hold skilled work. Female medical practitioners, too, as suggested in Monica Green's essay, encountered energetic competition from men interested in the profits of gynecological care. Even elite women, who enjoyed the considerable economic privileges of their social rank, suffered relative economic deprivation; in this collection, Sarah Westphal-Wihl's essay on *The Ladies' Tournament* emphasizes the constraints of the dowry system on these women.

In some instances, men clearly sought to benefit from women's lack of economic power. The Southwark ordinances discussed by Karras starkly illustrate how intervention in prostitutes' trade helped the territorial lord, the Bishop of Winchester, to consolidate his political power. For example, by prohibiting women from living in the stews (as the brothels were called), the bishop was able to assert his power over stewholders by making them franchisers within his monopoly rather than independent rent-payers. As discussed by

Kowaleski and Bennett, various guild ordinances—especially those that legislated against the work (and hence, the competition) of women–show the direct benefits of male economic privilege.

Even an expanding economy did not substantially alter the economic disabilities of women. Over the course of the Middle Ages (and especially after the eleventh century), trade expanded, specialization increased, and towns grew. Although the medieval economy always remained primarily rural, the economy of urban areas became increasingly important. The effects upon women of these economic developments (and the consequent development of a rural/urban dichotomy) need to be examined much more carefully. What we know thus far, however, suggests that these economic changes altered the specific experiences of some women but did not significantly alter men's economic power over women generally. For example, the complexion of women's monasticism began to change dramatically with the flourishing of city life from the twelfth century onward. As both Neel and McLaughlin demonstrate, women instrumental in the formation of women's religious communities from the twelfth through mid-fifteenth centuries often came from the newly prosperous urban middle classes. The communities they founded—such as beguinages or informal communities like the original Corpus Domini—were less structured than female monasteries in the early Middle Ages. But these urban women faced economic challenges similar to those of early medieval women religious; their communities were often poorly endowed, and their abilities to generate income were limited.

Familial obligations also constrained the lives of medieval women. Although the essays in this collection are not about families per se (whatever that term may have meant to medieval people), the theme of familial responsibility emerges with persistence and force. Many medieval women doubtless found much comfort and joy in their families—the intimacy of marital affection, the satisfaction of childrearing, the comfort of parents and siblings. Indeed, some of the pleasures of family life can be seen in the patterns of mother-daughter book owning traced by Susan Groag Bell. Yet, familial obligations and familial ideology also limited women's options. Schulenburg suggests that the establishment of new women's monasteries began to decline after the seventh century because such establishments no longer suited the family strategies of elite women and their relations. Westphal-Wihl describes an aristocratic debate about honor that ascribes men's honor to public action and women's honor to familial passivity and faithfulness. Kowaleski and Bennett show how the familial responsibilities of medieval townswomen often precluded full involvement in guilds and guild-supervised work.

The medieval writings explored in this collection suggest that medieval people were aware of familial constraints upon at least some women. Women like the convert Thecla, whose story is explicated by Ross Kraemer, appear to have recognized that the ascetic life offered a life free of marriage and childbearing. The story reported by Michael Shank of a woman who dressed as a man in order to acquire a university education in late medieval Krakow illustrates a similar awareness that the standard familial roles of daughter, wife, and mother limited the opportunities of women. These stories may or may not describe the actual experiences of historical persons, but they nevertheless reveal an ongoing discussion in the Middle Ages that questioned the idea of an exclusively familial role for women. Certainly, some historical women—such as the early beguines described by Neel, who tried to avoid the marriages planned by their parents—sought alternatives to expected familial roles.

Ideological understandings of women's proper roles were a third force that defined the experiences of medieval women. With its focus on late antiquity, Kraemer's study provides crucial insights into ideas about women that would persist throughout the Middle Ages. Kraemer shows that women were defined by social roles that prescribed heterosexuality, concluding that "to be a woman is to be a wife" (202). This notion was so strong that Thecla's conversion story reports that she was sentenced to death not because she succumbed to a sorcerer (as Paul of Tarsus was called by her community) but because she refused to marry. Throughout the Middle Ages, the proper fate of secular women was marriage alone: it can be seen in the plight of the dowryless maiden in *The Ladies' Tournament*, in pressure on Mary of Oignies and other beguines to marry, and in guild regulations that subsumed female labor into the labor of their husbands.

Even though early converts to Christianity rejected the idea that "to be a woman is to be a wife," women's religious experiences were described in terms of marriage and sexuality. In the early Christian centuries, female converts "married" Jesus, and throughout the Middle Ages, nuns described their mystical experiences in terms of marriage to and sexual union with Jesus. Thus, even in the context of Christian asceticism and monasticism, a woman was a wife—she was just spiritually rather than carnally married. The story of *The Ladies' Tournament*, too, only superficially challenged established roles for women. It tells of women fighting in a tournament with great bravery, of women freely taking the names of favored men, of women speculating about a life separate from men and family. Yet it ends when the bravest female fighter is finally married, an outcome that fully reaffirms women's familial roles.

The history of medieval women, then, is in part a history of the constraints of economic disadvantage, familial duty, and prescribed social roles. But it is also in part a history of women's agency within and against these constraints. Some women clearly sought alternatives that challenged patriarchal norms—the female converts to Christian asceticism, the cross-dressed woman at Krakow University, doubtless some beguines and nuns, and perhaps some prostitutes. These sisters and workers did not, as far as we know, explicitly criticize the sexual politics of their world, but they took action to avoid, alter, or minimize the constraints that were placed upon them as women. Like one of the greatest female saints of the Middle Ages, Jeanne d'Arc, they sought new social roles in which they could, as women, find greater power and satisfaction.

Many of these women sought out the company of their own sex to sustain themselves economically, spiritually, and intellectually within religious or secular communities that were better able to withstand the pressures of patriarchal oppression. In most cases their communities were more informal and transitory than the comparable communities of men. The women who worked in the London silk trade formed a loosely structured association; men in similar crafts formed guilds with firm charters, firm regulations, and firm structures. Women religious often sought relatively unorganized and informal forms of association (like the beguines who gathered around Mary of Oignies or the women who joined Bernardina Sedazzari); men were more likely to form communities that were not only religious but also clearly linked to the organized Church. Medical treatment of women, long handled informally by generations of women who privately passed on their craft, slowly became part of the expertise claimed by formally educated, licensed physicians. Even the fictive tournament of ladies was more ephemeral and informal than the male associations it mimicked.

Although most of these communities were comparatively informal and shortlived, community structures allowed many women to shape their lives in inspiring, if humble, ways. For example, as McLaughlin explains, Lucia Mascheroni, the heiress to the founder of Corpus Domini, found herself caught in an impossible situation: although she wished to maintain the independence of her religious community, she eventually was forced to forfeit its autonomy in order to ensure its continuity. Although our sources suggest that she was perhaps mercurial and instable in temperament, they also show that she was a loyal friend of her benefactress, that she nurtured the community left in her charge through many difficult years, and that she inspired love and devotion from her sisters. Lucia Mascheroni's hopes for Corpus Domini eventually fell victim to the imperatives of the patriarchal Church, but she lived courageously, full of faith and vision. Doubtless many other medieval women—from guilds-women to prostitutes to abbesses and queens—demonstrated similar dignity and courage.

Indeed, women's communities often actively contributed to the sustenance and expansion of medieval society. As Schulenburg's study shows, women's assistance was often particularly welcome at times of social upheaval or crisis; in the seventh century, when the Church's authority was weak and tenuous, the missionary activity of religious women was a welcomed and encouraged part of Christian life. As a result, the early medieval Church was built by both men and women. Yet, as the Church became securer in later centuries, women religious were increasingly seen more as liabilities than as resources for the Church. As a result, new foundations of women's monasteries were fewer, and all women's foundations were poorer and less powerful than in earlier centuries. Whenever the opportunity for full religious life was available to women, they responded with great enthusiasm and in relatively large numbers. Whenever these opportunities contracted, women persevered not only by pressuring the Church for greater acceptance but also by building extra-ecclesiastical communities, such as the beguinages of the thirteenth century.

Collectively, women also shaped the cultural milieu of medieval times. Bell's study of female book owners shows that elite women played a crucial role by carrying books (and ideas) across regions, bringing the culture of their parents' homes to the homes of their husbands. As mothers, moreover, they undertook responsibility for the literary and moral education of their children, selecting and using favored texts. And, as pious women, many of whom were unable to read Latin, they encouraged the development of vernacular devotional literature, thus contributing to the growth of the popular religious ideas that underlay the Reformation.

The literary and artistic texts these women read and distributed also sometimes challenged the apparent permanence of what medieval society considered a woman to be. The manuscript illuminations of the reading Virgin, described by Bell, not only advanced the standard ideals of female piety and chastity but also suggested that women—at least those with social and economic privilege—might have had extensive and distinctive relations with literature and literary production. Similarly, the medieval stories described by Westphal-Wihl and Shank—about jousting women and a woman who dresses as a man in order to attend university—suggest alternatives for women, even though their endings reassert social norms. In so doing, they reveal how literary and artistic representations of women both reflect and reject a patriarchal "reality."

Thus, these representations suggest the importance for any discussion of medieval women of addressing the relationship between extant sources and the lived experiences of women. In this volume the authors examine women's lives through the documentation found in land charters, spiritual memoirs, saints' *vitae*, civic codes, medical treatises, literary texts, and many other sources. Although these materials are richly diverse, none of them can be read as straightforwardly informative. Indeed, they suggest that the relation between medieval texts and the lives of medieval women ranges from nearly opaque to nearly transparent. Karras, for example, finds that we can only speculatively infer information about the lives of medieval prostitutes from the written restrictions that controlled their lives. Kraemer, similarly, notes that her examination of conversion narratives is "admittedly and consciously speculative" (p. 199). Green also observes the absence of testimony from women patients, yet, she claims, the ancient topos of female modesty may actually have served women's interests in providing them a rationale "to *make* women's health women's business" (74). Neel, more optimistic than these three authors, finds that some saints' lives, though written by men, reveal the "experiences and aspirations" of their women subjects (260). And McLaughlin ends her reconstruction of the community of Corpus Domini with a note of promise, calling for future studies that will, like hers, revise the "perhaps overly pessimistic judgment" that we cannot know what women thought and felt (218).

Our difficulty in deciphering the relation between the actual and the symbolic acknowledges the contradictions within medieval ideology itself. Medievalists have long recognized that the notion of woman as Eve—an evil, corrupting figure, associated with exile and death—existed side-by-side with the notion of woman as the Virgin Mary—a virtuous, purifying figure, associated with birth and salvation—and that this contradiction was central to medieval discourse on women. This double bind both constrained women's lives within oppressive patriarchal structures and offered sites of resistance, gaps—in texts as well as in society—wherein women could imagine and implement change.

Medieval ideology was especially contradictory in its views of women's sexuality. It stipulated that all women should be wives (and presumably mothers) of either men or Jesus, and in this way women's sexuality was accepted for its reproductive value (and sometimes redirected to religious ends). But women's sexuality was also a powerful and fearful thing. As exemplified in Brundage's reconstruction of the ideas of canonists about female sexuality, medieval people believed that women were always eager for sexual intercourse, inconstant by nature, and quickly yielding to stray desire. (Men, in contrast, were believed to boast a sexuality that was more mature, more controlled, and more contained.) Women were at the same time expected—as daughters, as wives, as widows, as nuns—to exhibit greater sexual self-control than men, but they were nevertheless suspected of failing to exhibit that control. As seen in the fabliaux and their German analogue, the Mären, discussed by Westphal-Wihl, wives were accused of using all manner of wiles to cuckold their husbands. As discussed by Schulenburg, nuns were sometimes charged with "whoredom" and consequently evicted from their monasteries, which were then sometimes appropriated by male orders. And, as Karras and Brundage tell us, prostitutes were assumed to be acting in accordance with the uncontrollable sexual nature of women, but they were nevertheless segregated as far as possible from other women, lest "contamination" occur.

One example of medieval society's contradictory expectations of women can be seen by comparing the canonists' relatively tolerant discussions of prostitutes to the much more severe civil codes of the same period. According to Brundage, the canonists claimed that prostitutes should be dealt with "rather leniently," whereas prostitutes' customers should be "subject to stringent repressive measures." Yet the actual way in which prostitutes were treated, as described by both Brundage and Karras, belies the benevolence of the canonists. Prostitutes could not inherit property; they could not sue in a court of law; they often could not seek redress for rape; they could not always protect themselves from beatings, forced work, undue debts; they suffered distinctive dress, tight curfews, and religious censure. Their male clients, who (according to the canonists) deserved strict punishment, were in actuality treated quite lightly. Some men, especially lay bachelors, could visit prostitutes with complete impunity, and prohibitions against brothel-visiting by other men—especially clerics and married men—were, Karras tells us, not well enforced. The teachings of the canonists suggested a new toleration of prostitutes; the actual regulation of the trade marginalized and stigmatized them.

Contradictory expectations of women within any single ideology clearly are not unique to medieval times—indeed, this is only one of many parallels that scholars of women's experiences in other time periods may draw from these essays. This central paradox both shaped the lives of medieval women and allowed medieval women themselves to shape, to some extent, the content of their own experiences. It also has allowed scholars to interpret these ideologies and experiences in positive, negative, and ambivalent ways. Any single interpretation belies the multidimensionality of medieval women's lives, just as any single scholarly definition of "woman" belies the diverse, indeed, contradictory notions of "woman" held by medieval people. Thus, the essays collected here broaden and deepen our perspectives not only on the contribution of medievalists to women's history but also on the nature of women's lives within the Middle Ages. In adding our voices to those of other feminist scholars who are altering the patriarchal and antifeminist traditions of academia, we hope to honor sisters and workers throughout our collective history.

CRAFTS, GILDS, AND WOMEN IN THE MIDDLE AGES: FIFTY YEARS AFTER MARIAN K. DALE

MARYANNE KOWALESKI AND JUDITH M. BENNETT

Of the many forms of community life in the Middle Ages, urban gilds were among the most common and most influential. Gilds joined together persons engaged in the same trade or craft for their mutual economic, social, and religious benefit.[1] As a rule, only persons involved in skilled work, merchants or artisans, formed gilds, and they controlled access to their work through these organizations. Only members of a gild could engage in the trade or craft supervised by that gild. Although the main purpose of merchant or craft gilds was economic (they provided training for apprentices, regulated wages and prices, and stipulated trade practices and quality), they also exercised important social, religious, and charitable functions. They held annual feasts, buried the dead, cared for the families of deceased members, and participated in religious processions. Gilds often accrued political clout as well; in many towns, membership in certain gilds was a prerequisite to civic enfranchisement.[2]

---

[1] In addition to merchant and craft gilds, other gilds joined together persons for religious benefit (parish gilds) or social purposes (drinking confraternities).

[2] The literature on gilds is vast and often contentious. Introductions to the subject may be found in Sylvia L. Thrupp, "The Gilds," in *The Cambridge Economic History*

This essay originally appeared in *Signs*, vol. 14, no. 2, Winter 1989.

The treatment of working women by medieval gilds is a complex and varied story. On the one hand, gilds can be seen as positive forces in women's lives. Gild membership allowed women to participate in a vital form of community life that offered its members economic security, spiritual comfort, and social privilege. No doubt, many townswomen enthusiastically sought gild privileges, and insofar as they were successful, they enjoyed a type of community unique to their urban milieu; gilds and their privileges were seldom part of the lives of either peasant women or women of noble birth. On the other hand, the history of working women and gilds is often a disheartening tale. First, most trades and crafts were dominated by men, and the gilds formed by these occupations tended to treat women as second-class workers and second-class members. Second, most "women's work" in medieval towns was either too low-skilled or too low-status to merit a gild. Most women in medieval towns worked as domestic servants, petty retailers, spinsters, midwives, prostitutes, and the like, all occupations never recognized as skilled, much less organized into gilds.[3] Third, even skilled women's occupations often failed to organize into gilds. This is the situation described by Marian K. Dale in the study of the silkworkers of London presented here; although they worked at skilled and valued tasks, they never gathered together into a gild.[4] Despite some notable exceptions—particularly the few female-dominated gilds found in Rouen, Paris, and Cologne—most skilled "women's work" never came under gild structure and supervision. The silkworkers of Lon-

of Europe, ed. M. M. Postan, E. E. Rich, and Edward Miller (Cambridge: Cambridge University Press, 1963), 3:230–80; Émile Coornaert, Les corporations en France avant 1789 (Paris: Gallimard, 1968); George Unwin, The Gilds and Companies of London (London: George Allen & Unwin, 1938); Stella Kramer, The English Craft Gilds (New York: Columbia University Press, 1927); Charles Gross, The Gild Merchant (Oxford: Clarendon Press, 1890); Toulmin Smith and Lucy Toulmin Smith, eds., English Gilds, Early English Text Society 40 (London: Oxford University Press, 1870), esp. Lujo Brentano's "Preliminary Essay," xlix–cxcix.

[3] For the prevalence of this type of work in medieval English towns, see Rodney Hilton, "Women Traders in Medieval England," in Class Conflict and the Crisis of Feudalism (London: Hambledon, 1985), 205–15; Maryanne Kowaleski, "Women's Work in a Market Town: Exeter in the Late Fourteenth Century," in Women and Work in Preindustrial Europe, ed. Barbara A. Hanawalt (Bloomington: Indiana University Press, 1986), 145–64. See also Judith Brown's theories about the Florentine sexual division of labor (which placed women in less skilled occupations), in "A Woman's Place Was in the Home: Women's Work in Renaissance Tuscany," in Rewriting the Renaissance, ed. Margaret Ferguson, Maureen Quilligan, and Nancy J. Vickers (Chicago: University of Chicago Press, 1986), 206–24.

[4] Marian K. Dale, "The London Silkwomen of the Fifteenth Century," Economic History Review, 1st ser., 4 (1933): 324–35.

don, then, provide one example of a general trend. Their story is both specific to their own situation and exemplary of the experiences of all; for most medieval townswomen, gilds were male communities in which women had little or no role.

In most towns, gilds formed in the High and later Middle Ages. Merchant gilds organized first, usually in the twelfth and thirteenth centuries, and craft gilds followed, usually within a few generations.[5] By the fourteenth century, most urban trades and industries were organized and regulated by gilds. Although gilds included all members of a trade or craft, they were not egalitarian. Only the "masters" of a gild could maintain workshops, hire apprentices and other workers, and participate in gild politics and decisions.[6] Usually masters were also the only gild members allowed to wear the full "livery," the distinctive dress or badge of each gild. Subject to the control of masters were trained wage workers, called journeymen or journeywomen, whose wages, working hours, social obligations, and gild privileges were set by the masters and their elected officers. At the bottom of the gild hierarchy were apprentices, adolescents indentured to a master of the gild for a period of about seven years. Masters provided room, board, and training to their apprentices, and when the term of service ended, they sponsored their apprentices' formal admission to the gild as journeymen or journeywomen.

Since most medieval crafts and trades were dominated by men, the institutions that structured their work—craft and merchant gilds—were also male dominated. The treatment of women within such gilds varied considerably according to time, place, and occupation, but women were seldom full members.[7] In many trades, young

[5] The history of gild formation varies tremendously from town to town. Most of the early merchant gilds included traders who received privileges from local lords, such as freedom from toll or trade monopolies. As commerce intensified and specialized in subsequent decades, traders often divided into separate gilds. Many of these specialized merchant gilds survived into the later Middle Ages as the "greater" gilds of their towns, endowed with more prestige, wealth, and power than the "lesser" craft gilds. The exact origin of craft gilds and their relationship to merchant gilds is a matter of considerable debate among medievalists (see n. 2 above). In general, it is agreed that they formed at a later date than merchant gilds, that they were often born of political and economic conflict with merchants, and that they eventually outlived merchant gilds.

[6] "Master" is the term for men and "mistress" the equivalent for women; we use "master" generically in this essay because to do otherwise would imply greater female involvement in gilds than was actually the case. As is argued throughout this essay, there were very, very few gild mistresses.

[7] The complex history of women in craft gilds has not been at the forefront of scholarship on gilds, urban work, or indeed women in the Middle Ages. For the

women were accepted as apprentices under terms of service identical to young male apprentices, but their numbers were extremely small compared to those of men. Furthermore, the gilds they entered usually centered on the textile trades, and more often than not the master's wife, rather than the master himself, took responsibility for their training. When female apprentices finished their training, moreover, they seldom became fully independent journeywomen; instead they usually remained with their masters until they married.[8] There is no female parallel in popular literature to the familiar figure of the itinerant, carousing, bachelor journeyman or apprentice.[9]

Once married, a woman often obtained new gild privileges. Wives of gild masters could work alongside their husbands, and they some-

English evidence on women in gilds, see A. Abram, "Women Traders in Medieval London," *Economic Journal* 26, no. 2 (1916): 276–85; Sylvia L. Thrupp, *The Merchant Class of Medieval London, 1300–1500* (Ann Arbor: University of Michigan Press, 1948), 169–74; Levi Fox, "The Coventry Guilds and Trading Companies with Special Reference to the Position of Women," in *Essays in Honour of Philip B. Chatwin* (Oxford: V. Ridler, 1962), 13–26; Eileen Power, *Medieval Women* (Cambridge: Cambridge University Press, 1975), 57–65; Kay E. Lacey, "Women and Work in Fourteenth and Fifteenth Century London," in *Women and Work in Preindustrial England*, ed. Lindsey Charles and Lorna Duffin (London: Croom Helm, 1985), 24–82, esp. 45–56. For the Continental evidence, see Martha C. Howell, *Women, Production, and Patriarchy in Late Medieval Cities* (Chicago: University of Chicago Press, 1986), esp. 124–37, 152–58, 168–73; Grethe Jacobsen, "Women's Work and Women's Role: Ideology and Reality in Danish Urban Society, 1300–1550," *Scandinavian Economic History Review* 31, no. 1 (1983): 3–20; Edith Ennen, *Frauen im Mittelalter* (Munich: C. H. Beck, 1984), esp. 141–93; Margret Wensky, *Die Stellung der Frau in der stadtkölnischen Wirtschaft im Spätmittelalter* (Cologne: Böhlau Verlag, 1980), esp. 61–186, and "Women's Guilds in Cologne in the Later Middle Ages," *Journal of European Economic History* 11, no. 3 (1982): 631–50; Brown (n. 3 above); Merry Wiesner, *Working Women in Renaissance Germany* (New Brunswick, N.J.: Rutgers University Press, 1986), and "Spinsters and Seamstresses: Women in Cloth and Clothing Production," in Ferguson et al., eds. (n. 3 above), 191–205. For a summary of women's work in medieval towns, see Shulamith Shahar, *The Fourth Estate: A History of Women in the Middle Ages*, trans. Chaya Galai (New York: Methuen, 1983), 189–201.

[8] Information about journeywomen is very rare in medieval records, suggesting that very few of them freely sold their labor to gild masters.

[9] With the development of a secular, popular, and frequently urban-oriented literature in the sixteenth century, this stereotype can be seen plainly. See, e.g., Louis B. Wright, *Middle Class Culture in Elizabethan England* (1935; reprint, Ithaca, N.Y.: Cornell University Press, 1958), esp. 25–29, 170–200; Charles W. Camp, *The Artisan in Elizabethan Literature* (New York: Columbia University Press, 1924); Laura Caroline Stevenson, *Praise and Paradox: Merchants and Craftsmen in Elizabethan Popular Literature* (Cambridge: Cambridge University Press, 1984), esp. 161–79.

times obtained membership in their husbands' gilds as "sisters." In this capacity, wives enjoyed many of the religious, social, and charitable benefits of gild membership. But sisters were clearly second-rank gild members; they often paid lower admission fees, were barred from wearing gild livery, and participated in only selected religious and social occasions.[10] Women were accepted in their husbands' gilds because their work was needed, but their involvement in such gilds was limited. Indeed, the extension of such privileges to women reflected more the interests of the masters than any recognition of women's work. In medieval London, for example, the wives and widows of masters in the most influential gilds in the city were often granted exceptional perquisites of gild membership, such as the right to wear gild livery or to attend important gild banquets. The context here is crucial; the masters of these gilds were the wealthiest and most powerful men in London, and the rights they gave their wives and widows were a reflection of their elite social privileges, not an endorsement of women's role within their gilds.[11]

Widows of gild masters who continued their husbands' businesses were accorded the most extensive gild privileges available to women; they supervised workshops, took on apprentices and journeymen, and participated in most social and religious celebrations. But few women ever enjoyed this privileged position; widows of gild masters who remained active within the gild usually represented only 2–5 percent of the total membership of any one gild.[12] Even these privileged widows, moreover, were rarely allowed to participate in gild politics. In the vast majority of gilds, no woman could vote for gild officials, serve as a gild officer, or take part in gild political and judicial activities.[13] And, although many men gained

[10] See, e.g., William Herbert, *The History of the Twelve Great Livery Companies of London*, 2 vols. (London, 1834–37), 1:83–84, 465–66; Charles Phythian-Adams, "Ceremony and the Citizen: The Communal Year at Coventry, 1450–1550," in *Crisis and Order in English Towns, 1500–1700*, ed. Peter Clark and Paul Slack (Toronto: University of Toronto Press, 1972), 57–85, esp. 57–58, 66–67; Abram, 284–85.

[11] See Herbert, 1:59, 68–71, 84–85, for the right of female members to wear the livery of powerful London gilds like the Grocers and Fishmongers.

[12] This figure is confirmed in early modern accounts, which offer more exact figures for gild membership. See, e.g., Mary Prior, "Women and the Urban Economy: Oxford, 1500–1800," in *Women in English Society, 1500–1800*, ed. Mary Prior (London: Methuen, 1985), 93–117, esp. 103–9; Steve Rappaport, *Worlds within Worlds: Structures of Life in Sixteenth-Century London* (Cambridge: Cambridge University Press, in press), chap. 2.

[13] Exceptions to the political exclusion of women were very rare, especially in England. Abram, 284–85, notes that the 1452 ordinances of the London Shearmen

civic enfranchisement through gild membership, women—no matter how influential within their gilds—did not enjoy via gild membership the right to participate in civic politics. Finally, the privileges
of widows were fragile ones; remarriage to a person who was not
a member of the gild, or to a master of another craft, could result
in expulsion from the gild.[14]

The experiences of widows emphasize the underlying principle
behind the treatment of women within male-dominated gilds. Most
crafts and trades in the Middle Ages operated out of household
workshops; within the household, materials were processed, goods
were produced, and commodities were sold. Because of the central
importance of this "household economy," women had to be incorporated into the gilds that regulated these economic activities. But
they were brought into gilds more as members of households than
as workers. Widows obtained their relatively high gild status not
through training, work, or service but through a change in marital
status, widowhood. Remarriage outside the gild was discouraged
because its results were usually disruptive; either a widow had to
change trades (moving into her second husband's workshop), or her
new husband gained control of a workshop in an irregular fashion.
Wives and daughters were also treated more as household members
than as workers. Because the family formed the basic unit of production, many gilds exempted the wives and children of masters
from regulations about the number or types of apprentices and craft
workers that could be hired.

Hence, although male-dominated gilds offered women important protections and privileges, they also severely restricted wom-
en's full involvement in gilds and women's work opportunities
overall. The secondary status of women in such gilds, for example,
left them particularly vulnerable when trade diminished or competition increased. Gilds often responded to adverse economic developments by placing further restrictions on the employment of
women in the craft, in some instances prohibiting masters from

---

imply that female members could participate in gild elections. Women sometimes
worked as technical supervisors in gilds (see, e.g., the "isolated incident" of the
London Leather Dyers in 1372, who appointed three men and their wives as overseers [Abram, 285]). But no evidence suggests that women actually elected officers.
In any case, the joint appointment of wives as overseers emphasizes more the household basis of production and trade in the medieval economy than a recognition of
women's rights in the craft. Nor is there any firm evidence that the female officers
present in some of the female-dominated gilds of Paris were elected by gild members; instead, they were appointed by the provost of the city.

[14] Brentano (n. 2 above), cxxxii; Jacobsen (n. 7 above), 14.

employing any women at all (except for their wives and daughters).[15] Although as members of households women could seldom be excluded entirely from gilds, their participation was limited to the minimum necessary to maintain the household economy.

For work defined as women's work, the situation was slightly different. Medieval townswomen worked in a wide variety of low-skilled, low-status, low-paid occupations that never formed into gilds. Only skilled trades and crafts organized gilds, and those who worked in nonskilled sectors—whether male or female—worked outside of gild control.[16] Some women's trades, however, were recognized as skilled, and even these rarely formed into gilds. The London silkworkers described by Marian Dale provide the best example of this phenomenon. Dale shows that the London silkwomen pursued a skilled craft and trade. As throwsters, they turned raw silk into yarn; as weavers, they produced ribbons, laces, and other small silk goods; as handworkers, they made up silk laces and other trappings; and as traders in silk, they undertook large and lucrative contracts. Moreover, the work of silkworkers was not a mere sideline to domestic duties, something a wife pursued in moments free from housework, child care, and labor in her husband's workshop. Girls served long apprenticeships to learn the silkworking craft, and wives often continued to work in silk, no matter what the occupations of their husbands. Silkworking was a true "mystery" (or, as Dale spells it, "mistery"), a skilled craft with secrets of production and trade passed only from mistress to apprentice. The women who worked in this craft had many of the attributes associated with high-status work: they had valued skills, ran workshops and trained apprentices, invested large amounts of money in purchases of raw materials and trading ventures, and stayed in the same craft throughout their working lives. They also banded together for mutual aid. On six occasions between 1368 and 1504, the London silkworkers sought protection of their craft and trade through petitions (presented to either Parliament or

[15] Abram, 282–84; Power (n. 7 above), 60–62; Shahar (n. 7 above), 198–201; Charles Phythian-Adams, *Desolation of a City: Coventry and the Urban Crisis of the Late Middle Ages* (Cambridge: Cambridge University Press, 1979), 87–94. There is some disagreement among historians about the effect of urban economic prosperity or decline on women's work and their activities in gilds. See, e.g., P. J. P. Goldberg, "Female Labour, Service and Marriage in the Late Medieval Urban North," *Northern History* 22 (1986): 18–38; Prior, 93–117; Rappaport, chap. 2.

[16] To be sure, women worked at many skilled tasks—as spinsters, brewsters, midwives, cooks, etc.—that were not considered skilled by their contemporaries. In part, this assessment probably reflected a tendency to undervalue women's work; in part, it reflected the fact that such tasks, although skilled, employed skills that were widely available and widely known.

the mayor of London), and most of their requests were granted.[17] But, despite their valued skills, large investments, lifelong commitments, and common petitions, the silkworkers of London never organized into a formal gild. In Dale's words, silkworking was "pursued on the lines of the craft gilds of male workers" but was "not recognized as a definite gild."[18]

The absence of gild organization among the London silkworkers is typical; in most medieval towns and cities, even the most skilled female trades and crafts never formed gilds. The only exceptions known to date are found in large Continental cities: Rouen, Paris, and Cologne. At least five female-dominated gilds existed in medieval Rouen, but little is known of their histories. All focused on the textile trades, particularly in luxury items or linen (one of the city's major exports), and women had some measure of political power as gild officials in at least one of the gilds.[19] In late thirteenth-century Paris, seven gilds (out of more than one hundred) were exclusively female or female dominated.[20] These gilds specialized in detailed

---

[17] Dale (n. 4 above), 324–25, 331–33; Kay Lacey, "The Production of 'Narrow Ware' by Silkwomen in Fourteenth and Fifteenth Century England," *Textile History* 18, no. 2 (1987): 187–204, esp. 188.

[18] Dale, 324. Lacey, in "The Production of 'Narrow Ware,' " has extended Dale's research on the London silkworkers, identifying by name some 123 silkworkers and confirming Dale's general conclusions.

[19] Charles Quin-Lacroix, *Histoire des anciennes corporations d'arts et métiers et des confréries religieuses de la capitale de la Normandie* (Rouen: Lecointe Freres, 1850), 106–7, 120–26, 580–84, 646–61, 684–88. In the early fourteenth century, the spinners, over 80 percent of whom were women, were ruled by eight *gardes*, two of whom were women. Quin-Lacroix discusses all of the Rouen gilds but never focuses on the almost exclusively female membership (which is obvious in the gild statutes he reproduces) of the spinners, linen merchants (two types), ribbon makers, and embroiderers. Further archival work is necessary both to uncover the complex history of these women's gilds in medieval Rouen and to discover whether such female-dominated gilds existed in other Continental cities. The eighteenth-century history of some of these women's gilds in Rouen has been investigated by Daryl Hafter; see "Conference Reports: Economic History Association 46th Annual Meeting, Hartford, CT, 26–28 September, 1986," in *Urban History Yearbook* (Leicester: Leicester University Press, 1987), 91–92.

[20] The ordinances of five of these gilds were noted in Étienne Boileau's late thirteenth-century survey of the Parisian gilds (René de Lespinasse and François Bonnardot, eds., *Les métiers et corporations de la ville de Paris, XIII siècle: Le livre des métiers d' É. Boileau*, Histoire générale de Paris, 5 [Paris: Imprimerie Nationale, 1879], 68–72, 74–75, 83–84, 207–8). The ordinances of another two female gilds (the embroiderers and the makers of fancy embroidered purses) were recorded slightly later, in the last decade of the thirteenth century (René de Lespinasse, ed., *Les métiers et corporations de la ville de Paris, XIV–XV siècle*, Histoire générale de Paris, 17, 3 vols. [Paris: Imprimerie Nationale, 1886–97], 2:166–67, 3:9–10). Many other gilds in Paris were mixed gilds, and some of these—like the linen merchants,

handwork and luxury textiles—spinning silk, weaving silk ribbons, and producing various types of fancy headgear and purses decorated with silk, gold thread, and pearls. The women in these gilds operated independently of their husbands, sons, and other male relatives, and they could become gild mistresses regardless of their marital status. Of the ninety-three members (eighty-one women and twelve men) of the embroiderers' gild, for example, none of the twenty-five women identified as wives had husbands in the same trade, and none of the twelve women identified as daughters had fathers in the trade. Indeed, ties between women might have been more important in such crafts than ties between women and men; the embroiderers' gild included four sets of mothers and daughters and four sets of sisters.[21] The relative independence of the working activities of these women is confirmed in the membership roll of the gild of purse makers. Although most medieval lists regularly identified women in terms of their dependent relationships to men (i.e., as a daughter, wife, or widow), only seven of the 124 female purse makers were identified by a relationship to a man (four wives, two daughters, one niece).[22]

Some of these gilds were also governed by female *jurés*, the gild officials in Paris responsible for supervising apprenticeship contracts, inspecting work for quality, and generally enforcing gild ordinances. But only one of these gilds (the weavers of silk headdresses) was actually managed exclusively by women; in all the others, women shared power or played no role at all in the gild's governing structure. The subordinate political role played by women in their own gilds is especially striking in the case of the silkspinners and purse makers; despite their all-female memberships, these gilds were supervised by male *jurés*, who presumably had no practical experience in the craft.[23] All the *jurés* of these women's gilds, more-

---

bath-house keepers, and the makers of pins, rosaries, and various types of silk adornments—clearly included large numbers of women. See also E. Dixon, "Craftswomen in the *Livre des Métiers*," *Economic Journal* 5, no. 2 (1895): 209–28.

[21] G. B. Depping, ed., *Réglemens sur les arts et métiers de Paris, rédigés au 13e siècle et connus sous le nom de Livre des Métiers d'Étienne Boileau* (Paris: Imprimerie de Crapelet, 1837), 379–80.

[22] Ibid., 383–84. There were also two women who were sisters, an aunt and her niece, and a mother and her daughter in this gild.

[23] There were two gilds of silkspinners, differentiated by the size of the spindle used. The language of their ordinances indicates their memberships were exclusively female, as does the membership list of the purse makers. Nevertheless, all three gilds were governed by appointed male *jurés* (although the silkspinners who used a small spindle also had two *preudesfames*, who possessed some powers of supervision); Lespinasse and Bonnardot, eds., 69–72; Depping, ed., 382–84.

over, were appointed by the city provost, unlike many of the male-dominated gilds, which frequently elected their own officials.[24]

In late medieval Cologne, three gilds—silkmakers, linen yarn finishers, and gold thread spinners—were women's gilds.[25] Like the women's gilds of Rouen and Paris, these Cologne gilds specialized in luxury goods and textiles. And like the women's gilds of Paris, these Cologne gilds were subordinated to the male power structure—men were appointed to administer gild affairs, and the women's gilds were the only ones excluded from participation in civic government.[26] The mistresses of these Cologne gilds ran profitable businesses, trained their own apprentices, and supervised the technical aspects of their crafts, but their control of their work was nevertheless limited by their place within and dependence on the family-based economy. In most cases, the mistress-wife produced a valuable export commodity that was then marketed by her husband or another close relative. The Cologne silkmakers provide the best example of this family-based economy. Almost all silk mistresses were married, only their husbands could be elected to supervise their craft, and many of these husbands were employed as silk merchants who exported the silk fabrics manufactured by their wives. The mistresses of the Cologne gilds worked at a skilled, prestigious, and lucrative craft, but their work was structured—at least in part—by men, both within the household economy and within their craft gilds.

The women's gilds of Rouen, Paris, and Cologne are exceptional instances of skilled women who organized and regulated their crafts. As gildswomen, they had to endure more external supervision (from males) than did gildsmen, but they nevertheless exercised considerable economic power. They controlled craft secrets, trained apprentices, determined prices and quality, and hired journeywomen. They suffered some restrictions not imposed upon male gilds, but "their powers over their craft were real."[27] If these women were able to take advantage of their skills to organize into gilds, why did most other skilled female workers—like the silkworkers of Lon-

[24] There is no indication that in the Middle Ages any of these female gilds elected their own officials. In the early modern period, however, the female gilds of linen merchants in both Paris and Rouen elected their own officials; Lespinasse, ed., 3:45–49; Quin-Lacroix, 120–23, 684–88.

[25] Wensky, Die Stellung der Frau (n. 7 above), and "Women's Guilds in Cologne" (n. 7 above); Howell (n. 7 above), 124–33.

[26] There were female officials in the women's gilds of Cologne, but they did not have the "broad supervisory and judicial roles" that male officials had; Howell, 129.

[27] Ibid., 130.

don—fail to organize into gilds? Dale speculates that the artistic nature of the silkworker's craft might have discouraged the sorts of quality and price controls that were characteristic of gilds.[28] But the Parisian women who embroidered jewels and rich threads onto head-coverings did similarly artistic work, and they nevertheless formed a gild. And other medieval crafts—such as that of the gold-smiths (a craft dominated by men)—had significant artistic components, and they too developed gild organizations. Dale also suggests that silkworkers eschewed gilds because they enjoyed the social and religious benefits of gild membership through their husbands' gilds. To be sure, most skilled townswomen were married to gild members, but Dale's rationale ignores not only the situation of unmarried silkworkers[29] but also the importance of the economic functions of gilds to any skilled worker, regardless of sex or marital status. Social and religious benefits aside, silkworkers had much to gain from organizing their "mystery" into a gild.

Since Dale finished her study of London silkworkers, others have sought to explain the failure of skilled women to organize into gilds. Martha Howell has emphasized the importance of the pa-triarchal household as the basic unit of production; because pro-duction was located within the patriarchal structure of the household, women could participate in skilled labor only within the limits prescribed by male power. Creation of independent female gilds would have threatened the authority of men as husbands, as gild masters, and as civic governors. Natalie Zemon Davis has argued that women were taught to have strong identities as members of families but weak identities as workers; even the most skilled fe-male workers were expected to have flexible careers that could accommodate changes in marital status. Merry Wiesner has ob-served that the very nature of gilds discouraged the participation of women; by emphasizing skilled training and by restricting access to only those privileged enough to receive that training, gilds in-herently hurt women and other underprivileged groups. Grethe Jacobsen has suggested that women might have actively resisted gilds not only because gild organization and regulation acted to the disadvantage of women (who often preferred to work on a casual basis) but also because "a trade gild attracted men who would surely

[28] Dale (n. 4 above), 335.
[29] There were far more women than men in late medieval towns (sex ratios ranged from 75 to 90 males per 100 females), and many women remained single or never remarried after their husbands died; see Maryanne Kowaleski, "The History of Urban Families in Medieval England," *Journal of Medieval History* 14, no. 1 (1988): 47–63, esp. 54–56; Power (n. 7 above), 53–55; Karl Bücher, *Die Frauenfrage im Mittelalter*, 2d ed. (Tübingen: H. Laupp, 1910), 5–7.

dominate it." And Judith Brown has supported the idea of an antagonistic relationship between women and gilds, observing that there is "an inverse relation between the ability of guilds to regulate economic activity and the extent of female participation in the labor force."[30]

All of these observations have come, as did the observations of Dale, from specific case studies—Howell on Cologne and Leiden, Wiesner on south German cities, Davis on Lyons, Jacobsen on Danish towns, Brown on Florence. Comparative work on crafts, gilds, and women is virtually nonexistent, and it is through such comparative work that we will eventually understand the unusual relationship between women and gilds in medieval towns. The examples of Rouen, Paris, and Cologne suggest that women's gilds were most likely to form in crafts that produced luxuries and export goods. They also suggest that the high social status of female workers in such crafts probably facilitated gild formation. But the London silkworkers also produced luxury goods and came from prosperous merchant families. Why were they different? Unlike silkworkers in Cologne, the London silkworkers produced only for the (less profitable) domestic market, and they also did not represent just one segment of a family-based trade. Not all London silkwomen were married, and even when they were, their work was not necessarily linked to the trade of their husbands.[31] In Cologne, the integration of the silkworkers' craft with the trade of their husbands was crucial to the gild's formation.[32] The relative independence of the London silkworkers may thus have worked to inhibit gild formation. This same independence did not hinder the formation of women's gilds in medieval Paris, but the thirteenth-century Parisian economy was more oriented to the production of luxury goods than was the economy of London. The remarkable success of women in Parisian gilds probably resulted in large part from governmental measures to reg-

[30] Howell (n. 7 above); see also her "Women, the Family Economy, and the Structures of Market Production in Cities of Northern Europe during the Late Middle Ages," in Hanawalt, ed. (n. 3 above), 198–222; Natalie Zemon Davis, "Women in the Crafts in Sixteenth-Century Lyons," *Feminist Studies* 8, no. 1 (1982): 47–80; Wiesner, *Working Women in Renaissance Germany* (n. 7 above), 3; Jacobsen (n. 7 above), 11; Brown (n. 3 above), 212. One major study of women's work, Alice Clark's *Working Life of Women in the Seventeenth Century*, was published before Dale studied the London silkworkers (1919; reprint, London: Routledge & Kegan Paul, 1982). Clark only briefly discussed skilled women's crafts (195–96), emphasizing her judgment that the family-based economy of medieval towns encouraged women's work. She did not deal specifically with the issue of gild organization in the Middle Ages.

[31] Lacey, "The Production of 'Narrow Ware'" (n. 18 above), 193–94, 200–204.

[32] Howell, *Women, Production, and Patriarchy*, esp. 130–33.

ulate luxury crafts, crafts whose products were used by the realm's wealthiest and most powerful people. The craft gilds in Paris, moreover, formed earlier than did those in London, and this might have worked to women's advantage. By the fifteenth century, many of the women's gilds in Paris had either disappeared or amalgamated into larger gilds, and women, although still active workers in the crafts, appear to have lost much of their political and judicial power as *jurés*.[33]

Whatever the reasons why most skilled female workers did not organize into gilds, the results were clearly devastating. Dale does not carry her story of the London silkworkers into the sixteenth and seventeenth centuries, but if she had, she would have shown the consequences of the silkworkers' lack of formal organization. Over the course of these two centuries, men slowly took over control of silkworking. This change reflects both changing economic conditions and the vulnerability of the unorganized female silkworkers; because the female silkworkers of London had not formed a gild to protect their craft, they lost that control to men. When men took over the craft, they formed a gild to protect their trade.[34]

[33] The later history and ordinances of these gilds may be found in Lespinasse, ed. (n. 20 above), 2:170–77; 3:1–4, 13–39, 296–300. By the late Middle Ages, the ratio of female masters and journeywomen may also have changed. The relative number of women working in late medieval Parisian crafts probably was the same, but women may have been more likely to be employed as wage workers rather than as masters. Indeed, further research on female-dominated gilds should address not only the numbers of women in particular crafts but also their relative power and place in the gild hierarchy (and how their position might have changed over time). If the possibilities for advancement to a mastership became increasingly limited in the late Middle Ages, the continued gild membership of wage-working women actually may have aided their exploitation. Wensky, "Women's Guilds in Cologne" (n. 7 above), 649–50, e.g., notes how exploitation of the silkspinners by the silkmakers became worse "as a result of the adoption of capitalist practices."

[34] By 1555, silkweaving had come under the control of the powerful Weaver's gild, which forbade anyone of the silkweaver's craft from taking on women as apprentices. Similar ordinances occurred in 1577, and in 1596 no woman was allowed to work as a silkweaver unless she was the widow of a gild member. A 1595 complaint of the Yeoman Weavers against immigrant weavers also singled out for criticism the foreigners' willingness to share the secrets of the trade with women (who then married men and brought them into the trade, thus adding to the competition in the trade); for all these ordinances, see Frances Consitt, *The London Weavers' Company* (Oxford: Clarendon Press, 1933), 1:229–30, 292, 312–14, 320. Separate male livery companies were established for silkthrowers in 1630 and silkmen in 1631 (W. Carew Hazlitt, *The Livery Companies of the City of London* [1892; reprint, New York: Benjamin Blom, 1969], 138–39). Women were probably still employed in these crafts, particularly in the handwork associated with silk adornments, but their work was clearly much more controlled and their opportunities to run their own businesses as silkmistresses were severely curtailed. See also Clark (n. 30 above), 138–43. A

The silkworkers of London, then, serve as a somber reminder of how some medieval notions of "community" worked to the disadvantage of women. Since most skilled work prone to gild organization was done by men, most gilds were male dominated, and if women were tolerated within them, they were second-class members. They enjoyed some of the religious, social, and charitable benefits of gild membership, but they were firmly excluded not only from its political perquisites but also from many of its more important economic and social privileges. Although some women's crafts and trades had sufficiently high status or sufficiently skilled workers to make gild organization possible, few gilds were actually formed. In some towns, such as Rouen, Paris, and Cologne, such women did form gilds, but even these were less autonomous than the gilds of men. In most other towns, like London, such women did not organize into gilds and were thus vulnerable to competition and loss of trade.

Marian Dale's study is important not only for what it exemplifies about the working status of medieval townswomen but also for what it illustrates about the history of women who have studied the lives of medieval women. In the late nineteenth and early twentieth centuries, as the study of history was becoming less a pastime and more a profession, a significant number of women not only gained training and prestige as recognized medievalists but also undertook, in some cases, to study the experiences of medieval women.[35] Mar-

---

crucial factor in these changes within the silk industry seems to have been a technical shift to broadloom weaving of silk cloths; see Lacey, "The Production of 'Narrow Ware,' " 187; and Eric Kerridge, *Textile Manufacturers in Early Modern England* (Manchester: Manchester University Press, 1985), 127–32.

[35] Perhaps the most outstanding example is Eileen Power, author of *Medieval English Nunneries, 1275–1535* (Cambridge: Cambridge University Press, 1922), and the posthumously published collection *Medieval Women* (n. 7 above). Others are E. Dixon, author of "Craftswomen in the *Livre des Métiers*" (n. 20 above); Emily James Putnam, author of *The Lady: Studies of Certain Significant Phases of Her History* (London: G. P. Putnam's Sons, 1910); Annie Abram, author of "Women Traders in Medieval London" (n. 7 above); and Florence Griswold Buckstaff, who published "Married Women's Property in Anglo-Saxon and Anglo-Norman Law," *Annals of the American Academy of Political and Social Sciences* 4 (1893): 233–64. Alice Clark's book (n. 30 above) also includes considerable work on women in medieval trades and industries. And a late representative of this early interest in women's history is Doris Mary Stenton, author of *The Englishwoman in History* (London: George Allen & Unwin, 1957). Among those female medievalists of these generations who chose not to study primarily women are Lucy Toulmin Smith, Mary Bateson, Alice Stopford Green, Eleanor Carus-Wilson, Bertha Phillpotts, Sylvia Thrupp, Helen Cam, Bertha Putnam, and Nellie Nielson. For information on the careers of some of these women,

ian Dale, who in 1928 completed her M.A. thesis on women in the fifteenth-century English textile trades, was part of this distinguished group.[36] Since these women were themselves exercising new options and roles for women, they sought positive images of women in their research, emphasizing the strengths of medieval women's lives rather than the restrictions. Today's generations of feminist medievalists tend to view the same evidence in a different light, seeing more constraints than independence.[37]

Department of History
Fordham University (Kowaleski)

Department of History
University of North Carolina at Chapel Hill (Bennett)

---

see Barbara A. Hanawalt, "Golden Ages for the History of Medieval English Women," 6–12; and Susan Mosher Stuard, "A New Dimension? North American Scholars Contribute Their Perspective," 86–90, both in *Women in Medieval History and Historiography,* ed. Susan Mosher Stuard (Philadelphia: University of Pennsylvania Press, 1987). Bonnie G. Smith has undertaken a study of earlier generations of female historians; for her preliminary observations, see "The Contributions of Women to Modern Historiography in Great Britain, France, and the United States, 1750–1940," *American Historical Review* 89, no. 3 (1984): 709–32.

[36] Marian K. Dale, "Women in the Textile Industries and Trade of Fifteenth-Century England" (M.A. thesis, University of London, 1928).

[37] Some contemporary medievalists do continue to extoll the work experiences of medieval women, but more recent work has focused on the limitations and restrictions faced by these women. For a review of recent literature, see Judith M. Bennett, "'History That Stands Still': Women's Work in the European Past," *Feminist Studies* 14, no. 2 (Summer 1988): 269–83.

* * *

THE LONDON SILKWOMEN OF
THE FIFTEENTH CENTURY[1]

MARIAN K. DALE

In giving some account of the London silkwomen it is the purpose of this article to illustrate the usual practices among female participants in trade and industry at this time, and to show that although this mistery was not recognized as a definite gild, it was pursued on the lines of the craft gilds of male workers.

Although there are evidences of silkwomen at the beginning of the reign of Edward III., it is not until the succeeding century that they appear in any numbers and can be said to have approached a monopoly in their work. London silkwomen were much later in establishing their art than the silkwomen of Paris, whose ordinances are to be found in "Le Livre des Métiers," a thirteenth-century digest of the Parisian crafts,[2] but by 1368 they were sufficiently organized, and important, to present a petition to the mayor against a Lombard who was cornering all raw and coloured silks.[3] During the second half of the fifteenth century, as a body, they were responsible for several petitions to Parliament, with the result that acts were passed protecting their work against foreign competition, which they suffered in common with other crafts at this time.[4] The

---

[1] The following abbreviations have been used throughout the footnotes: E.C.P., Early Chancery Proceedings; P.C.C., Wills proved in the Prerogative Court of Canterbury.

[2] "Craftswomen in the 'Livre des Métiers,'" E. Dixon (Economic Journal, v., 1895, p. 209).

[3] Calendar of Plea and Memoranda Rolls of the City of London, 1364-81, ed. A. H. Thomas (1929), pp. 99-106.

[4] Between 1455 and 1504 five acts were passed forbidding the importation of certain silk goods for periods ranging from four to twenty years. The petitions may have been part of an anti-alien movement, into which it is possible that the silkwomen were drawn at the instigation of other craftsmen. In 1455 and 1463, the occupation was said to be a luxury trade; in 1482 it was pleaded that many men and women had been thrown out of work.

This article first appeared in the Economic History Review, 1st ser., 4 (1933): 324–35. Reprinted with the permission of the Economic History Review.

first petition to Parliament, of 1455, was sent from the "Sylke-wymmen and Throwestres of the Craftes and occupation of Silke-werk,"[5] which had long been women's crafts within the city; in 1482 the preamble of the petition shows that those interested were "menne and women of the hole craft of Silkewerk of the Cite of London and all other Citeis, Townes, Boroghes, and Vilages of this Realme of Englond."[6] At present, this indication of so great a spread of the industry has not been supported by information from other sources, but the records of other towns, as they become available, may bring to light the work of the silkwomen outside London. The demand, however, is more likely to have been supplied by mercers, or by women such as a certain Edy Lucas of Salisbury, who sold other goods as well as silk.[7] Girls apprenticed to London silkwomen came from counties as far away as Warwickshire and Yorkshire,[8] and if these women returned to their native town they would work not under special regulations of the craft, but under the local customs in force for other female workers.[9] Thus, while it is probable that they were working elsewhere, it is in London that we can best study these women who in 1455 maintained that by their craft they "lyved full honourably, and therwith many good Householdes kept, and many Gentilwymmen and other in grete noumbre like as there nowe be moo than a M, haue be drawen under theym in lernyng the same Craftes and occupation ful vertueusly." Such contemporary generalizations, though doubtless exaggerated for the purposes of the petitions to Parliament, can be substantiated by incidents re-corded elsewhere.

Apprenticeship, the product of the craft gilds, had become an integral element of the whole industrial system; therefore the same practice was found in the mistery with which we are dealing. In this respect, the silkwomen kept the same rules and worked under the same conditions as the men. Following the usual custom, the prospective apprentice was bound by an indenture between her parent or guardian and her future mistress. In the collection of ancient deeds at the Public Record Office are two of these agree-ments made on the behalf of one girl from Yorkshire and another

[5] Rotuli Parliamentorum (Rec. Comm., 1832), V, p. 325 a.

[6] *Ibid.*, VI, p. 222 b.

[7] E.C.P., 100/73-78.

[8] P. and M. Rolls, A. 57, m. 36. *Ancient Deeds*, C. 2314. Other girls came from Norfolk, Buckinghamshire, Lincolnshire, and Bristol.

[9] The work would be pursued in the home and the woman would trade "covert de baron," or as "feme sole" under the regulations of the borough.

from Lincolnshire, both of whom were bound to London citizens and their wives, to learn the craft of the wife, who was a silkwoman.[10] The term of service in each case was seven years and the obligations on both sides were similar to those demanded on the occasion of the binding of a male apprentice. It was the girl's duty to cherish the interests of her master and mistress, not to waste their goods, or merchandise with her own or those of another without permission, to behave well, and not to withdraw unlawfully from their service. For their part, her future master and mistress promised to "teach, take charge of, and instruct, their apprentice, or cause her to be instructed" in the craft of the wife, to chastise her in meet fashion, and to find her food, clothing, footwear, a bed, and all other suitable necessaries.

In neither of these two deeds is there any suggestion that payment was made for the instruction given. That this sometimes happened is evident from a bill among the chancery proceedings, which was presented towards the end of Henry VIII.'s reign.[11] A man brought a plea of debt against a woman for £5 which he said she owed for board during the time that she was in his service; whereas, according to her petition, this was contrary to the agreement made by her mother, which provided that her mistress should teach her "the crafte and misterie of a Silkewoman & sewyng," wherein she was "expert and Connyng," finding the girl "mete and drynke and all other thinges convenyent." For this teaching her mother was to pay 20s. yearly, while the girl was to do service for her board. Without the contract itself, no comparison at all conclusive can be made between this agreement and the terms of the indentures referred to above. The period of service was much shorter than that usually required of apprentices. Indeed the word apprentice does not occur; although in view of the fact that such phrases as "apprenticeship and service," and "servant and apprentice" were fairly common, this point cannot be stressed too much. Yet the fee for instruction and service for board suggest something less comprehensive than apprenticeship, and this perhaps accounted for the money payment.

It is evident that those silkwomen who took apprentices were expected to keep the city's regulations. For several of them appear amongst the women against whom complaints were made before the mayor and aldermen, when female apprentices asked for ex-

[10] *Ancient Deeds*, C. 2314. *Ibid.*, D. 1176.
[11] E.C.P., 274/12.

oneration from service because they had not been enrolled within the appointed time of a year and a day.[12]

In addition to learning the craft itself, the girls were sent on various errands and entrusted with money transactions. Often, like Joan Woulbarowe, who "stode prentice" with Katherine Dore, silkthrowster, they must have delivered silk or made purchases. This girl's apprenticeship did not end happily. She alleged that her mistress, "immagening sotelly to haue hold vppon" her and to cause her to remain in service when her term was finished, found means to have her imprisoned until she became bound in an obligation for £12 13s. 4d. Of this, £8 was the value of silk and ware which Joan had delivered to two women dwelling in Soper Lane, "customers & werkers to ye said Katherine." A dozen years or so later the trouble was still unsettled. Joan, by then a silkwoman on her own account, petitioned the Chancellor because her former mistress had begun an action against her on the obligation. Katherine maintained that her apprentice had unjustly taken "throwen[13] sylke vncoloured and sylke dyed" amounting to £12 4s. 10d. and more; whereas Joan stated that Katherine had long since recovered for her goods, but that she owed her £7 10s. which Joan had paid to different people of whom she had, "in the tyme of her Prentyshode bought silke by the Commaundement," and for the use of her mistress. The case, which lasted throughout two terms, was decided in favour of the petitioner.[14]

The very nature of such strained relationships has been the cause of their remaining on record for us, but it is possible from wills, at least, to find a recognition of satisfactory service. Isabel Fremely, silkwoman, in 1456, appointed one legacy outside her circle of kinsfolk and this comprised a pair of sheets and her girdle of green silk garnished with silver, left to her female apprentice.[15] A woman of some note, Agnes Brundyssch, who called herself "citizen and silkwoman" of London, remembered several women who may have belonged to her household at some time, while to her apprentice she gave certain goods, adding, "I pardon and remit to the same Alice Seford the rest of her term of apprenticeship to me."[16] Another,

---

[12] P. and M. Rolls, A. 47, m 4d; A. 51, m. 5, m. 8d; A. 57, m. 3d, m. 6; A. 71, m. 1; A. 72, m. 3. This regulation was re-enforced by proclamation of March 21, 3 Hen. VI., addressed to "every man and woman having apprentices." *Calender of Letter Books of the City of London*, I. (ed. R. R. Sharpe, 1909), p. 134.

[13] Technically called "thrown" silk—*i.e.*, ready for weaving.

[14] E.C.P., 27/482; 28/83-84; 75/106.

[15] Somerset House, Commissary Court of London. Register Sharpe, f. 193.

[16] *Ibid*. Register More, f. 187d.

possibly also a member of the household, was styled "operaria mea." The apprentice who had finished her term presumably remained with her mistress until marriage, when, whatever her husband's occupation, she could work as a throwster or weaver or deal generally in silk goods.[17]

A few women figure in the chancery proceedings and wardrobe accounts as trading with large quantities of goods. The activities of women silk dealers can be illustrated by the petition of Jane Langton, widow of a saddler, who became involved in transactions with two merchants of Genoa, in which she agreed to become bound for payment for silk goods to the value of £300 15s. in the place of her daughter-in-law Agnes, who had died while away at Stourbridge fair.[18] In this case, since so large a purchase was made, Agnes Langton may have been a middleman, but there is nothing to show whether the silk was to receive further working, or whether it was merely intended for resale. Jane Langton herself is called silkwoman in her will dated 1475, not long after the events cited above.[19] It is of interest to note that she mentions her son John and Elizabeth his second wife, also engaged in the craft, since the latter must be the silkwoman of that name who, during 1503, supplied quantities of silk and other goods amounting to £101 17s. 5¼d. for members of the royal family.[20]

The transactions described above indicate that the women interested were expected to share in the necessary financial obligations, a position fairly common in the fifteenth century, when husbands and wives, for varied reasons, were frequently named jointly in pleas of debt brought either by them or against them. It is probable that many of the silkwomen, especially the poorer sisters in the craft, remained "covert de baron" so far as concerned their business dealings; which meant that their husbands were always responsible for payment of their debts. In general, to use words from the bill of a woman who was imprisoned in Canterbury, it was not usual "to make a woman that hath a husband to answere as a woman sole."[21] The somewhat different practice of London was set

---

[17] There are occasional references to "singlewomen"—e.g., Joan Litster of Nottingham, who bought and sold grain; Christian Baxster of London, who brought an action of debt first against a draper and then against his wife. But, if Conventry can be taken as an example, society had no room for the unattached woman, whom it considered to be an evil. Cf. the regulations in its Leet Book, ed. M. D. Harris (E.E.T.S., 1907–13), i., pp. 545, 568.

[18] E.C.P., 48/507.

[19] P.C.C., 18 Wattys.

[20] John Langton's will (P.C.C., 28 Blamyr) was proved by his wife Elizabeth in 1502.

[21] E.C.P., 32/344. The nature of the debt is not stated.

forth in certain chancery proceedings in which one of the parties stated that "the commune gise within the saide Citie is, and for long tyme hath been that the wyfes of men of worship and thrifte infraunchised in the same Citee haue by the sufferaunce of their husbondes in thabsence of them vsed to by and selle all manere of marchandise towardes thencreece and lyving of them and their household, the dutees of alle whiche bargaines commyng or gowyng hath alwey ben contente by suche wifes; or for nowne paiement of them by their husbondes."[22] But that it was by no means an unusual custom for the woman who worked alone to be answerable for her contracts as "feme sole" is seen in the provision made for such a trader in the ordinances of other towns as well as London.[23]

In the city of London women could make public declaration that they intended to trade as "sole merchants"; the records of such declarations, however, appear to be far too few, compared with the number of women so designated,[24] for this to have been the usual procedure. The Guildhall journal for 1457 shows that two silk-women at different times in the year came before the mayor, affirming that they were sole merchants, and seeking that in the future they should enjoy the benefits of the custom touching such traders.[25] This, as set forth in the Liber Albus, enabled a married woman pursuing a craft alone, to be charged as "feme sole," in all things touching her occupation; yet both of these silkwomen said that for a long time they had carried on the craft as sole merchants, so that perhaps they made this public avowal because they purposed to confine themselves to one craft, or to work on a much larger scale than before. On more than one occasion, the creditor of a silkwoman could not maintain an action for debt against her because there was no record that she had ever been admitted as sole merchant. In one case the woman was said to have beguiled a creditor by affirming that she was sole merchant, whereas there was no record that she had such power.[26] Therefore it may be that the two women mentioned above thus acquired prestige, or were the better enabled to trade satisfactorily by means of their guarantee.

The purchase of silk goods imported by Italian and other merchants into England was sometimes made through a broker, a practice common to traders at that time. Thus Isabel Norman, "trading for herself in the craft of a silkwoman," bought "gold of Cyprus on

---

[22] *Ibid.*, 43/293.
[23] Cf. *Borough Customs*, ed. M. Bateson (Seldon Soc., xviii., 1904), i., pp. 227–9.
[24] The usual phrase is "mercatrix sola in arte de . . ."
[25] Guildhall Journal, vi., ff. 182*d*, 184.
[26] E.C.P., 201/32.

a pipe" from a Genoese merchant through a certain David Galganete who acted as a broker between them.[27] That these merchants also dealt directly with the silkwomen is evident from the views of the hosts of foreigners, chiefly Venetians, for the years 18 to 22 Henry VI., which give the names of twenty-three women who bought silk from them during that period.[28] The silks included fardels of raw silk, raw silk by the pound and "papers of silk" of divers kinds. The size or quality of the fardels must have varied considerably, since of those sold by Leonard Conterin to eight women during one year no two were of the same value, their prices ranging from £30 18s. 9d. to £57 12s.[29] Further glimpses of these direct transactions are provided by cases from the chancery proceedings, where merchants who had sold silk to women for considerable sums had not been able to recover debts, or were asking for better security.[30]

The industry of the silkwomen included three processes, and consisted in converting the raw silk into yarn, weaving the lesser silken materials (but not whole cloths), and making up goods of different descriptions. First, they were engaged upon throwing the raw silk, which came principally direct from the hand of the Italian reeler.[31] This was then ready for further manufacture, or could be sold, possibly after special treatment, by the ounce or pound, as a finished article, for sewing silk and for other purposes. Private individuals such as the Paston women sometimes bought it in this form, while it also figures in the accounts of the King's wardrobe.[32] Its colour and quality varied, as can be seen from payments made by the clerk of the Queen's household in 1419 to a silkwoman who supplied, amongst other goods:

Silk of divers colours	.. .. ..		18d.	the oz.
Fine black and blue silk	.. .. ..		17d.	the oz.
Fine black silk	.. ..		2s. 10d.	the oz.
Black and blue silk	.. .. ..		1s. 4½d.	the oz.[33]

[27] P. and M. Rolls, A. 50, m. 10; see also A. 78, m. 4.

[28] Exchequer K. R. Accounts, Various, 128/30.

[29] See also *ibid.*, 128/31.

[30] E.C.P., 48/507; 64/1131; 110/125.

[31] The strands from several cocoons were gathered by the reeler into one thread, thus producing the raw silk of commerce. *Cf.* J. E. Staley, *The Guilds of Florence* (1906), pp. 204–235.

[32] There are many small items of silk purchased from Anne de London in the account of the bailiff of John Mowbray, Duke of Norfolk, for the year 1423 (Brit. Mus. Add. Roll, 17209).

[33] Exchequer K. R. Wardrobe Accounts, 406/30, f. 9*d.*

But apart from the distinction "fine," and differences in price, there is little here to show variety of texture.[34] According to a late fifteenth-century document relating to weights and measures, the silks produced in England were of an inferior quality to those of the Paris silkwomen.[35] Thus the dearer silks sold before the acts forbidding the importation of thrown silk may well have been prepared overseas. Among the lists of purchases from Elizabeth Langton in 1505 is a group of special interest as throwing some light on the materials used in her own workshop. Under one warrant she received money for the following goods, for the use of "the Lady Mary":

1 oz. of "open silk"[36] of divers colours	.. ..	16d.
1 oz. of "twyne silk" of divers colours	.. ..	16d.
1 oz. of Venice gold	.. ..	4s.
1 "weving stole cum sleys pro eodem"	.. ..	3s.
1 oz. "webbe silk"	.. ..	16d.
"a quarter hedelyng[37] threde pro le webbe"	..	5d.
1 oz. of gold "de damask"	.. ..	5s.[38]

Further processes of the industry were those of weaving the thrown silk into corses, ribbons and laces,[39] and of making up the materials into goods both useful and decorative, such as cauls for the hair, points for silk laces,[40] and other trappings of all kinds. Fringe and tassel of different qualities were in considerable de-

[34] Also it has not been possible to discover from any other source whether the silk was ever dyed by the silkwomen. Customs accounts do not always show if the silk imported was already coloured; but one bill among the chancery proceedings mentions "throwen sylke vncoloured and sylke dyed," said to have been stolen from a mistress by her apprentice (E.C.P., 28/84a).

[35] MS. Cotton, Vesp., E., ix., ff. 86–110. A treatise called "The Noumbre of Weyghtes," part of which has been included in *Select Tracts and Table Books relating to English Weights and Measures*, ed. Hubert Hall and Frieda Nicholas (Camden Miscellany, xv., 1929, pp. 12–20).

[36] This was perhaps used as a weft thread, which was composed of two or three strands of raw silk, not thrown.

[37] *I.e.*, to make loops to which the warp was attached, and by means of which the warp threads were separated into two sets to allow the weft to pass between them. (See *N.E.D.* under Heddle.)

[38] Exchequer K.R. Wardrobe Accounts, 416/3, f. 10.

[39] While the ribbon was a finished article, the corse generally served as a foundation for further work of embroidery or other form of decoration. Its commonest use was in the making of girdles. Lace, or twisted silk cord, fulfilled many purposes, such as the hanging for a sword, the attachment for seals of charters, and, very generally, the fastening together of different parts of dress.

[40] *E.g.*, Exchequer K.R. Wardrobe Accounts, 431/1, in which is the payment of 22s. 2d. for the pointing of sixteen dozen silk laces, and for nine gross nine dozen points of silk at 2d. the dozen.

mand, in the royal household at least, and at times the goods were more elaborate, as when the wardrobe keeper paid for quantities of laces "botons & tassel" of silk, and laces "cum knoppes & tassell," or "cum Botons & knoppes." Occasionally he delivered from his stock the material for some specific task. Thus we find him paying 75s. 8d. to have 4 ½ lbs. of gold of Cyprus mixed with 2 lbs. 2 ¼ ozs. of silk fringe, the latter being supplied by the woman who did the work.[41] Besides these delicate smaller productions made up from the silk thrown and woven by them together with the gold and silver from Venice, Cyprus, or elsewhere, the later wardrobe accounts show that some silkwomen were selling articles of clothing, and from the evidence of a letter written by John Paston to his brother at Norwich, it can be assumed that such goods came sometimes from their own workshops. He says: "as for Stoctons doghte, she shall be weddyd in haste to Skeerne, as she tolde hyrselfe to my sylkemayde, whyche makyth perte of suche as she shall wear, to whom she brake hyr harte, and tolde hyr that she sholde haue hadde Master Paston, . . ."[42] Here is disclosed the medieval dressmaker carrying gossip from one customer to another. The interest lies in the work she was doing and in the suggestion that her business with John Paston was no casual task, but that he was one of her regular customers.

Before turning to the problem of organization, it is necessary to consider two questions which have received no comment in passing—the male worker, and the making of piece silks. The active interest of a certain proportion of men might be expected from the 1482 petition, which represented that the petitioners, "aswell men as women, and yonge Damesels, beying servaunts and apprentises to the said Craft of Silkewerk" had, during the period of protection, gained a reasonable living by their work. But whereas men, as well as women, were selling silk fringe and other silks by the pound for the great wardrobe of Edward III. and Richard II., with one exception, no examples of men dealing with the silkwomen's goods have as yet come to light in the fifteenth-century records, apart from the mercers in London who sold Cyprus gold and silver as well as piece silks.

The petitions of the silkworkers asked for protection for all "wrought" silk in any way connected with their craft. The imports named as those which they wanted to keep out of the country were twined silk and silk goods of the lesser variety. It is improbable

[41] *Ibid.*, 406/9, f. 3*d*.
[42] *Paston Letters*, ed. J. Gairdner (1910), iii., p. 118.

that they were at this time interested in piece goods, to which reference is first made in this connection in the act of 19 Henry VII.,[43] which stated that no person might bring into England for sale "eny maner of Sylke, wrought by hyt selfe or w^t eny other stuffe in eny place ou^t of this Realme, in Ribandes laces gyrdylles Corses Calles[44] Corses of tissues or poyntes," but gave at the same time freedom to any person, denizen or stranger, to import "all other maner of Sylkes, aswell wrought as rawe, or unwrought to sell at pleasour." In his *Life of Henry VII.*, first published in 1632, Francis, Lord Bacon, commenting on this statute, says that it does not refer to "stuffs of the whole piece," because "the realm had of them no manufacture in use at that time."[45] Under Edward IV. an Italian was assigned a house at Westminster for the weaving of cloths of damask, velvet and gold, and other cloths of silk, thereby arousing opposition from merchant strangers, who tried to prevent him from teaching his art in the land.[46] That this attempt to set up the craft in England had no permanent success is clear from the suggestions for introducing Italian silkweavers, made in the reigns of Henry VIII. and Elizabeth.[47]

The assumption that no whole cloths were made in the country in this period removes the possibility that the petition of 1482 refers to the mercers, or to weavers of piece silks, who would have been interested in keeping out these goods, which are not specifically mentioned. Indeed, it is difficult to conceive that the mercers would not have named their company in the petition, or that any appreciable number of craftsmen could have existed without some of them appearing in the records, as the silkwomen have done. The male workers referred to must signify an occasional corse-weaver, such as the one who became a freeman of York in 1499.[48] It is certain that in London women alone were selling the lesser silk articles with which the craft was concerned, and the delicate nature of the work supports the other evidence that they were also mainly responsible for the manufacture of these goods.[49] There is no trace

---

[43] 19 Hen. VII., cap. xxi.

[44] *I.e.*, cauls for keeping the hair in place.

[45] Francis, Lord Bacon, *The Life of Henry VII.* (Pitt Press Edition, 1876), p. 195.

[46] *Cal. of Chan. Proc. Eliz. (Rec. Comm.)*, ii., p. ciii.

[47] *Cal. of Letters and Papers of Henry VIII.*, vol. ix., p. 203; vol. xiii., pt. i., p. 206. *S.P. Dom Eliz.*, vol. viii., nos. 32–5.

[48] *Register of the Freemen of York*, ed. F. Collins (Surtees Society, 1897), p. 224.

[49] The materials produced did not require large looms. *Cf.* the ordinances of Norwich worsted weavers of 1511, in which women were forbidden to weave certain cloths because they had not sufficient strength for the work (*Records of the City of Norwich*, ed. W. Hudson and J. C. Tingey, 1906, vol. ii., p. 377).

that here men were weaving the corses, ribbons and laces with which the women traded, and at the end of the century the act of 19 Henry VII. protecting these commodities was merely headed "For Silkewomen."

The use of the general terms silk and silkwomen, and the fact that those buying and selling silken materials also received payments for making up silk for specific purposes, make it difficult to decide if the women usually confined themselves to one branch of the industry.[50] This difficulty is seen in the evidence from proceedings concerning the debt of a throwster. William Hull, mason, was sued for silk worth £22, sold to his late wife Agnes by Ellen, wife of William Lovell, vintner.[51] Agnes was called a "Throwster" by one woman witness, and said by another to have been "accustomed to by and sell silk in her lyfe and bought and sold divers tymes of and to divers persones." This case discloses trafficking in silk by a group of women, most of whom worked independently of each other. Since Agnes Hull was also said to have bought corses worth £19, she must have been a trader as well as a throwster. But in practice a number of women were doubtless occupied in their own homes solely as throwsters. These were either independent, preparing yarn which they sold to a fellow craftswoman, or they worked on the goods of another like the "custumers" of Katherine Dore already noted. Perhaps throwing and weaving went on side by side in the workshops of some of the bigger traders, for the stock-in-trade of these women covered the whole range of goods, from coloured silks or gold and silver thread sold by the ounce, to the more elaborate decorative articles or ribbons and similar woven silks. So that while the term "throwster" suggests workers at one process only, it seems likely that the other handicraft and trading functions were often combined in the activities of one craftswoman. On the other hand, from the quantities sold by one or two women

[50] While details of bigger transactions suggest the middleman buying for resale, the smaller purchases must have been made by craftswomen for manufacture and sale. The wording of their petitions, with reference to silkwomen and throwsters, would suggest two main divisions of the industry, just as later, under Charles I., there were the separate gilds of the silk-throwsters and silkmen; but while throwster clearly signified a spinner of yarn, the term silkwoman was a general one applied to those who were in any way interested in the production or sale of the commodity. Some girls were apprenticed to silkwomen to learn their craft, the particular branch not being stated, others were bound to women who were distinguished as throwster or corseweaver. Sometimes a woman was called "lace-wheuere." (P. and M. Rolls, A. 51, m. 8d; A. 72, m. 3. *Ibid.*, A. 50. m. 6d; A. 71, m. 1. Guildhall Journal, ii., f. 27d.)

[51] E.C.P., 31/476; 43/158–60; 43/291–4.

to the King's wardrobe, it may be that these were occupied as retailers of goods which they themselves bought from several sources—
viz., the importer, the throwster and the corseweaver.[52]

Although the number of "good and notable Householdes" who
were engaged in this industry must always remain an obscure question, it is certain that members of the craft were women of standing
in the city. Thus one girl was apprenticed to a woman called a
throwster, whose first husband was a goldsmith, and whose second,
of the same craft, was also an alderman.[53] The wife of a citizen and
fishmonger bought £46 worth of Venice ribbon from a Genoese
merchant,[54] while the widow of William Horne, knight and alderman, received silk amounting to the value of £56 from John Fynkell,
knight, who believed her to be trading as "feme sole."[55] From these
examples it can be seen that their transactions were by no means
on a small scale, and the households of such women may well have
included more than the usual number of persons because of the
handicraft pursued there as a regular business.[56] From the scale
upon which some of them traded, and from the evidence of their
activities described above, it is clear that their work cannot be
dismissed as a mere domestic occupation. Indeed, perhaps its most
important characteristic, considered in the light of the wider question of the economic position of women at that time, is that it shows
them working, not as wives (or widows), but as artisans who were
wage-earners, or as traders, supplying a market.

The evidence examined above is sufficient to demonstrate that
the "mistery and craft" of the silkwomen followed the usual practices of industry and trade at the time, although it was not recognized as a regular craft gild of the city. The women received
apprentices and employed workers; they undertook their own busi-

---

[52] From wardrobe accounts throughout the century one or two women always
stand out as supplying a greater quantity of goods than any others, but at the same
time there are usually single items for one or more of their fellow-craftswomen. The
practice of appointing one person to "the rowme or office of our sylkwoman," which
happened later under Queen Mary, had not yet been adopted.

[53] P. and M. Rolls, A. 72/3, and her will, P.C.C., 32 Vox.

[54] E.C.P., 64/1131.

[55] Ibid., 301/32.

[56] In the will of a mercer's widow, known from other sources to have been a
silkwoman, are references to three female servants, one of whom was appointed
executrix, and to "Margaret Taillour myn Apprentice," "Alice my Mayde," and a
male servant who was to gather in her debts (P.C.C., 24 Milles). Another silkwoman
of importance was Elizabeth Stokton, who was first the wife of John Stokton, mercer,
mayor in 1471 and knighted in that year, and who afterwards married Gerard Can-
iziani, the wealthy Florentine merchant with whom she may have become ac-
quainted through her dealings in silk.

ness transactions, and they were sufficiently organized among themselves to present petitions (as a body) concerning their work. Yet they have left little trace of the craft consciousness that is obvious in the gilds of male workers. They had no ordinances of their own, and there was apparently no strict attempt to keep up the standard of work among them. This absence of a definite gild may be due to two considerations. The work, being more of an art than a craft, could not be submitted to regulations directed towards standardization of quality and prices; and what was of greater importance, religious and social needs would be satisfied by the gilds or companies to which the husbands of these women belonged.

WOMEN'S MEDICAL PRACTICE AND HEALTH CARE IN MEDIEVAL EUROPE

MONICA GREEN

It is a commonplace—both in histories of medicine and histories of women—that throughout the Middle Ages "women's health was women's business."[1] Midwives, it is claimed, were the sole providers of women's health care, and they maintained an unchallenged monopoly on this specialty of medicine until it was gradually wrenched away from them by so-called man-midwives in the course of the seventeenth and eighteenth centuries. At least two assumptions lie embedded in statements such as these: first, that "midwife" is necessarily synonymous with "caretaker of all of women's health

My thanks to the many colleagues who brought to my attention both their own and others' recently published works, and to the Interlibrary Loan staff at Duke University who performed wonders in tracking down the more elusive books and articles. I am particularly indebted to Michael McVaugh, Katharine Park, and the late John F. Benton for their suggestions and especially for sharing their research-in-progress with me. Very special thanks go to Kate Cooper for seeing the glimmer of light in my cloudiest thoughts. *Dedico questo contributo a Marta e Saro.*
    [1] For example, Beryl Rowland, *Medieval Woman's Guide to Health: The First English Gynecological Handbook* (Kent, Ohio: Kent State University Press, 1981), xv, who uses the formulation "women's illnesses were women's business."

. This essay originally appeared in *Signs*, vol. 14, no. 2, Winter 1989.

concerns,"[2] and, second, that in the Middle Ages there existed a sexual division of medical labor so absolute that men did not concern themselves with women's medical conditions (particularly gynecological or obstetrical matters), nor (as some would suggest) did women medical practitioners concern themselves with men. These assumptions are enticing in their simplicity, yet it is astounding how little historical evidence has been brought forth to substantiate them.

Since the purpose of this essay will be to challenge assumptions such as these, let me be clear about an assumption of my own: that most women in the Middle Ages required medical care at some point in their lives. Reproduction was one of the most taxing labors a woman's body had to bear, and it brought with it all manner of risks of infection and other complications. Even women neither gestating nor lactating—whether for reasons of age, infertility, circumstance, or personal choice—may have been subject to innumerable afflictions of the reproductive organs, including menstrual difficulties, infections, and cancers, all of which might be further complicated by malnutrition (which was almost certainly a chronic factor of medieval life). And all women, of course, may have been subject to the same general diseases and injuries that afflict men and children.[3] I assume, therefore, that women's need for health care was more or less constant[4] and that at least some of this need was addressed by specialized caretakers.

[2] Actually, there is a pernicious ambiguity with which "women's health" is discussed. Although the term is not usually defined explicitly, in actual use "women's health" is generally discussed solely in terms of childbirth or other matters directly concerned with it. There may be many reasons for this almost exclusive focus on the birth event (evident in the primary as well as the secondary sources), e.g., patriarchal concern over ensuring women's capacity to reproduce or the fact that birth is one of the few points in a woman's life when her health becomes a matter of public concern. However, if our interest is in the history of women rather than the history of childbirth, we should be asking how women's health as a whole was attended, not simply how the few hours of birth were supervised. Thus, even if we do find that midwives did not treat all of women's diseases, it is still legitimate (indeed imperative) to ask who did.

[3] For an excellent summary of the general medical landscape of medieval Europe, see Katharine Park, "Medicine and Society in Medieval Europe, 500–1500," in *Medicine in Society*, ed. Andrew Wear (Cambridge: Cambridge University Press, in press). For an interesting argument on how technological innovation may have affected women's health, see Vern Bullough and Cameron Campbell, "Female Longevity and Diet in the Middle Ages," *Speculum* 55, no. 2 (April 1980): 317–25.

[4] I am by no means suggesting that morbidity patterns are historically unvarying (as any study of plague, puerperal fever, syphilis, AIDS, or countless other diseases will show). Nevertheless, I do assume that the biomedical experience of medieval women was close enough to that of twentieth-century women to permit comparison.

But precisely who were these caretakers of women? Was the division of medical labor in the Middle Ages so simple and straightforward that the history of women's health care can be considered coextensive with a history of women medical practitioners? The history of the medical treatment of women in fact extends far beyond the question of whether it was provided exclusively by other women; likewise, the history of women's medical practice is by no means limited simply to determining whom they treated. Nevertheless, the history of women patients and the history of women practitioners in medieval Europe are inextricably interwoven: to understand what sort of health care women received, we also need to know what sort of health care they were allowed to give.

Only two monographs have been written on medieval women healers and women's health care, and the few articles published thus far on specific issues do not, even when taken together, constitute a comprehensive history of the subject.[5] Nevertheless, by analyzing the findings of these disparate studies together with the results of recent work on the general social history of medieval medicine, the outlines of a composite picture of women's medical care and medical practice in the Middle Ages begin to emerge. This picture, sketchy as it may be, shows that the assumptions we have accepted so uncritically about women's health care and the sexual division of medical labor in the Middle Ages have masked a reality far more complex than hitherto imagined. It also suggests directions that future research will have to take if we are to see past the prejudices that have

---

[5] Muriel Joy Hughes, *Women Healers in Medieval Life and Literature* (1943; reprint, Freeport, N.Y.: Books for Libraries Press, 1968); and Paul Diepgen, *Frau und Frauenheilkunde in der Kultur des Mittelalters* (Stuttgart: Thieme, 1963). The general works of Melina Lipinska and Kate Campbell Hurd-Mead on women healers throughout history contain substantial sections on the medieval period; see Lipinska, *Histoire des femmes médicins depuis l'antiquité jusqu'à nos jours* (Paris: G. Jacques, 1900), and her later summary, *Les femmes et le progrès des sciences médicales* (Paris: Masson & Cie, 1930); and Hurd-Mead, *A History of Women in Medicine* (1938; reprint, New York: AMS Press, 1977). The latter work, though admirably ambitious, is sadly unreliable in many of its particulars. Walther Schönfeld, *Frauen in der abendländischen Heilkunde vom klassischen Altertum bis zum Ausgang des 19. Jahrhunderts* (Stuttgart: Ferdinand Enke, 1947), offers a useful summary of biographical data on individual women. Most recently, see Margaret Wade Labarge, *Women in Medieval Life: A Small Sound of the Trumpet* (London: Hamish Hamilton; Boston: Beacon, 1986 [the title and the subtitle have been reversed in the U.S. edition]), chap. 8; and Gundolf Keil, "Die Frau als Ärztin und Patientin in der medizinischen Fachprosa des deutschen Mittelalters," in *Frau und spätmittelalterlicher Alltag: International Kongress, Krems an der Donau, 2. bis 5. Oktober 1984* (Vienna: Österreichischen Akademie der Wissenschaften, 1986), 157–211.

rendered this fundamental aspect of women's history into a topic so trivial as to be unworthy of critical investigation.[6]

Although narrow in its primary focus on women's gynecological and obstetrical health care and its providers in Western Christian society after the eleventh century,[7] in other ways this essay extends

[6] Barbara Brandon Schnorrenberg ("Is Childbirth Any Place for a Woman? The Decline of Midwifery in Eighteenth-Century England," Studies in Eighteenth-Century Culture 10 [1981]: 393–408) notes that the Victorian stereotype of the midwife as a "fat, dirty, drunken old woman" has "passed from fiction into fact to encompass all midwives in all periods in many serious works" by even the most respected historians (393). This attitude might also be part of the reason why there are few serious, comprehensive histories of gynecological and obstetrical practice. A welcome indication of change is Yvonne Knibiehler and Catherine Fouquet, La femme et les médecins: Analyse historique (Paris: Hachette, 1983).

[7] For late antiquity and the early Middle Ages, see Monica Green, "Obstetrices litteratae: The Audience of Gynecological Literature in the Late Antique West" (paper presented at the International Conference on "Lebensbedingungen, Lebensnormen und Lebensformen für Frauen in Spätantike und Frühmittelalter," Freie Universität, Berlin, February 18–21, 1987), "The Transmission of Ancient Theories of Female Physiology and Disease through the Early Middle Ages" (Ph.D. diss., Princeton University, 1985), and "The De genecia Attributed to Constantine the African," Speculum 62, no. 2 (April 1987): 299–323; Gerhard Baader, "Frauenheilkunde und Geburtshilfe im Frühmittelalter," in Frauen in der Geschichte, vol. 7, Interdisziplinäre Studien zur Geschichte der Frauen im Frühmittelalter, ed. Werner Affeldt and Annette Kuhn (Düsseldorf: Schwann, 1986), 126–35. Other than Diepgen's survey (n. 5 above), only a handful of works on Byzantium and the Islamic world can be recommended. For late antique Byzantium, see Giorgio del Guerra, Il libro di Metrodora sulle malattie delle donne e il ricettario di cosmetica e terapia (Milan: Ceschina, 1953), and "La medicina bizantina e il codice medico-ginecologica di Metrodora," Scientia Veterum (Pisa) 118 (1968): 67–94. Also, Timothy Miller's The Birth of the Hospital in the Byzantine Empire (Baltimore and London: Johns Hopkins University Press, 1985) contains some information on women's medical care and practice in medieval Greek hospitals. On the Islamic world, see 'Arib ibn Sa'id, Le livre de la génération du foetus et le traitement des femmes enceintes et des nouveau-nés (Arabic text with French translation), ed. and trans. Henri Jahier and Nourredine Abdelkader (Algiers: Librairie Ferraris, 1956), and the new Spanish translation, Antonio Arjona Castro, ed., El libro de la generación del feto, el tratamiento de las mujeres embarazadas y de los recien nacidos de 'Arib ibn Sa'id (Tratado de ostetricia y pediatria hispano árabe del siglo X) (Cordoba: Publicaciones de la excma. diputacion provincial, 1983); the uneven article by R. L. Verma, "Women's Role in Islamic Medicine through the Ages," Arab Historian 22 (1982): 21–48; and the brief anecdote about "The Midwife of Khumarawaih and Her Sister," in Land of Enchanters: Egyptian Short Stories from the Earliest Times to the Present Day, ed. Bernard Lewis (London: Harvill, 1948), 105–7. For the history of one aspect of Islamic medicine fundamental to women's lives, see Basim F. Musallam, Sex and Society in Islam: Birth Control before the Nineteenth Century (Cambridge: Cambridge University Press, 1983), esp. chap. 2. For women practitioners within the Jewish communities of medieval Europe, see Harry Friedenwald, "Jewish Doctoresses in the Middle Ages," in his The Jews and Medicine: Essays, 2 vols. (1944;

broadly: geographically, to include all of western Europe; chrono-logically, to include some pertinent research from the early modern period (which can often only be separated from the medieval period by arbitrary and ultimately unhelpful boundaries); and categori-cally, to include discussion of female medical practitioners in gen-eral for reasons that will soon become apparent.

Women as medical practitioners

When it concerns the Middle Ages, a simple (but hardly insignifi-cant) equation is often made between "woman medical practi-tioner" and "midwife."[8] The danger of such an equation is not merely semantic inaccuracy, for such a blurring of categories frus-trates any attempt to grasp the realities of the gynecological and obstetrical care women received or the expectations made by medi-eval society of both women and men in medical practice. More important, it is simply not true. Several major prosopographical studies provide a preliminary body of data on medieval medical

reprint, New York: Ktav, 1967), 1:217–20; Marcello Segre, "Dottoresse ebree nel medioevo," *Pagine di storia della medicina* 14, no. 5 (September/October 1970): 98–106, though note that not all the women he includes have been securely identified as Jewish; and A. Cardoner Planas, "Seis mujeres hebreas practicando la medicina en el reino de Aragón," *Sefarad* 9, no. 2 (1949): 441–45. Joseph Shatzmiller of the University of Toronto is currently engaged in a comprehensive study of Jewish women practitioners (personal communication, February 1988). S. D. Goitein, in his exhaustive study of Jewish life in medieval Egypt, has noted how surprisingly rare it is to find accounts of midwives and childbirth (*A Mediterranean Society: The Jewish Communities of the Arab World as Portrayed in the Documents of the Cairo Geniza* [Berkeley: University of California Press, 1978], 3:232). However, Ron Barkai has recently identified several medieval Hebrew gynecological works; his edition of one of these, the *Sefer ha-Toledet*, is forthcoming from Les Editions du Cerf, Paris.

  [8] For example, in her study of a fifteenth-century gynecological text, Helen Lemay occasionally uses the terms "midwife" and "old woman" (i.e., "old woman medical practitioner") as if they were completely interchangeable; see Lemay, "Anthonius Guainerius and Medieval Gynecology," in *Women of the Medieval World: Essays in Honor of John H. Mundy*, ed. Julius Kirshner and Suzanne F. Wemple (Oxford and New York: Blackwell, 1985), 317–36, esp. 326–27. See also C. H. Talbot and E. A. Hammond, *The Medical Practitioners in Medieval England: A Biographical Register* (London: Wellcome Historical Medical Library, 1965), 211, where they describe Matilda la Leche as "*probably* the 'sage femme' of Wallingford" (emphasis added). This may be mere assumption rather than a fact supported by the evidence. "Leech" was a generic term for "healer," and it is unwarranted to assume that just because Matilda was a woman, her practice must necessarily have been limited to midwifery. (Since writing this, I have found that A. L. Wyman makes the same point in a letter to the editor, *History Today* 36 [October 1986]: 59, suggesting that the interpolation was on the part of the Victorian editor of the document.)

practitioners, data that demonstrate that numerous medical specialties were recognized in the High and late Middle Ages, as evidenced both by the terminology used to designate different practitioners and by legislation and guild organization. Although they were not represented on all levels of medicine equally, women were found scattered throughout a broad medical community consisting of physicians, surgeons, barber-surgeons, apothecaries, and various uncategorizable empirical healers.[9] Midwives, then, were part of a much larger community of women practitioners, and it will be useful to discuss female healers in general in order to set a context for the specific historical details of women's medical care.[10]

[9] The distinctions between these categories of healers were roughly as follows: physicians, who could often boast of a university training, claimed as their province the general business of diagnosis and treatment of internal diseases; surgeons carried out most of the manual aspects of the medical art (bone setting, amputations, etc.), while barber-surgeons were largely confined to more minor surgical procedures, particularly bloodletting. Apothecaries would be responsible for dispensing medications, though this role took on real medical import when advice was dispensed as well. "Empiric" is a generic term used loosely to signify all those individuals who took up medical practice on their own, independent of university sanction, state licensure, or guild regulation. It should be emphasized, however, that these categories were much more fluid and subjectively defined than in the modern, highly regulated medical industry of Westernized societies. (Indeed, even the vocabulary to distinguish these specialties does not begin to take shape until the tenth and eleventh centuries.) The possibility of overlap in function was enormous, hence the intensity with which certain practitioners fought to solidify hazy boundaries.

[10] I should stress that I am limiting the following discussion to women who can in some sense be called medical specialists or "professionals"—i.e., women who at some point in their lives would have either identified themselves in terms of their medical practice or been so identified by their communities. "Professional" should be understood in its loosest sense. On this point, see the important insights of Margaret Pelling, who has recently stressed that in preindustrial times few medical practitioners relied *solely* on medicine for their livelihood: Pelling, "Medical Practice in Early Modern England: Trade or Profession?" in *The Professions in Early Modern England*, ed. Wilfrid Prest (London: Croom Helm, 1987), 90–128. Furthermore, I do not pretend to be discussing all the situations in which women gave or received health care (e.g., in hospitals); on the contrary, I imagine that most of the medical care women gave and received in the Middle Ages would probably have been in a familial context where few of the issues discussed here would have come into play. For some indication of what this familial context looked like in a later period, see Adrian Wilson, "Participant or Patient? Seventeenth Century Childbirth from the Mother's Point of View," in *Patients and Practitioners: Lay Perceptions of Medicine in Pre-industrial Society*, ed. Roy Porter (Cambridge: Cambridge University Press, 1985), 129–44. Findings from anthropological studies of modern nonindustrial societies might be of comparative value; see Sheila Cosminsky, "Cross-cultural Perspectives on Midwifery," in *Medical Anthropology*, ed. Francis X. Grollig and Harold B. Haley (The Hague and Paris: Mouton, 1976), 229–48. A final limitation of this essay is the omission of miraculous cures and religious healers, which, though important elements of medieval medical practice, involve issues too complicated to be properly addressed here.

Although in all the prosopographical studies conducted thus far women's numbers are remarkably small,[11] the data nevertheless demonstrate conclusively that women's medical practice was by no means limited to midwifery. For example, of the 7,647 practitioners documented by Ernest Wickersheimer and Danielle Jacquart in France for the twelfth through fifteenth centuries, 121 (approximately 1.5 percent) were women.[12] Of these, forty-four are identified by terms we might translate as "midwife" (*matrone, sage-femme, ventrière, mère-aleresse*), while the rest (close to two-thirds) practiced as barbers, surgeons, trained physicians, or untrained empirics. Three are referred to as *sorcières*.[13]

As sparse as the data for France are, the silence of the records for England is positively deafening. C. H. Talbot and E. A. Hammond's biographical register of medical practitioners in England, Scotland, and Wales covers the period from Anglo-Saxon times up to the beginning of the sixteenth century. In these eight centuries, the authors found records of only eight women: six identified as physicians, or more literally, "healers" (*medica* or *leche*), one as a surgeon (*la surgiene*), and one as a midwife (*obstetrix*).[14] Although Edward Kealey's in-depth study of medical practitioners during the Norman period (1100–1154) has not added any new entries to Talbot and Hammond's list of women for that period,[15] he has identified three more names to add to the roll of women practitioners in later twelfth- and thirteenth-century England: the two sisters, Solicita and Matilda, each of whom is designated *medica*, and Euphemia (d. 1257), abbess of Wherell, whom Kealey describes as "an active physician."[16] Talbot and Hammond's register has recently been supplemented for the later medieval period (1340–1530) by Robert Gottfried, who claims to have found evidence for a total of twenty-eight women practitioners (eight "leeches," sixteen barbers, and four apothecaries) in the

[11] Aside from those of Danielle Jacquart and, to a limited extent, Robert Gottfried, none of the following studies have attempted quantitative analyses of the data on women. Most of the figures and interpretations that follow reflect my own tabulations drawn from indices and a rapid survey of the compiled data.

[12] Danielle Jacquart, *Le milieu médical en France du XIIe au XVe siècle: En annexe 2e supplément au "Dictionnaire" d'Ernest Wickersheimer* (Geneva: Librairie Droz, 1981). To this total of 121 can be added the six (not five as stated on p. 47 of her work) additional women whom Jacquart lists in her app. C.

[13] Ibid., 47–54.

[14] Talbot and Hammond (n. 8 above). See the index (502) under "Women Practitioners," though note that Pernell (241) was inadvertently omitted here.

[15] Edward J. Kealey, *Medieval Medicus: A Social History of Anglo-Norman Medicine* (Baltimore and London: Johns Hopkins University Press, 1981), 35.

[16] Edward J. Kealey, "England's Earliest Women Doctors," *Journal of the History of Medicine and the Allied Sciences* 40, no. 4 (October 1985): 473–77.

two centuries of his survey. Yet even these women constitute only
1.2 percent of the 2,282 entries in Gottfried's "doctor's data bank."[17]

No comprehensive survey of female practitioners has yet been
made of medieval Italy,[18] though several localized studies of individual cities or regions provide evidence of women's varied medical
practice. Alcide Garosi, for example, has documented 550 Sienese
medical practitioners between 774 and 1555, two of whom are
women—both physicians (mediche).[19] Ladislao Münster has found
documents regarding seven women who practiced medicine in Venice in the first half of the thirteenth century, including a physician
who was accorded the title "master" (magistra); a surgeon's widow
(no specific practitioner label is attached to her own name) who
was fined for malpractice on "many people, men and women"; and
a specialist of gout and eye problems.[20] None of the documents
suggest that these women concentrated on women's diseases. Katharine Park, in her study of the late medieval Florentine Guild of
Doctors, Apothecaries, and Grocers, explicitly acknowledges that
midwives, barbers, and other practitioners on the medical periphery
have not been included in her research. Park finds only four women
doctors who were members of the guild and only two others who
are documented in contemporary tax records.[21]

[17] Robert S. Gottfried, *Doctors and Medicine in Medieval England, 1340–1530*
(Princeton, N.J.: Princeton University Press, 1986), esp. 87, 89, and 251. Gottfried's
study is of little use in learning more about women's medical practice since he gives
no specific information on these women (he does not even provide their names and
dates) nor does he include midwives among his categories of practitioners.

[18] Ladislao Münster, "Women Doctors in Mediaeval Italy," *Ciba Symposium* (English ed.) 10, no. 3 (1962): 136–40, is the only available survey. Unfortunately, Münster's brief study was published without any documentation, and his findings, therefore,
need to be rechecked against the original sources.

[19] Alcide Garosi, *Siena nella storia della medicina (1240–1555)* (Florence: Leo
S. Olschki, 1958); see 356–98 for his biographical list. The two women were Cha-
telana (fl. late fourteenth century) and Giovanna di Paulo (fl. ca. 1410). One wonders
how Garosi focused his research, however, for the absence of barbers and apothecaries (not to mention midwives) from his list suggests that he did not define "healer"
very broadly.

[20] Ladislao Münster, "Notizie di alcune 'medichesse' veneziane della prima metà
del Trecento," in *Scritti in onore del Prof. A. Pazzini* (Saluzzo: Edizioni Minerva
Medica, 1954), 180–87. For further information on the broader context of medical
practice in Venice, see Ugo Stefanutti, *Documentazioni cronologiche per la storia
della medicina, chirurgia e farmacia in Venezia dal 1258 al 1332* (Venice: Ferdinando
Ongania, 1961).

[21] Katharine Park, *Doctors and Medicine in Early Renaissance Florence* (Princeton, N.J.: Princeton University Press, 1985), 8, 71–72. Park (personal communication,
December 10, 1986) informs me that she has since found one, perhaps two, additional
women doctors in the guild. Other women in the guild were grocers, apothecaries,
leatherworkers, metal workers, painters, etc.

Women practitioners in the south of Italy were, if not more numerous, at least more visible in the documents that have been examined. Salvatore De Renzi's nineteenth-century study of the famous medical center of Salerno mentions several women practitioners: the so-called Salernitan women (*mulieres Salernitanae*) who are frequently mentioned in Salernitan medical literature of the twelfth century, as well as four other women (who are known by name) who not only practiced medicine but also are said to have written learned treatises.[22] Of these, the most famous is the eleventh- or twelfth-century physician Trota, whose existence and authorship have been the subject of a centuries-long, largely sterile debate that, as Susan Mosher Stuard has observed, has told us more about the prejudices of the disputants than about the woman herself.[23] Happily, the controversy has been brought to a close by John Benton's recent discovery of Trota's genuine work (a practical book of medicine) and his demonstration that the texts which circulated under her name were falsely attributed.[24]

Licenses of women who practiced between the thirteenth and fifteenth centuries also provide important evidence. Raffaele Calvanico's study of medicine in the Kingdom of Naples from 1273 to 1410 provides evidence for a total of twenty-four women surgeons, thirteen of whom were explicitly licensed to practice on women. Most interesting is the fact that some of these thirteen were not limited to treating women's peculiar diseases (i.e., those of the

---

[22] Salvatore De Renzi, *Collectio salernitana,* 5 vols. (Naples: Filiatre-Sebezio, 1852–59), 1:159–60, regarding the *mulieres Salernitanae;* on Abella, Rebecca Guarna, and Mercuriade (none of whose dates have yet been established), see De Renzi, 372–73, where the fourteenth-century physician Costanza Calenda is also mentioned. On Costanza, see also Paul Oskar Kristeller, "Learned Women of Early Modern Italy: Humanists and University Scholars," in *Beyond Their Sex: Learned Women of the European Past,* ed. Patricia H. Labalme (New York: New York University Press, 1984), 115, n. 52. On Trota, see John F. Benton, "Trotula, Women's Problems, and the Professionalization of Medicine in the Middle Ages," *Bulletin of the History of Medicine* 59, no. 1 (Spring 1985): 30–53. Benton also cites evidence for two other women healers at Salerno (38–39).

[23] Susan Mosher Stuard, "Dame Trot," *Signs: Journal of Women in Culture and Society* 1, no. 2 (Winter 1975): 537–42; see also Benton for an extended review of this protracted debate.

[24] Benton, esp. 41–46. Only one manuscript of Trota's genuine work, the *Practica secundum Trotam,* is now known to exist. Although the three other works that circulated widely under her name (the *Trotula* treatises) are spurious, that they were attributed to her is palpable evidence of her fame—much the way Hippocrates is associated with the ancient Greek Hippocratic Corpus even though he probably did not author any part of it.

breasts and genitalia) but seem to have been expected to perform a whole variety of surgical operations on women.[25]

The mass of documentation for the social history of medieval Spanish medicine has only begun to be studied, yet some preliminary results are available. Michael McVaugh has been undertaking an exhaustive study of the archives of the Crown of Aragón between 1285 and 1335. As rich and complete as these archives are, McVaugh has not been able to document a single woman medical practitioner attached to the royal household.[26] In contrast, studies of the wider medical community in fourteenth-century Valencia by Luis Garcia Ballester, McVaugh, and Augustin Rubio Vela reveal several women who were practicing both as unofficial, empirical healers (*curanderas*) and as licensed physicians (*metgesses*), the latter often being Muslim women who practiced within the ruling Christian community.[27] Like their Italian counterparts, it is clear that their practice was not limited exclusively to gynecological and obstetrical problems, and they may even have had more freedom to treat both men and women than did their Italian sisters.[28]

To my knowledge, no comprehensive archival study has yet been done of medical practitioners in the medieval German prin-

---

[25] Raffaele Calvanico, *Fonti per la storia della medicina e della chirurgia per il regno di Napoli nel periodo angioino (a. 1273–1410)* (Naples: L'Arte Tipografica, 1962). Since these women cannot all be readily identified in Calvanico's index, I list them here with their entry numbers: Adelicia da Capua (3006); Bona di Guglielmo di Odorisio da Miglionico (3119); Clarice di Durisio da Foggia (3127); Costanza da Barletta (1168, 1209); Francesca, wife of Matteo di Romano da Salerno (1451, 1872, 1874); Francesca, wife of Vestis (916); Gemma da Molfetta (1981); Isabella da Ocre (3195); Lauretta, wife of Giovanni dal Ponte da Saracena (1413, 2023, 2026); Letizia di Manso da Friano (3072); Mabilia di Scarpa da S. Maria (3327, 3371, 3406); Margherita di Napoli, da S. Maria (3534); Margherita de Ruga (3572, 3620); Margherita da Venosa (3226); Maria Gallicia (1165, 1234); Maria Incarnata (3571); Polisena de Troya (3598, 3610); Raymunda de Taberna (3643); Sabella di Ocro (or de Erro) (3071); Sibilia d'Afflicto di Benevento (3407); Sibilia da S. Giovanni Rotondo (3227); Trotta di Troya (966); Venturella Consinata (1875); Vigorita da Rossano (3512). Calvanico's notes on Clarice indicate that she was licensed to practice as a surgeon for women's eye problems (*chirurga oculista per le donne*).

[26] Michael McVaugh, personal communication.

[27] Luis Garcia Ballester, Michael McVaugh, and Augustin Rubio Vela, *Licensing, Learning and the Control of Medical Practice in Fourteenth-Century Valencia* (Philadelphia: American Philosophic Society, in press). Although a full tabulation of all the known Spanish women practitioners has not yet been made, McVaugh has indicated to me that most appear only after 1350.

[28] One woman, Bevenguda, was licensed by the king in 1394 with the explicit recognition that she already had experience "treating and curing many men and children of both sexes of serious conditions and illnesses" (Garcia Ballister, McVaugh, and Rubio Vela).

cipalities, though here again the few data that have been assembled indicate that women performed a variety of medical functions, not simply midwifery. Walther Schönfeld, for example, has found evidence for fifteen women practitioners (most of them Jewish) in Frankfurt am Main between 1387 and 1497, several of whom specialized in eye diseases. None is referred to as a midwife.[29]

These data on medieval Europe as a whole thus offer us tangible evidence for the existence of all kinds of women healers.[30] Still, we are left wondering why the evidence for these women—and especially for midwives—is so sparse, forming (in those instances where percentages can be tabulated) no more than the tiniest fraction of the medical populace as a whole. Is it really possible that there was only one midwife in the whole of England or that there were none at all in Italy? Obviously, beyond the general poverty of sources all medieval researchers must face, there is need to acknowledge the special limitations of the historical record for research on women, for apart from medical licenses, the principal sources used have been wills, property transfers, court records, and similar documents, all of which traditionally underrepresent women.[31] Indeed, it is generally the unusual woman—the one who has acquired enough personal wealth to leave a will or be taxed, the one who is brought to court on civil or criminal charges—that finds her way into the historical record, not her less conspicuous colleague.[32] The absence of women may also be due to the parameters by which some researchers themselves have chosen to define their investigations. Focusing on the upper echelons of "learned" medicine, sometimes to the complete exclusion of empirics and other healers on the legal and social fringes of medical practice (where most women would have been found), these studies by their

[29] Schönfeld (n. 5 above), 75. Schönfeld's list and other documents on German women's medical practice have been collected by Peter Ketsch in *Frauen im Mittelalter*, Band 1: *Frauenarbeit im Mittelalter, Quellen und Materialien*, Studien materialien Band 14: Geschichtsdidaktik, ed. Annette Kuhn (Düsseldorf: Schwann, 1983), 1:259–307.

[30] Gundolf Keil (n. 5 above, 204–6) suggests that women who translated, copied, and illustrated medical texts should also be included in assessing women's involvement in medicine. Keil would also include women for whom special tracts were written or to whom treatises were dedicated, since, in those cases where they actually commissioned the works to be written, these women were very obviously displaying an active interest in women's health care.

[31] Werner Gerabek has recently suggested the potential value of letter collections as a source for the history of medicine; see "*Consolida maior, Consolida minor* und eine Kräuterfrau: Medizinhistorische Beobachtungen zur Reinhardsbrunner Briefsammlung," *Sudhoffs Archiv* 67, no. 1 (1983): 80–93, esp. 92.

[32] Even these women often only surface in the records as widows or unmarried women, i.e., only when they are no longer legally "covered" by a husband or father.

very nature offer limited hope of documenting the existence of women practitioners.

The advantages of broadening the definition of "medical practitioner" are immediately apparent in Margaret Pelling and Charles Webster's study of sixteenth-century London and Norwich. Instead of focusing solely on officially recognized and licensed physicians, barbers, and surgeons, Pelling and Webster use as their working definition "any individual whose occupation is basically concerned with the care of the sick."[33] The dramatic increase in the number of women practitioners who can thus be identified cannot be attributed solely to demographic or social changes in the early modern period.[34] In London, Pelling and Webster have found an estimate made circa 1560 of sixty women practitioners in the city at that time (only thirty years after the ending date of Gottfried's survey). Although this may be a slightly exaggerated figure, it still poses a striking contrast to Gottfried's total of twenty-eight women throughout the whole of England for the two previous centuries. In Norwich in the two decades between 1570 and 1590, ten women practitioners are known by name, again a high figure compared to the sparse medieval data gathered thus far (though still seemingly low for a town of 17,000 people).[35]

Clearly, then, the definition of "medical practitioner" used in such studies must be as broad as possible if we are to catch more than a handful of women in our analytical net.[36] Yet prosopography

[33] Margaret Pelling and Charles Webster, "Medical Practitioners," in Health, Medicine and Mortality in the Sixteenth Century, ed. Charles Webster (Cambridge: Cambridge University Press, 1979), 165–235, esp. 166.

[34] Obviously, changes in the type and amount of records available for the early modern period would contribute to these differential findings. This, however, does not warrant (and if anything, it counterindicates) drawing arguments from the silence of the medieval records.

[35] Pelling and Webster, 183–84, 222–26. Seven of the Norwich women were employed by the city corporation to perform a variety of cures; one was a licensed surgeon. Only one was explicitly referred to as "obstetrix," though one other woman was described more vaguely as a spinster "that helped women."

[36] A similar critique was made by Luke Demaitre in his review of Jacquart's, Le milieu médical (Speculum 58, no. 2 [April 1983]: 486–89, esp. 488), where he notes the complete absence from Jacquart's study of any vetulae ("old wives") "who appear so frequently in the literature." See also Jole Agrimi and Chiara Crisciani, "Medici e 'vetulae' dal duecento al quattrocento: Problemi di una ricerca," in Cultura popolare e cultura dotta nel seicento: Atti del convegno di studio de Genova (23–25 novembre 1982) (Milan: Franco Angeli, 1983), 144–59. An example of such vetulae is "a certain old woman" I discovered who had been called before King William (William the Conqueror or William Rufus?) to explain one of her cures. Cambridge, Trinity College MS 903 (R.14.30), 13th or 14th cent., fol. 121r (olim fol. 227r): "Quidam quartanarius a nullo medico liberari potuit cui quedam uetula succum

may have limitations even more fundamentally rooted in the method itself, which usually restricts the admissible data to persons known by name in order to properly individuate and identify them. The problem this poses for any study of women in the medieval period is obvious, for even when they are introduced into the historical record women are all too often nameless (witness the otherwise indistinguishable "Salernitan women").

In sum, while the prosopographical data do demonstrate the variety of women's medical practice in medieval Europe, because of their paucity they tell us little more. Indeed, such meager data have encouraged an unsatisfactory, anecdotal sort of history that unfortunately is still characteristic of the field.[37] There is, nevertheless, still hope of bringing greater nuance and sophistication to our understanding of medieval women healers. For this, we need to bring analyses developed in other areas of women's history into play as we explore the wider social context of women's health care and medical practice. We need, in short, to raise questions of power, of economic rivalry, of literacy and the control of knowledge. When these are set into a chronological framework, certain striking patterns emerge.

Professionalization and the restriction of women's medical practice

In her recent book on women's work in early modern Germany, Merry Wiesner argues that women's participation in health care was seen as "natural and proper, part of women's sphere." She goes on to claim that women working in health care were rarely viewed as economically, socially, or politically threatening.[38] Whether or not Wiesner's idyllic picture is accurate for sixteenth- and seventeenth-century Germany,[39] the medieval data for the rest of Europe present no such uniform image of a clearly defined sexual division of labor that allowed women complete freedom of movement within their "natural

---

tapsi barbati tribus diebus ante accessionem dedit et statim liberatus est. Quam rex Williamus iussit uocari et confessa est quomodo fecit."

[37] See, e.g., Rowland (n. 1 above), introduction; and the works by Hughes and Labarge (n. 5 above).

[38] Merry E. Wiesner, *Working Women in Renaissance Germany* (New Brunswick, N.J.: Rutgers University Press, 1986), 37. Wiesner's findings on midwives also appear (in somewhat expanded form) in "Early Modern Midwifery: A Case Study," in *Women and Work in Preindustrial Europe*, ed. Barbara A. Hanawalt (Bloomington: Indiana University Press, 1986), 94–113.

[39] Some of the evidence Wiesner presents calls her own picture into question. In *Working Women*, Wiesner recounts the persecution of female physicians, sur-

sphere" or that freed men from any threat of competition. On the contrary, medieval Europe was a battleground for all medical practitioners—women being caught in the crossfire—and it is here, not in the seventeenth or eighteenth centuries, that the foundations were laid for the eventual (though hardly inevitable) exclusion of women from independent medical practice.

Although its timing and degree of effectiveness varied greatly, most of western Europe witnessed the implementation of medical licensing by secular and religious authorities between the twelfth and sixteenth centuries. Moreover, medical practitioners themselves often banded together to form guilds or protective societies that attempted to control who could practice and under what conditions they could do so. These developments resulted in fierce tensions between physicians trained in the universities, surgeons and apothecaries trained by apprenticeship, and empirics with no formal training at all.[40] Viewed from the perspective of women, these first attempts to control nonuniversity-trained practitioners are notable in that they were initially sexually egalitarian. Why, then, at a certain historical moment should women have been explicitly singled out and excluded?

In France from the late thirteenth century on, physicians of the Parisian faculty of medicine made concerted efforts to control the medical practice of surgeons, barbers, and empirics. This led in 1322 to the oft-recounted trial of several unlicensed healers, including one Jacoba (or Jacquéline) Felicie who clearly was treating both women and men.[41] A principal argument used by the prose-

geons, barbers, and empirics, noting that "during the course of the sixteenth century, many [German] cities passed regulations expressly forbidding 'women and other untrained people' to practice medicine in any way" (49–55, esp. 50).

[40] For a general discussion of these developments, see Vern Bullough, *The Development of Medicine as a Profession: The Contribution of the Medieval University to Modern Medicine* (Basel and New York: Karger, 1966); and Park, "Medicine and Society in Medieval Europe, 500–1500" (n. 3 above). How the process of the professionalization of medicine in late medieval Europe specifically affected women has never been thoroughly analyzed.

[41] The best accounts of this trial are Eileen Power, "Some Women Practitioners of Medicine in the Middle Ages," *Proceedings of the Royal Society of Medicine* 15, no. 6 (April 1922): 20–23; and Pearl Kibre, "The Faculty of Medicine at Paris, Charlatanism and Unlicensed Medical Practice in the Later Middle Ages," *Bulletin of the History of Medicine* 27, no. 1 (January/February 1953): 1–20, reprinted in *Legacies in Law and Medicine*, ed. Chester R. Burns (New York: Science History Publications, 1977), 52–71, and in P. Kibre, *Studies in Medieval Science: Alchemy, Astrology, Mathematics and Medicine* (London: Hambledon, 1984), art. 13. A partial translation of the proceedings can be found in James Bruce Ross and Mary M. McLaughlin, eds., *The Portable Medieval Reader* (1949; reprint, New York: Viking, 1959), 635–40.

cution against Jacoba was that as it was forbidden for women to practice law, so much the more should they be barred from practicing medicine where their ignorance might result in a man's death rather than the simple loss of his case in court. Yet the statute of 1271 which Jacoba allegedly violated said nothing that restricted women more than men from medical practice. On the contrary, the statute was phrased in such a way that put the female surgeon, apothecary, or herbalist under the very same restrictions as her male counterpart[42]—a formulation that assumes both that these women exist and that they have the possibility of meeting the same requirements as men in order to practice legally.[43]

In Valencia, Luis Garcia Ballester and his colleagues have shown that prior to 1329 (and in some cities, even afterward) all the ordinances regulating medical practice simply applied to anyone "who has not learned the science of medicine, be they men or women, Christian, Jew, or Saracen."[44] As they note, this precedent of "egalitarianism" makes the new law of 1329 all the more curious. It stipulated that "no woman may practice medicine or give potions, under penalty of being whipped through the town; but they may care for little children and women to whom, however, they may give no potion."[45] Garcia Ballester and his coauthors suggest that this severe and unprecedented prohibition of women's practice may have been motivated by a simple desire to control the practice of

[42] Henri Denifle, ed., *Chartularium Universitatis Parisiensis* (Paris, 1891–99; reprint, Brussels: Culture et Civilisation, 1964), 1:489: "Idcirco firmiter inhibemus ne aliquis cirurgicus seu cyrurgica, apothecarius seu apothecaria, herbarius seu herbaria per juramenta sua limites seu metas sui artificii clam vel palam seu qualitercunque excedere presumat." A full translation of the statute can be found in Lynn Thorndike, *University Records and Life in the Middle Ages* (New York: Columbia University Press, 1944), 83–85.

[43] It is, of course, conceivable that the inclusive phrasing of the statute was motivated by a formulaic need to cover all possibilities rather than by a straightforward recognition of current realities; nevertheless, other sources leave no doubt that women were in fact practicing in these fields. The one field that was virtually closed to women was the practice of "physic" (general internal medicine), which was generally limited to those having attended a university, which normatively women could not do. Neither, however, could Jews or (in Spain) Muslims or even (in practical terms) most Christian men, so the emphasis on university education cannot be seen as a restriction directed solely toward women.

[44] Garcia Ballester, McVaugh, and Rubio Vela (n. 27 above). The text quoted is from an ordinance from the town of Valls, redacted in 1299 and again in 1319. Religious diversity did raise its own complications, however. In 1338, concern over the potentially corrupting influence of intimate contact between religious groups prompted a regulation that "any Saracen woman who acts as *metgessa* to women" could not bring a Christian woman into her house for treatment.

[45] Ibid.

gynecology and obstetrics by Muslim *metgesses*. We should not, however, overlook the fact that it is simultaneously excluding them (and all other women) from other forms of practice.[46]

In England, where the physicians became organized only much later, it was not until 1421 that a petition was put before Parliament requesting, among other measures to ensure the physicians' hegemony, "that no Woman use the practyse of Fisyk [medicine] undre the same payne" of "long emprisonement" and a fine of forty pounds.[47] That this measure was ultimately ineffectual does not diminish the fact that the desire to prohibit women's medical practice was obviously real.

Interestingly, the one area of medicine generally thought of as "women's work," midwifery, was affected by the trend toward licensing only at the very end of the Middle Ages.[48] Currently there

[46] This law does not guarantee women a monopoly in gynecology and pediatrics, however, since the stipulation that women could not administer "potions" would, theoretically, have severely limited their independence of practice; any internal medicines (which were a major component of all medieval medical care) would have to be administered by a (male) physician.

[47] Power (n. 41 above), 23. Wiesner, *Working Women* (n. 38 above), argues that restrictions on women's practice in Germany came only in the sixteenth century.

[48] By "licensing" I mean the granting of official permission to practice according to prescribed regulations on training and ethical principles, which were usually assessed by means of examinations and/or oaths. This needs to be distinguished from other forms of official recognition of a practitioner's competence and/or right to practice. For example, the employment of midwives by municipal authorities to provide free or subsidized services to women of the city is known in Frankfurt am Main from 1302, in Nuremberg from 1381, in Basel from 1455, and in other German municipalities; see Gordon P. Elmeer, "The Regulation of German Midwifery in the 14th, 15th and 16th Centuries" (M.D. thesis, Yale University School of Medicine, 1964), esp. 8. Isaac De Meyer has similarly documented the employment of municipal midwives in Bruges from 1312; see Isaac De Meyer, *Recherches sur la pratique de l'art des accouchements à Bruges depuis le XIVe siècle jusqu'à nos jours* (Bruges: 1843), 9–11. In France, the Hôtel Dieu of Paris was appointing midwives to work at its maternity hospital from at least 1378; see Richard L. Petrelli, "The Regulation of Midwifery during the *Ancien Régime*," *Journal of the History of Medicine and the Allied Sciences* 26, no. 3 (July 1971): 276–92, esp. 279. In the absence of licensing, however, criteria that might have been used to appoint these individuals would not necessarily have applied to other practitioners. In Frankfurt am Main, e.g., municipal midwives were first examined for their medical knowledge only in 1491, 189 years after the office was instituted; examination of other midwives began eight years later (Elmeer, 9). Licensing also needs to be distinguished from the employment of midwives as "expert witnesses" in legal proceedings to determine pregnancy or virginity. Indeed, it is not clear that it was only publicly recognized (let alone licensed) midwives who performed this function. In England from the early thirteenth century, legal determinations of pregnancy were conducted by juries of matrons, "lawful and discreet women," no mention being made of their medical knowledge; see Thomas R. Forbes, "A Jury of Matrons," *Medical History*

is no indication that medieval midwives attempted to organize or control themselves by means of guilds or other formal associations in the same way that many male practitioners did. On the contrary, all currently available data show that licensing, which apparently began in the mid-fifteenth century (the earliest known example is from Regensburg in 1452), was imposed on midwives from the outside, either by local municipal or ecclesiastical authorities, or by both.[49] Most of these early regulations were meant to control not the midwives' medical skills but, rather, their moral character. When these regulations do focus on strictly medical matters, they usually reflect an attempt to monitor, restrict, and control midwives' practice, often requiring them to turn first to other midwives and then to male physicians and surgeons for help.[50]

32, no. 1 (January 1988): 23–33. Similarly, the committee of "matrones tres-expertes" appointed to confirm Joan of Arc's virginity in 1431 consisted of aristocratic women rather than practicing midwives; see Thomas G. Benedek, "The Changing Relationship between Midwives and Physicians during the Renaissance," *Bulletin of the History of Medicine* 51, no. 4 (Winter 1977): 550–64, esp. 561.

[49] Histories of midwifery have mostly been limited to local or regional studies. For England, see J. H. Aveling, *English Midwives: Their History and Prospects* (1872; reprint, London: Hugh K. Elliott, 1967); and Thomas R. Forbes, *The Midwife and the Witch* (1966; reprint, New York: AMS Press, 1982). More recently, see the introductory chapter of Jean Donnison's excellent study, *Midwives and Medical Men: A History of Inter-Professional Rivalries and Women's Rights* (New York: Schocken, 1977), which has in no way been superseded by Jean Towler and Joan Bramall, *Midwives in History and Society* (London: Croom Helm, 1986). The first known English midwife's license dates from 1588; see James Hitchcock, "A Sixteenth-century Midwife's License," *Bulletin of the History of Medicine* 41, no. 1 (January–February 1967): 75–76. Studies on German-speaking territories abound: in addition to Elmeer, see Georg Burckhard, *Die deutschen Hebammenordnungen von ihren erstern Anfängen bis auf die Neuzeit* (Leipzig: W. Engelman, 1912), which prints the texts of many early German midwife ordinances; Elseluise Haberling, *Beiträge zur Geschichte des Hebammenstandes*, vol. 1, *Der Hebammenstand in Deutschland von seinen Anfängen bis zum Dreissigjährigen Krieg* (Berlin: Elwin Staude, 1940); Katharina Meyer, *Zur Geschichte des Hebammenwesens im Kanton Bern*, Berner Beiträge zur Geschichte der Medizin und der Naturwissenschaften, Neue Folge, 11 (Bern: Hans Huber, 1985); and Merry Wiesner's studies (n. 38 above). Popular overviews can be found in Wolfgang Gubalke, *Die Hebamme im Wandel der Zeiten: Ein Beitrag zur Geschichte des Hebammenwesens* (Hannover: Elwin Staude, 1964), and Jean-Pierre Lefftz, *L'art des accouchements à Strasbourg et son rayonnement européen de la Renaissance au Siècle des Lumières* (Strasbourg: Editions Contades, 1985). In addition to De Meyer, data on midwives and women's medical care in the late medieval Netherlands can be found in Myriam Greilsammer, "The Condition of Women in Flanders and Brabant at the End of the Middle-Ages" (Ph.D. diss., Hebrew University, Jerusalem, 1984).

[50] The controlling function of midwifery regulations has been pointed out with particular clarity by Dagmar Birkelbach, Christiane Eifert, and Sabine Lueken, "Zur

The timing of these midwifery regulations, which coincide with the first stirrings of the early modern wave of witch persecutions, has prompted several theses that argue for a direct connection between the two phenomena.[51] These arguments suffer from numerous shortcomings, not least of which is the failure to distinguish between midwives and female medical practitioners in general or to recognize that midwives seem to have constituted no more than a minority of the women convicted of witchcraft. Richard and Ritta Jo Horsley have recently stressed the importance of distinguishing between "wise women" and midwives, and especially of distinguishing between official formulations of witchcraft theory and the actual beliefs of the people who made accusations against individual women.[52] What little evidence for the medieval period that has been brought forward seems to support their conclusions, for despite the vitriolic accusations made against midwives in Jakob Sprenger and Heinrich Kramer's *Malleus Maleficarum* ("The Hammer of Witches") in 1486, the rhetoric of witchcraft seems to have been used not so much against midwives as against *vetulae* ("old women") and empirics, and even here it is not clear how widespread such accusations were. [53]

Entwicklung des Hebammenwesens vom 14. bis zum 16. Jahrhundert am Beispiel der regensburger Hebammenordnungen," in *Frauengeschichte: Dokumentation des 3. Historikerinnentreffens in Bielefeld, April 1981* (Munich: Verlag Frauenoffensive, 1981), 83–98. See also Knibiehler and Fouquet (n. 6 above), esp. chap. 6; and Benedek (n. 48 above).

[51] Barbara Ehrenreich and Deirdre English, *Witches, Midwives and Nurses* (Old Westbury, N.Y.: Feminist Press, 1973); Gunnar Heinsohn and Otto Steiger, "The Elimination of Medieval Birth Control and the Witch Trials of Modern Times," *International Journal of Women's Studies* 5, no. 3 (May/June 1982): 193–214, and *Die Vernichtung der weisen Frauen: Beiträge zur Theorie und Geschichte von Bevölkerung und Kindheit* (Herbstein: März, 1985); and Anne Barstow, "Women as Healers, Women as Witches," *Old Westbury Review*, no. 2 (Fall 1986), 121–33.

[52] Richard A. Horsley, "Who Were the Witches? The Social Roles of the Accused in the European Witch Trials," *Journal of Interdisciplinary History* 9, no. 4 (Spring 1979): 689–715; and Ritta Jo Horsley and Richard A. Horsley, "On the Trail of the 'Witches': Wise Women, Midwives and the European Witch Hunts," in *Women in German Yearbook 3: Feminist Studies and German Culture*, ed. Mariane Burkhard and Edith Waldstein (Washington, D.C.: University Press of America, 1987), 1–28.

[53] For a summary of Jakob Sprenger and Heinrich Kramer's accusations against midwives in the *Malleus Maleficarum*, see Towler and Bramall (n. 49 above), 33–39. Although they place their discussion of witches in a chapter entitled "The Dark Ages and Medieval Period," none of the texts Towler and Bramall cite associating witches and midwives predates Sprenger and Kramer's 1486 tract; most are from the sixteenth century. Although Wiesner (*Working Women*, n. 38 above) does not really tackle this issue directly, the rarity of prosecutions for witchcraft among the

This rapid survey of legislation and other attempts to restrict and control women's medical practice demonstrates the complexity of the tensions within the wider community of medical practitioners to which women belonged: tensions not only between male and female, but also between Christian and Jew (and in Spain, Muslim as well), between those in positions of political power (the physicians and, to a lesser extent, guild members) and those relatively lacking in power (empirics and "old women"). To these must also be added the often conflicting needs and goals of municipal, royal, and ecclesiastical authorities. These multiple axes of tension and rivalry make it particularly difficult to determine the true motives and causes of developments affecting women's medical practice. There is, however, one strand of this complex tapestry that makes the question of professionalization unique for women—the sexual division of labor. This is itself a difficult issue, but in order to address it briefly, let me explore one deceptively simple question: Who was responsible for the care of women?

---

legal cases involving midwives in early modern Germany suggests that the rhetoric of witchcraft was not normally used against midwives, who on the whole were a well-respected community. Wiesner mentions in passing some cases in Württemburg but stresses that "these are really witchcraft cases in which the woman accused *happened* to be a midwife" (69; emphasis added). On the association of *vetulae* and witchcraft, see Agrimi and Crisciani (n. 36 above); and, in the same volume, Paola Zambelli, "Vetula quasi strix?" 160–63. For documents on several such women, see Josep Perarnau i Espelt, "Activitats i fórmules supersticioses de guarició a Catalunya en la primera meitat del segle XIV," *Arxiu de Textos Catalans Antics* 1 (1982): 47–78, which includes the case of Geralda Codines, who was brought in for questioning in 1304, 1307, and again in 1328 in Barcelona. Clearly quite knowledgeable about general medical theory, Geralda was questioned about her use of religious charms and prayers in her medical practice. (I am indebted to Michael McVaugh for bringing this article to my attention.) Other studies on women's medical practice provide only random incidents of alleged magical practices: Charles Talbot ("Dame Trot and Her Progeny," *Essays and Studies* [The English Association], n.s., 25 [1972]: 1–14, esp. 13–14) cites the case of a Viennese woman who in 1470 was forced to confess that she had practiced medicine "having been deceived by the devil." A. L. Wyman, "The Surgeoness: The Female Practitioner of Surgery, 1400–1800," *Medical History* 28, no. 1 (January 1984): 22–41, cites the Act of 1511 in England, by which physicians tried to limit the practice of empirics (27). The preamble to the act condemns "Women [who] boldly and accustomably take upon them great Cures, and things of great difficulty, in the which they partly use Sorcery and Witchcraft." Wyman notes, however, that a later act in 1542 removed many of these restrictions, allowing "divers honest men and women" to carry on their practice unimpeded. Only two witches, Margaret Neale and Elizabeth Clerke, are mentioned in Pelling and Webster's survey of sixteenth-century London and Norwich practitioners (n. 33 above, 231–32).

The care of women and the sexual division of labor

Up till now, the standard answer, as I stated at the outset of this essay, has been unequivocal: "women's health was women's business." In this vein, Charles Talbot has argued that at least in the case of the women practicing at Salerno, "It seems quite clear that [women's medical practice] was restricted to the fields of gynecology and paediatrics, in which medical men showed no interest."[54] Talbot thus envisions a simple sexual division of labor: women treated women, men treated men—the unambiguous line of sex (of both the patient and the practitioner) defining whose turf was whose, with neither men nor women desiring to cross that divide. (How Talbot imagined women's nongynecological problems were treated is unclear.) Obviously, the evidence for women practitioners surveyed above already casts serious doubt on these assumptions. To judge from Trota's genuine work, for example, her practice was not so limited as Talbot imagines, for only about one-quarter of it deals with gynecological or obstetrical concerns, the rest of the text being devoted to various ailments such as fevers, wounds, and internal disorders.[55] Similarly, the Italian and Spanish data indicate that, even for those female physicians and surgeons who were restricted by their license to treating only women, their practice was rarely limited to just gynecological or obstetrical problems.[56]

But even if we restrict our discussion to gynecological and obstetrical care, can we still maintain that "women's health was women's business" and particularly that it was *midwives'* business? Let me return to the issue of definition I addressed briefly above. Thus far, I have been treating the term "midwife" as if its definition were commonly agreed upon and unproblematic. Yet if "midwife" was

[54] Talbot, 2.

[55] See Benton (n. 22 above), 41. Professor Benton was kind enough to share with me his transcription of Trota's *Practica* which he was in the process of editing at the time of his death. Of the other Salernitan women noted for their writings, Abella was said to have written *On Black Bile* and *On the Nature of the Seed*, Rebecca Guarna *On Fevers*, *On Urines*, and *On the Fetus*, and Mercuriade *On Critical Days*, *On Pestilential Fever*, *On the Care of Wounds*, and *On Unguents*; see De Renzi (n. 22 above), 1:372–73. As with Trota, these attributions need to be reconfirmed in accordance with modern scholarly standards.

[56] It is important to stress, however, that modern Western medical beliefs about what does or does not constitute a condition or disorder of the reproductive system were not necessarily shared by medieval people. Work on medieval theories of female physiology and disease (as represented in medical literature) suggests that the spectrum of diseases thought to have their origin in the reproductive system was very broad indeed; see Green, "Transmission" (n. 7 above).

not simply a generic name for any female practitioner, how did medieval people actually define it?[57] Was it someone who assisted women with all their medical problems or just with those having to do with the reproductive organs? Or was this role even more narrowly defined as someone who assisted only with birth itself, leaving all prenatal and postpartum conditions to the care of others? Was the midwife a woman who functioned independently, or was she subservient to another (perhaps male) practitioner? Was she, indeed, always a woman? Was her role exclusive, that is, did she have a monopoly on whatever it was she did, or did she face competition from other healers? Was "midwife" a term used to refer to someone formally trained as a healer, or was it used more loosely to designate a woman who, in a specific situation, merely performed the function of "standing by" at birth (the original sense of the Latin term, *obstetrix*)?[58] Was there, in fact, any single definition of "midwife" in medieval Europe, or was it, rather, a variable concept whose definition changed in different social and medical contexts?

Michel Salvat, one of the few scholars to have raised the question of definition, found the following description of the midwife's function in the thirteenth-century Latin encyclopedia of Bartholomew the Englishman (which was subsequently translated into various

[57] Michel Salvat ("L'accouchement dans la littérature scientifique médiévale," *Senefiance* 9 [1980]: 87–106) distinguishes between midwifery as a simple activity that would be the shared responsibility of kinswomen and neighbors, and midwifery as a true craft or profession in which certain women would specialize and on which they would rely for income. In other words, this distinction would be between *midwives* (i.e., acknowledged specialists) and *midwifery* (i.e., a simple stock of skills and knowledge that was freely and informally shared among the whole community of women—and perhaps even some men). Salvat argues that informal, familial traditions of medical care predominated throughout most of the Middle Ages, whereas the midwife strictly defined cannot be found before the second half of the thirteenth century and then only as an urban phenomenon. This proposed chronology (which is based solely on French evidence) is probably a conservative estimate since it refers to when professional midwives first appear in the historical records. Nevertheless, Salvat is probably right to stress the urban aspects of midwives' practice, since any type of specialization requires a minimum concentration of population to support it. A profitable contrast might be made with the abundant evidence for professional midwives in the highly urbanized world of antiquity; see, e.g., the literature cited in Valerie French, "Midwives and Maternity Care in the Greco-Roman World," in *Rescuing Creusa: New Methodological Approaches to Women in Antiquity*, a special issue of *Helios* edited by Marilyn Skinner, n.s. 13, no. 2 (1987): 69–84; and Green, "*Obstetrices*" (n. 7 above).

[58] Adrian Wilson raises similar issues of the complexity of definition in his study of eighteenth-century male midwifery; see "William Hunter and the Varieties of Man-Midwifery," in *William Hunter and the Eighteenth-century Medical World*, ed. W. F. Bynum and Roy Porter (Cambridge: Cambridge University Press, 1985), 343–69.

vernacular languages): "A midwife [Latin, *obstetrix;* Italian, *obsti-tris;* Provençal, *levayritz;* Spanish, *partera;* French, *ventriere*] is a woman who possesses the art of aiding a woman in birth so that [the mother] might give birth more easily and the infant might not incur any danger. . . . She also receives the child as it emerges from the womb."[59] This would seem to conform with the most narrow definition above, yet Salvat does not mention that Bartholomew's passage occurs within the context of a larger discussion of the "ages of man" where there is no reference whatsoever to women's general health care.[60] Nor does Salvat examine the profound implications of this definition for the actual treatment of women. Looked at from the perspective of the patient, the midwife of Bartholomew's definition (if taken literally) provides an extremely limited service: both before and after the baby is born, the woman must call on some other health care provider for all her medical needs.

One might contrast Bartholomew's concept of the role of the midwife with that found in the sixth-century gynecological work of Muscio, which circulated throughout the Middle Ages. Here it is assumed that midwives (*obstetrices*) would be responsible for *all* gynecological and obstetrical concerns—a definition that would consequently have radically different ramifications for the woman patient.[61]

Neither of these definitions may be fully representative of medieval understandings of the term (Muscio because he reflects late antique realities more than medieval, Bartholomew because of the limited context of his discussion), yet their agreements and disagreements are instructive. Both take it for granted that the midwife is a woman,[62] and both identify the midwife as a trained healer who specializes in the care of other women's reproductive concerns. They disagree, however, on how extensive that province of specialty is. Most interestingly, neither definition either states or implies that the midwife's province of medical practice is exclusively hers,[63] an

---

[59] Salvat, 90–91, 101.

[60] "Man" as Bartholomew uses it is ostensibly meant to refer to humans, though the specificity of most of his discussion suggests that he is really just talking about the male.

[61] Valentin Rose, ed., *Sorani Gynaeciorum vetus translatio latina* (Leipzig: Teubner, 1882), 6: "What is a midwife? A woman learned in all the diseases of women, and also expert in medical practice" (Quid est obstetrix? femina omnium muliebrium causarum docta, etiam medicinali exercitatione perita).

[62] The grammatical gender of all the terms for "midwife" in the various European languages is feminine.

[63] There are other indications in Muscio's text that obstetrics and gynecology are definitely not the exclusive monopoly of midwives; see Green, "*Obstetrices*" (n. 7 above).

issue of monopoly that is important for a proper historical understanding not only of midwives' practice (which might have faced
competition from or subordination to other practitioners) but also
of the options available to women patients when they had to choose
a medical attendant.[64] If midwives did not have a monopoly on the
whole field of obstetrics and gynecology (and if my assumption is
accepted that a constant need for this care existed), then obviously
there must have been other practitioners caring for women. Who,
then, were they?

Those who argue that "women's health was women's business"
assume that the treatment of women, especially for "women's diseases," constituted the exclusive domain of women practitioners
either because of social convention or because (as Talbot would
argue) male practitioners simply lacked interest in such matters.
There is, in fact, evidence to support both these views. Many of
the Italian licenses that limited women to a female clientele stipulated that this was done for reasons of propriety, as it was more
seemly that women be treated by other women than by men.[65] As
for male practitioners' lack of interest in women's affairs, Beryl
Rowland cites the statement of the fourteenth-century French surgeon, Guy de Chauliac, who remarked on the topic of multiple
births that "because the matter requires the attention of women,
there is no point in giving much consideration to it."[66]

Yet despite certain indications to the contrary, women were not
immune to male competition even in the field considered "naturally" theirs. When Jacoba Felicie argued that she should be allowed to continue her practice on the grounds that as a female she
would not threaten women's modesty, the court dismissed her arguments as "worthless" and "frivolous."[67] That the medical faculty
refused to engage in a debate about sexual "propriety" strongly
suggests that they were not willing to so easily cede the treatment

[64] The choice of medical attendant may, of course, have been made not by the
woman herself but by her husband or male guardian; this is another question in
need of study.

[65] See Münster, "Women Doctors" (n. 18 above), 139; and Talbot (n. 53 above),
11–13. While it could be argued that this enforced specialization would have the
benefit of encouraging practitioners to learn the peculiar anatomy and physiology
of their female patients better, in the case of many practitioners (e.g., the woman
eye surgeon mentioned by Calvanico [n. 25 above] who worked in a field where
sex specialization would hardly seem relevant or medically useful), it must have
simply limited their potential clientele and hence their economic viability.

[66] Rowland (n. 1 above), 24.

[67] Denifle, ed. (n. 42 above), 2:267. Jacoba may have used this argument simply
for its rhetorical force since obviously it would not have justified her practice on
male patients.

of female patients to women practitioners.[68] Indeed, contrary to Talbot's claim that gynecology was a field "in which medical men showed no interest," there is abundant evidence that male practitioners *were* interested in the care of women's reproductive health. This becomes readily apparent from an examination of medieval gynecological literature.

Texts and audiences

Toward the end of the sixteenth century, Scipione Mercurio received advice on how to ensure a successful career as a physician in Venice. All he needed to know, he was told, were two things: how to get on well with pharmacists and how to make women fertile.[69] The potential for profit in gynecological practice was not lost on Mercurio's medieval predecessors. In her superb study of the medical careers of a group of north Italian male physicians of the late thirteenth and early fourteenth centuries, Nancy Siraisi has found evidence that the treatment of gynecological problems was often a fundamental part of their practice. In the writings of a leading Bolognese physician, Taddeo Alderotti, Siraisi notes a "large number of gynecological remedies and cosmetics . . . [which] perhaps implies an extensive practice among women and a situation in which upper-class males were prepared to spend frequently and generously for the medical treatment of their wives and daughters."[70]

Another recent work that demonstrates the gynecological activity of male physicians is Helen Lemay's study of the *Treatise on the Womb* by a fifteenth-century Pavian professor of medicine, Anthonius Guainerius.[71] Lemay convincingly argues that Guainerius was actively involved in the medical care of women, diagnosing and treating them for a variety of gynecological ailments both di-

---

[68] Although it is unlikely that this ever happened (though compare Clarice, the Italian eye surgeon mentioned in n. 25 above), the argument of modesty could, if carried to its logical extreme, preclude men from treating any of women's medical problems, not simply those of "the shameful parts."

[69] Richard Palmer, "Pharmacy in the Republic of Venice in the Sixteenth Century," in *The Medical Renaissance of the Sixteenth Century*, ed. A. Wear, R. K. French, and I. M. Lonie (Cambridge: Cambridge University Press, 1985), 100–117, esp. 105.

[70] Nancy G. Siraisi, *Taddeo Alderotti and His Pupils: Two Generations of Italian Medical Learning* (Princeton, N.J.: Princeton University Press, 1981), 279–80, 282–83, esp. 278. An individual case history of a gynecological problem is discussed in Ynez Violé O'Neill, "Michael Scot and Mary of Bologna: A Medieval Gynecological Puzzle," *Clio Medica* 8, no. 2 (June 1973): 87–111, and 9, no. 2 (June 1974): 125–29.

[71] Lemay (n. 8 above).

rectly and through the use of midwives as his assistants.[72] Lemay's reading of Guainerius's treatise does not, however, exhaust the questions that need to be asked if this fascinating document is to tell us all it can about women's medical care and practice in this period.

For example, the question of rivalry between different medical practitioners could be addressed with far greater nuance. Lemay writes that "Guainerius clearly recognizes the necessity of distinguishing himself from the lay healer"—a concern Lemay attributes to "professional decorum."[73] To treat a certain disorder, Guainerius recommends that whereas "old women" use burned hair and feathers, the physician ought instead to use asafetida or castoreum. What Lemay does not realize (but which Guainerius clearly did) is that the distinction between these two sets of medicinal substances is solely economic: hair and feathers are valueless yet readily available, while asafetida and castoreum can be obtained only at considerable cost; all of these substances had been recommended in virtually every medical account of this disease from antiquity on.[74] Guainerius's innovation was to use something as seemingly neutral as *materia medica* to construct a social distinction between himself and a "lower" class of healers who in reality practice a medicine not so very different from his own.

Also crucial to understanding Guainerius's text is an analysis of its intended purpose and audience. The title itself is revealing: it is called a "Treatise on the Womb," not "On the Diseases of Women." This reductive focus is clearly evident in Guainerius's dedicatory preface to Filippo Maria, the duke of Milan: this is a treatise motivated not by a concern for the suffering of women (though Guainerius is not indifferent to this) but by an explicitly male desire for progeny.[75] Guainerius's treatise, obviously written with the self-serving goal of his own social advancement, is rife with subtle

---

[72] Lemay notes a similar relationship between male physician and female midwife in her study of the thirteenth-century physician, William of Saliceto (Helen Lemay, "William of Saliceto on Human Sexuality," *Viator* 12 [1981]: 165–81). I do not see, however, how the midwife's role as manual assistant to the physician demonstrates that she had "ultimate responsibility for the practice of gynecology and obstetrics in thirteenth-century Italy" (181). As Lemay herself notes, according to William, the midwife even had to be taught the anatomy of the vagina by the physician (180).

[73] Lemay, "Anthonius Guainerius" (n. 8 above), 326–27.

[74] Compare Green, "Transmission" (n. 7 above).

[75] I have examined a microfilm copy of Milan, Biblioteca Ambrosiana, MS A 108 inf., at Notre Dame University. The apparent popularity of the work suggests that Guainerius struck a responsive chord among the patriciate of fifteenth- and sixteenth-century Italy. There are at least fourteen extant manuscripts dating from the fifteenth and sixteenth centuries. The work was also printed at least three times before 1500.

polemics that, though they make interpretation more difficult, have a great deal to tell us about why male practitioners were interested in reproductive medicine. My point, then, is that Guainerius was writing within the context of a specific social and cultural environment that subtly pervaded even the most technical aspects of his work; understanding that environment is crucial to making proper sense of his medicine and of the way he describes his relations with other practitioners and his own patients.

Peter Biller offers other examples of male interest in gynecological and obstetrical matters, bringing up many of the complex issues of the relations between medieval males (scientific writers, practicing physicians, and even clergy) and midwives.[76] Biller refers (somewhat hyperbolically) to "the massive presence in the west of learned books" that describe how birth ought to be handled, noting, however, the possible disjunction between such learned discussions (of which there is abundant evidence) and orally transmitted midwifery (about which there is virtually none). Even so, male medical literature was not simply scholastic speculation, Biller argues, but was derived at least in part from actual practice or discussion with midwives and was intended, in its turn, to be used to instruct them. He cites the Dominican friar Thomas of Cantimpré (d. ca. 1280), for example, who included discussion of midwifery in his general encyclopedia of learning "because of the danger of still-births and the ignorance of midwives. . . . We exhort therefore . . . that they [those with care of souls] should call together some more discerning midwives, *and train them in secret,* and others may be trained by them" (my emphasis).[77]

There are many other instances in medieval medical literature that prove the active interest in gynecological matters among male practitioners.[78] Even obstetrics was not beyond the pale of male

[76] Peter Biller, "Childbirth in the Middle Ages," *History Today* 36 (August 1986): 42–49.

[77] Ibid., 45–46.

[78] Much of this material has been collected in the undeservedly neglected article of Carl Oskar Rosenthal, "Zur geburtshilflich gynaekologischen Betätigung des Mannes bis zum Ausgange des 16. Jahrhunderts," *Janus* 27 (1923): 117–48. For the text of a criminal inquest, held in 1326, against a male practitioner accused of gynecological malpractice, see Joseph Shatzmiller and Rodrigue Lavoie, "Médecine et gynécologie au moyen-âge: Un exemple provençal," *Razo: Cahiers du Centre d'Études Médiévales de Nice,* no. 4 (Nice: Université de Nice, Faculté des Lettres et Sciences Humaines, 1984), 133–43. The story of a miracle at St. Thomas à Becket's shrine involves a parish priest who personally observed a difficult birth and gave technical advice to the midwife; cited in Peter Biller, "Birth-Control in the West in the Thirteenth and Early Fourteenth Centuries," *Past and Present,* no. 94 (February 1982), 3–26, esp. 19, n. 69. Biller also cites evidence of priests' manuals which depict the priest as a source of advice on breast feeding and child care.

interest, as indicated by the quotation from Thomas of Cantimpré. Indeed, despite his dismissive statement that there was "no point" in giving attention to certain matters of birth, Guy de Chauliac himself nevertheless saw it as his duty to advise both the mother and the midwife on what they ought to do in case of difficulties.[79] However, as I already suggested in the case of Anthonius Guainerius, it must be kept very clearly in mind that this is, after all, literature, and if we are to treat it as historical evidence we need to subject it to the same analyses as any other form of literary material meant to inform and persuade its audience, keeping in mind all the various ways in which language can hide or misrepresent reality. How much, for instance, do these writings reflect real experience, and how much are they simply reiterating beliefs and practices the authors have found in other writings? How much, in other words, of what we find in these texts is merely "armchair gynecology"? What role do rhetoric and polemic play, and how are we to filter out their influences? Who wrote this literature? And even more important, who read it?

John Benton has argued that the gynecological treatises ultimately attributed to "Trotula" were written both by and for men. Further, he argues that the false attribution to a woman author was equally an indication of and an aid toward the takeover of "women's medicine" by male physicians and the gradual exclusion of women themselves from medical practice.[80] I believe, however, that the "victimization" of women both as practitioners and as patients was not so absolute as Benton supposes; particularly, I believe it is incumbent upon us to distinguish between the purpose with which a text is written and the purpose to which it is later put. This distinction is absolutely crucial if we are to determine the relationship women—either as practitioners or patients—had to gynecological literature.

One critical problem in Benton's thesis that the "Trotula" texts were written for men is that he does not explain the meaning of the preface to the longest of the three works, the *Cum auctor* (or *Trotula major*). In that preface, the author (who very well may have been male) states her or his reasons for writing. Recounting the numerous reasons why women are afflicted with diseases of their reproductive organs, she or he adds that "shame-faced on account

[79] See the text of the *Cyrurgie*, ed. Margaret Ogden (London: Oxford University Press for the Early English Text Society, 1971), 529–32, for Guy's discussion of gynecological and obstetrical ailments.

[80] Benton (n. 22 above), esp. 48–52.

of their fragile condition and the diseases which afflict them in such a private place, women do not dare reveal their distress to a male physician." It was out of recognition of their misfortune (and particularly "for the sake of a certain woman") that she or he was impelled to write the book.[81]

If women "do not dare reveal their distress to a male physician," how could the author possibly intend that this work be solely for the use of male physicians? While it is conceivable that the work was meant to educate male physicians so that they would not have to press a woman patient with questions she was too embarrassed to answer, it is also conceivable (and to my mind quite plausible) that the author meant her or his work to be read by women themselves; who actually did read it and who controlled its later transmission is an entirely different matter. Benton notes the condescension and distancing with which the author speaks of both women patients and midwives, yet these same features can be found in the sixth-century work of Muscio that was very clearly intended to be used by midwives.[82] Furthermore, Benton himself concedes that the short work on cosmetics also attributed to "Trotula" was written explicitly for women.[83] If, as this one instance suggests, men were willing to write texts specifically for women and women were eager (and able) to read them,[84] why could this not be true of the gynecological texts as well? This problem of intended audience becomes all the more difficult when we turn to the multitude of vernacular gynecological treatises dating from the fourteenth and fifteenth centuries.

An anonymous late medieval Flemish translation of the "Trotula" texts has recently been edited by Anna Delva, who argues that the translation was made by a practicing midwife critical of

[81] Paris, Bibliothèque Nationale, MS lat. 7056, fol. 77r: "Et ipse conditionis fragilitatis rubore faciei egritudinum suarum que in secretiori loco eis accidit, medico angustias reuelare non audent. Earum igitur miseranda calamitas et maxime cuiusdam mulieris gratia animum meum sollicitans impulit ut contra egritudines earum euidentius explanarem." Although this passage was subject to frequent scribal alteration in the manuscripts, its sense remains substantially the same.

[82] Benton, 46; compare Green, "Obstetrices" (n. 7 above).

[83] Benton, 48.

[84] Little is known about women's literacy in the Middle Ages, especially among women outside the cloister. On the one hand, it would be presumptuous simply to assume, without positive evidence, that women were illiterate. On the other hand, even in the case of a woman author such as Trota, we cannot be sure that she was literate, since it is possible that she dictated her work rather than writing it herself. Still, we should not dismiss this realm of "quasi-literacy"; even if women "wrote" only by dictating and "read" only by having works read to them, they were still functionally participating in literate culture.

male university masters.[85] Various translations of "Trotula" and other Latin sources were also made into Irish, French, English, German, and Italian, and at least one entirely new gynecological tract was composed in Italian.[86] The English translator of the "Trotula" makes explicit the value of the vernacular: "Because whomen of oure tonge donne bettyr rede and undyrstande thys langage than eny other and every whoman lettyrde rede hit to other unlettyrd and help hem and conceyle hem in her maledyes, withowtyn shewyng here dysese to man, i have thys drauyn and wryttyn in englysh."[87]

How are we to explain the contemporaneous appearance of "men's texts" such as Guainerius's and "women's texts" like these vernacular ones? Are the vernacular texts addressed to women an active response, as Delva would argue, by women themselves to the increasing male intrusion into gynecological affairs? If so, did only women read them?

[85] Anna Delva, *Vrouwengeneeskunde in Vlaanderen tijdens de late middeleeuwen*, Vlaamse Historische Studies 2 (Brugge: Genootschap voor Geschiedenis, 1983). This edition is not without its defects; see the (excessively hostile) review by Albert Derolez in *Scriptorium* 38, no. 1 (1984): 175–77. Delva provides a French résumé of her conclusions on 201–6. Here she repeats the argument that "women's health was women's business": "Enfin notre étude a établi avec certitude que jusqu'à environ [!] 1550 tous les aspects de la médecine pour les femmes étaient confiés à des femmes" (205). Male involvement, she argues, was solely theoretical or in the guise of counsel offered in emergency situations.

[86] See Benton, nn. 12 and 52, for references to these works. To this list can be added B. Kusche, *Das Frauenbild in Gebrauchsprosatexten aus dem 15. Jahrhundert (3 mittelniederländische Handschriften gynäkologisch-obstetrischen inhaltes)* (Stockholm: Deutsches Institut, 1982). An unedited Italian text on the diseases of the breasts exists in MS 38 of the Boston Medical Library. Another Italian text (mistakenly identified in the catalog as a translation of pseudo-Cleopatra) is found in London, Wellcome Institute Library, MS misc. med. II; like the English text it, too, is intended "maximamente per le done [*sic*]" (fol. 64r). On the general question of the use of the vernacular for gynecological texts, see Audrey Eccles, "The Early Use of English for Midwiferies, 1500–1700," *Neuphilologische Mitteilungen* 78, no. 4 (1977): 377–85. Faye Marie Getz ("Gilbertus Anglicus Anglicized," *Medical History* 26, no. 4 [October 1982]: 436–42) has some useful cautions about assuming too much about the class or even the profession of the readers of vernacular medical literature. The problematic question of male vs. female audiences is also addressed in the recent editions of two early modern German translations of the *Secreta mulierum* (falsely attributed to Albertus Magnus), which seems to have been intended, not as a practical gynecological text, but as a "natural history of women" to inform curious male audiences. (One, the version of Hartlieb, was definitely intended for the use of the aristocracy, while the other was probably intended for the urban bourgeoisie.) See Kristian Bosselman-Cyran, ed., *"Secreta mulierum" mit Glosse in der deutschen Bearbeitung von Johann Hartlieb* (Pattensen/Hannover: Horst Wellm, 1985); and Margaret Schleissner, "Pseudo-Albertus Magnus: *Secreta mulierum cum commento*, Deutsch. Critical text and commentary" (Ph.D. diss., Princeton University, 1987).

[87] As cited in Rowland (n. 1 above), 14.

One of the fifteenth-century Middle English works, transcribed by Beryl Rowland, begins with a preface which, like that of the *Trotula major*, mentions women's reluctance to bare their ills to a male doctor, although in this case the intended audience is explicitly declared: "Because there are many women who have numerous illnesses—some of them almost fatal—and because they are also ashamed to reveal and tell their distress to any man, I therefore shall write somewhat to cure their illness. . . . And so, to assist women, I intend to write of how to help their secret maladies so that one woman may aid another in her illness and not divulge her secrets to such discourteous men."[88] In addition to its intriguing preface, the intended audience of this anonymous text is further indicated, Rowland argues, by the inclusion of material on obstetrics—a topic that (she believes) was of little interest to men and was not usually found in standard medical texts.[89] From this, Rowland suggests that at this time "women were the sole obstetricians," arguing further that "the debt to the experience of women, whether such material was originally recorded orally or written down, is obvious throughout the work."[90]

Rowland edited her text from only one of at least six manuscripts now extant, two of which are identical to the copy she used in all substantive details.[91] The other three are exemplars of a second version of the text; a transcription of one of these latter manuscripts has now been produced by M.-R. Hallaert.[92] Although both Row-

[88] Ibid., 59. This edition is marred by numerous errors of presentation and interpretation. The reader wishing to make use of it should refer to the important critiques in the reviews by Jerry Stannard and Linda Voigts, *Speculum* 57, no. 2 (April 1982): 422–26; Nancy Siraisi, *American Historical Review* 87, no. 2 (April 1982): 435–36; and Faye Marie Getz, *Medical History* 26, no. 3 (July 1982): 353–54. For some reason, Rowland insists on calling her text an "English Trotula" even though she knew it was not an English translation of the Latin *Trotula* texts (48). Peter M. Jones (*Medieval Medical Miniatures* [London: British Library, 1984], 54) has now demonstrated that Rowland's text is for the most part a translation from the Latin of a general book on practical medicine by Roger Baron. Copies of the "genuine" Middle English translation of *Trotula* (actually, a compilation made from *Trotula* and other texts) can be found in Oxford, Bodleian Library, MSS Bodleian 483 and Douce 37; and London, British Library, MSS Additional 12195 and Sloane 421A. All have an incipit more or less as follows: "Our Lord God when he had stored the world" (cf. *Trotula major*: "Cum auctor universitatis deus in prima mundi origine").
[89] Rowland, 23–26.
[90] Ibid., vxi.
[91] Rowland transcribed London, British Library MS Sloane 2463. Other manuscripts with the same text are London, British Library, MS Sloane 249, and London, Royal College of Physicians and Surgeons, MS 129 a.i.5.
[92] See M. R. Hallaert, *The 'Sekenesse of wymmen': A Middle English Treatise on Diseases of Women*, Scripta: Mediaeval and Renaissance Texts and Studies, no.

land and Hallaert knew of the existence of these other manuscripts, neither made any attempt to compare them systematically with the copy each transcribed. [93] Had they done so, they might have realized that the two versions of this text together have a lot more to tell us about the creation and dissemination of gynecological knowledge than a superficial reading would suggest.

The second version of this Middle English text (which for convenience I will call "Hallaert's version") not only is rearranged in parts and substantially "abbreviated," but it also lacks much of the obstetrical material (including the illustrations of the fetus in utero) and other sections found in the first version ("Rowland's version"; see table 1).[94] Most important, Hallaert's version lacks the poignant, almost feminist preface that was the sole *explicit* indicator in Rowland's version that women were the intended audience. Without the preface, the text becomes superficially "neutral." The scribe of one manuscript in Hallaert's version, however, had a very clear idea of who his (or her) audience would be and emended the text accordingly: she or he simply began "*Sirs,* we shall understand that women's bodies have less heat" (emphasis added).[95]

How are we to explain the simultaneous existence of the two versions of this text, one (Rowland's) ostensibly a "women's version," the other (Hallaert's) a neutral or "men's version"? Which came first, and who appropriated from whom? These, unfortunately, are questions that must wait until a competent specialist in Middle English can produce a critical edition of all the manuscripts and determine the text's origins.[96] It is not necessary to know which version was prior, however, to see that Rowland's claim that "the debt to the experience of women . . . is obvious throughout the work" is unfounded, for the obstetrical material, no less than many other parts of the text, clearly derives in large part from previous Latin sources—all of them (in those cases where authorship can be de-

---

8 (Brussels: Omirel, URSAL, 1982), which is a transcription of New Haven, Connecticut, Yale Medical Library, MS 47. Other copies of the same text are London, British Library, MSS Royal 18A.VI and Sloane 5.

[93] Both Rowland (47) and Hallaert (20) do nothing more than refer vaguely to "similarities" or "resemblances."

[94] I say "first," "second," and "abbreviated" only provisionally since at this point it is impossible to know which version is original and which represents the alterations of a later medieval editor.

[95] London, British Library, MS Sloane 5, fol. 158r: "Sires, we shulle vnderstonde that womene hau lesse hete."

[96] This task will be greatly aided by the catalog of all medical and scientific writings in Middle English currently being prepared by Linda Voigts, Department of English, University of Missouri at Kansas City.

TABLE I **COMPARISON OF MIDDLE ENGLISH TEXTS EDITED BY ROWLAND[a]
AND HALLAERT[b]**

Middle English Text[c]	Page Numbers	
	Rowland	Hallaert
For as muche as ther ben manye women [preface]	58	[lacking]
Therfore ye schal understonde [text of treatise proper]	58	27–29[d]
Withholdyng of this blode	60–64	29–33
For to helpe women of these sekenesses	66–70	33–39
Good electuaries for this sekenesse	70	39
Also a worschipfull serip	70–74	[lacking]
To moche flowyng of blode	74–86	43–49
Suffocacion of the moder is when	86–96	49–55
The precipitacioun of the moder	98–104	55–59
Moche wynde ther is also in the moder	104–8	59–61
Ydropsie of the moder	108–10	41
A good suppositorie to purgen the moder	110–12	41
The moder semyth ofte flayne & rawe	112–14	41
Apostume of the moder	114–18	61–65
Ache of the moder	118–20	65–67
Yff a woman be with childe	120–22	[lacking]
Greuances that women haue in bering [includes 17 figures of fetus in utero]	122–34	[lacking]
And the greuaunces that women have in beryng	134–38	67–71
Mola matricis is in two maners	140–44	[lacking]
Secondine is a litell skynne	144–46	71–73
Fyrst, yf she be repleted	146	[lacking]
The women that bleden otherwhiles	146–48	73
Wowndes of the marice	148–50	65 [one-tenth of text]
Cancryng and festres of the marice	150–52	65 [approximately one-third of text]
Women whan they ben with childe	152	[lacking]

TABLE I (*Continued*)

Middle English Text[c]	Page Numbers	
	Rowland	**Hallaert**
(Several pages of Latin text on such topics as provoking the menses, anaphrodisiacs, tumors of the breasts)	152–62	[lacking]
(Several more pages of Middle English recipes)	162–72	[lacking]

[a]Beryl Rowland, *Medieval Woman's Guide to Health: The First English Gynecological Handbook* (Kent, Ohio: Kent State University Press, 1981). Rowland's text is based on only one manuscript of the work: London, British Library, MS Sloane 2463. The same text is also found in London, British Library, MS Sloane 249, and London, Royal College of Physicians and Surgeons, MS 129 a.i.5.

[b]M.-R. Hallaert, *The "Sekenesse of wymmen": A Middle English Treatise on Diseases of Women*, Scripta: Mediaeval and Renaissance Texts and Studies, no. 8 (Brussels, 1982), a reproduction and transcription of the text in New Haven, Connecticut, Yale Medical Library, MS 47. Two other copies also exist of this version: London, British Library, MSS Sloane 5 and Royal 18A.VI.

[c]The Middle English chapter incipits (i.e., opening phrases) cited are those of Rowland's text.

[d]Although it lacks a preface, Sloane 5 nevertheless makes its intended audience explicit: "*Sires, we* shulle vnderstonde" (fol. 158r; emphasis added).

termined) written by men. Aside from two unnamed women said to have cured their own illnesses, no women are ever mentioned as authorities in the text.[97] Nor, aside from the preface, is the text in any way addressed to either women patients or midwives; both are referred to solely in the third person. All second-person references and imperatives are reserved for the practitioner reading the book who, apparently, is assumed to be neither laywoman nor midwife.[98] In what sense, then, whether we talk about its audience or its sources, can we unambiguously speak of this work as a "medieval *woman's* guide to health"? Clearly, this was a text shared (fought over?) by men and women, and it reflects men's accumulated knowledge of gynecological and obstetrical medicine as much as (if not more than) women's. Even if the text was originally intended for women,[99] the fact that the manuscript Rowland edited is known to

[97] Rowland, 110/111 and 144/145. Although "Trotula" is mentioned (168/169), it is not clear whether the author understood the word to be a woman's name or simply the title of a text; the name "Lilie" on 102/103 is not a woman but rather a reference to the *Lilium medicinae*, a general textbook of medicine by Bernard of Gordon. The male authorities cited are not merely the traditional figures (e.g., the Arabic authors, Avicenna and Rhazes); on pp. 76/77, e.g., a remedy for uterine flux is described which was taught to a woman by the prior of Bermondesey!

[98] Although, as I suggested earlier in reference to the *Trotula major* and Muscio, this does not entirely exclude the possibility that women (either practitioners or patients) were the original intended audience, it does raise serious doubts.

[99] If the argument that "whomen . . . donne bettyr rede and undyrstande" English than Latin is to be accepted, then the presence in this text of an extended section

have been owned by a male surgeon within a century after its creation underscores how tenuous women's possession of texts might have been.[100]

In light of all the apparent male involvement in this Middle English text, what is to be made of the rhetoric of the preface of this or, for that matter, any of the other vernacular translations ostensibly addressed to women? Should it be dismissed as false and meaningless on the assumption that the content of these works, because it came from texts either written or transmitted by men, could not possibly have reflected the gynecology and obstetrics practiced by women themselves?

Some scholars, in discussing both modern and premodern times, have suggested that men and women lived in such completely separate cognitive universes that gynecological theories formulated by men would in no way correspond to the "female medicine" practiced by women. Helen Lemay suggests that such an assumption is inappropriate. Granted, she relies for her argument on a comparison of the text Rowland edited (which as I have just argued can only tenuously be said to represent "women's medicine") and Guainerius's work (which, as I have also suggested, presents a very biased view of what "women's medicine" was). Nevertheless, Lemay's observation that medieval women as well as men may have fully accepted the cultural and scientific assumptions of their time is a point worth heeding.[101]

Benton, in contrast, believes that there is such a difference and that the "Trotula" texts, despite their (false) attribution to a woman, nevertheless reflect "male medicine," which he assumes was both less effective and more harmful than that practiced by women. Benton argues that male physicians took comfort in the thought that they were reading what a woman, speaking as a woman, had to say about gynecology, though he suggests that if medieval male physicians had really wanted to know "what women think," they could have looked at the medical writings of the twelfth-century German abbess, Hildegard of Bingen.[102] While studies of these works show

---

in Latin (Rowland, 152–62) raises further doubts that it represents an original "women's text."

[100] See Rowland (46) for the later history of this manuscript. The other contents of the codex (which was created as a unit) are surgical, suggesting that it was intended to be used by a surgeon. There is no evidence to indicate whether the original owner was male or female, though the "de luxe" quality of the codex suggests at the very least that she/he was well-to-do.

[101] Lemay, "Anthonius Guainerius" (n. 8 above), 325–26.

[102] Benton (n. 22 above), 51–52.

that Hildegard was indeed a remarkably innovative thinker (particularly with regard to notions of female nature), her writings still evince a fundamental dependence on the dominant medical theories of her day.[103] Furthermore, if Delva is correct in arguing that women themselves were responsible for and used at least some of the vernacular translations of the "Trotula," this would suggest that they viewed the contents of the texts as an acceptable interpretation of their diseases.[104]

The connection (or disjunction) between literature and reality is also relevant when interpreting rhetoric. Despite the hoary antiquity of the theme of women's modesty in gynecological and other literature,[105] this topos may still have been meaningful to medieval people, both male and female. Carl Rosenthal notes that, although male physicians considered themselves competent to treat the full range of gynecological disorders (even to the point of instructing the midwife!), he was able to find no instance of a man manually examining a woman's vagina for a gynecological disorder.[106] This deeply ingrained social taboo would have insured women a place in the medical care of other women, if only in the role of manual assistant to the male physician (as can be seen in Guainerius and other writers) and in the rarely challenged role of birth attendant.[107]

---

[103] See Gertrude M. Engbring, "Saint Hildegard, Twelfth Century Physician," *Bulletin of the History of Medicine* 8, no. 6 (June 1940): 770–84; Bernhard W. Scholz, "Hildegard von Bingen on the Nature of Woman," *American Benedictine Review* 31, no. 4 (December 1980): 361–83; Michela Pereira, "Maternità e sessualità femminile in Ildegarda di Bingen: Proposte di lettura," *Quaderni storici*, no. 44 (August 1980), 564–79; and Joan Cadden, "It Takes All Kinds: Sexuality and Gender Differences in Hildegard of Bingen's 'Book of Compound Medicine,'" *Traditio* 40 (1984): 149–74. Cadden writes that "Hildegard of Bingen's views on the physical constitution of men and women were generally consistent with the scientific outlook of twelfth-century male medical and philosophical authors" (150). What is fascinating is how Hildegard used and manipulated those ideas in such a different fashion from that of her male contemporaries.

[104] It would be interesting to know whether in the vernacular translations of "Trotula" addressed to women emphasis was given to the fact that the author was (allegedly) female, leading women readers (as it had led men) to believe they were reading a woman's own theories and practices. Other than Trota's *Practica*, no other extant gynecological text is known to have been composed by a woman until the early modern period. The later texts show that women did accept many prevailing views of their physiology and diseases; see Natalie Zemon Davis, "Women on Top," in her *Society and Culture in Early Modern France* (Stanford, Calif.: Stanford University Press, 1975), 124–51, esp. 125. Perhaps class needs to be used as an analytical variable as well as gender.

[105] See Green, "*Obstetrices*" (n. 7 above).

[106] Rosenthal (n. 78 above), esp. 146–47.

[107] There is a very long tradition (which itself needs to be explored) of surgeons being called in in cases of difficult labor when the child often had to be sacrificed

The rhetoric of women's modesty is not used by Jacoba Felicie and the authors of the vernacular prefaces to support these merely ancillary roles, however. Rather, their employment of the rhetoric of modesty might be seen as a conscious attempt to actively turn the taboo to their own advantage and thereby resist the increasing circumscription of women's sphere of medical practice. Their desire may have been to *make* women's health women's business because it was women's interests that there be a sexual division of medical labor that would ensure them a field of practice where men could neither claim competence nor offer competition. The rhetoric of modesty could equally have served the purposes of women patients who may very well have preferred to be treated by attendants of their own sex. Indeed, in this sense, to speak of modesty in terms of "rhetoric" may be slightly misleading, for it is at least possible that women really felt the shame these statements attribute to them.[108] Unfortunately, since we do not yet have any testimony from women patients themselves telling us how they perceived this complex world of medical practice, for now we can only guess whether the sentiments we find in the vernacular gynecological literature ad- dressed to women—having passed through who knows how many filters—do not in some way truly reflect women's desire "to help and counsel themselves in their maladies, without showing their diseases to men."

---

to save the life of the mother. It would be interesting to know whether, when there was a female surgeon at hand, she would be preferred to a male. If so, what would her relationship to the midwife be? Besides the traditional use of surgeons as the attendant of last resort in difficult labors, men apparently assisted births only of the upper classes. Labarge (n. 5 above) notes this but then quickly dismisses it as a relatively insignificant indicator of male obstetrical practice (179). Its rarity may not be the sole criterion with which to assess its importance, however. Because of con- cern over succession, the births of royalty and the nobility are great matters of state; for kings and nobles to consider university-trained male physicians competent to supervise these births indicates faith that they were indeed the best available at- tendants. For example, Michael McVaugh has demonstrated that King Jaime II of Aragón/Catalonia placed such high faith in university training that he went to great lengths to make sure that his wife, Blanca, was attended by a (male) physician at almost all of her ten births; see Michael McVaugh, "The Births of the Children of Jaime II," *Medievalia* 6 (1986): 7–16. Whether these physicians acted alone or in concert with an assisting midwife is not clear; there are no traces of any female midwives in the royal archives. Male involvement in gynecological surgery is also documented. The fifteenth-century anatomist, Berengario da Carpi, recalls a hys- terectomy performed by his father, a barber surgeon; see R. K. French, "Berengario da Carpi and the Use of Commentary in Anatomical Teaching," in Wear, French, and Lonie, eds. (n. 69 above), 42–74, esp. 43.

[108] The social inculcation of shame would be well worth exploring, particularly from an anthropological perspective.

Other sources, other questions

Awareness of the deep tensions between men and women might help us decipher other aspects of women's health care and medical practice in medieval Europe. Here we are especially in need of interdisciplinary studies, such as Grethe Jacobsen's exemplary analysis of pregnancy and childbirth in medieval Scandinavia.[109] Jacobsen has taken virtually every sort of evidence imaginable—archaeological findings, laws, sermons, folk ballads, theological and scientific literature, even language itself—to reconstruct a picture of how women themselves experienced pregnancy and childbirth. Sensitive both to the different perspectives of what she terms "women's sources, men's sources, and common [or neutral] sources" and to the limitations of traditional periodization, Jacobsen describes among other things the *Kvindegilde* (Women's feast), a postpartum gathering of women which, "in its most raucous form, . . . ended with a tour of the village where women upset carts, split wagons, knocked over gates, destroyed haystacks, stripped the men they encountered and forced them to dance."[110] This may at first sight seem to show women's power and control of their reproductive capacities, yet as Natalie Zemon Davis has demonstrated for the sixteenth century, such ritualized reversals of the sexual order—as dramatic, even violent, as they may be—in fact can have very ambiguous meanings.[111]

As with Davis's work on inversion rituals, methodological techniques developed in other areas of women's history have tremendous potential to inform the history of medicine. For example, Merry Wiesner's discussion of female healers in her study of women in early modern Germany has the inestimable virtue of placing these women in the context of workers, where questions of economic rivalry, guild regulations, and municipal and state control can properly be addressed.[112] Alison Klairmont Lingo's study of charlatans

[109] Grethe Jacobsen, "Pregnancy and Childbirth in the Medieval North: A Topology of Sources and a Preliminary Study," *Scandinavian Journal of History* 9, no. 2 (1984): 91–111.

[110] Ibid., 106–7.

[111] Davis (n. 104 above).

[112] Wiesner, *Working Women* (n. 38 above). Wiesner's admirable reconstruction of the training, practice, and social position of midwives in early modern Germany, one hopes, will serve as a model for similar regional studies; see also Natalie Zemon Davis, "Women in the Crafts in Sixteenth-century Lyon," in Hanawalt (n. 38 above), 167–97. Although she does not discuss women healers specifically, the general conclusions of Martha Howell, *Women, Production and Patriarchy in Late Medieval*

in sixteenth-century France shows how potentially useful the concept of "Otherness" can be to assessing the development of professionalization in medicine.[113] Such conceptual approaches might also be used to explore many other important questions, such as the development of a rhetoric about the ignorance of midwives and other women practitioners,[114] or the role of women's literacy in determining their access to certain areas of medical knowledge, or the possible impact of the vernacular translations of gynecological literature.[115] Literate sources are of only limited utility, however, in chronicling the history of a society that was predominately illiterate. One particularly fruitful form of evidence not yet fully exploited is artistic depictions of childbirth and other medical encounters, though

<hr>

Cities (Chicago: University of Chicago Press, 1986), might usefully be set against the developments of women's increased restrictions in medicine, their access to medical guilds, and questions of the sexual division of medical labor. For example, in her study of the effects that the Black Death had on late fourteenth- and early fifteenth-century Florentine physicians, Katharine Park (n. 21 above) notes that she could find no evidence of women matriculating as physicians in the Guild of Doctors, Apothecaries, and Grocers before 1353 or after 1408; between those two dates, however, Park documents a notable opening-up of the profession to otherwise marginal practitioners. By contrast, women's access to guilds of surgeons and especially barbers in England seems always to have been quite free; cf. Gottfried (n. 17 above), 50–51. Although Gottfried's explanation for the relative freedom in the barbers' guilds is hardly satisfactory, he is nevertheless quite right to note that attention should be paid to whether these women gained access to the guild in their own right or only because, as widows, they were allowed to take the place of their dead husbands; see also Wyman, "The Surgeoness" (n. 53 above), 26–27.

[113] Alison Klairmont Lingo, "Empirics and Charlatans in Early Modern France: The Genesis of the Classification of the 'Other' in Medical Practice," *Journal of Social History* 19 (Summer 1986): 583–603.

[114] Ignorance had always been an argument used by university-trained physicians to distance themselves from other practitioners, but this theme seems to take on particular virulence when applied to women. This is noted briefly by Biller, "Childbirth in the Middle Ages" (n. 76 above), 44. While some would argue that for all their elaborate theories university physicians were in no better position to cure their patients than empirical healers, great caution is needed when addressing questions of medical efficacy, for it is both presumptuous and simply unhelpful to criticize medieval healers for not having thought and acted in ways that only make sense in light of modern medical discoveries.

[115] For example, when Perretta Petonne was prosecuted in 1411 by the master surgeons of Paris for unlicensed practice, she was ordered to deposit her books on surgery with the provost for examination by the physicians; cf. Wyman, "The Surgeoness," 25; and Denifle, ed. (n. 42 above), 4:198–99. Thomas Benedek (n. 48 above) cites a late fifteenth-century German ordinance that also assumes women's literacy: "So that the midwives be better informed in all aspects [of their practice] *they should read their professional books diligently* and, when necessary, make use of the information of a physician" (554; emphasis added).

here, too, we need to beware mistaking topoi (in this case, icono-graphic ones) for historical realities.[116]

These desiderata could be continued ad infinitum. Clearly, the most pressing need is for extensive work based on the primary sources themselves. Benton's discovery of the genuine work of Trota (after more than four hundred years of empty speculation about her existence) could not have been accomplished without extensive manuscript research. Critical editions of medical texts are also essential if we are to avoid the danger of premature generalizations drawn from insufficient information. In all of this, we must remain sensitive to chronological, regional, religious, and class distinctions—in short to all the factors that create historical specificity and diversity.

Paying attention to such diversity allows us to realize how far we have been misled by simplistic assumptions, seeing uniformity where there may in fact have been much variety: in the roles mid-wives played, in the ways other women practiced medicine, in the medical needs women had beyond assistance at birth, and in the sources from which they obtained that medical care. Even though such findings do not radically alter the accepted view that the majority of births were probably attended by women up until the eighteenth, perhaps even the twentieth century, or that an all-female world of birthing ritual did exist,[117] once we move beyond a reductive focus on the birth event, we see that there was also a world of interface between male practitioners and female patients—a world where women practitioners were gradually being restricted to a role as subordinate and controlled assistants in matters where, because of socially constructed notions of propriety, men could not practice alone. Women's health was women's *and* men's business, the latter being interested if for no other reason than their concern

---

[116] See Loren MacKinney, "Childbirth in the Middle Ages, as Seen in Manuscript Illustrations," *Ciba Symposium* 8, nos. 5/6 (December 1960): 230–36; Volker Lehmann, *Die Geburt in der Kunst: Geburtshilfliche Motive in der darstellenden Kunst in Europa von der Antike bis zur Gegenwart* (Brunswick: Braunschweiger Verlagsanstalt, 1978); Danièle Alexandre-Bidon and Monique Closson, *L'enfant à l'ombre des cathédrales* (Lyon: Presses Universitaires de Lyon, 1985); Jones (n. 88 above), esp. 123–24; and Biller, "Childbirth in the Middle Ages." A study on the history of medieval illustrations of caesarian sections by Renate Blumenfeld-Kosinski is forthcoming from Cornell University Press. An index of medieval medical images is now being created at the Medical History Division, Department of Anatomy, University of California at Los Angeles.

[117] See, e.g., Wilson, "Participant or Patient?" and "William Hunter" (nn. 10 and 58 above); and Nadia Maria Filippini, "Levatrici e ostetricanti à Venezia tra Sette e Ottocento," *Quaderni storici*, no. 58 (April 1985), 149–80, and the literature cited therein.

as husbands and fathers for the production of healthy (and legitimate) heirs or, as medical practitioners, for the potential profit to
be made in treating the wives and daughters of their wealthier
clients. As many other studies in the history of women have shown,
the superficially simple dichotomies of sex and gender often mask
very complex and tension-fraught realities of the relations between
women and men. Making sense of such complexity is no easy task,
but it is one that will inevitably enrich and deepen our understanding of the history of women's medical practice and health care in
medieval Europe.

Department of History
Duke University

PROSTITUTION IN THE MEDIEVAL CANON LAW

JAMES A. BRUNDAGE

Prostitution has been called the oldest human profession,[1] and it is certainly true that virtually every known system of positive law has had something to say about the prostitute, the pimp, the procurer, and the conduct of their business.[2] My purpose here is to examine the treatment of the harlot and her trade by the lawyers and lawgivers of the medieval church.

One difficult question must be faced at the outset: the definition of the term itself. What is prostitution, so far as the medieval canonists were concerned? The answer to this fundamental question involves two

1. It has even been suggested that prostitution may be older than humanity: investigators have characterized some forms of sexual behavior among chimpanzees and other primates as prostitution (see Vern L. Bullough, *The History of Prostitution* [New Hyde Park, N.Y.: University Books, 1964], p. 4, and the literature cited there). The antiquity and ubiquity of prostitution among human societies has often been remarked upon, although Bullough points out (p. 14) that just how universal it may be depends upon one's definition of what behavior prostitution includes. It is clear that sexual promiscuity may be discovered in virtually every human society. Promiscuity and prostitution, however, are not necessarily synonymous, although the medieval canonists tended to identify the one with the other.

2. Thus although forbidden in the Mosaic law (Lev. 19:29, 21:7), prostitution obviously was practiced in ancient Israel (e.g., Gen. 38:12–26, Judges 11:2, 1 Kings 3:16–28, etc.). Sacral prostitution is implied, though not explicitly described, in the laws of Hammurabi (see *The Babylonian Laws,* ed., with translation and commentary, G. R. Driver and Sir John C. Miles, 2 vols. [Oxford: Clarendon Press, 1955], 1:360–61, 366–67). Throughout the paper I have used synonyms for "prostitute" such as "harlot," "whore," "tart," "trollop," and the like. "Prostitute" is a relatively neutral, almost clinical term, while the other terms carry a certain amount of judgmental freight. Since the sources I have used employ terms which are more judgmental than neutral, it seemed appropriate to try to convey some sense of that fact by using English terms of a similar sort. The word *meretrix* in Latin, for example, carries about as much judgmental weight as "whore" does in English; it is certainly less neutral than "prostitute."

This essay originally appeared in *Signs,* vol. 1, no. 4, Summer 1976.

strands of thought. Prostitution may be treated as a moral category, in which case the element of sexual promiscuity will be prominently emphasized in the definition. Or prostitution may be treated primarily as a legal category, a type of trade which has implications for public order and policy. In this case, the element of gain, the cash nexus of the transaction, will tend to be emphasized. The moralist will mainly be concerned about the ethical problems of indiscriminate intercourse for the sake of gain; while the jurist will tend to analyze prostitution in terms of the hire-sale situation, will be concerned about the quasi contract established between the harlot and her customer, will have something to say about the property rights conveyed in the transaction, the price paid, and the value received in the exchange.

This contrast in viewpoints is particularly intriguing in the treatment of prostitution by the canonists, the lawyers of the medieval church. The canonists constructed an elaborate and closely reasoned system of jurisprudence to regulate all the branches of human activity that touched upon the moral interests, the business activities, and the social concerns of the church in medieval Europe. Since the church was far and away the largest and most intricate institutional structure in medieval society, its legal system was immensely influential in shaping the attitudes and dictating the limits of action and policy of medieval people at every level of society. Monarchs, monks, and merchants; bishops, businessmen, and bureaucrats; popes, princes, and pimps—all needed to know how to comply with or, if necessary, to evade, the legal sanctions devised by the canonists. Consequently, canon lawyers played critically important roles in determining the ways in which medieval society functioned. Partly for this reason, no doubt, the ranks of the canonists included some of the ablest and most powerful minds of the twelfth and thirteenth centuries. The ingenuity and originality of their work is not always easy to perceive because of the technical medium in which they worked. Their insights and ideas tend to be embedded in lengthy and often tortuous legal treatises. Thus the ideas of a canonist are neither so immediately perceptible nor so pleasurable to read as, say, those of a poet. On the whole, though, the ideas of the canonists often had far greater impact on the functioning of governments, the enforcement of social policy, and the workings of business than the ideas of any comparable group of writers.

The canon law in its origins was an offshoot of moral theology and never wholly escaped its moralistic heritage. Yet the canonists also drew upon the Roman law as a major source of their arcane science, and they employed both legal and moral concepts in their writing. This duality accounts for some of the peculiarities in their treatment of prostitution.[3]

3. Prostitution is, in fact, extremely difficult to define satisfactorily. The problem is discussed by Bullough, pp. 1–2. A classic definition is given by Iwan Bloch, *Die Prostitution*, 2 vols. Handbuch der gesamten Sexualwissenschaft (Berlin: Louis Marcus, 1912–25), 1:38.

How, then, did the canonists define prostitution? As one might expect, both of the basic criteria, promiscuity and gain, were involved. The fundamental definition which they employed was coined by Saint Jerome (ca. 342–420): "A whore is one who is available for the lust of many men."[4] In the mid–twelfth century, when the canon law first began to take coherent shape, its founding father, the monk Gratian, incorporated Saint Jerome's definition in his *Decretum* (ca. 1140). Gratian thereby set the framework within which later canonists were to deal with the whole problem of prostitution. For Gratian and the later lawyers of the medieval church, then, promiscuity was the controlling factor in determining who was a prostitute. There is much sense in this: it may be possible to be promiscuous without being a prostitute; but it is hardly possible to be a prostitute without being sexually promiscuous. The notion of promiscuity was further clarified by the decretists, the writers who commented on Gratian's *Decretum*. The ordinary gloss, which became the standard exposition of the *Decretum* used in the universities as a textbook, defined the notion through a biological analogy: "Promiscuous: that is, she copulates indifferently and indiscriminantly, as in canine love. Dogs indeed copulate indifferently and indiscriminantly."[5] Other canonistic writers mentioned some additional considerations in their discussions of what prostitution meant. One of the most prominent thirteenth-century canonists, Cardinal Hostiensis (d. 1271) stressed the element of notoriety: a prostitute was not only sexually promiscuous, she was openly and publicly promiscuous.[6] Both Hostiensis and an equally

---

Fernando Henriques, *Prostitution in Europe and the Americas*, 2 vols. (New York: Citadel Press, 1962), 1:17, attempts a slightly more explicit definition. A common-law definition of prostitution was set down by Justice Darling in Rex v. de Munck, [1918] 1 K.B.635: "We are of the opinion that prostitution is proved if it be shown that a woman offers her body commonly for lewdness for payment in return"; cited by T. E. James, *Prostitution and the Law* (London: Heinemann, 1951), p. 2.

4. D. 34 c. 16, citing Saint Jerome, *Epist*. 64.7 ad Fabiolem: "Vidua est, cuius maritus mortuus est. Eiecta, que a marito uiuente proicitur. Meretrix, que multorum libidini patet." The conventional canonistic citation system is employed throughout this paper. For explanations, see Javier Ochoa Sanz and Aloisio Diez, *Indices canonum, titulorum et capitulorum corporis iuris canonici*, Universa Bibliotheca Iuris, Subsidia, vol. 1 (Rome: Commentarium pro Religiosis, 1964), pp. iv–v. The texts of the various parts of the *Corpus* are cited from the standard edition by Emil Friedberg, 2 vols. (Leipzig: B. Tauchnitz, 1879; reprint ed., Graz: Akademische Druck- und Verlagsanstalt, 1959). The *glossa ordinaria* will be cited from the Venice, 1605, edition in 4 vols.

5. C. 27 q. 1c. 41 *glos. ord.* ad v. *promiscuum:* "Promiscuum, id est, indifferenter et indistincte comisceret scilicet canino amore. Canes enim indifferenter et indistincte comiscerentur." Also Rolandus (later Pope Alexander III), *Summa* to C. 27 q. 1 c. 41 ad v. *promiscuum*, ed. Friedrich Thaner (Innsbruck: Wagner, 1874), p. 125.

6. Hostiensis (Henricus de Segusio), *In quinque Decretalium libri commentaria* (= *Lectura*) to X 4.1.20, no. 4; 5 vols. in 2 (Venice: apud Iuntas, 1581; reprint ed., Turin: Bottega d'Erasmo, 1965), vol. 4, fol. 6ᵛᵇ: "Publicas id est meretrices, que multorum libidini patent, et melius xxxiiii dist. vidua [D. 34 c. 16], vel quarum publice venalis est turpitudo, xxxii q. iiii meretrices [C. 32 q. 4 c. 11]."

renowned canonistic writer of the next generation, Joannes Andrea (ca. 1270–1348), agreed that an element of deception is also involved in prostitution: the harlot systematically deceives those whom she serves.[7] The deception that these lawyers had in mind was presumably the simulation of love or at least of emotional intimacy between the prostitute and her client.

When the canonists dealt with the element of gain in prostitution, they drew heavily upon the Roman law. The classical Roman law had defined prostitution as the offering of the body for sexual intercourse in return for money or other remuneration, at least so long as the woman made herself available to more than one or two lovers.[8]

The widespread practice of concubinage also complicated the attempts both of canonists and of medieval writers on the Roman law to define prostitution. The ancient Roman jurists, whose ideas were heavily relied upon by medieval lawyers, had assigned the concubine a status quite distinct from that of the prostitute. They considered the concubinage relation a relatively stable one, in contrast to the transient relationship of the prostitute and her customers. Thus the status of the concubine was closely related to that of the married woman in the Roman law, and concubinage might be treated as an informal type of marriage. The concubine and her lover were considered bound to one another, not simply by lust and sexual attraction, but also by "marital affection."

---

7. Joannes Andrea, *In quinque Decretalium libros novella commentaria* to X 3.2.6, no. 2; 5 vols. in 4 (Venice: apud Franciscum Franciscium, 1581; reprint ed., Turin: Bottega d'Erasmo, 1963), vol. 3, fol. 8[rb], following Hostiensis, *Lectura* to X 3.2.6, no. 2 (vol. 3, fol. 6[rb]): "Fornicarias, dicitur fornicaria, quasi carens forma nitida, unde versus: 'nec meretrix munda, nec cornix alba sit unda.' Et dicitur concubina quasi simul cubans. Et meretrix quasi mere, id est vere tricans, vel quasi merens quando non tricat, id est decipit."

8. Esp. Ulpian in *Dig.* 23.2.43; cf. also Modestinus in *Dig.* 23.2.24 and Marcellinus in *Dig.* 23.2.42. The conventional Roman law citation system is employed throughout this paper. For explanations, see Javier Ochoa Sanz and Aloisio Diez, *Indices titulorum et legum corporis iuris civilis,* Universa Bibliotheca Iuris, Subsidia, vol. 2 (Rome: Commentarium pro Religiosis, 1965), pp. x–xi. The texts of the *Corpus* are cited from the standard critical edition by P. Kruger, T. Mommsen, R. Schoell, and G. Kroll, 3 vols. (Berlin: Weidmann, 1872; many times reprinted). The *glossa ordinaria* will be cited from the Lyons, 1584, edition in 5 vols. The basic definitions set forth in the Roman law texts cited here identify as prostitutes the inmates of brothels, those who offer their bodies for hire in taverns and elsewhere, those who make their living by furnishing sex for pay, and other promiscuous women in general, whether they take remuneration for their services or not. Public display was an important ingredient in the Roman jurists' notions about prostitution. The medieval jurists tended to identify certain occupations with prostitution and to take the view that actresses, for example, could be presumed to be prostitutes (see *Cod.* 5.4.23.1 *glos. ord.* ad v. *scenicis*). This was not a view to which the classical jurists necessarily subscribed (see Riccardo Astolfi, "Femina probrosa, concubina, mater solitaria," *Studia et documenta historiae et iuris* 31 [1965]: 15–60, at 20). The theologians sometimes attempted to define how many men a woman must have intercourse with to merit classification as a prostitute. Bloch, 1:18, mentions opinions ranging from a low minimum of forty to a high minimum of 23,000.

The lawyers used this latter term to signify either an intention eventually to contract marriage or else an emotional quality, not wholly unlike the concept of love.[9] Marital affection, in fact, was treated in Justinian's legislation as excluding promiscuity, which was essential to the definition of prostitution.[10] Thus concubinage and prostitution were mutually exclusive.

The medieval canonists, although conscious of these Roman law texts, faced a theological problem in adopting wholesale the Roman law definitions. By the lights of Western theology in the twelfth century, all extramarital sexual relations involved fornication, which was a species of sin. Concubinage, from this viewpoint, was an aggravated type of fornication, since it implicitly involved a long-term, continuing, nonmarital sexual relationship.[11] On the other hand, some of the decretists preferred to treat concubinage as a type of marriage,[12] a temporary marriage, perhaps, as Bishop Rufinus (d. 1192) called it,[13] or an informal, clandestine marriage, as the law professor Huguccio (d. 1210) thought of it.[14] The canonistic doctrine on concubinage, in short, was not wholly clear or consistent. Yet although the canonists clearly thought concubinage undesirable, it was less undesirable than prostitution, and they felt it necessary to draw a sharp distinction between prostitution and concubinage. The distinction that they drew was based on the element of promiscuity, not on the element of gain in the relationship.[15]

9. *Dig.* 25.7.1, 3, 4; 34.9.16.1; 50.16.144; *Cod.* 5.26. The various senses of the term *maritalis affectio* are discussed by John T. Noonan, Jr., "Marital Affection in the Canonists," *Studia Gratiana* 12 (1967): 482–89.

10. *Nov.* 89.12.4-5; Noonan, p. 489.

11. Adhémar Esmein, *Le mariage en droit canonique*, 2 vols. (Paris: L. Larose & Forcel, 1891; reprint ed., New York: Burt Franklin, 1968), 2:114–15; J. A. Brundage, "Concubinage and Marriage in Medieval Canon Law," *Journal of Medieval History* 1 (1975): 1–17.

12. D. 34 d.a.c. 4.

13. *Summa decretorum* to D. 33 d.p.c. 1 and D. 34 d.a.c. 7 ad v. *Certum si non talis,* ed. Heinrich Singer (Paderborn: F. Schöningh, 1902; reprint ed., Aalen: Scientia Verlag, 1963), pp. 77, 81.

14. Huguccio, *Summa* to D. 34 c. 3 (Paris, Bibliothèque Nationale, MS lat. 3892, fol. 41vb; hereafter cited as B.N.): "Sed concubina dicitur illa uxor quam quis clandestine, non adhibita preterita sollempnitate maritali affectu sibi copulat." Also his *Summa* to D. 33 d.p.c. 1 (ibid., fol. 41ra): "Concubina: hic similiter distinctio [*scil.:* ab uxore] nullius est momenti quia potes . . . intelligere concubina uulgariter, sed grauius intelligit concubinam uxorem clandestine post uel ante aliam ductam." Again, *Summa* to D. 33 c. 6 ad v. *concubinam relicet* (ibid., fol. 41rb): "Ego uulgariter intelligo, sed grauius intelligit concubinam scilicet uxorem clandestine ductam ante uel post aliam uxorem." See also the *Summa 'Elegantius in iure diuino' seu Coloniensis*, pt. 2, sec. 36, ed. Gérard Fransen and Stephan Kuttner, Monumenta Iuris Canonici, Corpus Glossatorum, vol. 1 (New York: Fordham University Press, 1969), pp. 58–59.

15. *Summa Coloniensis*, pt. 2, sec. 37 (ed. Fransen and Kuttner, p. 59); *Summa Parisiensis* to D. 33 pr., ed. Terence P. McLaughlin (Toronto: Pontifical Institute of Mediaeval Studies, 1952), p. 32; Joseph Freisen, *Geschichte des kanonischen Eherechts bis zum Verfall der Glossenliteratur*, 2d ed. (Paderborn: F. Schöningh, 1893; reprint ed., Aalen: Scientia Verlag, 1963), p. 58.

When one looks beyond the matter of definition, one finds other anomalies in the ways in which the canonists dealt with prostitution. On the one hand, they flatly disapproved of prostitution. It was morally offensive, theologically repugnant, and ought to be repressed. For these views they could find adequate basis in the Scriptures,[16] in the natural law,[17] and in the Roman law.[18] Yet the medieval canonists' treatment of prostitution was strangely ambivalent. Although they disapproved of it in principle and thought that it should be prohibited, still in practice they were prepared to tolerate prostitution and to justify its toleration in a Christian society.

The origin of this policy of practical toleration seems to go back to Saint Augustine (354–430), who observed that if prostitutes were not available, established patterns of sexual relationship would be endangered. Therefore, he thought, it was better to tolerate prostitution, with all of its associated evils, than to risk the perils which would follow the successful elimination of the harlot from society.[19] In Augustine's attitude one can arguably find the wellsprings of later medieval and even modern attitudes toward prostitution, the notion that it is a necessary evil and that its elimination, if possible at all, would disturb and dislocate the social order.[20] Augustine's views on prostitution, as on other matters of sexual conduct, were accepted by theologians as well as by the canonists. Some of them even made the argument that prostitution was necessary for the public good.[21]

16. Esp. in the Mosaic law, e.g.; Deut. 23:17, Lev. 19:29, 21:7, 9. Cf. the scriptural *glossa ordinaria* to Deut. 23:17: "Non erit meretrix a filiabus Israel, et non erit fornicans a filiis Israel. Manifeste prohibet viros et feminas fornicari, etiam cum non alienis conjugibus suis, quando et meretrices esse, et ad eas prohibet accedere, quarum publice venalis est turpitudo" *(Biblia sacra, Penteteuchus cum glossis interlineari et ordinaria, Nicolai Lyrani Postilla et Moralitates* [Lyon, 1545], fol. 358[ra]). Also Huguccio, *Summa* to C. 32 q. 4 c. 11 (B.N. lat. 3892, fol. 313[va]): "Ubi dicitur, non erit meretrix de filiabus Israel, neque scortator de filiis Israel . . . cum dicitur 'non erit meretrix,' prohibi meretrices esse; cum enim dictum 'non erit scortator,' prohibi accedere ad meretrices."

17. D. 1 c. 7 *glos. ord.* ad v. *ius naturale.*

18. *Dig.* 48.5.11(10): *Cod.* 1.4.14, 33; *Nov.* 14.1.

19. Augustine, *De ordine,* 2.4, in J. P. Migne, ed., *Patrologiae cursus completus . . . series latina,* 221 vols. (Paris: Garnier, 1844–64), 32:1000, (hereafter cited as *PL*): "Aufer meretrices de rebus humanis, turbaveris omnia libidinibus: constitue matronarum loco, labe ac dedecore dehonestaveris."

20. Bloch, 1:640. See e.g., N. M. Haring, "Peter Cantor's View on Ecclesiastical Excommunication and Its Practical Consequences," *Mediaeval Studies* 11 (1949): 101; Saint Thomas, *Summa Theologica* 2[a] 2[ae] q. 10 a. 11; Hostiensis, *Lectura* to *X* 4.1.20, no. 7 (vol. 4, fol. 6[vb]).

21. Nicholas of Lyra, *Postilla* to Matt., proem., quoted by Gaines Post, *Studies in Medieval Legal Thought: Public Law and the State, 1100–1322* (Princeton, N.J.: Princeton University Press, 1964), p. 553, n. 151. Similar views were current in the sixteenth century (see Joost de Damhouder, *Subhaustationum compendiosa exegesis,* c. 5, in Benvenuto Straccha, *De mercatura decisiones et tractatus varii* [Lyon, 1610; reprint ed., Turin: Bottega d'Erasmo, 1971], p. 763; A. W. Small, *The Cameralists: The Pioneers of German Social Policy* [Chicago, 1909; reprint ed., New York: Burt Franklin, 1967], p. 37).

But there is more to it than this. The practical toleration of prostitution, coupled with the moral condemnation of it, was also rooted in medieval notions about the nature of sexuality itself. The medieval lawyers construed sexual intercourse as a part of the natural law, a notion which stemmed from the Roman jurists.[22] Although they knew that sexual urges are strong and universally shared, the canonists were also aware that sexual desire could lead to sin—and usually did. Few adults are not guilty of fornication, they observed,[23] and the ordinary gloss to the *Decretum* noted that people are commonly more inclined to fornicate than to steal.[24] The canonists also suspected that sexual desires might be of diabolical origin, a product of original sin and man's subsequent fallen state.[25] While they taught that the only legitimate outlet for sexual desire was to be found in marriage, some canonists believed that even in marriage sexual pleasure was sinful.[26] The major differences of opinion among them on this matter concerned the question of the sinfulness of intercourse if the reason for the sexual act was enjoyment rather than the procreation of children. Huguccio, an influential twelfth-century canonist, thought that even procreative sex was morally wrong; his more liberal brethren allowed that sexual relations might be morally admissible between married persons when the object of their relations was to beget offspring.[27] There was general agreement, however, that excessive intercourse, even within marriage, was sinful, although there was some dispute as to whether the sin involved should be equated with simple fornication or with the more serious sin of adultery.[28] Sex outside of marriage, however, was clearly wrong, and intercourse with a prostitute compounded the wrong: it involved the bad use of an evil thing, as the ordinary gloss put it.[29]

22. *Dig.* 1.1.1; D. 1 c. 7; cf. *Summa Parisiensis* to D. 1 c. 7 ad v. *coniunctio* (ed. McLaughlin, p. 2); *Summa Coloniensis*, pt. 1, sec. 5 (ed. Fransen and Kuttner, 1:2).

23. D. 50 c. 16; C. 15 q. 8 c. 1 *glos. ord.* ad v. *caetera;* Huguccio, *Summa* to D. 25 d.p.c. 3 ad v. *sine peccato* (B.N. lat. 3892, fol. 29va): "Immo pauci adulti inueniuntur sine carnali delicto, scilicet fornicationis, ut di. 1 quia sanctitus [D. 50 c. 16], et ita nullus potest eligi sine peccato, unde patet quod non sic accipitur ibi in epistola Pauli nomen criminis, sed sensus est ibi."

24. D. 2 de pen. c. 5 *glos. ord.* ad v. *ex qua minus.*

25. D. 13 c. 2 *glos. ord.* ad v. *nervi, testiculorum;* C. 32 q. 2 d.p.c. 2 *glos ord.* ad v. *sine ardore;* cf. Peter Lombard's views in his *Sententiae* 2.20.1 (*PL,* 192:᷀592).

26. D. 5 c. 2; *Summa Parisiensis* to C. 32 q. 4 c. 14 (ed. McLaughlin, p. 244); see also Rudolf Weigand, "Die Lehre der Kanonisten von den Ehezwecken," *Studia Gratiana* 12 [1967]: 443–78).

27. D. 13 d.a.c. 1 *glos. ord.* ad v. *item adversus;* D. 13 c. 2 *glos. ord.* ad v. *et quia;* D. 25 d. p. c. 3 and *glos. ord.* ad v. *excepto;* C. 27 q. 1 c. 20 *glos. ord.* ad v. *peiores;* C. 27 q. 2 c. 10 *glos. ord.* ad v. *non poterat;* C. 33 q. 4 c. 7 *glos. ord.* ad v. *voluptate; Summa Parisiensis* to D. 5 c. 4 ad v. *prava* (ed. McLaughlin, p. 5). For the view of Saint Thomas, see *Summa Theologica* 3 Supp. q. 49 a. 2 ad 1.

28. C. 32 q. 7 c. 11; the *Summa Parisiensis* to C. 32 q. 2 d.p.c. 2 ad v. *item immoderatus* (ed. McLaughlin, p. 241), equates it with adultery, while D. 13 c. 2 *glos. ord.* ad v. *maiora* treats it as fornication.

29. C. 32 q. 1 c. 11 *glos. ord.* ad v. *usus mali.*

The canonists were quite aware that the sexuality of women differed from that of men. For this they found a theological reason: woman was not created in the image of God, as man was.[30] The chastity of women, particularly young women, they held, was always suspect,[31] and women, they observed, are always ready for sexual intercourse. Cardinal Hostiensis illustrated his comments on these points with the story of a priest who was journeying with two girls, one riding in front of him, the other behind. The priest, said Hostiensis, could never swear that the girl in back was a virgin.[32] Young girls were thought to be particularly susceptible to the call of sexual desire: the less they knew about it, the sweeter they thought it, as Saint Jerome put it.[33] Since women were considered so susceptible to sexual temptations, great care had to be taken to confine their sexual activities within a properly structured marriage relationship. Women usually sigh when their men are not available, Hostiensis observed,[34] and so husbands had a moral obligation to keep their wives sexually satisfied, lest they be tempted to stray to other beds.[35] The canonists treated this obligation as a debt, and, like other debts, it was enforceable at law.[36] Nonetheless, women commonly

30. X 1.33.12 glos ord. ad v. iurisdictionis: "[S]ed contra videtur quod mulier iudicare non potest. . . . Praeterea mulier non debet habere talem potestatem, quia non est facta ad imaginem Dei, sed vir, qui est imago et gloria Dei, et mulier debet subesse viro, et quasi famula viri esse, cum vir caput sit mulieris, et non econverso. . . ." Cf. Andrea, Novella to X 1.33.12, no. 6 (vol. 1, fol. 267[vb]): "Et ibi, imago: sicut enim a deo procedit omnis creatura, sic et ab Adam omnis humana et ab eo solo, et non ab Eva sola, cum ipsa Eva processerit ab Adam et sic ipsa non est imago Dei in creatione."

31. X 3.32.18 glos. ord. ad v. talis etas de qua suspicio.

32. Hostiensis, Lectura to X 4.13.11, no. 1 (vol. 4, fol. 27[ra]): ". . . hoc ex parte mulieris, cuius vas semper paratum est. secundum Gof. Unde et consuevit dici vulgariter adeo magnum rostrum habet pericula sicut pica. Exemplum de sacerdote qui portabat duas filias, una ante se et aliam retro, qui dixit, quod de illa, quem retro deferebat, nullatenus iuraret, quod virgo esset; secus in viro, qui non potest tanto tempore pervenire, salvo eo, quod narrat Gregorius in dialogo, de puero ix annorum qui impregnavit nutricem suam. Etiam hoc idem reperi ego de puero xi vel xii annorum in castro sancti Michaelis systaricensis diocesis. Et idem legitur de Salamone, scilicet quod in xi anno genuit filium." Andrea, Novella to X 4.13.11, no. 5 (vol. 4, fol. 42[vb]) follows Hostiensis virtually word for word.

33. Quoted in C. 27 q. 1 c. 2 glos. ord. ad v. viae sunt: "Dicit Hieronymus: Libido in virginibus maiorem patitur famem, dum dulcius esse putant quod nesciunt."

34. Hostiensis, Lectura to X 3.34.7, no. 15 (vol. 3, fol. 127[rb]): "Suspira. Loquitur per similitudinem, cum enim mulier, propter recessum et absentem viri consueverit suspirare, vult dicere quod idem facit Trecen. ecclesia, que est sponsa sua, supra de translatione episcopi ca. ii [X 1.7.2] et repete. in contrarium allegabant."

35. Thus, e.g., C. 33 q. 5 c. 3,4,11, d.p.c. 20; D. 5 c. 4 glos. ord. ad v. ablactetur. This was an especially acute problem for Crusaders, whose extended absence might expose their wives to sexual temptations. On the canonists' treatment of this problem, see my study, "The Crusader's Wife: A Canonistic Quandary," Studia Gratiana 12 (1967): 425–42.

36. This usage is common form, based on 1 Cor. 7:3–6 (see Esmein, 1:84, 110; 2:8–13; John T. Noonan, Jr., Contraception: A History of Its Treatment by the Catholic

yielded to stray sexual desires, for a variety of reasons: they were overly trusting and put faith in the dubious promises of unworthy men; they were ignorant, sometimes so ignorant that they were unaware that adultery was sinful; or they might be separated from their spouses and despair of their return.[37] Moreover, they were fickle and inconstant creatures by nature.[38] They were soft of heart,[39] moreover, and susceptible to sensual stimulation, which easily led them into sexual sins.[40] In addition, the canonists were aware that females reach the age of sexual readiness earlier than males: girls are *viripotentes* from age twelve, according to Hostiensis, who cited the Roman law to prove his point.[41] They reach sexual maturity earlier than males, he thought, because they are warmer and quicker by nature than men and hence attain their natural perfection at an earlier age. Hostiensis also observed, rather ungallantly, that women are like weeds, which mature earlier than desirable plants—he quotes Plato to prove this point—but also die earlier.[42]

Despite all these handicaps—and one might have thought from some of the discussions that chastity in a woman was virtually impossible—women were nonetheless expected to observe a more austere standard of sexual conduct than were men, as at least some of the canonists were quite aware. They taught a double standard of sexual morality: they were aware of it and they had reasons for it, mainly

Theologians and Canonists [Cambridge, Mass.: Harvard University Press, Belknap Press, 1965], pp. 283–85). Peter Herde, *Audientia litterarum contradictarum: Untersuchungen über die päpstlichen Justizbriefe und die päpstliche Delegationsgerichtsbarkeit vom 13, bis zum Beginn des 16, Jahrhunderts*, 2 vols., Bibliothek des deutschen historischen Instituts in Rom, vols. 31–32 (Tübingen: Max Niemeyer, 1970), 2:304, gives the form for delegation of trial on such a complaint.

37. Hostiensis, *Lectura* to *X* 4.15.6, no. 6 (vol. 4, fol. 33ra).

38. Hostiensis, *Lectura* to *X* 5.40.10 (vol. 5, fol. 125vb).

39. Hostiensis, *Lectura* to *X* 3.33.2, no. 10 (vol. 3, fol. 124rb).

40. C. 27 q. 1 c. 4; C. 32 q. 5 c. 11 *glos. ord.* ad v. *aliam;* Hostiensis, *Lectura* to *X* 2.13.10, no. 13 (vol. 2, fol. 51rb).

41. Hostiensis, *Lectura* to *X* 4.2.1, no. 3 (vol. 4, fol. 10ra): "Duodecim vero anni in muliere expectantur [*scil.*: ad contrahendum matrimonium], infra eodem continebatur [*X* 4.2.6]. Unde versus: 'Iam matura thoro plenis adoleverat annis' [cf. Aeneid 7.53; 12.428]. Nunc ergo dicitur viripotens, ff. ut in possessionem legatorum, 1. pen. [*Dig.* 36.4.16] et si quandoque ante hos annos cognoscatur, sed tunc dicitur immatura, ff. de iniuriis, si stuprum [*Dig.* 47.10.25]."

42. Hostiensis, *Lectura* to *X* 4.2.4, no. 2 (vol. 4, fol. 11rb): "Si quaeretur ratio quare mulier citius quam homo pubescat? Respondeo quia ingeniosior et calidior est, unde et citius impetrat venam etatis, quam masculus: quia mulier in 18 anno masculus vero in 20, C. de his qui veniam aetatis impetraverunt, omnes adolescentes [*Cod.* 2.44(45).2]; sed et naturaliter debilior est sexus muliebris, unde communiter minus vivit: quia et minus habet caloris naturalis, ideo quanto citius finitur, tanto citius naturaliter perfici debet. Et sicut etiam dicunt aliqui naturales in xii anno omnino apta est mulier ad concipiendum. Plato vero dixit, quod hoc ideo est: quia citius crescit mala herba, quam bona, sed et dici potest quod facilius est mulieri pati quam homini agere, unde et semper mulier est parata, non idem in homine. . . ."

theological.[43] Modesty, they taught, was woman's glory.[44] Therefore a woman who was sexually desirous and ardent, who did not blush at sex, was at heart a whore, though she need not legally be classified as one so long as she remained faithful to her husband.[45] The adulteress, on the other hand, was more reprehensible than her partner in sin, and sexual promiscuity was considered more detestable in women than in men, according to Joannes Teutonicus in the ordinary gloss on the *Decretum*.[46] Even within the marriage relationship a woman should not use the sexual wiles of a prostitute, and a matron who dressed like a tart could legally be classed as one.[47]

As for male sexuality, it was no secret to the canonists that men have a natural appetite for carnal relations with women.[48] The lawyers were also aware that casual conversation with members of the opposite sex might easily lead to greater intimacy,[49] an outcome which became even more likely when conversation was enlivened by intemperate drinking.[50]

43. Innocent IV, *Apparatus toto orbe celebrandus super V libris Decretalium* to X 1.21.5, sec. 3 (Franfurt, 1570), fol. 112ᵛ: "Sed quare magis exigitur in uxore quam in viro? Nam maritus corrupte promoveri non potest, 34 dist. curandum [D. 34 c. 4] praecipimus. Sicut si vir: ille autem qui post uxorem habuit concubinam promoveri potest, 34 dist. Fraternitatis [D. 34 c. 7]. Ugolinus dicit, quod vir significat ecclesiam, quae saepe adulteratur exorbitando a fide et ita non deest significatio sacramenti, licet vir adulteretur; uxor autem significat Christum, qui nunquam ecclesiam dimisit: ipse enim est fons vivus, cui non communicat alienus. Ego credo quod vir significat Christum quo sibi copulavit synagogam, et post ecclesiam, et ideo non nocet, si vir dividit carnem suam in plures; uxor autem ecclesiam, quae semper virgo permansit saltem mente: unde despondi enim vos uni viro, et cap. 27 quaestio i nuptiarum [C. 27 q. 1 c. 41]; unde si uxor in plures carnem suam dividat deficit in ea sacramentum, 33 dist. Valentino [D. 33 c. 20]."

44. Andrea, *Novella* to X, prol., no. 7 (vol. 1, fol. 6ʳᵃ).

45. Hostiensis, *Lectura* to X 4.13.11, no. 2 (vol. 4, fol. 27ʳᵃ), followed *ad litteram* by Andrea, *Novella* to X 4.13.11, no. 1: "Carnis stimulis: frons meretricis sibi facta est, noluit erubescere. Hie. iii b., quamvis nec propter hoc meretrix sit, immo caste vivit, dummodo ab aliis abstineat, 31 di. nicena [D. 31 c. 12], alioquin non excusaretur, licet diceret se rem naturalem passam esse, in Auth. de restitutionibus et ea quae parit xi mense, sec. unum siquidem, col. iiii [*Nov.* 39.1, 1 in c. = *Auth.* 4.6.1]; neque pretextu paupertatis, ut patet in his que no. supra eodem distinctionem."

46. C. 12 q. 2 d.p.c. 58 *glos. ord.* ad v. *capitali:* "Sed numquid servus potest accusare dominam suam si cum alio servo adulteratur? Respondeo quod non, quia de proprio tantum servo; similiter nec domina virum suum potest accusare, si cum ancilla sua iacet vel cum aliena, cum hoc cautum non invenio hoc immo, quia detestabilius est hoc crimen in muliere quam in viro. Jo. Maledicit Jo., quia accusari potest mulier, et vir, si cum ancilla sua fornicetur, aut femina si adulterium committat, ut extra de divor., ex litteris [X 4.19.5]. B."

47. Rufinus, *Summa* to C. 32 q. 2 d.p.c. 2 (ed. Singer, p. 479); X 5 39.25 *glos. ord.* ad v. *meretricali.*

48. E.g., Huguccio, *Summa* to D. 1 c. 7 ad v. *ut uiri et femine coniunctio* (B.N. lat. 3892, fol. 2ᵛᵃ): "Mouetur enim homo quodam naturali appetitu sensualitatis ut carnaliter commisceatur femine."

49. *Cod.* 5.27.1.1 *glos. ord.* ad v. *venenis:* "Ut veneno occiditur corpus, sic animas istarum conversatione. Accursius."

50. *Cod.* 9.9.28(29) *glos. ord.* ad. v. *intemperantia vina:* "Id est ex quibus oritur intemperantia et incontinentia unde illud, 'Nolite inebriari vino, in quo est luxuria.' [Eph. 5:18] Venter enim mero affluens, facile despumat in libidinem" (cf. Eccles. 19:2).

So rampant was male attraction to women that the ordinary gloss to the *Decretum* observed that some scholars even went to church services more in order to ogle the women who attended than to worship God.[51] It was obvious to the canonists, too, that religion and sex did not mix well together: a man who had sexual gratifications readily available could not give his whole attention to God.[52] This being so, clerics were especially exhorted not to have dealings of any kind, even the most innocuous conversations, with women whose morals were suspect. Those who did so were liable to excommunication.[53] Still, the canonists cautioned their students to give a benevolent interpretation to the association of clerics with members of the opposite sex. A cleric found embracing a woman is presumed to be blessing her, according to the ordinary gloss[54]—to which a later commentator jestingly added: "God save us from such blessings!"[55]

Given such views of male and female sexuality, with a far higher standard of sexual conduct demanded from women than from men, it may seem somewhat surprising to find that the lawyers generally, both civilians and canonists, wasted very little time detailing punishments to be dealt out to prostitutes. The prostitute, in the eyes of the canonists, was culpable, but not severely culpable, for her conduct. She was, after all, simply acting in accord with her sexual character, as the canonists viewed it. When it came to punishments, they gave most of their attention to the penalties to be inflicted upon those who used the prostitute's services and upon the pimps, procurers, and brothel keepers who made those services regularly available.[56]

The canonists saw financial need as one root cause of prostitution,

51. C. 24 q. 1 c. 28 *glos. ord.* ad v. *sed suas:* "Argumentum contra scholares, qui vadunt ad ecclesiam ut videant dominas: quia ibi potius attendunt causam suam quam Dei."

52. Hostiensis, *Lectura* to X 2.23.15, no. 3 (vol. 2, fol. 124va).

53. X 3.2.2 (= *Comp. I* 3.2.3); cf. D. 81 c. 22.

54. C. 11 q. 3 c. 14 *glos. ord.* ad v. *sinistrum:* "Si ergo clericus amplectitur mulierem, interpretabitur quod causa benedicendi eam hoc faciat, ut 96 dist. in scripturis [D. 96 c. 8]."

55. Hippolytus de Marsiliis, *Tractatus de fideiussoribus,* in Straccha, p. 689: "Et facit glossa in ca. absit 11 quaest. 3 [C. 11 q. 3 c. 14], quae dixit, quod si clericus osculatur mulierem, praesumitur causa benedictionis hoc facere, quam glossa ad hoc refert Angelus de Aretinis in tractatu maleficio in verbo, *Che hai adulterata a la mia donna,* versi, an patri liceat: ubi iocose subdit, quod a tali benedictione clericorum liberet nos Deus."

56. Punishment for those who frequented harlots, especially for clerics who did so, is frequently prescribed: e.g., D. 28 c. 9; D. 33 c. 6; D. 51 c. 5; Rufinus, *Summa* to D. 33 pr. (ed. Singer, p. 77); D. 32 *glos. ord.* ad v. *audiet;* Gulielmus Durantis, *Speculum iuris,* lib. 4, partic. 4, De adulteriis et stupro, no. 5; 2 vols. in 1 (Frankfurt a/M.: Sumptibus heredum A. Wechli & J. Gymnici, 1592), 2:477. The law dealing with pimps, procurers, and brothel keepers is extensive. See, *inter alia, Dig.* 3.2.4.2, 13.7.24.3, 48.5.2.6; *Cod.* 1.4.12, 14, 33; 4.56.1,2,3; 7.6.1.4; 9.9.2; 11.41.6; *Nov.* 14 (=*Auth.* coll. 3 tit. 1); Rolandus, *Summa* to C. 32 q. 1 c. 4 (ed. Thaner, p. 60); Goffredus de Trani, *Summa super titulis Decretalium* to X 5.16.4 (Lyon: Roman Morin, 1519; reprint ed., Aalen: Scientia Verlag, 1968), fo. 216ra; X 5.16.3 *glos. ord.* ad v. *reus sit;* Hostiensis, *Summa aurea una cum summariis et adnotationibus Nicolai Superantii,* lib. 5, De adulteriis et stupro, no. 14 (Lyon, 1537; reprint ed., Aalen: Scientia Verlag, 1962), fol. 245ra.

but they did not consider poverty or economic necessity as mitigating circumstances.[57] No matter how hungry she might be or how desperate her situation, a woman was not justified in turning to prostitution in order to earn even the necessities of life.[58] Although poverty and desperation might excuse a man who committed theft, for example, and under certain circumstances even homicide could be justified, the canonists admitted no circumstances to excuse fornication and prostitution.[59] Nor was a natural craving for sexual gratification a mitigating circumstance;[60] some theologians indeed taught that the more pleasure a prostitute derived from her sexual encounters, the more serious was her offense.[61] Some authors tended to link prostitution with greed and saw an inordinate desire for wealth and opulence as a cause of harlotry, but this was not a theme on which the legal writers had much to say.[62] The only mitigating situation which the canonists would admit for the prostitute occurred if the girl had been forced into prostitution by her parents or someone who exercised legitimate control over her actions.[63] In such a situation, the prostitute herself was not accountable for her actions, and those who forced her into a life of sin bore the guilt for any actions which she was forced to perform.[64]

Perhaps the principal disability felt by the medieval prostitute was her inability to attain any form of significant social status. This she shared in common with her predecessors in Roman antiquity.[65] It has

57. X 4.1.20 glos. ord. ad v. publicas; the opinions of Laurentius and Vicentius are given by Stephan Kuttner, Kanonistische Schuldlehre von Gratian bis auf die Dekretalen Gregors IX, Studi e testi, vol. 64 (Vatican City: Biblioteca Apostolica Vaticana, 1935; reprint ed., 1961), p. 298, n. 1.

58. Hostiensis, Lectura to X 4.1.20, no. 6, and 4.19.4, no. 3 (vol. 4, fol. 6vb, 43vb).

59. Hostiensis, Lectura to X 5.18.3, nos. 2–4, 9 (vol. 5, fol. 55ra-rb).

60. Hostiensis, Lectura to X 4.19.4, no. 3 (vol. 4, fol. 43vb).

61. Leopold Brandl, Die Sexualethik des heiligen Albertus Magnus: Eine Moralgeschichtliche Untersuchung, Studien zur Geschichte der katholischen Moraltheologie, vol. 2 (Regensburg: F. Putest, 1955), p. 244; Dennis Doherty, The Sexual Doctrine of Cardinal Cajetan, Studien zur Geschichte der katholischen Moraltheologie, vol. 12 (Regensburg: F. Putest, 1966), pp. 102–3.

62. Saint Thomas Aquinas, Summa Theologica, 2a 2ae q. 118 a. 8 ad 4; Jacques de Vitry, Historia occidentalis, c. 18, ed. John F. Hinnebusch, Spicilegium Friburgense, vol. 17 (Friburg: University Press, 1972), p. 99. Some modern writers have suggested that avarice is a factor in modern marriage and that the principal economic difference between marriage and prostitution lies in the nature of the return: prostitution involves the rendering of sexual services for a specified fee, while marriage provides continuous support in return for assured availability of sexual gratification (Max Weber on Law in Economy and Society, ed. Max Rheinstein, Twentieth Century Legal Philosophy Series, vol. 6 [Cambridge, Mass.: Harvard University Press, 1954], p. 134).

63. Dig. 13.7.24.3; Cod. 1.4.12, 14, 33; 4.56.1–3; 7.6.1.4; 11.41.6; Azo, Summa super Codicem to Cod. 11.41, Corpus glossatorum jures civilis, vol. 2 (Pavia: Per Bernardinum et Ambrosius fratres de Rouellis, 1506; reprint ed., Turin: Bottega d'Erasmo, 1966), p. 437.

64. Summa Parisiensis to C. 32 q. 5 c. 1 ad v. tolerabilius (ed. McLaughlin, p. 245).

65. Hans Herter, "Die Soziologie der antiken Prostitution im Lichte des heidnischen und christlichen Schrifttums," Jahrbuch für Antike und Christentum 3 (1960): 70–110; Dig. 9.9.28(29) glos. ord. ad v. et stupri et adulterii; Dig. 23.2.47.

been suggested that even in modern societies the harlot's loss of social status remains one of the major disabilities of the prostitute's role, and that the fees she receives should be interpreted as compensation not only for her sexual services but also for her impaired social standing.[66] Certainly the medieval canonists considered the harlot's status debased: it was so vile, according to Hostiensis, that she was not even required to obey the law—the inference being that she was beneath the law's contempt.[67] She was so base that she was canonically debarred from accusing others of crimes, according to one conciliar canon,[68] save for the crime of simony, which the canonists considered a particularly depraved offense.[69] The Roman law doctrine that prohibited a harlot from inheriting property was still considered applicable law in the Middle Ages.[70] Likewise, the harlot who had charges brought against her was not allowed to answer them in person but had to employ a representative to respond to them, just as did madmen and monsters.[71]

When it came to dealing with the property and property rights of prostitutes, the canonists followed very closely the doctrine of the classical Roman lawyers, which was still current law in many secular jurisdictions in the Middle Ages. Money given to a prostitute could not be reclaimed by the donor, according to this doctrine: the client had no right to take back the money he had paid for her sexual services. She, for her part, committed no wrong in accepting the money. What she did in return for her fee might be wrong, but the taking of money for it was no crime.[72] The customer who paid the harlot her fee might be held wrong to give money to her; but her acceptance was perfectly legal.[73] Once she had taken the fee, it became her property outright and her rights to it were legally valid, a validity which at least one medieval lawyer sustained because of the harlot's "usefulness."[74] Cardinal Cajetan, incidentally,

66. Vern L. Bullough, "Problems and Methods for Research in Prostitution and the Behavioral Sciences," *Journal of the History of the Behavioral Sciences* 1 (1965): 247.

67. Hostiensis, *Lectura* to X 3.30.23, no. 3 (vol. 3, fol. 100vb) and 4.1.20, no. 5 (vol. 4, fol. 6vb); *Cod.* 9.9.28(29).

68. C. 4 q. 1 c. 1.

69. C. 6 q. 1 d.a.c. 1, *glos. ord.* ad v. *quod autem:* "In simonia quilibet auditur accusans contra laicum, etiam meretrix, ut 89 dist. si quis papa [*recte:* D. 79 c. 2] et ext. de simonia, tanta [X 5.3.7] . . . secus si accusatus sit clericus et bonae famae. . . ."

70. *Dig.* 29.1.41.1; 37.12.3 pr.

71. X 2.1.14 *glos. ord.* ad v. *factum proponat:* "Item universitas per alium respondet. . . . Item furiosi, prodigi, et mulier luxuriosa, ff. de curatoribus furioso, 1. et mulieri [*Dig.* 27.10.15]. Ber."

72. *Dig.* 12.5.4, quoting Ulpian, who relies on the doctrines of Labeo and Marcellus in this passage.

73. Huguccio, *Summa* to C. 14 q. 5 d.a.c. 1 (B.N. lat. 3892, fol. 119ra): "Unde dicit lex meretrix turpiter facere in eo quod est meretrix, sed nec turpiter accipit cum sit meretrix, ut ff. de con. ob tur. c. idem esti quotiens [*Dig.* 12.5.4.2]"; cf. D. 86 c. 7 *glos. ord.* ad v. *talibus;* Hostiensis, *Lectura* to X 3.30.23, no. 7 (vol. 3, fol. 100vb).

74. Azo, *Summa Codicis* to *Cod.* 4.7 (p. 115): "Turpitudinem enim meretricis non dignatur lex respicere propter utilitatem sui, ut infra ad legem iuliam de adulteriis, 1. que

stipulated that a prostitute, in order to be entitled lawfully to retain what she earned, must charge only a just price for her services. He did not specify how this was to be determined. He also considered it unlawful for a prostitute to practice deception in the display of her wares.[75]

If a whore was legally entitled to retain what had been paid to her, she was on shakier ground in seeking fulfillment of promises made to her. The customer who paid in cash could not reclaim what he had paid to her. The wilier customer, who paid in promises of future gifts, could renege on his promises and the prostitute could not legally secure enforcement of them.[76]

Another vexing question concerned the liability of prostitutes for the payment of the tithe. On this matter opinions were divided. Some canonists held that since the harlot lawfully possessed the money she received for her services, she must pay tithes from her earnings.[77] Hostiensis, however, thought otherwise: the earnings of the whore, although lawfully held, were nonetheless the wages of sin, and tithes could not legally be collected from them.[78] Saint Thomas (1224–74), as usual, distinguished: the harlot must be required to pay the tithe from her earnings—but the church might not accept the payment until she had reformed.[79]

If the harlot's liability for payment of the tithe was disputed, her

---

ad adulterium [*Cod.* 9.9.28(29)], nec obstat quod legitur ff. de furtis, 1. verum [*Dig.* 47.2.25], quia ibi non meretricis turpitudinem spectat licet eius qui accessit ad eam."

75. Doherty, p. 102, no. 35.

76. *Cod.* 5.3.5 *glos. ord.* ad v. *non potes;* Azo, *Summa Codicis* to Cod. 4.7 (p. 115).

77. The solution of Joannes Teutonicus, *Apparatus* to *Comp. III* 3.23. 5 (= X 3.30.28) is particularly ingenious: "Set numquid meretrix uel ystrio dabit decimam? Non uidetur, quia ut dixi honorandus est dominus de iustis laboribus, et decime tantum de licitis dantur, ut supra eodem ex transmissa lib. ii [*Comp. II* 3.17.7 = X 3.30.23]. Item quia scriptum est non accipies mercedem prostibuli [Deut. 23:18] et est arg. ad hoc xiiii q. v elemosina [c. 7] et xxxii q. iiii sic non sunt [c. 10]. Nam illicite quesita non sunt in bonis nostris, ut ff. pro socio cum duobus sec. ult. [*Dig.* 17.2.52.18]. Ad hoc dicunt quidam quod a talibus non est sumenda decima, ne ecclesia uidetur approbare delictum eorum, arg. ad hoc xxiii q. i Paratus, in fine [c. 2], ff. de inoffic. testa, si pars, in fine [*Dig.* 5.2.10]. Alii dicunt quod decima sumenda est potius ab eis quam apud eos remaneat, arg. xxii q. i. Considera [c. 8]. Melius dicas quod si transfertur dominium in aliquos ita quod non competit repetitio licet ille peccent, tamen tenentur dare decimas. Et licet ecclesia petat decimam a talibus, non tamen approbat officium eorum quia conuenit eos tamquam quemlibet possessorem lucri, unde de iustis spoliis danda est decima exemplo Abrahe, ut xxiii q. v. Dicat [c. 25]. Jo" (Admont, Stiftsbibliothek, MS 22, fol. 209ʳ. I wish to thank Professor Kenneth J. Pennington, Jr., for calling this passage to my attention and for his transcription of the manuscript). Cf. the argument of Panormitanus, *Commentaria,* 9 vols. (Venice: Apud Iuntas, 1588) to X 3.30.23 (vol. 6, fol. 231ʳʰ).

78. Hostiensis, *Lectura* to X 3.30.23, no. 2 (vol. 3, fol. 100ᵛʰ): "De omnibus quae licite, etc. Ergo videtur quod de illicite acquisitis non tenetur quis solvere decimam, ar. i q. i Non est putanda [c. 27] et sic meretrix de meretricio suo ad decimam non tenetur: Deut. xxiii, 'Non offeres mercedem protibuli nec pretium carnis in domum domini Dei tui [Deut. 23:18]; Prouer. iii, 'Honora dominum tuum de tua substantia' [Prov. 3:9]."

79. Saint Thomas Aquinas, *Summa Theologica* 2ᵃ 2ᵃᵉ q. 87 a. 2 ad 2.

ability to give freewill alms was likewise in doubt: most canonistic authorities agreed with Huguccio that the church could not accept alms
from ill-gotten goods, such as the gains derived from usury, the earnings
of actors, the stipends of *mathematici,* the profits of extortioners, or the
fees of prostitutes.[80] Others distinguished between various types of ill-
gotten gains, commonly on the grounds that some were wrongly acquired by force or the threat of force (e.g., the profits of robbers, extortioners, or advocates, who prey on the poor and ignorant), while other
ill-gotten gains were derived from more-or-less generous, if misdirected
impulses; the earnings of prostitutes and actors fell into this class.[81] The
ordinary gloss distinguished on still other grounds. According to this
view, alms should not be given from ill-gotten gains if ownership of the
goods was retained by the original giver, with mere possession passing
into the hands of the receiver but if both ownership and possession
passed to the recipient (as was the case with fees given to prostitutes)
then alms could be given and received from such goods.[82]

Hostiensis posed a particularly tantalizing case—that of the Crusading harlot. What would the legal situation be if a whore took the Cross?
She would surely be followed by many men, since nothing is stronger
than love; and this would clearly bolster the defensive forces of the Holy
Land. Should the Crusading harlot therefore be obliged to fulfill a
Crusading vow? Hostiensis thought not: the motivation of her followers,
after all, was not likely to be a spiritual one. Should she then be allowed
to redeem her vow by making an offering for the defense of the Holy
Places? Hostiensis thought that this, too, would be unacceptable.[83] The
appropriate conclusion seemed to be that harlots should not take
Crusading vows.

Although prostitutes were acknowledged to have some property
rights, their power to protect those rights was extremely limited, so far as
the canonists were concerned. A prostitute could not denounce a criminal, nor were the courts to hear a harlot's complaints about wrongs done
to her.[84] This attitude was consistent with the teaching of the Roman

80. Huguccio, *Summa* to C. 14 q. 5 d.a.c. 1 (B.N. lat. 3892, fol. 119[ra]): "Et indistincte
dicunt quod in nulla re illicite acquisita potest fieri elemosina, ergo nec de acquisita per
furtum, uel per rapinam, uel per usuram, uel symoniam, uel lusum, uel meretricium, uel
per opus ystrionicum, uel mathematicum, uel per extorsionem sicut sepe fit a rusticis, et his
ius ar. infra eodem questione elemosina [C. 14 q. 5 c. 7]." Cf. the *glossa ordinaira* to Deut.
23:18 ad v. *non offeres* (fol. 358[ra]): "De mercede meretricis videtur repulisse, quia superius
prohibuit esse meretricem de filiabus Israel, aut quenque filiorum Israel uti meretrice, et
ne quis posse hoc expiari si aliquid in templum offeret, dicendum fuit, quod domino
abominatio sit."
81. Rufinus, *Summa* to C. 14 q. 5 pr. (ed. Singer, pp. 342–43).
82. D. 90 c. 2 *glos. ord.* ad v. *dona,* ad fin.; C. 1 q. 1 c. 27 *glos. ord.* ad v. *ex illicitis rebus;* C.
14 q. 5 d.a.c. 1 *glos. ord.* ad v. *quod vero.*
83. Hostiensis, *Summa aurea,* lib. 3 tit. De voto et voti redemptione, no. 11 (fol. 177[rb]).
84. X 5.1.20 and *glos. ord.* ad v. *concubinarios.*

lawyers.[85] Alberto dei Gandini (ca. 1245–ca. 1310) discussed this situation in the context of a case which is said to have occurred at Mantua. One Armanius, clearly no gentleman, entered the house of a woman and attempted to have intercourse with her, against her will. Charged with this offense, Armanius proved in his own defense that the woman he had assaulted was a public prostitute, of bad condition, ill famed, and known by many men. Indeed, Armanius himself was one of her regular customers and frequently had intercourse with her. Under these circumstances, could he be punished for attempting to rape her? The subtlety of the question taxed the wits of lesser lawyers, and a famous jurist, Dino Mugellano, was consulted on the matter. Dino gave it as his opinion that if it were proved that the woman had put her body up for hire, then Armanius could not be punished for an attempt to rape her.[86] Alberto cited another case: an unnamed man broke down the door of a harlot's house, *libidinis causa*. Thieves subsequently entered the house through the broken door and made off with the furnishings. Was the sex-crazed door breaker liable for damages for the stolen goods? Alberto thought not—his motive was lust, not theft and he could not be held responsible for what he had not intended.[87]

If whores abounded everywhere in medieval Europe—and the available evidence strongly suggests that they did—one problem which faced public authorities was how to distinguish them visibly and clearly from respectable women. The canonists tended to think that distinctive dress was the best solution to the problem.[88] Municipal authorities commonly reverted to ancient practice by sequestering their prostitutes in specified portions of their cities and establishing quasi-public control over the practice of their trade.[89] The whores of Paris are said even to have founded a guild—perhaps in an attempt to restrain competition, as other guilds commonly did.[90]

Attempts at regulation, identification, and isolation were made easier for the authorities by the fact that prostitution in medieval Europe was most commonly practiced in the setting of a brothel.[91] Streetwalkers were not unknown, but brothels were everywhere, even in small towns

85. *Dig.* 47.2.39; 47.10.15.15; *Cod.* 9.9.22.
86. Alberto dei Gandini, *Tractatus de maleficiis*, ed. H. Kantorowicz, in *Albertus Gandinus und das Strafrecht der Scholastik*, 2 vols. (Berlin: J. Gutentag, 1907–26), 2:360–61. In contrast, the monarchs of Sicily protected prostitutes in their kingdom from such attacks (see Frederick II, *Constitutiones regni Siciliae* [= *Liber Augustalis*] 1.21[24], ed. J. L. A. Huillard-Bréholles, *Historia diplomatica Friderici II*, 6 vols. in 12 [Paris: Plon, 1852–61; reprint ed., Turin: Bottega d'Erasmo, 1963], 4, pt. 1: 23–24.
87. Gandini, 2:214.
88. E.g., Hostiensis, *Lectura* to X 5.6.15, no. 4 (vol. 5, fol. 32vb).
89. Bullough, *History of Prostitution*, pp. 113–14; Richard Lewinsohn, *A History of Sexual Customs*, trans. A. Mayco (New York: Harper & Bros., 1958), p. 145.
90. Bullough, *History of Prostitution*, p. 112.
91. Bloch (n. 3 above), 1:690.

and large-sized villages.[92] In many towns the local brothels were acknowledged civic corporations, regulated minutely by local ordinances, even supervised by public officials: often enough the local executioner doubled as supervisor of whorehouses in his off hours.[93]

Despite sporadic local efforts to outlaw brothels and prostitution,[94] whorehouses apparently flourished everywhere, often under the guise of bathhouses and frequently under the supervision of barbers.[95] For this reason, canonists frequently warned Christians in general and clerics in particular not to frequent bathhouses, since they were apt to be morally dangerous.[96] Bathhouses and barbershops might not be the only occasions of sin. Jacques de Vitry, writing in the first quarter of the thirteenth century, gives a vivid description of the Parisian prostitutes of his day. They were everywhere in the city, soliciting passing clerics to sample their delights and crying out, "Sodomite!" after those who passed up the invitation. Both a brothel and a scholar's hall might occupy the same premises: while the master delivered his lectures in an upper room, the trollops exercised their trade below. It is likely that the twain sometimes met, as the arguments between the harlots and their pimps rose to mingle with the disputations of the schools.[97]

Bold and brazen though she might be, the medieval law viewed the prostitute as a largely powerless person, socially degraded, but in actual practice tolerated and allowed to exercise some limited property rights in her earnings. Still she could redeem her situation through reform. For this there were illustrious examples—had not Jesus himself said to the Pharisees of his time that repentant tax collectors and whores would take precedence over them in the kingdom of heaven?[98] And the example of Saint Mary Magdalene demonstrated that the believing and repentant harlot could achieve salvation.[99] In some circumstances the

92. Ibid., 1:740–45, lists seventy-five towns and cities in Germany which had brothels between the thirteenth and fifteenth centuries.

93. Ibid., 1:670. For a more detailed account of a slightly later period, see Ruth Pike, *Aristocrats and Traders: Sevillian Society in the Sixteenth Century* (Ithaca, N.Y.: Cornell University Press, 1972), pp. 195, 203–6.

94. E.g., Jean de Joinville, *The Life of St. Louis*, trans. René Hague (New York: Sheed & Ward, 1955), chap. 36, sec. 171, p. 66; Gandini, 1:243–44 (Urk. 30), 252–54 (Urk. 35); Bullough, *History of Prostitution*, p. 113. There were older—and equally ineffectual —precedents (see *Nov.* 14.1 [= *Auth. coll.* 3, tit. 1]).

95. Bullough, *History of Prostitution*, p. 115; also his *The Development of Medicine as a Profession: The Contribution of the Medieval University to Modern Medicine* (New York: Hafner Publishing Co., 1966), p. 88; Lewinsohn, p. 148. Bloch, 1:747–50, gives a lengthy—and eloquent—list of words used to designate brothels in the middle ages.

96. D. 81 c. 28 *glos. ord.* ad v. *omnino;* C. 24 q. 1 c. 24 *glos. ord.* ad v. *balneas;* Rufinus, *Summa* to D. 81 c. 20 (ed. Singer, p. 172).

97. *Historia occidentalis*, c. 7 (ed. Hinnebusch, p. 91); cf. the harlots at the door of the tent of meeting: 1 Sam. 2:22 (= 1 Kings 2:22).

98. Matt. 21:31–33.

99. Luke 7.37.

church stood ready to assist girls to leave a life of sin. Involuntary prostitutes (i.e., girls who had been sold into prostitution by their parents or masters) could petition the local bishop or other authority to liberate them from their carnal bondage.[100] Other harlots could also look to the church for help in efforts at self-reform. Still the canonists recognized realistically that the chances of successful reform were slim and that a repentant strumpet might continually be tempted to take up her former life.[101]

Nonetheless the hope of reform was there. Two major avenues of reform were contemplated. The favorite with most reformers was to induce the repentant harlot to enter the religious life, to become a nun. From at least the twelfth century onward, religious houses were established with the particular purpose of serving as havens for reformed prostitutes.[102] In 1224 an effort began to create a special religious order of penitential nuns to harbor reformed whores, and in 1227 Pope Gregory IX (1227–41) gave the highest ecclesiastical sanction to the Order of Saint Mary Magdalene, which subsequently established convents in numerous cities. The sisters wore a white habit, whence they were sometimes known as "the White Ladies."[103] Subsequent official patronage and encouragement was given to the Magdalenes by the fourteenth-century popes.[104] Similar convents, not necessarily affiliated with the Magdalene order, received endowment and support from monarchs, such as the pious Louis IX of France (1226–70), who was subsequently elevated to the altars of the church for this and other saintly actions.[105]

For the harlot who wished to reform but who was not inclined to embrace the religious life, there was another alternative: marriage. The canonists required, however, that a number of conditions be fulfilled before a prostitute might marry. In this area of the law, a gradual change of attitude and policy took place. The doctrine of the early church had tended to discourage such marriages: one of the canons in Gratian's *Decretum* characterized the man who kept a whore as his wife as idiotic and unreasonable.[106] Even the reformed prostitute, who had done solemn public penance for her sins, might be forbidden to marry,

100. Durantis, *Speculum iuris*, lib. 4, partic. 4, De adulteriis et stupro, no. 8–9 (2:377) gives examples of such petitions.
101. D. 34 d.p.c. 8; C. 32 q. 1 d.p.c. 13.
102. *Historia occidentalis*, c. 8 (ed. Hinnebusch, pp. 99–100); Milton R. Gutsch, "A Twelfth-Century Preacher—Fulk of Neuilly," in *The Crusades and Other Essays in Honor of Dana C. Munro*, ed. L. J. Paetow (New York: Appleton-Century-Crofts, 1928), pp. 190–91; Bullough, *History of Prostitution*, p. 115.
103. Max Heimbucher, *Die Orden und Kongregationen der katholischen Kirche*, 3d ed., 2 vols. (Munich: F. Schöningh, 1965) 1:646–48.
104. Bernard Guillemain, *La Cour Pontificale d'Avignon, 1309–1376: Etude d'une société* (Paris: E. de Boccard, 1966), pp. 485–86.
105. De Joinville, p. 210.
106. C. 32 q. 1 c. 1, taken from an apocryphal work ascribed to Saint John Chrysostom. Gratian, in his *dictum* before this canon, appears to equate harlotry with adultery.

unless she first obtained a special dispensation for this purpose,[107] a provision which was consistent with Roman imperial law on the subject.[108] Still, marriage to a prostitute, although dubious, was not held to be actually sinful.[109] And a man who married a prostitute, believing her to be a chaste virgin, was held to be validly married, according to the leading theologian of the twelfth century.[110]

Gratian was inclined to take a cautiously more permissive view of the matter, although he observed gloomily that one could not trust the word of a harlot.[111] He distinguished between the situation in which a man married a whore who continued her trade and that in which a man married a whore in order to reform her. In the first situation the marriage was not allowed; in the second it was permitted.[112] The decretist commentators accepted Gratian's distinction. They also commonly insisted that the reformed prostitute must demonstrate her intention of changing her ways by doing penance prior to the marriage.[113] Rolandus, a famous twelfth-century canonist who later became Pope Alexander III, remarked that in his day it was considered praiseworthy to marry reformed prostitutes.[114] Pope Innocent III (1198–1216), in a decretal issued during the first year of his pontificate, confirmed Rolandus's observations. The pope lauded those who married harlots in order to reform them and described their actions as "not least among the works of charity." Further, he assured those who rescued public prostitutes and took them to wife that their actions would count for the remission of their own sins.[115] Bernardus Parmensis, the author of the ordinary gloss to the thirteenth-century canonical code known as the *Decretals*, was apparently more dubious about this matter than was the pope: "This [decretal] concerns her who freely wishes to be chaste—if someone can be found who wishes to take her as a wife."[116] Other commentators on the *Decretals* also insisted that corrigibility was an essential criterion: the incorrigible prostitute was not allowed to marry, and the man who kept such a one as his wife was classified as a pimp.[117]

107. C. 33 q. 2 c. 11-12; Esmein, 1:210.

108. *Cod.* 5.4.29.6; 9.9.20.

109. C. 32 q. 1 c. 14.

110. Peter Lombard, *Sententiae* 4.30 (*PL*, 192:917); Esmein, 1:312–13.

111. C. 32 q. 1 d.p.c. 13.

112. C. 32 q. 1 c. 10, again equating whores with adulteresses; C. 32 q. 1 d.p.c. 13; Freisen (n. 15 above), pp. 621–22.

113. E.g., Paucapalea, *Summa* to C. 32, ed. J. F. von Schulte (Giessen: E. Roth, 1890), p. 125; *Summa Parisiensis* to C. 32 q. 1 c. 1 ad v. *sicut crudelis* (ed. McLaughlin, p. 240); Rufinus, *Summa* to C. 32 q. 1 pr. (ed. Singer, p. 475); Rolandus, *Summa* to C. 32 q. 1 (ed. Thaner, pp. 158–59); Huguccio, *Summa* to C. 32 q. 1 d.a.c. 1 (B.N. lat. 3892, fol. 308ra).

114. Rolandus, *Summa* to C. 32 q. 1 (ed. Thaner, p. 162).

115. X 4.1.20 (= *Comp. II* 4.1.5).

116. X 4.1.20 *glos. ord.* ad v. *in uxores:* "Hic de ea, quae continere libenter vellet, si invenerit qui eam ducere vellet in uxorem. Ber."

117. E.g., Innocent IV, *Apparatus* to X 4.1.20 (fol. 465v); Hostiensis, *Lectura* to X 3.32.19, no. 3, and X 4.1.20, no. 8 (vol. 3, fol. 121vb; vol. 4, fol. 6vb).

The man who wished to marry a prostitute, even one who had reformed her life, also faced certain problems. If he had previously had intercourse with her himself, there was some question whether he could marry her at all: Gratian raised the matter at two points in the *Decretum*, but left the solution unclear. He apparently believed that such a marriage would be licit, but that the woman must do penance.[118] Once the marriage had been contracted, she could be put aside only if she reverted to her old ways and refused to do penance.[119] If the husband were a cleric, he was further penalized for his choice of a wife: he could not be ordained to major orders even after the death of his wife,[120] and he was barred from any sort of promotion in the ecclesiastical hierarchy,[121] although presumably it was possible to receive dispensation in such cases.[122] Even after Innocent III's approval of marriage with harlots for purposes of reform, for ecclesiastical purposes[123] the ordinary gloss to the *Decretals* continued to classify men who married harlots as bigamists.

What does this survey of the canonistic jurisprudence tell us about the theory and practice of medieval prostitution?

The writings of the canonists underscore what other sources indicate about the prevalence of prostitution in medieval society. It is also clear that one reason for the frequency of prostitution in a society which was heavily influenced, not to say dominated, by ecclesiastical institutions and the doctrinal attitudes of the church, may well have been a fundamental ambivalence in the church's own law about prostitution. Although theologically denounced, prostitution was viewed by the lawyers as an evil which had to be tolerated in order to avert the greater evils which would follow from the abolition of prostitution. Further, medieval notions about male and female sexuality, as reflected in the lawyers' writings, led the church's legal functionaries to require women (whom they thought highly susceptible to sensual stimuli) to adhere to a higher standard of sexual morality than men. Conversely, however, the woman who fell into a life of prostitution was not overtly punished by harshly repressive measures, while men who frequented prostitutes were subject to more numerous and more severe punishments than were the ladies of joy whom they patronized. Ironically, then, the lawyers treated the pros-

118. C. 31 q. 1 c. 1–7; C. 32 q. 4 d.a.c. 1; Esmein, 1:208–10.

119. C. 32 q. 1 c. 1 *glos. ord.* ad v. *patronus.*

120. D. 33 c. 2; D. 34 c. 11, d.p.c. 14, c. 15.

121. Rufinus, *Summa* to D. 33 c. 2 (ed. Singer, p. 77); D. 33 d.a.c. 1 *glos. ord.* ad v. *sed queritur;* D. 34 d.p.c. 8 *glos. ord.* ad v. *meretricari.*

122. Rufinus, *Summa* to D. 34 pr. (ed. Singer, pp. 79–80).

123. X 1.21.1 *glos. ord.* ad v. *in bigamis.* Bigamy in the ecclesiastical law had a number of peculiarities (see Stephan Kuttner, "Pope Lucius III and the Bigamous Archbishop of Palermo," in *Medieval Studies Presented to Aubrey Gwynn, S.J.,* ed. John A. Watt, J. B. Morrall, and F. X. Martin [Dublin: Colin O'Lochlainn, 1961], pp. 409–53).

titute as a necessary evil, to be tolerated and dealt with rather leniently, while at the same time they looked upon the use of her services as a relatively serious crime, subject to stringent repressive measures.

The canonistic jurisprudence dealing with prostitution also points up another characteristic of the canon law rather generally, namely, the way in which it accommodated moral principles to the realities of human behavior. This was, after all, the basic service which the canonist performed for the medieval church and for society at large. The canonist attempted to translate the abstract principles of the theologian into practical, workable, behavioral norms. The canonistic treatment of prostitution illustrates this function of the canon law, I think, very well indeed. Without abandoning the moral principle that prostitution was an undesirable form of sexual behavior, the canonists tried to work out a functional system of norms which also took into account the existing structures of society and the family, and the nature of male and female sexuality as they understood them. Many of their fundamental ideas about the nature and function of sexual relations in society are not ones which are nowadays shared by most people in the Western world. But given the data and the assumptions with which the canonists of the twelfth and thirteenth centuries worked, one can hardly fail to admire the ingenuity with which they reconciled reality with high principles in dealing with one of the most intimate and most difficult of all human behavioral situations.

University of Wisconsin—Milwaukee

THE REGULATION OF BROTHELS IN LATER MEDIEVAL ENGLAND

RUTH MAZO KARRAS

Medieval society recognized prostitution as a necessary evil. Sinful men, theologians held, would corrupt respectable women—even their own wives—or turn to sodomy if they did not have the prostitute as a sexual outlet: "Remove prostitutes from human affairs and you will destroy everything with lust."[1] Though they argued

Versions of this paper were presented to the Western European History Workshop at the University of Pennsylvania, the seventh Berkshire Conference on the History of Women, the Fordham University Center for Medieval Studies Conference on Gender and the Moral Order in Medieval Society, and the University of Oregon department of history. I thank the audiences there and the readers for *Signs* for their comments on earlier versions; Caroline Barron, Martha Carlin, and Maryanne Kowaleski for help, advice, and access to unpublished work; and J. B. Post for permission to use his edition of the Southwark customary. Travel funds for research in Britain were provided by a grant from the University of Pennsylvania Research Foundation.

[1] Augustine, *De Ordine* 2.4, *Patrologiae Cursus Completus Series Latina* (hereafter cited as *PL*), ed. J. P. Migne (Paris, 1845), 32:1000, quoted by Thomas Aquinas, *Summa Theologica*, 2.2.10.11, in *Opera Omnia* (Rome: Sacred Congregation for Propagation of the Faith, 1895), 8:93. Augustine held that it was better for a man to have nonprocreative sex with a prostitute than with his own wife because then he at least would not be corrupting an innocent woman (Augustine, *De Bono Conjugali* 11, *PL*, 40:382).

This essay originally appeared in *Signs*, vol. 14, no. 2, Winter 1989.

that prostitution was necessary because of men's natural, if sinful, sex drive, this did not lead to respect for the prostitute herself. The church considered her one of the worst of sinners: lust was considered the woman's sin par excellence and the prostitute epitomized it.[2] While the notion of woman as temptress might be expected among a celibate male elite, preachers in England as elsewhere spread the notion to the general public as well.[3]

Though medieval thinkers attributed the prostitute's choice of profession to her sinfulness, for many prostitutes the choice was dictated by the available alternatives. Many women were not able to marry—because of lack of dowries, because of sex ratios, because too few men were in a position to marry—and had to support themselves.[4] Opportunities for women in the labor market varied, but in late medieval Europe as population rose again after a period of labor shortage following the Black Death of 1348, their access to guild membership or other skilled work tended to be limited.[5] Not

[2] On women as more lustful than men, see, e.g., Charles T. Wood, "The Doctors' Dilemma: Sin, Salvation and the Menstrual Cycle," *Speculum* 56 (1981): 711–13. In the iconography of the sins, lust (*luxuria*) is often represented by a woman and depicted with avarice represented by a man (see, e.g., Adolf Katzenellenbogen, *Allegories of the Virtues and Vices in Medieval Art* [London: Warburg Institute, 1939], 58–59, 76). The woman whom Luke 7:37 identifies only as "a sinner" was identified in medieval hagiography as Mary Magdalen whose sin, it was assumed without scriptural basis, was lust. See Marjorie M. Malvern, *Venus in Sackcloth: The Magdalene's Origins and Metamorphoses* (Carbondale: Southern Illinois University Press, 1975); and Helen Meredith Garth, *Saint Mary Magdalen in Medieval Literature*, Johns Hopkins University Studies in Historical and Political Science, ser. 67, no. 3 (Baltimore: Johns Hopkins University Press, 1950), for references to medieval literary representations of Mary Magdalen.

[3] Women's sexual immorality, love of ornament, and shrewishness were common themes of medieval sermons (see, e.g., G. R. Owst, *Literature and Pulpit in Medieval England* [Cambridge: Cambridge University Press, 1933], 375–404).

[4] The "Western European marriage pattern" identified for early modern Europe, involving relatively late ages of marriage compared to other preindustrial societies and a high proportion of the population who never married at all, may have applied in the Middle Ages as well (Richard M. Smith, "Some Reflections on the Evidence for the Origins of the 'European Marriage Pattern' in England," in *The Sociology of the Family: New Directions for Britain*, ed. Chris Harris, Sociological Review Monograph no. 28 [Keele, England: University of Keele, 1979], 74–112).

[5] See P. J. P. Goldberg, "Marriage, Migration, Servanthood and Life-Cycle in Yorkshire Towns of the Later Middle Ages: Some York Cause Paper Evidence," *Continuity and Change* 1 (1986): 141–69, and "Female Labour, Service and Marriage in the Late Medieval Urban North," *Northern History* 22 (1986): 18–38, for the demographic situation in fifteenth-century towns that may have led women to turn to prostitution: a low sex ratio due to female in-migration, a decline in work opportunities, and a decline in nuptiality.

all, of course, turned to prostitution, but it was one of a limited range of options.[6]

The brothel, to medieval society, was the locus of this necessary evil, this societal safety valve. This article focuses on the regulations of brothels in medieval England. It deals mainly with regulations for the bathhouses of Southwark, a suburb of London, which date from the fifteenth century (see App.), but draws on other material from approximately 1350–1550. The regulation of brothels in England must be seen against the background of the tolerated and institutionalized brothels found elsewhere in Europe. Prostitution was not restricted to towns, but like any other service industry it was concentrated where people were concentrated. Municipal authorities all over Europe recognized the social value of prostitution but tried to keep it as unobtrusive as possible, placing it under strict control without abolishing it totally. In many parts of medieval and early modern Europe this meant establishing licensed, or even municipally owned, brothels or official red-light districts.[7]

[6] Personal as well as structural factors played a role. Jacques Rossiaud, "Prostitution, Youth and Society in the Towns of Southeastern France in the Fifteenth Century," trans. Elborg Forster, in Deviants and the Abandoned in French Society, ed. Robert Forster and Orest Ranum (Baltimore: Johns Hopkins University Press, 1978), 19, mentions rape victims turning to prostitution.

[7] The most complete list of towns with legal brothels, though not an analytical study, is found in Iwan Bloch, Die Prostitution, 2 vols., Handbuch der gesamten Sexualwissenschaft in Einzeldarstellungen, vol. 1 (Berlin: Louis Marcus, 1912), 1:740–47. See also Bronislaw Geremek, The Margins of Society in Medieval Paris, trans. Jean Birrell (Cambridge: Cambridge University Press, 1987), 211–41; Franz Irsigler and Arnold Lassotta, Bettler und Gaukler, Dirnen und Henker: Randgruppen und Aussenseiter in Köln 1300–1600 (Köln: Greven Verlag, 1984), 179–227; G. L. Kriegk, Deutsches Bürgerthum im Mittelalter nach urkundlichen Forschungen (1871; reprint, Frankfurt am Main: Sauer & Auvermann, 1969), 2:292–329; Leah Lydia Otis, Prostitution in Medieval Society: The History of an Urban Institution in Languedoc (Chicago: University of Chicago Press, 1985), hereafter cited as Prostitution, and Otis, "Prostitution and Repentance in Late Medieval Perpignan," in Women of the Medieval World, ed. Julius Kirshner and Suzanne Wemple (Oxford: Basil Blackwell, 1985), 137–60; Elisabeth Pavan, "Police des moeurs, société et politique à Venise à la fin du moyen âge," Revue historique, no. 264 (1980), 241–88; Mary Elizabeth Perry, "Deviant Insiders: Legalized Prostitutes and a Consciousness of Women in Early Modern Seville," Comparative Studies in Society and History 27 (1985): 138–58, and " 'Lost Women' in Early Modern Seville: The Politics of Prostitution," Feminist Studies 4 (1978): 195–214; von Posern-Klett, "Frauenhäuser und freie Frauen in Sachsen," Archiv für Sächsische Geschichte 12 (1874): 63–89; Lyndal Roper, "Discipline and Respectability: Prostitution and the Reformation in Augsburg," History Workshop, no. 19 (1985), 3–28; Rossiaud, "Prostitution, Youth and Society," 1–46; Jacques Rossiaud, "Prostitution, Sex and Society in French Towns in the Fifteenth Century," in Western Sexuality: Practice and Precept in Past and Present Times, ed. Philippe Ariès and André Béjin (Oxford: Basil Blackwell, 1985), 76–94;

The philosophy behind the official establishment and regulation of brothels in France, Germany, Spain, and Italy followed church doctrine in treating prostitutes as degraded and defiled but tolerated their activity because of male demand.[8] The medieval European towns that licensed or sponsored brothels did so not for the protection of the prostitutes but for the maintenance of social order. Recent scholarship on municipal or municipally regulated brothels in Florence, Seville, Dijon, Augsburg, and the towns of Languedoc in the medieval and early modern periods agrees that regulated brothels were seen as a foundation of the social order, preventing homosexuality, rape, and seduction.[9] They also could be important sources of income for the town itself or, in the case of licensed brothels, for wealthy individuals or institutions within the town.[10]

Richard C. Trexler, "La prostitution florentine au XVe siècle: Patronages et clientèles," *Annales economies sociétés civilisations* 36 (1981): 983–1015; Merry E. Wiesner, *Working Women in Renaissance Germany* (New Brunswick, N.J.: Rutgers University Press, 1986), 97–105; Gustav Wustmann, "Frauenhäuser und freie Frauen in Leipzig im Mittelalter," *Archiv für Kulturgeschichte* 5 (1907): 469–82. Often the toleration and official establishment of brothels followed unsuccessful earlier attempts to ban prostitution within the town.

[8] A similar philosophy grounded nineteenth-century licensing and policing movements. See Judith Walkowitz, *Prostitution and Victorian Society* (Cambridge: Cambridge University Press, 1980); Jill Harsin, *Policing Prostitution in Nineteenth-Century Paris* (Princeton, N.J.: Princeton University Press, 1985); Mary Gibson, *Prostitution and the State in Italy, 1860–1915* (New Brunswick, N.J.: Rutgers University Press, 1986); and Barbara Meil Hobson, *Uneasy Virtue: The Politics of Prostitution and the American Reform Tradition* (New York: Basic, 1987). See also Abraham Flexner, *Prostitution in Europe* (1914; reprint, Montclair, N.J.: Patterson Smith, 1969), for a discussion of regulated prostitution in Europe by a contemporary.

[9] Trexler, 983, suggests that in Florence the purpose of institutionalization was to shore up a declining birthrate by turning men away from homosexuality. By initiating men into the joys of heterosexual intercourse, the prostitutes would awaken in them a desire to marry. Perry, " 'Lost Women,' " 196 and 204–6, argues that prostitution was not only acceptable but a buttress of the moral order because of the necessary outlet it provided. Rossiaud, "Prostitution, Youth and Society," 13, suggests that the town of Dijon deliberately provided young men with opportunities for fornication with prostitutes as a remedy for an epidemic of rape that he sees as having been violence directed against the governing elite. Otis, *Prostitution*, 103–5, argues that the authorities thought institutionalized prostitution rid the streets of free-lance prostitution that set a bad example and encouraged respectable women to lasciviousness. Roper, 4, discusses how brothels in German towns fit into a male understanding of the "good of the community." Even where the brothel was supposed to benefit respectable women by making the streets safe for them, the women were defined in terms of their relationships to men. Roper, 5, and Rossiaud, "Prostitution, Youth and Society," 21–25, discuss apprentices or other young unmarried men as the main clientele.

[10] For examples, see Perry, " 'Lost Women,' " 209–10; Rossiaud, "Prostitution, Youth and Society," 3–4; Otis, *Prostitution*, 53–55.

While the regulation of prostitution and brothels varied across continental Europe, a number of characteristics were common. In most places, prostitution was forbidden except in particular streets or (especially in smaller towns) in one particular brothel. Prostitutes were either required to wear some sort of distinguishing clothing or else forbidden to wear certain types of garments or jewelry.[11] In many places they were forbidden to attend church with or speak to respectable women.[12] These provisions apparently aimed to protect nonprostitutes from being taken for prostitutes, although there is no evidence that this problem concerned the women themselves. Rather, men wanted to protect bourgeois wives by labeling prostitutes and restricting them to brothels.

The regulations generally gave the brothel keepers a great deal of control over the prostitutes. The brothel keeper in German towns was usually a man, sometimes a woman. In France some municipal brothels were farmed by women only, and even when a man held the farm a woman (known as *abbesse*) might administer it.[13] In Languedoc the prostitutes paid the brothel keeper for room and board, not according to the number of customers they had, while in Germany the payments from the prostitutes might vary according to their income.[14] The chances of a prostitute's owing money to the brothel keeper were great: she might have ended up in the brothel in the first place because of her own or her family's debts, or the keeper could have lent her money. Some of the continental regulations specifically authorized the brothel keeper to imprison a woman for debts she owed him; this was no doubt a factor in keeping a prostitute in the brothel on a permanent basis.[15] When she had no customers, the prostitute might also have to perform other work

[11] Otis, *Prostitution*, 79–80; Wustmann, 474–75; von Posern-Klett, 83–84; Geremek, 246; Bloch, 814–15; J. Brucker, *Strassburger Zunft- und Polizeiverordnungen des 14. und 15 Jahrhunderts* (Strasbourg: Karl J. Trübner, 1889), 459.

[12] Roper, 10; Otis, *Prostitution*, 81, 104; Wiesner, 102.

[13] Otis, *Prostitution*, 60–61. On women running official brothels in Germany, see Wustmann, 472; and Kriegk, 299; according to Wiesner, 97–100, they were mostly men.

[14] Otis, *Prostitution*, 82; Wustmann, 470 (in Leipzig, apparently a weekly charge only); Joseph Baader, ed., *Nurnberger Polizeiordnungen aus dem XIII bis XV Jahrhundert*, Bibliothek des Litterarischen Vereins in Stuttgart, vol. 63 (Stuttgart: Litterarische Verein, 1861), 119 (in Nuremberg, seven pfennigs a week plus one per customer and three for every man who spent the night); von Posern-Klett, 67; Bloch, 768; Roper, 6; Wiesner, 98.

[15] Italian regulations are cited in Otis, *Prostitution*, 83 (Venice was an exception). See Wiesner, 99; and Kriegk, 312, on German regulations forbidding keeping women in the brothels for debt; see also, for Strasbourg, Brucker, 469. In some towns it seems that women were put into the trade in the first place in order to repay capital lent to them or to a relative (see Roper, 7; Kriegk, 319; Perry, " 'Lost Women,' " 201).

for the profit of the brothel keeper.[16] In most cases the prostitutes were required to live in the brothel and, usually, had to board there too.[17] One exception was Paris, which had an official red-light district rather than a municipal brothel. There prostitutes had to leave the brothels before curfew and were not allowed to practice the profession from their homes after curfew.[18] In some towns the regulations protected the prostitutes from physical abuse, but in others, particularly in Italy, the brothel keepers were allowed to strike the prostitutes as long as they did not maim them.[19] On the whole, the keeper of a municipal brothel exercised a great deal of control over the lives of the prostitutes employed there, a control that was not even ostensibly for the protection of the prostitutes.

Despite their recognition that prostitution was a necessary feature of society, the municipalities of continental Europe still paid lip service to the Church's ideals of sexual purity. Regulations from municipal brothels in Languedoc and in Germany provide that the houses should not be open for business on holy days or that the women should all leave the brothel during Holy Week. During Lent and especially Holy Week the prostitutes were to listen to sermons intended to sway them from their life of sin.[20] Such rules can only be considered half-hearted given the official establishment of the brothels, but the appearance of religious orders for repentant prostitutes and movements to provide dowries so that poor women, including prostitutes, could marry did provide an alternative for at least a few.[21] Some towns' restrictions on who could visit the brothels—no clerics, no married men, no Jews—although not well enforced, also indicate some concern for standards of sexual morality.[22]

[16] In Ulm, the brothel keeper could require the prostitutes to spin yarn for him during the day or else reimburse him for lost earnings (Roper, 6).

[17] Sometimes they could have their dwelling elsewhere on payment of a special sum, although they still had to conduct their trade in the brothel. Otis, *Prostitution* (n. 7 above), 83, cites regulations from both France and Italy. An ordinance from Nuremberg, where women do seem to have lived in the brothels, provides that the prostitutes cannot be forced to board there (Baader, ed., 119). See Kriegk, 315, on varying German regulations on women boarding with the brothel keeper.

[18] Geremek (n. 7 above), 217. These rules were constantly infringed upon. See also Rossiaud, "Prostitution, Youth and Society" (n. 6 above), 3.

[19] Ordinances of Perugia and Foligno, cited in Otis, *Prostitution*, 82–83; for Germany, see Kriegk, 314.

[20] Otis, *Prostitution*, 85–87; Wustmann (n. 7 above), 473; von Posern-Klett (n. 7 above), 72; Wiesner (n. 7 above), 102.

[21] Otis, *Prostitution*, 72–76; Wiesner, 101; Irsigler and Lassotta (n. 7 above), 180; Rossiaud, "Prostitution, Youth and Society," 21; André Simon, *L'ordre des pénitentes de Ste. Marie Madeleine en Allemagne au XIIIme siècle* (Fribourg: Imprimerie et Librairie de l'oeuvre de Saint-Paul, 1918).

[22] Roper (n. 7 above), 5; Irsigler and Lassota, 190; Otis, *Prostitution*, 84; Kriegk, 316; Rossiaud, "Prostitution, Youth and Society," 23.

The municipal brothels were established to serve the necessary function of restraining male sexuality, but they also controlled the sexuality of the prostitute or at least denied her any control over it herself. She was not allowed in some places to support a procurer or even to have a favorite customer.[23] In some places, she was not allowed to reject any customer, indeed could not be raped because she was considered to belong to all men and thus had no right to withhold consent.[24] As a municipal service, prostitution was made available to all who qualified, and the women who provided it had no say in determining how their bodies were to be used.[25]

The officially regulated or municipally owned brothels in many Continental towns took away the prostitutes' mobility and their ability to set their own working conditions, restricted their right to leave the profession whenever they wished, and stigmatized them.[26] Yet, they provided the prostitutes with a roof over their heads and reduced the need for them to seek out their own customers. There are several examples from France of prostitutes from official brothels taking collective action to protest the replacement of a female brothel keeper by a man or to stamp out clandestine prostitutes not connected with the brothel.[27] The prostitutes themselves did not have any formal collective organization, but the official brothel did bring prostitutes together.[28]

Officially regulated brothels were not the rule in England, although the one well-documented instance of legal brothels there, in Southwark, has a good deal in common with general patterns in continental Europe. The regulations from the official brothels in Southwark are exceptional for England, but from them one may infer much about the manner in which other towns dealt with the

[23] Otis, *Prostitution*, 84–85; Wiesner, 98–99.

[24] Examples are given by Roper, 6, who also suggests that the sharing of prostitutes as common property strengthened male bonding. See also Wiesner, 99; Otis, *Prostitution*, 68–69.

[25] The Nuremberg regulation makes this particularly clear: the common women "should be common according to their name" (*nach irem namen gemin sein sollen*) (Baader, ed. [n. 14 above], 121). None of the regulations that I have read or seen reference to mention particular sexual acts even to prohibit them.

[26] Irsigler and Lassotta, 186–88, discuss how the stigma was worse for the women in the official house than for others.

[27] Otis, *Prostitution* (n. 7 above), 61; Rossiaud, "Prostitution, Youth and Society" (n. 6 above), 25.

[28] The often repeated statement that prostitutes formed an official guild in many towns has not been borne out by recent research (Otis, *Prostitution*, 69; František Graus, "Randgruppen der städtischen Gesellschaft im Spätmittelalter," *Zeitschrift für historische Forschung* 8 [1981]: 429). Bloch (n. 7 above), 670, speaks of prostitutes as an officially recognized corporate body but apparently only because the brothels were official; there is no evidence that they had any organization among themselves.

issue. Where prostitution was prohibited, illicit brothels flourished. English society was willing to tolerate them in practice if not in theory. Where brothels were permitted by law, the surviving regulations indicate that prostitution was to be tolerated only under the firmest control, control that would keep sexually active women from threatening the social order. The control was more pragmatic and less moralistic than elsewhere in Europe, but it involved a similar response to the threat of independent female sexuality.

In medieval England the regulation of prostitution and brothel keeping, like most other aspects of public order, was in the hands of local authorities. Boroughs (legally chartered towns) or manors (over which a territorial lord had jurisdiction) had their own courts and their own systems of fines for offenses. Sexual offenses of all sorts came under the purview of the ecclesiastical courts, but secular courts also dealt with any sexual offenses that affected public order: prostitution, rape, and sometimes even adultery or fornication. Often the same people were fined in both secular and ecclesiastical courts.[29] The ecclesiastical courts served a punitive rather than a regulatory function; their records provide some evidence for how brothels operated but not for the reasons behind the control of brothels.

The only surviving records about prostitution and brothels are the texts of municipal regulations and court records, and it is often difficult to tell precisely when they are referring to established houses of prostitution. The court records show that individuals were much more often accused of being prostitutes or procurers (in Latin usually *pronuba, leno,* or *lena,* in English usually *bawd*) than of keeping brothels. The procurers were probably pimps for individual women, or go-betweens for couples, rather than keepers of brothels. Those prosecuted for harboring prostitutes were probably merely renting premises to independently operating women. When the records state that a certain person "is a procurer for divers women living in her house," this is probably a brothel, but even the terms *bordellum, lenocinium,* and *lupanar* could refer to places where adulterous couples could meet, not just where prostitutes worked.[30] The term *prostibulum,* rare but occasionally used in En-

---

[29] See, e.g., Richard Wunderli, *London Church Courts and Society on the Eve of the Reformation,* Speculum Anniversary Monographs, no. 7 (Cambridge, Mass.: Medieval Academy of America, 1981), 99. The fact that someone had been charged with an offense in the secular court could be used as evidence against her or him in ecclesiastical court (see, e.g., Guildhall Library, London, Department of Manuscripts, London Commissary Court Act Books, 9064/1, fol. 6r, 27v).

[30] In Nottingham, e.g., the standard accusation was that someone "tenet bordellum et enormitatem [or 'tenet lenocinium'] infra domum suam" ("keeps a brothel and immorality in her [or his] house"). In some cases, however, the accusation mentions specific parties ("tenet bordellum inter x et y"), implying that the accused

gland, is a clearer indication of a brothel, as is *domus meretricum*.[31] The courts occasionally connected prostitution with taverns or gaming houses that may also have operated as brothels.[32]

Most English towns explicitly prohibited prostitution, whether connected with brothels or not. This does not necessarily mean that they seriously attempted to eradicate it.[33] In many places repeated fining of the same people for keeping brothels indicates not simply punishment of continuing offenders but also a system of de facto licensing fees; such fines appear in the same court rolls as fines for commercial activity that amounted to licensing fees.[34] This de facto

---

was not a brothel keeper but rather a go-between or facilitator (Nottinghamshire Record Office, Borough Quarter Sessions, CA/1 ff.).

[31] For example, in the records of Great Yarmouth (Norfolk Record Office, Y/C4/ 161, membrane 16d, Y/C4/162, membrane 15; and passim), and Ipswich (Suffolk Record Office, C8/1/20, membrane 1, C7/1/27, membrane 1: "William Porter is a procurer [*leno*] and Johanna Porter wife of the said William is a procuress [*pronuba*] and they keep a brothel and house of prostitutes [*prostibulum & domum meretricis*] in Ipswich . . . and foment, promote and aid adultery, fornication, and prostitution between men and prostitutes and continue to keep the house of prostitutes and brothel as a procurer and procuress").

[32] For example, Corporation of London Records Office (hereafter CLRO), Letter-Book D, fol. 131r–132r (*Letter-Book D* in *Calendar of Letter-Books Preserved among the Archives of the City of London at the Guildhall*, ed. Reginald R. Sharpe [London: Corporation of the City of London, 1902], 263–64)—books in this series will hereafter be referred to as *Cal. L-B* and their letter designation (e.g., *Cal. L-B D*); Public Record Office (hereafter PRO), SC2/191/55, membrane 2. Taverns and gambling dens are still connected with prostitution in 1542 (CLRO, Journals of the Court of Common Council, vol. 14, fol. 357r; Repertories of the Court of Aldermen [hereafter Rep.], vol. 10, fol. 300r). For innkeepers accused of procuring, see, e.g., Guildhall Library, 9064/1, fol. 153v, and 9064a, fol. 188v; Martha Carlin, "The Urban Development of Southwark c. 1200 to 1550" (Ph.D. diss., Centre for Medieval Studies, University of Toronto, 1983), 506–7.

[33] Legislation in many towns ordered brothels outside the city walls: e.g., Coventry in 1445 (Mary Dormer Harris, ed., *The Coventry Leet Book*, Early English Text Society, no. 134 [London: Early English Text Society, 1907], 1:219–20); Leicester in 1467 (Mary Bateson, ed., *Records of the Borough of Leicester* [London: C. J. Clay, 1901], 2:291). Bristol had similar ordinances referring to prostitutes in general and not brothels (Francis B. Bickley, ed., *The Little Red Book of Bristol* [Bristol: W. Crofton Hemmons, 1900], 1:33–34).

[34] See Maryanne Kowaleski, "Women's Work in a Market Town: Exeter in the Late Fourteenth Century," in *Women and Work in Preindustrial Europe*, ed. Barbara A. Hanawalt (Bloomington: Indiana University Press, 1986), 146, on fines as licensing fees for tradespeople. See also Derek Keene, *Survey of Medieval Winchester*, Winchester Studies, no. 2 (Oxford: Clarendon Press, 1985), 1:391, on the question of whether the fines for brothel keeping amounted to a licensing fee. In some instances (e.g., Alice Dymmok of Great Yarmouth [Norfolk Record Office, Y/C4/194 membrane 21, Y/C4/196 membrane 12, Y/C4/198 membrane 12, Y/C4/199 membrane 13, Y/C4/ 200 membrane 10, Y/C4/201 membrane 9]), repeat offenders were fined more heavily with each offense.

toleration, even if it was a result of failed attempts at eradication, shows a practical stance on the part of local secular authorities. Some element of punishment or stigma was involved, but fines were clearly not high enough to deter.

London, with four times as great a population at the next largest town, is where one might expect to find the highest concentration of, and the most highly organized, brothels in England.[35] Despite customs of the city that declared that no prostitute might stay within the walls on pain of forty days in prison, and a royal command in 1310 that all brothels in the city be shut down, city authorities by 1393 tolerated brothels in one part of the city, in Cock's Lane.[36] This was the only exception to the effort to make prostitutes stay in "the stews [bathhouses] on the other side of the Thames"—that is, in the liberty of the bishop of Winchester in Southwark, outside the city's jurisdiction.[37] In 1417 stews were forbidden in London and the suburbs under its control on the grounds of "many grievances, abominations, damages, disturbances, murders, homicides, larcenies, and other common nuisances" that occurred "by reason and cause of the common resort, harbouring, and sojourning, which lewd men and women, of bad and evil life, have in the stews."[38] Some bathhouses were later permitted in London if their keepers

[35] On population of medieval towns in Britain, see Josiah Cox Russell, *British Medieval Population* (Albuquerque: University of New Mexico Press, 1948), 282–302.

[36] H. T. Riley, ed., *Liber Albus*, vol. 1 of *Munimenta Gildhallae Londoniensis: Liber Albus, Liber Custumarum, et Liber Horn*, Rolls Series vol. 12, pt. 1 (London: Longman, 1859), 283; CLRO, Letter-Book A, fol. 130r (*Cal. L-B A*, 218: Assizes of the City of London, 1276–78); CLRO, Letter-Book D, fol. 116r (*Cal. L-B D*, 246); CLRO, Letter-Book H, fol. 287r, (*Cal. L-B H*, 402; trans. in H. T. Riley, *Memorials of London and London Life in the Thirteenth, Fourteenth and Fifteenth Centuries* [London: Longman, 1868], 535); see also Riley, ed., 459. The law was not entirely effective; an ordinance probably dating from 1483 again banned prostitutes from the city (CLRO, Letter-Book L, fol. 189v; *Cal. L-B L*, 206).

[37] CLRO, Letter-Book H, fol. 287r (*Cal. L-B H*, 402; trans. in Riley, 535). Southwark, across the Thames from London, came under the city's jurisdiction in 1327, but the territory held by the Bishop of Winchester remained separate, as did the liberties of other high churchmen (see David J. Johnson, *Southwark and the City* [London: Corporation of London, 1969], 43–60, on the evolution of the city's legal authority there).

[38] Individuals were still allowed to have bathhouses for the cleanliness of their own households (CLRO, Letter-Book I, fol. 193v [*Cal. L-B I*, 178; trans. in Riley, 647]). See also CLRO, journal 1, fols. 18v–19r, journal 2, fol. 41r–v, journal 8, fol. 120r. In 1428 the ordinance was changed so that those free of the city could keep stews but not foreigners (which included English people not citizens of London) (CLRO, journal 2, fol. 106v).

could assure the authorities that they kept an "honest stew" and did not permit women in a men's bathhouse. Fines for keeping unlicensed stews may reflect the use of these stewhouses as brothels.[39] Clearly the authorities did not succeed in banishing brothels to Cock's Lane and Southwark, but from the scanty evidence that survives, prostitution in the city itself does not seem to have been highly organized or connected with permanent houses.[40] There were many procurers operating at a higher level of the trade than the typical brothel keeper, who likely catered largely to a clientele of unmarried apprentices, journeymen, servants, and lower clergy.[41] These procurers served the individual customer rather than keeping a house open to all comers.[42]

[39] CLRO, Letter-Book K, fols. 54r, 64r (*Cal. L-B K*, 75–76, 95); Letter-Book L, fol. 114r (*Cal. L-B L*, 136); CLRO, Plea and Memoranda Roll A66, membrane 8 (*Calendar of Plea and Memoranda Rolls Preserved among the Archives of the Corporation of the City of London at the Guildhall*, ed. A. H. Thomas [Cambridge: Cambridge University Press, 1926], 5:17)—hereafter *Cal. PMR;* CLRO, journal 2, fols. 32v–33r, 34r, 35r, 55v, 68v, 108v, 113r–v. In 1446, Nicholas Croke, "stewmonger," was accused of being "a common procurer," although this involved arranging liaisons elsewhere than in his stew (CLRO, journal 4, fol. 134v). Some stewhouses were not organized brothels but meeting places, like the one in Grub Street indicted in 1422 "which is a common house of prostitution [*putre*] and bawdry, and in which thieves and also priests and their concubines are received" (CLRO, Plea and Memoranda Roll A51, *Cal. PMR* 4:154). The word "stew" comes from the same root as "stove," and originally meant a hot room, by extension a place where people took hot baths.

[40] Not many London court records survive. For only one ward (Portsoken, between 1465 and 1481 with some years missing) does a fairly full series of presentments exist, and those indictments name "common strumpets" and "common bawds" but not specifically brothel keepers. Scattered indictments for keeping brothels in other wards are extant, with the same people often indicted for receiving nightwalkers or stolen goods (e.g., CLRO, Letter-Book B, fol. 3r [*Cal. L-B B*, 6–7]; CLRO, Plea and Memoranda Roll A3, membrane 4b, membrane 14 [*Cal. PMR* 1:109, 124–6]; CLRO Plea and Memoranda Roll A5, membrane 2, membrane 11 [*Cal. PMR* 1:167, 188]; CLRO, journal 2, fol. 107v).

[41] There is little direct evidence for the involvement of apprentices, though servants appear in ecclesiastical court records as frequenters of prostitutes (Guildhall Library [n. 32 above], 9064/1–11).

[42] Several instances from the London city administration and ecclesiastical court records indicate how procurers operated. In 1385 Elizabeth Moryng was accused of recruiting women as apprentice embroidresses but then hiring them out as prostitutes to friars and chaplains. She sent the women out to the men's lodgings rather than having the men come to her house (CLRO, Letter-Book H, fol. 194v [*Cal. L-B H*, 271; trans. in Riley, 484–86]). In 1423 Alison Boston took apprentices whom "she hired out to various persons for various sums of money to execute and exercise with them the horrible vice of lechery" (CLRO, Letter-Book K, fol. 11v [*Cal. L-B K*, 17]; see also CLRO, journal 2, fol. 19r). Other examples with details are found, e.g., in CLRO, Plea and Memoranda Roll A66, membrane 5 (*Cal. PMR*, 5:14); Guildhall Library, 9064/1, fol. 24b.

Where prostitutes in London congregated in houses, they did not necessarily live under the supervision of a brothel keeper. Several cases from the London Eyre of 1276 deal with violent crimes that happened to have taken place at houses of prostitutes, who seem to have operated independently as a group. For example, Henry Peticors and Roger le Stedeman were killed in a quarrel with some foreign merchants at the house of six prostitutes. The woman from whom the six rented the house had to appear in court but was acquitted, probably indicating that the prostitutes were independent operators.[43]

The London urban area included more than just the city of London itself, and brothels in the suburbs no doubt served a London clientele. Many suburbs were under the jurisdiction of manorial lords, often monasteries, which administered their own justice. The court rolls for the manor of Westminster include accusations of receiving prostitutes and keeping brothels.[44] Most of the presentments in the extant East Smithfield manorial court rolls are either for keeping prostitutes in one's house or for gambling, both offenses that might have drawn undesirable customers from the city but also activities a manorial lord might profit from through fines.[45] The fines for these offenses had a fiscal as well as a punitive function and probably did not represent an attempt to wipe out the trade.

The suburb of London most connected with houses of prostitution was Southwark. There the bathhouses were so notorious that by the middle of the fourteenth century a whole neighborhood in the liberty of the bishop of Winchester came to be called "Les Stuwes."[46] This is one of two jurisdictions in England where there were legal, officially sponsored brothels and the only one about

---

[43] Martin Weinbaum, ed., *The London Eyre of 1276* (London: London Record Society, 1976), 34, see also 37–38. This is a court held before a special royal commission. For other examples of brothels, see A. H. Thomas, ed., *Calendar of Early Mayor's Court Rolls Preserved among the Archives of the Corporation of the City of London at the Guildhall a.d. 1298–1307* (Cambridge: Cambridge University Press, 1924), 110, 211.

[44] Westminster Abbey Muniments Room 50699–50773 (1364 to 1508). The manor of Westminster is fully discussed in A. G. Rosser, *Medieval Westminster 1200–1540* (Oxford: Oxford University Press, in press).

[45] PRO, SC2/191/56–59 (scattered years from 1418 to 1534). I thank Derek Keene and Martha Carlin for suggesting this manor.

[46] *Calendar of Close Rolls*, Edward III (London: His/Her Majesty's Stationery Office, 1904), 7:551 (1345); *Calendar of Patent Rolls*, Edward III (London: His/Her Majesty's Stationery Office, 1903), 9:184 (1351), 12:24 (1361). London customs, which may go back to the thirteenth century, prohibited any boat keeper from taking any man or woman to "les Estouves" at night (Riley, ed. [n. 36 above], 242; CLRO, Letter-Book H, fol. 264v [*Cal. L-B H*, 372]).

which much information survives. That the brothels were legal within that jurisdiction—a liberty where the bishop in his capacity as territorial lord took the place of a municipal government[47]—does not mean that church courts accepted them as legal: men were still prosecuted in ecclesiastical court for visiting them.[48] Repeated petitions and complaints from Southwark residents to king and Parliament indicate that there were brothels elsewhere in the suburb, too; people accepted the stews of the Winchester liberty but did not want them to spread.[49] The stews were eventually closed not by the bishop but by the central government: the eighteen legal stews were closed for a short time in 1506 and only twelve reopened, and in 1546 Henry VIII ordered all the bathhouses in Southwark, officially recognized or not, closed.[50]

The only other English town with an official or municipal brothel seems to have been Sandwich, a port town in Kent. In 1475 the mayor and commons of the town entered into an exchange of land in order "to make a common house of stews to be called the Galye."[51] This was not just a municipal bathhouse: in 1494 the council decreed "that a house shall be ordained for common women as has been the custom" and set the amounts the brothel keepers (*lenones*) could charge the prostitutes (*ancillae*) for room, board, and ale. Two brothel keepers, a husband and wife, were named along with four prostitutes.[52]

The fifteenth-century set of regulations surviving from the Southwark stews (see App.) provides the best information as to how brothels operated. The regulations cannot be taken as representative of brothels in those English towns where prostitution was il-

[47] By the fifteenth century the bishop had sold or granted ownership of all but two of the stewhouses to others but retained jurisdiction over them all (Carlin [n. 32 above], 60–69).

[48] At least, married men (e.g., Guildhall Library, 9064/6, fol. 70r).

[49] *Rotuli Parliamentorum*, 6 vols. (London: Record Commission, 1767–77), 2:282 (1390), 4:447 (1433), 4:511 (1436). Court records from those parts of Southwark under the jurisdiction of the city of London in 1539 indicate that brothels were being kept there (CLRO, 39C/SCM1, fol. 2r). See also Carlin, 506.

[50] On the 1506 closing and subsequent reopening of legal stews, see A. H. Thomas and I. D. Thornley, eds., *The Great Chronicle of London* (London: George W. Jones, 1938), 331. For more on the final closing in 1546, see Society of Antiquaries, London, Proclamations II/194: "A Proclamation to avoyde the abhominable place called the Stewes" (also in Paul L. Hughes and James F. Larkin, eds., *Tudor Royal Proclamations*, vol. 1, *The Early Tudors [1485–1553]* [New Haven, Conn.: Yale University Press, 1964], 365–66).

[51] Kent Archives Office, Sandwich Year Book 1 (Old Black Book), Sa/AC1, fol. 217v.

[52] Kent Archives Office, Sandwich Year Book 2 (White Book), Sa/AC2, fols. 33v, 35r–35v.

legal, but considered in the context of what is known from elsewhere, they do reveal something of English attitudes to prostitution and brothel keeping. The regulations placed strict controls on the prostitutes but did not allow the brothel keepers a free hand over them and at least made it possible for the prostitutes to operate without harassment from the London authorities.

The Southwark regulations required that the stewholders be men; they could be accompanied by their wives, but no unmarried woman could keep a stewhouse.[53] Nonetheless, fines assessed on stewholders in the Bishop of Winchester's liberty in 1505–6 show that women did run stewhouses. A list from 1519 of suspicious persons arrested at the stewhouses also lists the keeper of each house, and several are women.[54] The proportions of women to men who kept illicit brothels varied from town to town within England. Table 1 indicates the numbers of women, men, and married couples accused in several jurisdictions. Accusations against women alone range from 34 percent to 59 percent of total accusations.[55] That so many were women indicates that this was an important area for female entrepreneurship. It is possible, of course, that women were simply more likely than men to be accused, but it is more likely that the court rolls underestimate the proportion of brothel keepers who were women than the reverse. If a couple ran the operation, only the man might be accused and fined, or a man might be fined for activities carried out by his wife alone.[56] It is unlikely that a woman alone would be fined for activities carried out by her husband alone, or even by both partners, even when the offense was one often connected with women; the husband would probably be

[53] Number B22 of the ordinances (see the App.). Numerical references to these ordinances will hereafter be cited parenthetically in the text.

[54] Hampshire Record Office, Eccles. I 85/1; PRO (n. 32 above), SP1/18/365/5/iii, fol. 232. Of the twenty-two stewholders presented for various offenses in the Southwark court sessions in 1505–6, nine were women. I owe the reference to this court roll, the only one that survives from this manor, to Carlin, 491. In 1366 an apprentice brought a complaint against his mistress, Joan Hunt, who kept stews in Southwark, for abusing him, but it is not certain whether this stewhouse was in the Bishop of Winchester's liberty (CLRO, Plea and Memoranda Roll A11, membrane 2 [*Cal. PMR* 2:54]).

[55] Winchester is not included in the table. According to Keene (n. 34 above), 1:391, brothels there were run either by men, by prostitutes themselves, or by husband/wife partnerships.

[56] Kowaleski finds men being accused and fined for their wives' activities in Exeter, not just for brothel keeping but for other economic activities (Kowaleski [n. 34 above], 156; Maryanne Kowaleski, personal communication, London, July 1987).

TABLE I **BREAKDOWN BY SEX OF ACCUSATIONS OF BROTHEL KEEPING IN LATE MEDIEVAL ENGLISH COURT RECORDS**

Record Series and Dates	Women		Men		M. Couples		
	No.	%	No.	%	No.	%	Total
London, Plea and Memoranda Rolls, 1338–40*	12	57	9	43	...	...	21
Diocese of London, Commissary Court Act Books, 1470–1516†	121	53	50	22	57	25	228
East Smithfield Views of Frankpledge, 1422–1534‡	17	53	8	24	7	22	32
Westminster Views of Frankpledge, 1364–1508§	86	46	86	46	16	8	188
Nottingham Borough Sessions, 1453–1550‖	76	57	54	40	4	3	134
Exeter Mayor's Tourns, 1327–1445#	98	53	80	44	6	3	184
Great Yarmouth Courts Leet and Sessions of the Peace, 1367–1548**	73	59	46	37	5	4	124
Ipswich Courts Leet and Sessions of the Peace, 1415–1544††	32	34	57	60	6	6	95

NOTE.—The percentages given here should be taken only as rough guides. In addition to the small size of some of the samples, they are not complete; most of the series have big gaps, and the extant rolls are damaged and illegible in places. Because the types of records are so different and some are much more complete than others and because the time periods covered vary, the figures cannot be used to compare absolute numbers of accused brothel keepers in different towns.

*Corporation of London Records Office, Plea and Memoranda Roll A3, membrane 4b, membrane 14, Roll A5, membrane 2, membrane 11 (*Calendar of Plea and Memoranda Rolls Preserved among The Archives of The Corporation of the City of London at the Guildhall*, ed. A. H. Thomas [Cambridge: Cambridge University Press, 1926], 1:109, 124–26, 167, 188). These rolls contain presentments from several wards only, and what has survived is obviously only a small fraction of all such accusations from medieval London. This count includes only those listed for keeping a brothel (*bordellum*), not those accused of receiving prostitutes.

†Guildhall Library, 9064/1–11 and 9064a. These are ecclesiastical court records dealing with moral offenses, mostly either sexual offenses or defamation. Many refer to *pronubae* (procurers) accused of procuring for specific people, and I have not counted them as brothel keepers. Richard Wunderli (*London Church Courts and Society on the Eve of Reformation*, Speculum Anniversary Monographs, no. 7 [Cambridge, Mass.: Medieval Academy of America, 1981]), 92–93, explains, "Scribes used the word *pronuba* to refer indiscriminately to a male or female pimp; but on occasion they also used the words *fautor lenocinii* (or one who *fovet lenocinium*) for the same purpose. Court scribes never clearly indicate the difference between a *pronuba* and a *fautor lenocinii*, but it appears that a *pronuba* accepted money for providing a woman and a *fautor lenocinii* provided a place (for payment?) for the illegal act." "Procurer" is a better translation than "pimp" for *pronuba* because "pimp" in modern parlance is usually one who lives off a prostitute's earnings (rather than being paid by a client to provide a prostitute). I have included those who *fovent lenocinium*, and those accused of being *pronubae* for several women living in their house, as brothel keepers. The records do not give the disposition of most of the cases. See Wunderli for full discussion of these records. For published excerpts from these records, see William Hale Hale, ed., *A Series of Precedents and Proceedings in Criminal Cases, Extending from the Year 1475 to 1640. Extracted from the Act Books of Ecclesiastical Courts in the Diocese of London, Illustrative of the Discipline of the Church of England* (London: Francis & John Rivington, 1847).

‡This was a manorial court. The numbers include people listed as keeping prostitutes in their houses, not those only listed as procurers (Public Record Office), SC2/191/55–59.

§Westminster Abbey Muniments Room (hereafter WAM), 50699–50773. Those listed above include receivers of prostitutes. Many of those accused of receiving prostitutes were also accused of receiving thieves. Some of those listed as receivers may not be brothel keepers but keepers of cheap lodgings; e.g., Johanna de Bone and Margery Nayler were both listed as receivers of the same prostitute (WAM 50711). In some cases it is specified that people receive prostitutes in their tenements rather than their homes, probably renting to them rather than keeping brothels (WAM, 50716). Only a few entries specifically state that the offense is brothel keeping: e.g., "they keep a brothel, that is, unknown men and prostitutes in their houses" (WAM, 50739), or "they are common procurers and keep a common brothel" (WAM, 50753). Of these, seven are men and thirteen are women.

‖Nottinghamshire Record Office, CA/1–45b (the series continues, but only those up until 1550 were consulted for this article). Sessions of the Peace were held before Justices of the Peace, royally appointed local officials. These figures do not include those presented in the sixteenth century for "kepyng of bawdry," which might mean either brothel keeping or committing immorality themselves.

Devon Record Office, Mayor's Tourn Rolls, EC9, 1337–1445; Mayor's Court Rolls, K7, 1327–67. These court rolls contain presentments for municipal offenses. I thank Maryanne Kowaleski for sharing her expertise with the Exeter court rolls.

**Norfolk Record Office, Y/C4/81–249 (the series continues but only those up to 1550 were examined for this article). Courts Leet dealt with many of the same sorts of cases as Sessions of the Peace in addition to commercial offenses. Entries about receiving prostitutes are more common than those for keeping brothels; this table includes only the latter.

†† Suffolk Record Office, C7/1/3–27; C5/112–13; C8/1/5–34. This includes those presented for brothel keeping or for "supporting, abetting and receiving various persons committing prostitution [*scortum*] and adultery" in their houses. One presentment refers to a brothel as "comune lupanarium et apertu stue" (common brothel and open stew) (C7/1/5, membrane 1d).

in a better position to pay the fines.[57] In the case of the records from the London ecclesiastical courts, which also appear in the table, systematic error probably works in the opposite direction: these are accusations of moral offenses, less likely to be aimed only at those deemed fiscally responsible, and women's moral transgressions may have been presented more commonly (especially by their neighbors) than men's.[58]

When women did manage brothels, it may still have been men who owned them and profited from them. Records from Great Yarmouth indicate that women there often managed brothels that were the property of men. The male property owners were fined higher amounts, perhaps because they were accorded more blame or, perhaps, simply because the court thought they could better afford to pay, but the fact that they were fined at all indicates that the municipality considered them to be responsible parties, not just absent landlords.[59] Just as women were likely to enter occupations that required little capital, they were more likely to be involved in those aspects of the brothel business that used someone else's investment.[60]

In Southwark, where brothels were legal and officially established, brothel keeping was more likely to be a permanent occupation than elsewhere in England. In other towns, those presented as brothel keepers had other occupations as well. The Nottingham records, for example, name a wide range of occupations, including

[57] In medieval English law a husband could be held responsible for his wife's activities and not vice versa, though this does not mean that those women whose names appear were unmarried. On laws regarding women as entrepreneurs in London, see Kay E. Lacey, "Women and Work in Fourteenth and Fifteenth Century London," in *Women and Work in Pre-Industrial England*, ed. Lindsey Charles and Lorna Duffin (London: Croom Helm, 1985), 24–82, esp. 42–45. See also Kowaleski, 146–47.

[58] See Wunderli (n. 29 above), 81–102, on the prosecution of sexual crimes by London ecclesiastical courts.

[59] For example, Norfolk Record Office, Y/C4/199, membrane 15. From the same town, however, there are also instances of men who "let out their houses to farm to prostitutes," that is, rented to the prostitutes themselves rather than to brothel keepers, and were sometimes fined less than were brothel keepers (e.g., Norfolk Record Office, Y/C4/186, membrane 16d). This renting to prostitutes also shows up in sixteenth-century Sessions of the Peace (e.g., Norfolk Record Office, Y/C4/222, membrane 14d).

[60] This pattern holds true for most occupations in which women worked in the Middle Ages; denied entrance to many of the skilled trades and guilds, they worked at a wide variety of tasks (especially brewing and spinning), none of which required major capital investment or permanent, year-round activity (see Barbara Hanawalt's introduction to Hanawalt, ed. [n. 34 above], xii–xiii). Prostitution was a natural outlet for casual unskilled labor, and brothel keeping also may have allowed women to take advantage of available opportunities and the supply of prostitutes.

laborer, for the men accused; of the women, thirty-eight are listed as housewife (or as "wife of so-and-so"), nineteen as widow, seven as spinster (perhaps simply meaning unmarried woman), two as laborer, and one as tipler (tavern keeper).[61] In Exeter, of the seventeen women listed as brothel keepers during the period 1373–93, all are also listed in the court rolls as having other occupations.[62] Brothel keeping was a sideline and not a profession in itself, although the degree to which one could make a living at it alone would depend on the size of the town and the demand for prostitutes. Even the Southwark brothels probably did not have a very long-term staff.[63]

Foreigners, particularly from the Low Countries, were often accused of keeping brothels, perhaps in part because foreigners were generally distrusted, perhaps because foreign women had few other opportunities available to them, perhaps because there would have been a large foreign clientele for brothels as many foreign merchants in port towns would not have their families with them. "Dutch" brothel keepers seem to have been particularly common, for example, in Great Yarmouth, where a sizable Dutch community was settled.[64] The East Smithfield court rolls show several "Dutch" women as brothel keepers.[65] A Southwark stewhouse attacked during the Peasants' Rebellion in 1381 was run by "frows de Flaundres"; the Tudor chronicler John Stow explained that "English people disdayned to be baudes. Froes of Flaunders were women for that

[61] Nottinghamshire Record Office, CA/1–45b.

[62] Kowaleski (n. 34 above), 154, n. 53, and 143 for her table 1. Kowaleski's study of Exeter for this twenty-year period is based on a much wider range of documents than is my tabulation of brothel-keeping statistics for a longer period. See Keene (n. 34 above), 1:392, on prostitution as a secondary occupation; in the Winchester records he has found prostitutes who worked as spinsters, and a wool-comber, a dressmaker, a laundress, and a netmaker.

[63] Records of stewholders fined in 1506 show that six of twelve brothels had more than one keeper during the year (Hampshire Record Office, Eccles. I 85/1).

[64] For example, for 1381: "William Taylour, Dutchman, is a common receiver of thieves, prostitutes, and other malefactors, and is a common regrater of beer" (Norfolk Record Office, Y/C4/92, membrane 14d). "Dutch" people often appear in the Yarmouth records for other offenses as well, and their appearance as brothel keepers may simply reflect their importance in the population. The term "Dutch" can also include Germans or Flemings (see Sylvia Thrupp, "Aliens in and around London in the Fifteenth Century," in *Studies in London History*, ed. A. E. J. Hollaender and William Kellaway [London: Hodder & Stoughton, 1969], 251–72, esp. 259). The majority of those so labeled were in fact Hollanders or Brabanters.

[65] PRO, SC2/191/55, membrane 2, membrane 3 (these are cases where "Duchewoman" is given as a surname or appellative; some of the other names could also be Dutch or Flemish).

purpose."[66] The 1393 ordinance banishing prostitutes in London to Cock's Lane and to the stews specifically blamed "Flemish women, who profess and follow such shameful and dolorous life," for the disturbances causes by prostitution, a clear indication that there had been Flemish women involved in prostitution elsewhere than the Winchester liberty.[67]

The brothel keepers of the Southwark stews had a great deal of control over the working conditions of the prostitutes but not over all aspects of their lives. The ordinances forbade the prostitutes to live in the stewhouses (B1). The brothels had to close at certain times: the prostitutes had to leave not only the house but the entire lordship on holy days from 6:00 to 11:00 A.M. and 1:00 to 6:00 P.M. (the forbidden hours are shorter in the winter), and at night during the sitting of Parliament (B11, A3, B15, B16).[68] Not only did the prostitutes not live in the brothels, stewholders could not force them or even allow them to board there (A2, B10). London ecclesiastical court records refer to people harboring women from the Southwark stews, further evidence that the prostitutes did in fact live elsewhere.[69] Banning prostitutes from the liberty on religious holidays may have been a concession by the bishop of Winchester to the Church's disapproval of prostitution; during Parliament or a meeting of the king's council the bishop himself was likely to be at his Southwark residence next to the stews and may have wanted the

[66] V. H. Galbraith, ed., *The Anonimalle Chronicle, 1333–1381*, University of Manchester Historical Series, no. 45 (Manchester: Manchester University Press, 1927), 140; John Stow, *A Survey of London*, ed. Charles L. Kingsford (Oxford: Oxford University Press, 1908), 310. This quotation is a marginal rubric, which may have been inserted by the publisher of Stow's 1603 edition rather than by Stow himself. Trexler (n. 7 above), 986, has studied the geographical origins of women in Florentine brothels, as well as male employees of the brothels (not male prostitutes), and finds that the largest group is from Flanders. While this may be coincidental, it may also be that Flemish women had a general reputation for prostitution or that prostitutes were called Flemish in slang even if they were not actually from Flanders.

[67] CLRO, Letter-Book H, fol. 287r (*Cal. L-B H*, 402; trans. in Riley [n. 36 above], 535).

[68] The presentments of stewholders (Hampshire Record Office, Eccles. I, 85/1) show that closing on holy days was one of the regulations they were often accused of infringing.

[69] Harboring a prostitute meant allowing her to lodge, not necessarily sheltering her from justice. Juliana Colson, a widow, was accused of being a procuress for her daughter, "and allowing her to have access at night to the Stewsside and come back the next day" (Guildhall Library, 9064/3, fol. 215r); a woman of St. Michael of Wood Street parish was accused of being a prostitute in the Stews side (Guildhall Library, 9064/8, fol. 147v). Other Londoners accused of harboring unspecified prostitutes may also have been renting rooms to women from the stews (see, e.g., CLRO, Plea and Memoranda Roll A3, membrane 14 [*Cal. PMR* 1:124–25]).

area cleared up temporarily. The effect of forcing the prostitutes to have their actual dwellings elsewhere did minimize the women's ties to the brothel, perhaps giving them less group solidarity but also giving them more freedom of movement than if they had lived there.

The illicit brothels elsewhere in England may have operated similarly, with prostitutes working there and living elsewhere.[70] This may explain why, in so many court rolls, those who received or harbored prostitutes in their houses are mentioned separately from keepers of brothels. The brothel keeper did not directly employ the prostitutes and they did not live in her or his house; she or he merely rented to them their working premises. Even in the case of the legal brothels, the prostitutes may have picked up their customers elsewhere: there are references to men taking women to the stews, and these may be prostitutes who normally worked there.[71] The stewholders could also have rented rooms by the night to couples even if the women did not usually work there, but the regulations refer only to prostitutes paying a weekly rent.

In the Southwark brothels each woman was to pay 14d. a week for her room—her place of business and not her residence (B2). This was much higher than usual rents at the time.[72] The amount charged by brothel keepers in Sandwich was similar, 16d. a week for board and lodging.[73] The regulations give no indication that the stewholders received any money from the customers; the latter probably paid the prostitutes, who paid a high rent rather than a percentage of their fees. Procurers not connected with official brothels might make more favorable deals: for example, William Redwode and his wife Isabella were "procurers for divers women and received from divers men sums for these women, from some 20d.,

[70] For example, the London ecclesiastical court accused a woman of "being in a brothel all Monday night"; her residence is also given, implying that it was not the brothel (Guildhall Library, 9064/1, fol. 86r; see also fol. 169v). A Westminster court book entry from the reign of Henry VIII accuses Anne Warren of "keeping whores daily in her house," implying that they did not live there (Westminster Abbey Muniments Room, 50782, fol. 1v); in the same book others are accused of "keeping bawdry both day and night" (fol. 2r–2v).

[71] For example, Guildhall Library, 9064/6, fol. 69r.

[72] Carlin (n. 32 above), 487, n. 18, compares the 60s. 8d. paid annually by each prostitute for her room to the 20s. per annum for tenements owned by Sir John Fastolf in Southwark. The amount may also be compared to fifteenth-century wages of 1.5–2d. per day plus board for women agricultural workers, or 14–18s. per year plus board for laundresses in Oxford (James E. Thorold Rogers, *Six Centuries of Work and Wages* [New York: Putnam's, n.d.], 329, and *A History of Agriculture and Prices in England* [1866–1902; reprint, Vaduz: Kraus Reprint, 1963], 3:660–63).

[73] Kent Archives Office, Sa/AC2, fol. 35r.

from some 30d., from some 40d. and from some four shillings at the most."[74]

The regulations from both Southwark and Sandwich show a great concern that the prostitutes not be exploited financially. The Sandwich regulations limited the price the brothel keeper could charge the women for ale; the Southwark regulations prohibited all prostitutes from boarding at the brothel, thereby preventing the stewholder from overcharging them. The Southwark rule against the stewholder lending money to the women—if he did so, he could not bring suit for its recovery (A6)—seems intended to keep the women from falling into his debt and therefore into dependence on him. This regulation was breached in practice, as in at least one case a stewholder did succeed in having a woman imprisoned because she would not work for him to pay off a debt. Sometime between 1473 and 1475 Ellen Butler petitioned the chancellor for a writ of habeas corpus to release her from the bishop of Winchester's prison. She had been looking for a position as a servant and had met a man in London named Thomas Bowde who had asked if she wanted a good job. He took her to his house on the Stews side of the river and "would have compelled her to do such service as his other servants do there." When she refused, he brought an action against her in the court of the bishop of Winchester in Southwark to get a judgment for a sum she would never be able to pay, so that she would have to remain in prison unless she agreed to work for him as a prostitute.[75]

The Southwark stew regulations also aimed at protecting the prostitutes from other forms of exploitation. Prostitutes could not spin or card with the stewholder (B13). Spinning was the most common occupation for women in the later Middle Ages, particularly for single women.[76] This regulation, though it could be seen

[74] Guildhall Library, 9064/1, fol. 57r. Alexander Elwold kept two prostitutes in his house, "for whom he received weekly two shillings from a certain priest" (Guildhall Library, 9064/3, fol. 217r). A penny seems a more typical payment for a prostitute herself (Guildhall Library, 9064/1, fol. 80r). One woman received from a priest 4d. for one night and "a farthing cake and a farthing worth of single beer" for the second (Guildhall Library, 9064/6, fol. 21v). Eden Johnson was accused of being a procurer: she demanded payment from John Parnesse and his lover, saying "I have been bawd between you two a dozen times and thou owest me 16s.," to which he responded, "I paid thee at the stews side, thou whore" (Guildhall Library, 9064/8, fol. 79v).

[75] PRO, C/48/191. Her petition alleged not that he breached the regulations by suing her but rather that the action of trespass was false. The exact date of the petition is unknown, as is the result. The stewholder's surname is clearly Bowde rather than Bawde.

[76] The term "spinster" began to be applied to single women in general because it was so common an occupation. When the term "spinster inhabiting the stews"

as an attempt to limit the work options of prostitutes, did reduce the brothel keeper's ability to force the prostitutes to spin and card for his profit. In both Southwark (B40) and Sandwich the brothel keeper was forbidden to beat the prostitutes.[77]

The Southwark regulations place great stress on the free movement of the prostitutes. According to the preamble, the problem the regulations set out to solve was that the prostitutes' freedom of movement had been taken from them. The preamble presents the reissuance of the regulations as a way to prevent the prostitutes from being exposed to more "horrible sin" than necessary, by stressing that they might not be kept in the stews, or in a life of prostitution, against their wishes. Yet the regulations did not propose that the women should convert and give up prostitution; rather they took a practical approach that also benefited women who could not or did not want to leave the profession. The regulations required the bishop's officials to search regularly for women being kept against their will and stipulated that a pending legal action could not prevent a prostitute from leaving the stews and the life of prostitution whenever she wished (A5).

The abuses these regulations attempted to prevent were very real and continued after the issuance of the regulations. Margaret Hathewyk in 1439 arranged with "a certain gentleman" to have a young girl named Isabella Lane kept in the Southwark stews for four days "to be used in lustful acts." Nicholas Croke took Christiana Swynowe to the Southwark stews and forced her to remain there

---

was used in a 1543 ordinance (CLRO, 39C/SCM1, fol. 32r), it undoubtedly referred to single women, prostitutes in particular, and not specifically women who spun. This is not to say that all single women were equated with prostitutes, just that those from the Southwark stews were. The term "spinster" was used as the legal designation of an unmarried woman from the seventeenth century, according to the Oxford English Dictionary, s.v. "spinster," but appears to have meant the same in popular parlance even earlier.

[77] In Sandwich the regulations specified that any disputes between brothel keeper and prostitutes were instead to be brought before the mayor and jurats (Kent Archives Office, Sa/AC2, fol. 35r). The Southwark regulations as they survive do not contain a prohibition on beating the prostitutes, but the question about beating the prostitutes (B40) is the only one in the list of thirty-three questions that does not parallel the regulations themselves; a provision punishing the beating of women was probably once included but inadvertently omitted at some point in the manuscript transmission. Beating the prostitutes was clearly forbidden by the early sixteenth century as it was one of the offenses for which the stewholders were being fined (Hampshire Record Office, Eccles. I 85/1). The others were keeping their houses open on holidays, buying and selling women, and having women "to board," which all appear in the regulations.

nine days.[78] In 1490, Henry Whitehere was accused in ecclesiastical court of soliciting women to fornicate with other men; he also "took a certain Margaret to the Stews side, and there sold her to a certain procurer."[79] In 1517 John Barton was accused of taking a young girl on her first visit to London to the stews and making "covenant with a bawd to set the said maiden with the said bawd."[80]

Coercion, including the sale of young girls (*iuvenculae*) not only to brothel keepers but also to individual customers, often rich merchants from overseas, indicates both the demand for prostitutes and the problems facing unskilled young women, often new in the city and without connections, who saw no alternative to a life of prostitution. Though regulations might protect women from being forced into prostitution, they could not protect women from choosing that life out of economic necessity. In 1495 Thomas Togood, a "bawd of the Stews," was put on the pillory in London for having enticed two women "to become his servants and to have been common within his house at the Stews."[81] These women may have gone to be prostitutes in Togood's house voluntarily rather than by force or subterfuge, but they may have had little real choice.

The Southwark regulations had neither the sole intention nor the sole function of protecting the prostitutes. They also aimed to protect the customer from being harassed in the street (B13), being pulled into the brothel by his clothing (B7, B8), or having his person or belongings detained in the house because of debts (B3, B6). The stewholder could not sell food or other goods in his house (B29) or keep a boat (B21), probably in order to protect the customer from being forced to purchase food or transportation at inflated prices as part of his transaction with the prostitute. The banishment from the stews of any women with "burning sickness" (B25) protected the customer from disease.[82]

[78] CLRO, Plea and Memoranda Roll A66, membrane 5 (*Cal. PMR*, 5:13–14); CLRO, journal 3, fol. 15v, journal 4, fol. 134v.

[79] Guildhall Library, 9064/4, fol. 176v. Similarly, Anna Chester sold a young girl, her servant, to someone who took her to the Stews (Guildhall Library, 9064/9, fol. 108r).

[80] CLRO, Rep. 3, fol. 157v–158r; Letter-Book N, fol. 47v. The girl managed to escape, aided by the wife of the waterman with whom Barton left her while he went to negotiate with the brothel keeper. Barton was convicted and sentenced to the pillory.

[81] Thomas and Thornley, eds. (n. 50 above), 258.

[82] It is not clear whether the "burning sickness" is syphilis or some other venereal ailment; see Robert Gottfried, *Epidemic Disease in Fifteenth-Century England* (New Brunswick, N.J.: Rutgers University Press, 1978), 62, on the identity of the "French Pox" of the late fifteenth century. As Otis, *Prostitution* (n. 7 above), 41, points out,

Though London itself, and several other English towns, had legislation about certain types of clothing (e.g., striped hoods) that prostitutes had to wear, and prohibited them from wearing the dress of "good and noble ladies," the Southwark brothels had no restrictions on the dress of the prostitutes other than that they not wear aprons (B28).[83] The city of London complained in 1538 about "the evil example of the gorgeous apparel of the common women of the stews to the great temptation of young maidens, wives and apprentices," but the regulations from the fifteenth century were not concerned with restricting the prostitutes to keep them from tempting or contaminating respectable women.[84] As long as they were being controlled by their relation to the official brothels they did not need to be identified as a group.

The Southwark brothel regulations levied harsh punishments against the prostitute who had a paramour, especially if she supported him financially (B12, B50).[85] For this she could get three weeks of prison, a fine, the cucking-stool, and banishment from the lordship. The regulations may have been directed against pimping in order to protect the prostitute's control over her income, to which canon lawyers agreed she had a right, but a measure intended mainly

---

the Middle Ages had a long tradition of connecting prostitutes with disease, e.g., the closing of brothels in times of plague. There is no reason why this provision need even have referred specifically to venereal disease. It could be an acknowledgment that intimate contact could spread many diseases. An English treatise of the fourteenth century gives the danger of "meseles" (probably leprosy) as one reason for not visiting prostitutes (*Robert of Brunne's "Handlyng Synne,"* ed. Frederick J. Furnivall, Early English Text Society Original Series 123 [London: Kegan Paul, Trench, Trübner & Co., 1901], 2:238). The penalty for violating this regulation was higher in the later manuscript tradition. As J. B. Post, "A Fifteenth-Century Customary of the Southwark Stews," *Journal of the Society of Archivists* 5 (1977): 422, explains, this was probably due to a copyist's error, but it could possibly reflect higher penalties once the "French disease" had arrived.

[83] On restrictions concerning dress, see e.g., CLRO, Letter-Book A, fol. 130v (*Cal L-B A,* 220), Letter-Book F, fol. 208r (*Cal. L-B F,* 241, trans. in Riley [n. 36 above], 267), Letter-Book H, fol. 139r (*Cal. L-B H,* 176, trans. in Riley, 458). For other towns, see Bickley, ed. (n. 33 above), 2:229; Great Yarmouth Courts Leet, Norfolk Record Office, Y/C4/90, membrane 12. An apron was a linen garment worn over other clothing but could also be a garment worn by a bishop; it could be that women were mocking the bishop of Winchester by wearing this type of garment (*Middle English Dictionary,* ed. Sherman M. Kuhn [Ann Arbor: University of Michigan Press, 1975], s.v. "napron").

[84] The complaint by the city of London can be found in CLRO, Rep. 10 (n. 32 above), fol. 27r.

[85] The question based on this regulation (B50) indicates that the concern is with her maintaining the lover financially.

to protect the prostitute would hardly punish her so severely.[86] Some of the prostitutes of the stews did have people who drummed up business for them, but these were not necessarily their lovers.[87] This regulation also controlled the prostitute's choices about her own sexuality. To work in a public brothel she must not be attached to any one man. Similarly, wives or nuns, who belonged to a man or to God, were not to be received in the stewhouses (B4).

Probably the most central concern of both the Southwark authorities and city officials in other towns in shaping the regulations and prohibitions directed at prostitutes, brothels, and brothel keepers was the preservation of public order, which required control over female sexuality. The concern with public order appears, for example, in the preamble to London's antiprostitution legislation.[88] Prostitution was connected with other crimes: as a royal commission of 1460 put it, "owing to the number of prostitutes in Southwark and other places adjacent many homicides, plunderings and improprieties have occurred."[89] Not only legislation but also court rolls class receivers of prostitutes with receivers of thieves or, more generally, suspicious persons.[90] Disturbing the neighbors is often part of the formula for accusations of brothel keeping.[91] A provision in the Southwark stew regulations requiring a prostitute to spend the whole night with a customer is probably meant to discourage people from wandering around the area at night (B20).[92] The city of London

[86] For a discussion of medieval canon law as it pertains to prostitution, see James A. Brundage, "Prostitution in the Medieval Canon Law," *Signs: Journal of Women in Culture and Society* 1, no. 4 (Summer 1976): 825–45, esp. 837–38.

[87] Edward Newton and his wife Margaret were listed as procurers for prostitutes of the Stews, procuring both priests and laymen (Guildhall Library 9064/9, fol. 42v).

[88] CLRO, Letter-Brook H, fol. 287r (*Cal. L-B H*, 402; trans. in Riley, 535), Letter-Book I, fol. 193v (*Cal. L-B I*, 178; trans. in Riley, 647).

[89] *Calendar of Patent Rolls,* Henry VI (London: His/Her Majesty's Stationery Office, 1910), 6:610.

[90] For example, King's Lynn Inquisitions before the Constables, 1309, in Dorothy M. Owen, ed., *The Making of King's Lynn: A Documentary Survey,* Records of Social and Economic History, n.s. 9 (London: British Academy, 1984), 419; King's Lynn Borough Archives, King's Lynn Leet Roll KL/C17/21, membrane 2d; Nottinghamshire Record Office, Nottingham Mickletourn Jury Roll, CA 3011, 1408 (also in *Records of the Borough of Nottingham,* ed. W. H. Stevenson [London: Bernard Quaritch, 1883] 2:62); Norfolk Record Office, Y/C4/92, membrane 14d. A receiver (*receptator*) would be one who knowingly harbors the wrongdoer.

[91] An example from Great Yarmouth from 1436: "Isabell Merssh keeps a brothel and supports brawlers and vagabonds in her house, to the nuisance of her neighbors" (Norfolk Record Office, Y/C4/143, membrane 12). This type of accusation is formulaic but there is significance in the formula adopted.

[92] It can hardly have been the case that a prostitute had to spend a whole night with each customer since the stews were open during the day and the women must

forbade boat owners to take people to or from the stews at night "lest misdoers be assisted in their coming and going."[93] London was subject to a curfew and night-walking was a common offense, often connected with prostitution or frequenting brothels.[94]

Brothels might violate the public order because they fomented violent crime, but the simple presence of independent women might also violate order: prostitutes are very often accused of being scolds as well, or accused prostitutes are listed in court rolls along with accused scolds.[95] Any woman making public scenes and quarrels, or misbehaving sexually, was a threat to order. The regulations thus attempted not to stamp out prostitution as immoral but rather to control it as disorderly.

The Southwark regulations show remarkably little concern with sexual morality in general, not even paying lip service to the goal of making the prostitutes leave their sin. The church condemned prostitution and brothel keeping, as is apparent from the numerous accusations in ecclesiastical courts, but this did not deter the bishop of Winchester from sanctioning and regulating brothels, although not in his capacity as bishop.[96] Fines from the stews contributed to the bishop's income and probably formed a major motivation for

---

have had more than one customer per day. From the list of questions later in the manuscript (B54), it appears that the problem would arise only if she accepted money to spend the whole night and then did not do so.

[93] CLRO, Letter-Book H, fol. 264v (*Cal. L-B H*, 372). The regulation in Riley, ed. (n. 36 above), 277, does not give any rationale.

[94] For example, CLRO, Letter-Book B, fol. 3r (*Cal. L-B B*, 6), Letter-Book D, fol. 131r (*Cal. L-B D*, 63).

[95] In the London ecclesiastical court records, e.g., it is often the same women accused of scolding or defaming and of prostitution (Guildhall Library, 9064/1–11). The combination or juxtaposition is also found often in other court rolls, e.g., PRO, Sc2/191/55 membrane 1 (East Smithfield); Westminster Abbey Muniments Room, 50707, 50709, etc. (Westminster).

[96] Concerning accusations in ecclesiastical courts, see Wunderli (n. 29 above), 81–102. Brian Woodcock, *Medieval Ecclesiastical Courts in the Diocese of Canterbury* (London: Oxford University Press, 1952), 79–82, discusses sexual offenses as a proportion of ex officio cases treated by these courts but does not separate out prostitution. The Bishop of Winchester was not entirely unique in his sanctioning of brothels; the Bishop of Mainz, e.g., owned brothels. See Bloch (n. 7 above), 760, and Wiesner (n. 7 above), 97, on Germany; see also Keene (n. 34 above), 1:392, on ecclesiastics as landlords of brothels in the town of Winchester, although these were not officially condoned. Although the bishop himself would have been fully aware of what was going on in Southwark (many of the bishops of Winchester served as royal chancellors and spent a good deal of time at their London palace, adjacent to the stews), he was not personally concerned about it. His bailiffs and other officials enforced the regulations.

not just condoning but also actually encouraging the brothels: both prostitutes and stewholders paid fines for violations of the regulations, and stewholders paid rents well above market rate to those who owned the houses.[97] In addition, by regulating the stewholders' power over the prostitutes, the bishop or his representative asserted his own power over the stewholders. Indeed, the bishop of Winchester's regulation of brothels may have been a way of asserting his jurisdiction over the liberty. By allowing brothels to exist there that were illegal elsewhere, the bishop was proclaiming that in this corner of the London suburbs he was the lord of the manor: the brothel regulations also stipulate that all residents of the liberty must sue each other in the bishop's court rather than the king's (A7). The bishop's exclusive jurisdiction also permitted abuses of power by brothel keepers: because they were licensed and accepted, they could wield power in the bishop's courts. In a petition to the chancellor between 1475 and 1485, Henry Saunder complained that Thomas Dyconson, "a keeper of one of the unclean houses on the other side of the Thames," had had him arrested in the Bishop of Winchester's liberty on false charges and that Saunder's just defense had not prevailed because all the members of the jury were "occupiers and keepers of such unclean and infamous places as the said Thomas is."[98]

The bishop of Winchester was not the only powerful figure to profit from brothels; he was unique only in that his jurisdiction in Southwark made the brothels legal. Elsewhere in England, if leading citizens owned brothels, they could not make the brothels legal, but they could often ignore the law with impunity. William Walworth, Lord Mayor of London, owned the brothel attacked by the rebels in 1381.[99] Apparently Walworth was not the only leading London citizen to rent to prostitutes or brothel keepers; in 1417 the council decreed that "no Alderman, substantial Commoner, or other person whatsoever, shall receive as a tenant . . . any man or woman who has been indicted or charged as of, or known to be of, evil and vicious life."[100] Indeed, the ownership of brothels by powerful cit-

---

[97] Carlin (n. 32 above), 491–92, has collected evidence from the Winchester pipe rolls of the early sixteenth century about amercements of brothel keepers for various offenses. See also 487, n. 18, on high rents paid by stewholders to the owners of the houses, mostly ecclesiastical institutions. The Fraternity of the Assumption of the Virgin in St. Margaret's Church in Southwark, who owned one of the stewhouses, seems to have had some qualms about owning brothels since they inserted a clause in the leases of other tenements in the area forbidding their use as brothels (496).

[98] PRO, Cl/64/897. I owe this reference to Carlin, 499, n. 38.

[99] Galbraith, ed. (n. 66 above), 140.

[100] CLRO, Letter-Book I, fol. 194r (*Cal. L-B I*, 178, trans in Riley [n. 36 above], 649).

izens could be one reason why towns did not establish municipal brothels. The brothel keepers who were fined were usually those who actually managed the brothels, not those who owned them; but the example of Southwark shows that the landlord, charging high rents, could do very well out of the business. Such people might not look kindly on a municipal takeover of the trade and preferred illegality with ineffective enforcement.

The regulation of brothels in Southwark was in part an effort to keep female sexuality under the control of men. Female sexuality was to be kept within bounds: to disappear on holy days, to be unobtrusive, to stay indoors and not walk the streets. If women were not the property of a particular man, a husband, their sexual behavior must be strictly regulated by the male civil authorities. The regulations emphasize this by referring to the prostitutes as "single women."[101] If not the property of one, they were "common women," the property of the community, and could not choose their lovers. What made the prostitute less offensive to medieval morality than an adulteress or fornicatrix was that she was available to all men.[102] For her to have a particular lover would make her the property of one man and would make her sexual license much more morally offensive.

The prostitutes of the stews were publicly accepted as prostitutes and thus as promiscuous. The same principle probably underlay the treatment of illicit brothels elsewhere in England. The brothels were recognized as seedbeds of sin and disorder, the brothel keepers and prostitutes were fined and stigmatized by being labeled as such, but they continued to operate. Because brothels were illegal the authorities could enforce the laws strictly and close brothels when they so chose because of particular complaints, but in general the brothels provided a means for the authorities to control prostitutes and ensure that they would be available. The same social forces that legitimated their activity as the least of a number of evils seized control of that activity to place the women at the disposal of any man. The lack of restrictions on who could be customers means that the brothels were a sexual outlet for more than just unmarried apprentices. The clergy, who could not marry and who were often accused of adultery with Londoners' wives, may have been among the intended clientele.[103] As some men were excluded from the

---

[101] This does not mean that any unmarried woman was assumed to be a prostitute. In B22, for example, "single" clearly just means "unmarried."

[102] The financial element was less important to medieval theorists than that of promiscuity (see Brundage [n. 86 above], 825–29).

[103] See, e.g., CLRO, Letter-Book I, fols. 286–90 (*Cal. L-B I*, 273–77).

institution of the family, women not under the control of the family had to be tolerated to prevent these men from disrupting the families of others. But the women still had to remain under some sort of patriarchal control. The brothels fulfilled this function as intermediaries for the bishop of Winchester or other local authorities.

More than elsewhere in Europe the regulations of the Southwark brothels do seem concerned to help the prostitutes in practical ways. The control over their sexual behavior was delegated to the brothel keeper but he (or she, in practice) did not control their lives in other ways. They could leave the stews, both daily and permanently, and could not be made to pay the stewholder more than their rent. Even as their sexuality remained under the control of male society in general, they were protected from too strict control by a particular man. Prostitution for these women was a trade, as the regulations acknowledge: a prostitute was defined as a woman who lives by her body (B2). Like other trades in medieval towns prostitution was regulated. But the regulations of the trade were not concerned with the practitioners' lives outside the trade: that was for other authorities. In effect the Southwark brothel regulations made the prostitute's sexuality a commodity and controlled its sale. Though they were much more specifically concerned with the trade as trade than were regulations from elsewhere, they still existed within the same general context of seeing women's sexual activity as a threat to the social order and a defilement of the woman herself.

The Southwark brothel regulations provide frustratingly little information on the prostitutes themselves and how the brothels and brothel keepers shaped their experiences. There is no evidence as to whether the prostitutes of the stews felt any group identity in contrast with illicit prostitutes or other women. While we may surmise that the choice of work as a prostitute was dictated by economic constraints, we do not know what made a prostitute choose to work in the stews of Southwark rather than illicitly elsewhere: diminished harassment by the law and a steady stream of customers probably played a part, but some sort of group solidarity may have been involved. The restrictions under which they operated have left traces, but the prostitutes themselves have not, and one can only infer from their circumstances the choices they may have made.

Department of History
University of Pennsylvania

Appendix

Text of ordinances[104]

This act and ordinance was made, as hereinafter appears in this book, in the parliament held at Winchester in the eighth year of the reign of King Henry II [1162], by all the assent of the commons, and so confirmed by the king and all the lords of the said parliament, in the same year and time of parliament there so held, Theobaldus then being archbishop of Canterbury and Thomas Becket then being archdeacon of the same.[105]

We ordain and make to the said lord's [the Bishop of Winchester's] avail divers ordinances and constitutions to be kept forever more within the said lordship and franchise, according to the old customs that have been used and accustomed there out of time of mind, which now of late were broken, to the great displeasure of God and great hurt unto the lord, and utter undoing of all his poor tenants there dwelling, and also to the great multiplication of horrible sin upon the single women, who ought to have their free going and coming at their own liberty, as it appears by the old customs thereof made before, time out of mind, for the eschewing of these inconveniences and of all others thereof coming.

(A1) First, therefore, we ordain and make, according to the said old customs contained in the customary, that no stewholder nor his wife hinder any single woman to go and come at all times when they wish. And as often as they do the contrary, to forfeit to the lord at every court held within the said lordship when they are presented by the constables there, three shillings fourpence.

(A2) Also, we ordain and make that no great householder shall keep any women to board, but that they be expelled between now and Whitsuntide next coming after the date of this present writing, upon pain of losing to the said lord, at every default so made, a hundred shillings.

(A3) Also, we ordain and make that no great householder keep open his doors upon any holy days according to the old customs and customary,

---

[104] What follows is a modernization of the English text of the ordinances. Portions originally appearing in Latin are italicized. Several manuscripts of the ordinances survive: Bodleian MS. E. Mus. 229, from the late fifteenth century (clearly based on earlier material) and three in the British Museum, of which one, Harleian (hereafter Harl.) MS. 1877 contains two articles not in the Bodleian text. This translation follows the Bodleian manuscript except where Harl. 1877 has been used to supply missing material. The Bodleian MS. also contains ordinances made by the manorial Court Leet in the mid-fifteenth century; those that deal with prostitution have been included, the others omitted. The numeration is that used by Post in his edition of the Bodleian MS. (n. 82 above). For a discussion of the manuscript tradition and various textual problems, see Post.

[105] The date 1162 is clearly false (Parliament did not even exist then) (see Post, 420).

nor keep any of their women within the houses against their will, upon pain of a hundred shillings.

(A4) Also, we ordain and make that the bailiff of the said franchise for the time being shall see all the single women expelled every holy day out of the aforesaid lordship, according to the old custom thereupon made, and that he begin to do the same before the feast of Whitsuntide now next coming, upon pain of ten pounds to be forfeited to the said lord. And if any stewholder or his wife hinder him, that then they and either of them be brought into the prison, and forfeit unto the said lord forty shillings.

(A5) Item, we ordain and make that the bailiff and constables of same franchises four times in the year, that is to say once every quarter, shall make a due search in every great house, whether there be any single woman found and kept there against her will that would depart and leave her sin and never come there any more. It shall then be lawful to the said bailiff and constables and other honest men of the said lordship to expel the said women out of the said lordship without any hindrance or interruption from any great householder or his wife for any man's action, cause, or other matter against them, or any of them, to be taken or commenced in any way.

(A6) Item, we ordain and make that no great householder shall lend nor trust to any single woman more than the sum of six shillings and eightpence, and if they or any of them do the contrary thereof, that then their action or actions, condemnation or condemnations thereof shall utterly stand void and annulled, according to the old custom thereof had and made.

(A7) Item, we ordain and make that no man nor woman dwelling within the said lordship and franchise, of whatever degree he or they be, shall commence or take any action or process against another for no matter or cause in any court of the king, but only within the said lord's court, to be determined and ended there, without in any way removing out of the said court, except if it is for an obligation above the sum of forty shillings, upon the pain of forfeiting to the said lord at every time that they or any of them so do the contrary, ten pounds.

(B1) *There should be a wife, laundress and male ostler in the house, so many and no more.* First, that no stewholder that holds or keeps any stewhouse have nor keep any woman dwelling with him but his wife and a laundress and a man for his ostler, and no woman for ostler.

(B2) *Fourteen pence are to be paid every week for the room of each woman.* Item, that the women that are at common brothel be seen every day what they are, and a woman that lives by her body [be allowed] to come and go, as long as she pays her duty as old custom is, that is to say every week fourteen pence for her chamber, at all times [she] shall have free license and liberty without any interruption by the stewholders.

(B3) *Those who detain someone in their houses because of debts.* Item, if any of them that holds any stewhouse keeps any man against his will within his house as prisoner for any debt that he owes to him or for any other cause, unless the stewholder brings such persons to the lord's prison as the law wishes, there to answer as the court will award to every party that will say anything against him, he that does otherwise shall pay twenty shillings at every time and as often as he breaks this ordinance.

(B4) *Religious women and wives are not to be received in the stew-houses.* Item, that no stewholder receive any woman of religion, nor any man's wife, if it be known, but that they let the lord's officers know that such default is found, under pain of twelve pence.[106]

(B5) *Women who want to be kept secretly as though unknown.* Item, if a woman comes into this lordship and would be kept secretly within, and it is not the stewholder's wife,[107] they shall let the officers know upon the pain of forty shillings, and the same woman shall be taken and fined twenty shillings and be set three times upon the cucking-stool and then forswear the lordship.

(B6) *Those who have the goods of another in custody and do not want to give them back.* Item, if any man comes into this lordship to any stew-house and leave any belongings with the wife or with the ostler or any other woman therein, that he have deliverance of his belongings again at his going, or else the householder shall bring the ostler or the woman that has withheld it to prison and turn over the belongings to my lord and make satisfaction to the party. And if the ostler or the woman goes away with the belongings the householder shall answer for them and make a fine of twenty shillings.

(B7) *Women who draw men in by the clothing or otherwise.* Item, if any woman of the brothel hinders any man, other than sit still at the door and let him go or come, choose which they will, or if she draws any man by his gown or by his hood or by any other thing, she shall make a fine to the lord of twenty shillings.

(B8) *Wives of stewholders who draw men in similarly.* Item, if there be any stewholder's wife that draws any man into her house without his will, her husband and she shall be amerced to the lord in forty shillings.

(B9) *Those who hinder the officers in making their weekly searches.* Item, that the lord's officers, that is the constables, bailiff and surveyor, every week when they like best shall search every house of the stews, and if any man or woman hinder them he or she shall be amerced unto the lord in a hundred shillings.

(B10) *Those who have women at board contrary to the custom.* Item, that no stewholder hold any woman that lives by her body to board, but that they go to board elsewhere they wish, upon pain of twenty shillings at every time that this ordinance is broken.

(B11) *Those who do not keep their hours of absence on holy days.* Item, that no woman be found within the lordship on holy days from Michaelmas [September 29] to Candlemas [February 2] after eight o'clock in the morning until eleven o'clock at noon, and that they be expelled at one o'clock after noon until five o'clock at night, upon the pain contained in custom of the manor. And from Candlemas until Michaelmas that they be not found there on holy days from six o'clock in the morning until eleven o'clock at

[106] Twelve pence seems exceedingly low; it may be a mistake for twelve shillings. Harl. MS. 1877 has a fine of forty shillings.

[107] Reading "wif" for "wil."

noon, and then be expelled by one o'clock after noon and not come there until six o'clock at night upon the same pain.[108]

(B12) *Women who have their own lovers contrary to the custom.* Item, if any woman that lives by her body holds any paramour against the use and custom of the manor she shall be three weeks in the prison and make a fine of six shillings eightpence and then be set once on the cucking-stool and forswear the lordship.

(B13) *Women who spin contrary to the custom.* Item, if any woman that lives by her body spins or cards with the stewholder, or else casts any stone or makes any face at any man going by the way, either by water or by land, she shall make a fine of three shillings fourpence.

(B14) *Women who scold contrary to the custom.* Item, if any woman that lives by her body chides any man or makes a fray, she shall be in prison three days and three nights and make a fine of six shillings eightpence.

(B15) *Those who keep their houses on holy days.* Item, if any stewholder opens his door on holy days from the time of matins until noon, or from two o'clock in the afternoon until between five and six at night, he shall be amerced in twenty shillings at every time that that default is found.[109]

(B16) *Women who do not remove themselves at night in Parliament time.* Item, if any woman is found within the lordship after the sun is gone to rest, the king being at Westminster and holding there either Parliament or council, until the sun is up in the morning, after the custom of the manor, she shall make a fine at every time she does so of six shillings eightpence.

(B17) *Officers who conceal any of the above.* Item, if any officer, as constable, treasurer or bailiff, conceals any of the defaults above rehearsed, or do other than present them at every court, such officer shall be put in custody and kept in prison until the time that he makes a fine at the lord's will.

(B18) *Those who take ostlers for more than a half year contrary to the custom.* Item, if any stewholder takes any ostler in any way longer than from half year to half year, with reasonable hire for his service, he shall make a fine to the lord of twenty shillings.

Item, the steward as councillor to the lord's bailiff there shall have and take of every common woman for quarterage at each of the four quarters of the year, threepence, and at the like days of every of them and of every ostler fourpence toward his dinner, and of the lord by the hands of the bailiff six shillings eightpence for his said dinner.[110]

Item, he [margin: bailiff] shall have and take of every woman that is common, or is taken within any common hostel four times in the year, at every time threepence for her quarterage.

(B19) *Officials that allow anyone bail or mainprise.* Item, that no constable, treasurer or bailiff allow any man or woman bail, mainprise or other

[108] The MS. has "from Michaelmas to Candelmas" here, clearly an error.

[109] The amount of the amercement, twenty shillings, is omitted in the Bodleian MS. and in those that copy directly from it but found in Harl. 1877.

[110] This provision and the one that follows are found in Harl. 1877 but not in the Bodleian MS. or its direct copies.

pledge, but bring him to the lord's place to prison as they ought to do, upon the pain of losing, as often as they so do, six shillings eightpence.[111]

(B20) *Women who take money to lie with men and do not do it.* Item, if any woman takes any money to lie with any man, unless she lies still with him until it be the morning and then arise, she shall make a fine of six shillings eightpence.

(B21) *Those who hold or occupy boats contrary to the custom.* Item, if any stewholder holds or occupies any boat in any manner against the custom of the manor, he shall make a fine of six shillings eightpence.

(B22) *Women who keep stewhouses and do not have husbands.* Item, if any single woman holds or keeps any stewhouse within the lordship against the custom of the manor, she shall at every court make a fine of twenty shillings until the time that it is reformed.

(B23) *Pregnant women found in stews.* Item, that no stewholder nor any tenant within the lordship receive any woman that lives by her body if she be known to be with child, after reasonable warning, upon the pain of paying to the lord twenty shillings, and the woman to pay six shillings eightpence.

(B24) *The bailiff allowing bail without the license of the court.* Item, that the bailiff let no woman nor man make bail or mainprise without the leave of the court, upon the pain of paying a fine to the lord of a hundred shillings.

(B25) *Those who keep women who have a horrible disease.* Item, that no stewholder keep any woman within his house who has any sickness of burning, but that she be put out, upon the pain of making a fine unto the lord of twenty shillings.

(B26) *Arrests and pleas to be made for certain pence.* Item, that no bailiff nor constable shall take more than fourpence at the most for arrest, and the clerk twopence for the complaint, unless it be for a great sum or for a great trespass, upon pain of a fine to the lord.

(B27) *Those who keep bitches in heat within the lordship contrary to the custom.* Item, if any man within the lordship holds any bitch that goes into heat within the same lordship he shall make a fine for it to the lord of three shillings fourpence.

(B28) *Women using clothes which are called aprons.* Item, if any common woman wears any apron, she shall forfeit it and make a fine after the custom of the manor.

(B29) *Those who sell victuals out of the house to those who do not enter.* Item, that any man keeping a stewhouse neither sell nor retail out of the same house bread, ale, flesh, fish, wood, coal, candle or any other victual, upon pain of a fine to be made to the lord at the discretion of the steward and the constables.

Questions to be made of the stewholders and each of them:
(B30) Does he have any woman for ostler against the ordinance?
(B31) Does he have more laundresses than one?

[111] "Mainprise" is defined as surety.

(B32) Does he have any more servants in his house of women?

(B33) Does he take more for the women's chamber in a week than fourteen pence?

(B34) Does he prevent the women from coming and going freely?

(B35) Has he imprisoned any person in his house for debt or trespass?

(B36) Does he keep in his house any woman of religion or any man's wife?

(B37) Does he keep any woman secretly within his house?

(B38) Does he keep any man's belongings in distress for any debt or otherwise?

(B39) Does he hinder any officer in making his due search?

(B40) Does he beat any woman belonging to his house?

(B41) Does he keep any of the women to board against the ordinance?

(B42) Does he let his doors stand open on the holy days?

(B43) Does he hold any boat or vessel against the ordinance?

(B44) Does he keep any woman that is with child?

(B45) Does he keep any woman that has the perilous infirmity?

(B46) Does his wife draw any person into the stewhouse against his will?

Questions to be made of the common women and each of them:

(B47) Does she draw any man by his clothes against his will?

(B48) Does she hinder any officer from making his due search?

(B49) Does she not keep her hours on the holy days?

(B50) Does she hold or keep any paramour, against the ordinance?

(B51) Does she spin or card with any stewholder?

(B52) Does she chide with any person, or cast stones?

(B53) Is she absent in the parliament and council time?

(B54) Does she take any money to lie with men, and not perform it?

(B55) Is she single and keeps a stewhouse?

(B56) Is she known to be with child?[112]

(B57) Does she customarily wear any apron?

Questions of the officers to be answered by the surveyor and twelve men:

(B58) Does any constable bailiff or treasurer make any mainprise?

(B59) Do any of them take any person to bail without the court?

(B60) Does any officer take any more fees than are ordained by custom?

(B61) Does any person hold any bitch that is in heat?

(B62) Does any stewholder retail any victual or other necessity?

(B63) *Item, of those who falsely multiply gold and silver.*

(B64) *Item, prostitutes and their customers, with their procurers.*

---

[112] This question indicates that these were questions to be asked about the women, not directly of them, for clearly no one would be in a better position than the woman to answer the question "Is she with child?" not just "Is she known to be?"

(B65) *Item, of common scolds and causers of disputes among men, etc.*[113]

. . . .

(E1) Also, at the leet held the twenty-fourth day of April the thirtieth year of the reign of the king aforesaid [Henry VI, 1452], it was ordained that no person keeping any common hostel or stewhouse have or occupy any person for his ostler that before this time has been a soldier in the parts beyond the sea, under pain of forfeit of a hundred shillings unto the lord of the franchise as often as he does so.

(F1) Also, at the leet day held the last day of September the thirty-third year of the reign of the king abovesaid [1454], it was ordained that any constable or treasurer of the said franchise shall not keep any common woman to board or table at meat and drink under pain of forfeiting forty shillings to the lord.

(G1) Also, at the leet day held the seventh day of October, the twenty-fourth year of the reign of the king abovesaid [1445], it was ordained that no man keeping any common hostel or stewhouse shall disturb the common women of the same hostel from going to board and to have meat and drink where they wish, under the pain of six shillings eightpence to be paid to the lord as often as he so disturbs or hinders them or any of them, it being understood that they do not go to board within the common hostel wherein they are abiding, contrary to the old ordinance above rehearsed.

. . . .

(H1) Also, that no man's wife dwelling within the said lordship be brought into prison for scolding as the common women are, but that the constables yearly at the leets shall make their presentments of them, and they are to be inquired of by twelve men sworn for the king. This ordained at the leet day held the eleventh day of October in the thirty-sixth year of the king's reign above-said [1457] by twelve men sworn for the king.

[113] These last three items are given only in Latin rubrics.

MEDIEVAL WOMEN BOOK OWNERS:
ARBITERS OF LAY PIETY AND
AMBASSADORS OF CULTURE

SUSAN GROAG BELL

This boke is myne, Eleanor Worcester
An I yt lose, and yow yt fynd
I pray yow hartely to be so kynd
That yow wel take a letil payne
To se my boke is brothe home agayne.

[Inscription in a Book of Hours
belonging to the Duchess of Worcester,
ca. 1440][1]

Cultural changes of the later Middle Ages were characterized by a shifting relationship between the laity and traditional religious institutions leading eventually to the Protestant Reformation of the sixteenth century. The development of lay piety and the rise of vernacular literature were interrelated and were two of the more significant of these cultural changes. Expressions of lay piety have been attributed to a confluence of unsettling political, religious, demographic, and even climatological factors during the fourteenth and fifteenth centuries. The breakdown of

1. MS Harley, 1251, British Library, London.

This essay originally appeared in *Signs*, vol. 7, no. 4, Summer 1982.

institutional Christian unity, epitomized by the schism in the papacy, led concerned individuals to question the authority of the church. Repeated natural disasters (plagues and famines) created hysteria and an emotional need for religious support. This resulted in the widespread quest for spiritual certainties and a dramatic increase in recognized heresies in which women played a prominent part. The new spirit of inquiry was also evident in an upsurge of literacy and book ownership. Women's participation in this aspect of the new piety, however, has been overlooked.

I believe that the influence of laywomen in promoting cultural change can be assessed by looking at their special relationship to books, and I offer this article as a pioneer attempt to chart this area. Preliminary research suggests that book-owning women substantially influenced the development of lay piety and vernacular literature in the later Middle Ages. Women frequently bought and inherited religious as well as secular books, and spent considerable time reading them. In particular, as readers of vernacular literature, as mothers in charge of childhood education, as literary patrons who commissioned books and translations, and as wives who married across cultural and geographical boundaries, women had a specific and unique influence.

This essay is divided into three parts. The first deals with the facts of medieval laywomen's book ownership, including the acquisition of books through inheritance, commission, and patronage. The second part focuses on women's special relationship to books: (1) because of their inferior status in medieval Christian thought and their exclusion from scholarship and clerical life, women had an even greater need for the mental and spiritual nourishment offered by books than men did; (2) as

The earliest version of this essay was presented to the Associates of the Stanford University Libraries on February 13, 1977. I would like to express my gratitude to them and particularly to Byra Wreden, their most energetic founding member, for giving me the opportunity to think extensively about this topic and to present it to the public. The paper has also been read at the Medieval Conference at Western Michigan University, Kalamazoo, in 1978 and at the Berkshire Conference on Women's History at Vassar College in 1981. I must thank a large number of friends and colleagues for their encouragement, critical reading, help, and advice (not always followed). These include Charmarie Jenkins Blaisdell, Robert Brentano, George H. Brown, Kathleen Cohen, Stephen Ferruolo, Janet Gardiner, Michael Hackenberg, Maryanne Horowitz, Carolyn Lougee, JoAnn McNamara, Mavis Mate, Susan Noakes, Karen Offen, Mary O'Neil, Jean Preston, Nancy Roelker, Richard Rouse, Susan Stuard, Thomas Turley, and Margaret Williams. My greatest debt is to Natalie Davis, Joan Kelly, and Suzanne Wemple who, from the beginning and throughout much negative response, insisted that I continue to pursue this subject. I am grateful to Ronald L. Bell who has taught me how to photograph in the most difficult conditions and has a great share in my acquisition of hundreds of pictures representing medieval women as readers. Finally, I wish to thank the Djerassi Foundation under its Pamela Djerassi Visiting Artist program and friends in the Stanford community for the generous financial support that enabled us to pay the high price necessary to reproduce even a few of these illustrations in color. Acknowledgments to owners of the originals of these illustrations can be found at the end of the article.

mothers they were the primary teachers of the next generation and acquired books as teaching texts; and (3) untutored in Latin, they played an important role in the development of vernacular translations. The last section deals with the importance of women's relationship to books in the development of cultural change, including their influence on iconography as well as book content, and their role in the international movement of art and ideas through their ownership of books.

Patterns of Book Ownership

Many still regard the medieval book as a possession of the cloister or of the male of the family. Traditional textbooks and historiography emphasize medieval culture as a phenomenon associated with either monasticism or feudalism. Monks (rarely nuns) are depicted as scribes or as readers of religious books. Troubadours' tales of lovelorn knights sighing over unattainable ladies did not address these ladies' intellectual or spiritual pursuits, beyond a nod at Eleanor of Aquitaine as a patron of poets. Classic medieval historiography focuses on one of two male institutions—the church or chivalric feudalism. Even the authors of the most widely used recent Western civilization textbook, who are aware of the literacy of medieval laywomen, see those women as literary subject matter rather than as creators or users of books.[2] Scholarly articles concerned with book ownership also largely ignore women book owners. In her 1972 article on fifteenth-century books and their owners, Susan Connel observed, "Exceptional not for the contents, but for being found at all, are records of books owned by women."[3] Yet from the ninth to the fifteenth century, particularly in the latter portion of this period, there is solid evidence of individual European laywomen of the upper classes who read and owned books. Table 1 shows the numbers of laywomen identified by name to whom the ownership of at least one book can be traced. These women were identified in: (1) rare book library catalogs; (2) medieval wills; (3) medieval inventories of household goods or of libraries; and (4) dedications to patrons. The 242 women identified who lived between A.D. 800 and 1500 in no way constitute a representative sample, and their origins are geographically diverse—from Scotland in the north to Sicily in the south, and from the Atlantic in the west to Serbia and Poland in the east. The evidence, however, suggests that the number of laywomen book owners increased substantially by the fourteenth century and multiplied dramatically by the fifteenth century. This

2. Edward McNall Burns, Robert Lerner, and Standish Meacham, *Western Civilizations, Their History and Their Culture* (New York: W. W. Norton Co., 1980).

3. Susan Connel, "Books and Their Owners in Venice: 1345–1480," *Journal of the Warburg and Courtauld Institute* 35 (1972): 163–86, esp. 163.

Table 1

Identified European Laywomen Owning Books, A.D. 800–1500

				Number of Women, by Century				
Number of Books	Ninth Century	Tenth Century	Eleventh Century	Twelfth Century	Thirteenth Century	Fourteenth Century	Fifteenth Century	All Centuries
One book	3	3	6	9	12	41	76	150
2–10 books	1	…	5	6	3	6	29	50
11–50 books	…	…	…	…	…	7	13	20
51–200 books	…	…	…	…	…	1	13*	14
Unspecified number of books**	6	1	…	1	…	…	…	8
Total	10	4	11	16	15	55	131	242

*One of these women, Gabrielle de la Tour, owned 200 manuscripts in 1474. Nine others, indirect evidence indicates, may have owned between 51 and 100 manuscripts and printed books, although this cannot be positively documented.

**Each of these women was referred to as "owning books" or being "busy with her books," although no specific books could be traced to them.

preliminary exploration also strongly suggests that there may be rich, untapped evidence of women book owners between the ninth and fifteenth centuries. I wish to stress the tentativeness of all but the most general conclusions based on the figures shown in the table, and my awareness of the many avenues that are open for further work on this subject. That these women and their books originated in diverse European locations, while they often journeyed across the Continent and the English Channel on marriage, suggests important trends in the diffusion of medieval culture.

Various medieval developments facilitated the individual search for spiritual guidance through books. For example, M. T. Clanchy sees the shift "from memory to written record" that occurred over the eleventh and twelfth centuries as preparation for the growth of a literate mentality—for people ready to spend time and effort with books.[4] Technology also played an important part. The chimney flue and fireplace, developed in the early fourteenth century, provided safety and warmth indoors by allowing smoke to escape. The fireplace, substituting for the central open fire in large communal areas, also facilitated the development of smaller rooms which, together with the appearance of window glass, provided privacy for peaceful and comfortable indoor reading (pl. 2).[5] Further, by the thirteenth century eyeglasses became available: lenses to correct presbyopia, allowing the middle-aged to continue close work, had been introduced in the late thirteenth century, and concave lenses for myopia made reading a possibility for the nearsighted by the mid-fifteenth century.[6] Finally, cheaper production of manuscripts in the course of the fourteenth and fifteenth centuries and improvements in printing of small books by the end of the fifteenth century undoubtedly spurred the growth of individual book ownership and literacy.

Until the advent of incunabula (that is, the earliest printed books, published between 1453 and 1500), medieval books consisted of handwritten rolls or bound pages known as manuscripts. Most of these books owned by the laity that have survived were religious in content, covering sermons, selections of psalms (the Psalter), parts of the Old or the New

4. M. T. Clanchy, *From Memory to Written Record* (London: Edward Arnold, 1979).

5. LeRoy Joseph Dresbeck, "The Chimney and Fireplace: A Study in Technological Development Primarily in England during the Middle Ages" (Ph.D. diss., University of California, Los Angeles, 1971). The concept of reading by the fireplace in comfort is well illustrated by Robert Campin's Annunciation scene in the *Merode Altarpiece* (pl. 2); Campin's *Santa Barbara Reading*, at the Prado Museum, Madrid; or the *Woman Reading by the Fireplace While Stirring a Pot*, in Comestor, "Historia Scholastica," MS Reg. 15 D.I., British Library, London.

6. Vincent Illardy, "Eyeglasses and Concave Lenses in Fifteenth Century Florence and Milan: New Documents," *Renaissance Quarterly* 29 (Autumn 1976): 341–60. Also, E. Rosen, "The Invention of Eyeglasses," *Journal of the History of Medicine and Allied Sciences* 11 (January–April 1956): 13–46, and 183–218.

Testament, or a combination of all of these items in a "Book of Hours," which will be considered in detail later in this article.

While the actual cost of medieval books cannot be measured in modern terms, medieval women's accounts show not only that they bought books but that the books they bought were relatively expensive. We know, for example, that in the eleventh century the Countess of Anjou paid two hundred sheep; one bushel each of rye, wheat, and millet; and a quantity of marten pelts for one volume of the sermons of Haimo of Halberstadt.[7] But we do not know the circumstances of this exchange. The countess may well have accepted the book in part payment for the goods, or she may have made a donation to the monastery to which the scribe belonged and then received the book as an expression of thanks. Fourteenth-century accounts present less ambiguous figures. Thus, for example, the accounts of Mahaut, Countess of Artois, show that in 1308 she paid seven livres and ten sous for copies of the *Histoire de Troyes* and *Perceval;* in 1313 she paid eight livres for a copy of the *Consolations of Boethius.*[8] At about the same time, in 1324, the Countess of Clare paid a scribe eight shillings and his board and lodging for the four months it took him to copy the *Lives of the Church Fathers* for her.[9] It appears that the work of the scribe was a minor part of the total cost. Parchment and illuminations (especially those using gold leaf) largely accounted for the high cost of books. Mahaut, Countess of Artois, paid a female scribe, Maroie, twenty-five sous for writing a Book of Hours in 1312[10] and ordered an even less expensive Book of Hours costing six sous for her niece in 1320.[11] By the end of the fourteenth century, it was possible to acquire tracts, broadsides, and small devotional texts for less than one shilling in England.[12]

However, whether a book cost eight livres or six sous in the fourteenth century, it was still out of reach for anyone except the nobility or upper bourgeoisie. It would have taken a female agricultural laborer in southern France in the early fourteenth century about fourteen days to earn enough to buy the cheapest book purchased by the Countess of Artois between 1306 and 1330, and more than a year's daily labor to buy one of the more luxurious books. A male agricultural laborer could have purchased the cheaper book after seven days of labor, since he earned

7. See James Westfall Thompson, *The Medieval Library* (Chicago: University of Chicago Press, 1939), p. 640.

8. Jules Marie Richard, "Les Livres de Mahaut, Comtesse d'Artois et de Bourgogne, 1302–1329," *Revue des questions historiques* 40 (1886): 135–41.

9. Thompson, p. 645.

10. Richard, p. 237.

11. Ibid., p. 238. This may have been one of the mass-produced Books of Hours described by Dr. Pieter Obbema in a paper read at the University of California, Berkeley, in 1977 (Library, State University of Leiden, the Netherlands).

12. Malcolm B. Parkes, "The Literacy of the Laity," in *The Medieval World*, ed. D. Daiches (London: Aldus Books, 1973), p. 564.

twice as much as his female companions for the same type of work.[13] By the fifteenth century, however, it appears that such a book came within the reach of the lower bourgeoisie, some of whom were documented book owners.

Perhaps the clearest documentary evidence for the acquisition of books by medieval laywomen comes from bequests by fathers or husbands. It seems likely that the legator would be disposed to bequeath those items for which the legatee had expressed a preference in his lifetime. Such a bequest, then, may indicate a woman's preference for a book rather than some other object that might have been willed to her. Examples of the passage of books from fathers to daughters include the ninth-century Gisela, daughter of Louis the Pious, who inherited her husband's library. Her three daughters were also mentioned individually in the will as legatees of their father's books.[14] Three daughters of the Earl of Devon each inherited one book at his death in 1377.[15] Many of the most exquisite volumes of the Duc de Berry's collection were inherited or purchased by women from his estate in 1416. His famous *Très Riches Heures* was inherited by his daughter Bonne, the Countess of Savoy. Around 1504 Margaret of Austria carried it off to the Netherlands as part of the library she salvaged from her short marriage to the Savoyard Philibert le Bel.[16] Jean de Berry's younger daughter Marie, Duchess of Bourbonnais, specifically requested and received forty of the most prized books from his estate in 1417. These included nine religious books (four Bibles in French, one in Latin, a small Psalter, two copies of the *City of God* in French, two treatises on the Trinity, and at least one Book of Hours).[17] The duke's magnificent *Belles Heures*, now in the Cloisters Collection in New York, was purchased by his nephew's widow, Yolande of Aragon, Countess of Anjou and Queen of Sicily, for the vast sum of three hundred livres.[18] Anne of Brittany inherited the enormous library of her former royal husbands, Charles VIII and Louis XII, who had acquired large collections from Italian libraries through plunder and purchase during their Italian campaigns. But Anne had also collected and commissioned books of her own.[19] By the fifteenth century,

13. A male agricultural laborer in southern France during the same period earned between ten and fifteen deniers (or pence), double the daily earnings of a woman (Georges Duby, *L'Economie rurale et la vie de campagne dans l'occident medieval*, 2 vols. [Paris: Aubier, 1962], 2:562).

14. Thompson, p. 265.

15. Margaret Deanesly, "Vernacular Books in England in the Fourteenth and Fifteenth Centuries," *Modern Language Review* 15, no. 4 (1920): 349–58, esp. 351.

16. Jean Longnon, *The Très Riches Heures of Jean Duke of Berry* (New York: George Braziller, 1969), p. 25.

17. Leopold Delisle, *Recherches sur la Librarie de Charles V, Roi de France, 1337–1380*, 2 vols. (Amsterdam: G. Th. van Heusden, 1967), vol. 2.

18. Ibid., 2:239; and see also Millar Meiss, *The Belles Heures of Jean Duke of Berry* (New York: George Braziller, 1974), p. 267.

19. Ernest Quentin Bauchart, *Les Femmes bibliophiles de France*, 2 vols. (Paris: D. Morgand, 1886), 2:374–82.

the disposition of less expensive books written on paper in the vernacular was frequently mentioned in wills.[20]

Wills and testamentary settlements attest to women's inheritance of books from men. However, women's inheritance of books from women is of greater significance in this analysis of medieval women's book ownership. Solid evidence comes from the *Sachsenspiegel* [The Mirror of the Saxons], a collection of Saxon custom laws first compiled by Eike von Repgow in about 1215, which reflected the social mores of the previous three centuries. Book 1 of the *Sachsenspiegel* discussed the household items that were to be inherited by women. The "gerade" (or Roman "paraphernalia") were to be passed from mother to daughter; they included geese, small farm animals, beds, household furniture, linens, clothing, kitchen utensils—and books (pl. 3). The text enumerating items to be passed from woman to woman specifically includes all books connected with religious observance: "Alle Bücher die zum Gottesdienste gehöre [sic]."[21] An additional clause in the 1279 version that remained in later editions added that these devotional books were to be inherited by women, because it was women who were accustomed to reading them: "Bücher die Fraue phlege zu lese [sic]."[22]

The *Sachsenspiegel,* translated from its original Latin into German by Eike von Repgow, was frequently copied and recopied throughout the thirteenth and fourteenth centuries. It was also adapted for non-Saxon areas; the laws applied to wide geographic regions to the east of its birthplace near Magdeburg, reaching far into what is now the Soviet Union. The *Sachsenspiegel* clearly attests to women's role in the transmission of culture, especially lay religious culture, and to the different reading habits and religious observances of men and women.

Women's inheritance of books from women was not confined to *Sachsenspiegel* areas. A Dutch Book of Hours, inscribed with the names of six generations of women, indicates a Western European parallel to the *Sachsenspiegel* custom.[23] Examples in wills of women inheriting books from their mothers also exist.[24] However, testamentary evidence of

20. For example, in 1434 Agnes Paston, a member of the English wool trading gentry, inherited a religious tract, the "Prick of Conscience," from a burgess of Yarmouth. See Deanesly, p. 353. Occasionally a resigned notation in a will made it clear that since a woman had borrowed a book and kept it a very long time, she might as well inherit it permanently. The Countess of Westmorland, however, came close to losing her copy of the *Chronicles of Jerusalem* when King Henry V died before returning the borrowed book to her. See Thompson, p. 402.

21. Hans Hirsch, ed., *Der Sachsenspiegel* (Berlin and Leipzig: Walter de Gruyter, 1936), pp. 130–31.

22. Ibid., and see, e.g., the oldest dated *Sachsenspiegel* (May 7, 1295): Märta Äsdahl Holmberg, ed., *Der Harffer Sachsenspiegel* (Lund: C. W. K. Gleerup, 1957), p. 118.

23. *Books of Dyson Perrins*, 3 vols. (London: Sothebys Sales Catalogues, 1960), 3:98–100, esp. 98 (lot 139; present whereabouts of lot 139 unknown).

24. For example, Catherine Payenne inherited a *Book of Our Lady* from her mother Maroie. See Thompson, p. 265. Eleanor de Bohun, Duchess of Gloucester, died in 1399

women's bequests of devotional books to their daughters is scarce, which may suggest that such bequests were customary (as in the *Sachsenspiegel*) and required no documentation.

Fourteenth-century records increasingly reveal names of women who not only owned books but also collected numerous manuscripts of the same book and assembled libraries. Mahaut, Countess of Artois, an outstanding example, ordered thirty books of various types between 1300 and 1330.[25] The countess did not collect merely for the sake of owning luxurious and beautiful treasures. Her accounts indicate that she paid a large sum for a desk that enabled her to read in comfort. In the early years she preferred history and romances: the *Chronicles of the Kings of France, Perceval,* and the *History of Troy*. After the death of her only son in 1316, however, she ordered only books of religion and meditative philosophy. Between 1316 and 1328 she commissioned two different copies of the Bible, both in French; a two-volume Bible written on parchment and bound in red leather; two different copies of the *Lives of the Saints;* a roll of illuminated prayers in a silver container; three Books of Hours; the *Lives of the Church Fathers; Miracles of Our Lady;* and a French translation of Boethius's *The Consolations of Philosophy*.[26] Isabeau of Bavaria's accounts show that her thirty-three books included nine Books of Hours and sixteen other books of devotion.[27] She appointed Katherine de Villiers, one of her court ladies, to be in charge of her books. In 1393 Katherine de Villiers paid forty-eight sous to the trunk maker Pierre de Fou for a leather-covered wooden trunk with lock and key so that the books could be safely transported during Queen Isabeau's travels.[28] An inventory of Gabrielle de la Tour, Countess of Montpensier, found at her death in 1474, listed more than two hundred volumes according to their arrangement in cupboards and chests. At least forty of these were religious texts.[29]

---

and left a well-illustrated *Golden Legend* in French to her daughter Anne, and a "Book of Psalms" and other "Devotions," which she had used constantly, to her daughter Johanna. See *Collection of All the Wills Now Known to Be Extant* (London: Society of Antiquaries, 1780), pp. 182–83. Cicely, Duchess of York, left the *Life of Catherine of Siena,* the *Life of Matilda,* and a *Golden Legend* to her granddaughter Brigitta in 1495. See J. G. Nichols and J. Bruce, eds., *Wills from Doctors' Commons* (London: Camden Society, 1863), pp. 1–8.

25. Richard, pp. 235–41.

26. Ibid.

27. Valet de Viriville, "La Bibliothèque d'Isabeau de Bavière," *Bulletin du Bibliophile* 14 (1858): 663–87.

28. Ibid., p. 677.

29. A. de Boislisle, *Annuaire-Bulletin de la Société de l'Histoire de France,* vol. 17 (Paris: Société de l'Histoire de France, 1880), pp. 297–306. There were many other women collectors. Mechthild of Rottenburg, Countess of Palantine, who founded the universities of Tübingen and Freiburg, collected some one hundred books in the mid-fifteenth century. See Philipp Strauch, *Pfalzgräfin Mechthild in Ihren Literarischen Beziehungen* (Tübingen: H. Laupp, 1883). Jeanne d'Evreux received Jean Pucelle's now-famous Book of Hours at her marriage. Between 1325 and 1370 she ordered twenty devotional books,

As patrons of authors and of publishers, women also became interested in the new printing presses that sprang up in Western Europe late in the fifteenth century. Most women, as well as men, collectors still preferred the luxurious handwritten books, but some also bought or commissioned incunabula. Margaret of York and Isabella d'Este were notable for their connections with major early printers. While Duchess of Burgundy, Margaret of York encouraged William Caxton to translate from the French and later to print *The History of Troyes*—the first English book, printed in 1476. Caxton's preface describes how Margaret personally helped him through his initial difficulties with the translation and how she later rewarded him well.[30] However, Margaret also continued to collect artistic manuscripts of meditative religious philosophy, such as Boethius's *Consolations* (pl. 4). Isabella d'Este was one of many Italian women of the nobility and merchant aristocracy who, as children during the early humanist period, were taught to read Latin and Greek. As the Countess of Gonzaga at Mantua, she became an industrious collector of books. She commissioned the printing of many books, including in 1497 a copy of Jerome's *Letters*. Her regular correspondence with Aldus Manutius, the early Venetian printer and publisher, reveals that she was a determined collector who searched for rarities printed on the finest parchment, for special bindings, and for first copies of printing runs.[31] Isabella clearly encouraged high standards in both the textual and technical execution of Aldus' work.

By the end of the fifteenth century, then, women had become more frequent possessors of many types of books, which they had acquired

---

among them four breviaries and eight missals. See Paulin Paris, "Livres de Jehanne d'Evreux," *Bulletin du Bibliophile* (1838), pp. 492–94. Margaret, Duchess of Brittany, whose books were inventoried at her death in 1469, left eleven prayerbooks. See *Bibliothèque de l'Ecole des Chartes*, 5th ser., no. 3 (1862), p. 45. Bona of Savoy left forty books at her death in 1503, most of which were books of piety. See Theodor Gottlieb, *Die Ambrasser Handschriften: Beitrag zur Geschichte der Wiener Hofbibliothek* (Leipzig: M. Spirgatis, 1900), pp. 122–25, which is an inventory of Bona's books. Valentina Visconti, who had arrived in France with twelve books in her trousseau in 1388, left forty-three volumes at her death in 1408. At least twenty-six of these were books of devotion. See Pierre Champion, *La Librairie de Charles d'Orléans* (Paris: Honoré Champion, 1910), pp. 70–74. Marie de Clèves, second wife of the poet Charles d'Orléans, left about thirty books at her death in 1487; see Champion, pp. 115–17.

30. N. F. Blake, *William Caxton and His World* (London: André Deutsch, 1969).

31. See Julia Cartwright, *Isabella d'Este*, 2 vols. (London: John Murray, 1911). In 1501 Isabella ordered the first copies of the poems of Petrarch and Virgil to be printed by the Aldine press, and then had them bound for herself in Flanders. In 1505 she wrote to Aldus requesting books in Latin that he had printed in a small edition and added: "When you print other volumes, do not forget to print some on fine paper for us, and that as quickly as possible." Later that year she complained: "The four volumes which you sent us are pronounced by everyone who has seen them to be twice as dear as they ought to be. We have given them back to your messenger. . . . When you print some more, at a fair price and on finer paper, with more careful corrections, we shall be glad to see them." See Cartwright, 2:25, 27.

through inheritance, through outright purchase from scribes and book-sellers, and through commission.

Women and the Written Word

Throughout the Middle Ages, following the teachings of the early Christian fathers, women were exhorted to model themselves on biblical heroines. In order that they should do so, noble women were taught to read at an early age. "Let her take pattern by Mary," wrote Jerome.[32] Although Jerome had called on women to play an important part in Christianity, both in monastic communities and as mother-educators, the institutional clerical attitude throughout the following thousand years was ambivalent.[33] Women were excluded from established philosophical Christian debate and from the councils of the church. From the fourth to the twelfth century, however, women took a prominent part in monastic life and from the thirteenth century onward in the resurgence of institutional piety.[34] Women flocked to the leadership as well as the rank-and-file membership of female religious communities such as the Dominicans, the Poor Clares, and the Beguines. "Yet, the ecclesiastical attitude to women," writes Brenda Bolton, "was at best negative if not actively hostile."[35] In that same period, not surprisingly, women were also in the forefront of heretical movements.

Because women's public participation in spiritual life was not wel-comed by the hierarchical male establishment, a close involvement with religious devotional literature, inoffensive because of its privacy, took on a greater importance for women. Cicely, Duchess of York, repeated and commented upon her morning devotional reading to her supper com-panions at night.[36] Margaret Beaufort's confessor wrote that she had

32. Saint Jerome, *Selected Letters*, Loeb Classical Library (London: Putnam & Co., 1933), pp. 343–63. On women's education and learned women in the Middle Ages, see Patricia H. Labalme, ed., *Beyond Their Sex: Learned Women of the European Past* (New York: New York University Press, 1980); and Suzanne Wemple, *Women in the Frankish Kingdom* (Philadelphia: University of Pennsylvania Press, 1980).

33. See Clara Maria Henning, "Canon Law and Sexism," in *Religion and Sexism: Images of Woman in the Jewish and Christian Traditions*, ed. Rosemary Radford Ruether (New York: Simon & Schuster, 1974), pp. 267–91, esp. pp. 275–77.

34. Rosemary Rader, "Early Christian Forms of Communal Spirituality: Women's Communities," in *The Continuing Quest for God: Monasticism in Tradition and Transition*, ed. Daniel Durkin (Collegeville, Minn.: Liturgical Press, in press); Lina Eckenstein, *Woman under Monasticism* (Cambridge: Cambridge University Press, 1896); JoAnn McNamara, "Sexual Equality and the Cult of Virginity in Early Christian Thought," *Feminist Studies* 3, no. 3/4 (1976): 145–58; and Brenda M. Bolton, "Mulieres Sanctae," in *Women in Medieval Society*, ed. Susan M. Stuard (Philadelphia: University of Pennsylvania Press, 1976).

35. Bolton, p. 143.

36. J. Nichols, ed., *Collection of Ordinances and Regulations for the Government of the Royal Household* (London: Society of Antiquaries, 1790), pp. 37–39. See also, C. A. J. Armstrong, "The Piety of Cicely, Duchess of York: A Study in Late Medieval Culture," in *For Hilaire Belloc*, ed. Douglas Woodruff (London: Sheed & Ward, 1942).

"diverse books in French wherewith she would occupy herself [in meditation] when she was weary of prayer."[37] Of the 242 laywomen identified who owned books before 1500, 182, or 75 percent, included books of piety among their possessions (145, or 60 percent, owned books of piety written in the vernacular). In cases where only one book could be attributed to a woman, the book was almost invariably a devotional item. These books of piety included Gospels, Psalters, lives of the saints, and, in large part, Books of Hours.

A Book of Hours was composed of prayers to be read at certain hours of the day and included varied collections of biblical material and saints' lives. According to Victor Léroquais and J. M. L. Delaissé, the Book of Hours was the most popular devotional item developed in the twelfth century. Léroquais described the individual commissioning of Books of Hours as an "escape from Church control."[38] Delaissé contended that the development of Books of Hours implied "a greater concern for the layman by offering him devotional exercises with a more personal approach."[39] It seems likely that the laywoman would be even more interested in this escape from church control, which provided for private devotional reading; Books of Hours were traditional gifts for young girls learning to read and were often included in a bride's trousseau. Furthermore, the contents of Books of Hours could be varied to suit the individual.[40] Most Books of Hours consisted merely of standard versions of the written text embellished with a few ornamental letters. The more magnificent, however, were enhanced with colored illustrations. The margins were occasionally filled with frightening or charming vignettes of everyday life or with mythical and imaginary designs.

Catherine of Cleves's Book of Hours, made during the 1430s in the early years of her marriage to the Duke of Gelders, suggests that one item of devotional literature could cover the whole range of human experience. This book, although exceptionally luxurious, is a good example of the diverse material that might be packed into a Book of Hours and of the emphasis it could throw on women's duties and be-

37. John E. B. Mayor, ed., "Month's Mind of the Lady Margaret," in *The English Works of John Fisher*, Extra Series no. 27 of the Early English Text Society (London: H. Milford, 1876), p. 295.

38. Victor Léroquais, *Les Livres d'Heures*, 2 vols. (Paris: Protat Frères, 1927), vol. 1, introduction.

39. L. M. J. Delaissé, "The Importance of Books of Hours for the History of the Medieval Book," in *Gatherings in Honor of Dorothy E. Miner* (Baltimore: Walters Art Gallery, 1974), pp. 203–5.

40. There are innumerable examples of the varied compositions of Books of Hours. Some, including that given to Jeanne d'Evreux on her marriage in 1325, included the life of Saint Louis and the tale of his crusade to the Holy Land, which presumably was meant to impress upon the recipient the high achievements of the royal family into which she was marrying. See *The Hours of Jeanne d'Evreux* (New York: Metropolitan Museum of Art, 1957). Yolande of Aragon bought a Book of Hours from the estate of the Duc de Berry in 1416 that included an unusual story of how Saint Jerome was tricked into wearing a woman's dress by his envious companions. See Meiss, fol. 184v.

havior.[41] The Latin text was supplemented by hundreds of lively illustrations of Old and New Testament scenes and of saints' lives. One illustration showed the birth of Eve from Adam's rib, reminding the reader of woman's subordinate status.[42] Another pictured the crucifixion with Catherine, the book's owner, praying at one side of the cross, and the Virgin with milk spurting from her breast standing at the other, reminding Catherine of her expected duty as a merciful and chaste mother.[43] The illustrations reminded the reader of her duty as a charitable and competent economic manager by portraying her distributing alms, supervising the household production of food, supervising workers such as the dairy women, milking cows, and churning butter.[44] Finally, the book pointed to women's responsibility for their children's education, which included finding tutors for young sons; one of the illustrations showed a schoolmaster with his pupils.[45] It is clear that Books of Hours were much more than simple prayerbooks. They could bring spiritual consolation, edification, and perhaps peace of mind; they could also instruct, distract, and amuse. To dismiss medieval women's devotional books merely as books of piety would demonstrate a misunderstanding both of medieval women's need for spiritual nourishment and of the richly varied contents of their books of devotion.

During the fourteenth and fifteenth century, Books of Hours became the most popular devotional reading. While they were by no means exclusively women's books, women of the nobility and of the upper bourgeoisie were unlikely to be without one. The poet Eustache Deschamps, with whom Christine de Pizan corresponded in 1404 on the subject of men's injustice to women, satirized the ladies of the bourgeoisie for flaunting their luxurious Books of Hours. Queen Isabeau of France chose gold and azure for her daughter's Book of Hours in 1398, and Deschamps caught the brilliance of these colors in his satire of bourgeois women:

> A Book of Hours too must be mine
> Where subtle workmanship will shine
> of gold and azure, rich and smart
> Arranged and painted with great art
> Covered with fine brocade of gold,
> and there must be, so as to hold
> the pages closed, two golden clasps.[46]

41. John Plummer, ed., *The Hours of Catherine of Cleves* (New York: George Braziller, 1975).

42. Ibid., no. 88.

43. Ibid., no. 96.

44. Ibid., nos. 57, 93, 81, and 13.

45. Ibid., no. 56.

46. Translated in E. Panofsky, *Early Netherlandish Painting*, 2 vols. (Cambridge, Mass.: Harvard University Press, 1953), 1:68.

Deschamps was not interested in books as aesthetic objects.[47] But because organized medieval Christian ritual revolved around the greatest artistic treasures, perhaps laywomen, excluded from immediate contact with these treasures during Christian liturgical celebrations, wished their one item of devotion to be as beautiful as possible.

Book ownership probably had a second purpose as well. Beginning with Jerome in the fourth century, Christian moralists repeatedly declared that it was women's duty to concern themselves with the literary and moral upbringing of their children, and particularly of their daughters. Thus, in A.D. 403 Jerome wrote a letter to the mother of a newborn daughter:

> Have a set of letters made for her of boxwood or of ivory and tell her their names. . . . When she begins with uncertain hand to use the pen, either let another hand be put over hers or else have the letters marked on the tablet. . . . Let her every day repeat to you a portion of the Scriptures as her fixed task. . . . Instead of jewels or silk let her love the manuscripts of the Holy Scriptures, and in them let her prefer correctness and accurate arrangement to gilding and Babylonian parchment with elaborate decorations. Let her learn the Psalter first, with these songs let her distract herself, and then let her learn lessons of life in the Proverbs of Solomon. . . . Let her then pass on to the Gospels and never lay them down.[48]

Between 1247 and 1249 Vincent of Beauvais wrote a treatise entitled *De eruditione filiorum nobilium* (On the Education and Instruction of Noble Children) at the request of Queen Margaret of Provence, wife of Louis IX of France (Saint Louis). The queen's commission included details and some chapters specifically on the education of girls.[49] Vincent relied almost entirely on Jerome's letters concerning girls' education, insisting that by busying themselves in reading and writing, girls could escape harmful thoughts and the pleasures and vanities of the flesh.[50]

Some seventy years after Vincent of Beauvais's treatise, the Italian Francesco di Barberino wrote his *Reggimento e Costumi di Donna* (Rules and Customs for Ladies). Like Vincent of Beauvais and Jerome, Francesco di Barberino took it for granted that the mother would be concerned with children's primary and moral education. "And if it is

47. Daniel Poirion, *Le Poète et le Prince* (Paris: Presses Universitaires de France, 1965), p. 219. Deschamps's poetry was never assembled into an aesthetic object as were the collected poems of his contemporaries.

48. Saint Jerome, pp. 343–65.

49. The treatise was intended for the use of the royal children, Louis and his sister Isabelle. See A. Steiner, *Vincent of Beauvais "De eruditione filiorum nobilium,"* Medieval Academy of American Publications no. 32 (Cambridge, Mass: Medieval Academy of American Publications, 1938); and Astrik L. Gabriel, *The Educational Ideas of Vincent of Beauvais* (Notre Dame, Ind.: University of Notre Dame Press, 1956).

50. Steiner, pp. 172–76; Gabriel, p. 40.

fitting to her station," he wrote, addressing a mother on how to educate her daughter, "she should learn to read and write so that if it happens that she inherits lands she will be better able to rule them, and the acquired wisdom will help her natural wisdom. But here note well, that the person who teaches her be a woman or a person above suspicion, since too much intimacy is the occasion for many evils."[51]

The Italian-born author Christine de Pizan, who spent her life in Paris composing thirty books, among them a number of educational works, wrote in 1405 of the duties of women: "When her daughter is of the age of learning to read, and after she knows her 'hours' and her 'office,' one should bring her books of devotion and contemplation and those speaking of morality."[52]

In keeping with these prescriptions, many types of books—such as Psalters, Gospels, and educational treatises—were commissioned and used specifically for the education of children. First and foremost was the Psalter, or book of psalms, which often served as an alphabet book. Blanche of Castille followed the maxim of Jerome in ordering the now-famous Psalter, housed in the Morgan Library, to teach her son, the future Saint Louis, to read.[53] Isabeau of Bavaria's accounts show that she ordered a Book of Hours including psalms for her daughter Jeanne in 1398 and an alphabet Psalter, an "A,b,c,d, des Psaumes," for her daughter Michelle in 1403.[54] The girls were between six and seven years old when they received these books. A rare pictorial example of a medieval alphabet book can be found in a manuscript that belonged to the Countess of Leicester in about 1300, and is now in the Bodleian Library in Oxford.[55] One illustration shows the Virgin as a small girl holding her alphabet Psalter and standing within the shelter of her mother's ermine-lined cloak (pl. 5). "Put to my book, I had learned the shapes of the letters, but hardly yet to join them into syllables, when my good mother eager for my instruction arranged to place me under a schoolmaster," wrote the eleventh-century Guibert de Nogent, describing his mother's determination to educate him for the religious life.[56]

In choosing these books of instruction for their children, mothers pursued their individual interests and ideas. In 1395 Christine de Pizan

51. Francesco di Barberino, *Reggimento e Costumi di Donna* (Turin: Loescher-Chiantore, 1957), p. 344 and app., p. 15. Elsewhere in the book Francesco admitted that he sometimes thought girls should not be taught to read.

52. Christine de Pizan, *Le Trésor de la Cité des Dames* (Paris: Janot, 1536), fol. xxxiv. This book is sometimes known as "Le Livre des Trois Vertus" (The Book of Three Virtues).

53. Le Coy de la Marche, *St. Louis* (Tours: A. Mame et fils, 1887), p. 194; and Susan Noakes, "The Fifteen Oes, the 'Disticha Catonis' and Dick, Jane and Sally," *University of Chicago Library Bulletin* (Winter 1977), pp. 2–15.

54. Viriville, pp. 668–69.

55. MS Douce 231, fol. 3, Bodleian Library, Oxford.

56. John F. Benton, *Self and Society in Medieval France: The Memoirs of Abbot Guibert of Nogent* (New York: Harper & Row, 1970), p. 45.

wrote a book of moral instruction, the *Enseignements moraux,* for her son Jean. A copy of this manuscript, now in the British Library, belonged to Queen Isabeau of France, who may have read it to her own son, the Duc de Guienne.[57] Empress Eleanor of Portugal ordered a sumptuous copy of Pius II's *De Liberorum Educatione* for her son Maximilian I of Austria in 1466. Her interest in new artistic trends and ideas caused her to choose an Austrian scribe and an illuminator who followed the latest Italian ideas on art and architecture in their execution of the manuscript.[58]

It is important to consider as well the power and influence that women, as commissioners of educational volumes, were able to exercise in their choice of subject matter. By commissioning books and by instructing children they were able to influence both artistic and ideological developments. The choice between an alphabet Psalter, a Gospel, a Book of Hours, or an educational treatise may indicate steps in the growth of the student reader or the commissioner. The commissioner of a Book of Hours could choose whether to order Hours of the Cross, Hours of Saint Louis, or Hours of the Virgin. A patron could decide where to place the emphasis in the Testaments—whether, for example, to include the story of Solomon's judgment between the two mothers (emphasizing maternal unselfishness) or whether to include the story of Salome and the beheading of John the Baptist (demonstrating female power). A commissioner had to decide which vignettes of the numerous saints to include, and whether or not to concentrate on female saints' lives in a Book of Hours intended for a young girl.

Books of Hours were certainly used as works of primary education. As noted previously, Isabeau of Bavaria gave her daughter, Jeanne of France, a Book of Hours at the age of six.[59] This example of a commissioned Book of Hours ordered by a mother for her daughter, together

---

57. Maurice Roy, ed., *Oeuvres poetiques de Christine de Pisan,* 3 vols. (Paris: Société des Anciens Textes Français, 1886–96), 3:iv–ix, and 27–57; and MS Harley, 4431, British Library, London.

58. Franz Unterkircher, *A Treasury of Illuminated Manuscripts* (New York: G. P. Putnam & Sons, 1967), pp. 144–47. The primer ordered by Anne of Brittany for her six-year-old daughter Claude in 1505 begins with the alphabet and proceeds with the Lord's Prayer, the creed, grace to be said before meals, the story of the creation, and other short details from the New Testament. See M. R. James, *A Descriptive Catalogue of the Manuscripts in the Fitzwilliam Museum* (Cambridge: Cambridge University Press, 1895), item no. 159, pp. 356–59; and John Harthan, *Books of Hours and Their Owners* (London: Thames & Hudson, 1977), pp. 134–37. Gospels also may have served as reading exercises particularly for learning new languages; for example, English Gospels were especially translated for Anne of Bohemia when she arrived in London as a young bride in 1382. See Margaret Deanesly, *The Lollard Bible and Other Medieval Biblical Versions* (Cambridge: Cambridge University Press, 1922), p. 20. Vincent de Beauvais's educational treatise, *De eruditione filiorum,* was commissioned by Margaret of Provence, who also suggested what he should include for the education of her children, as we have seen.

59. Isabeau ordered the book from Perrin Cauvel in 1398, and paid eleven livres and four sous for it. Jeanne married at the age of six, like many aristocratic girls, and the book served educational purposes as well as being a wedding gift. See Viriville, p. 681.

with the existing evidence about women's involvement with devotional books and their concern for passing on their culture to the next generation, suggests that there may have been a general practice of mothers commissioning books as wedding gifts for their daughters. Through individual choice and collaboration with scribes and artists, women may have exerted a powerful influence on the contents of the Books of Hours handed on to their children.

Educating the young and choosing their reading material was but one aspect of medieval women's cultural contribution in their special relationship to books—another was their concern for vernacular translations. Most devotional literature in the early Middle Ages was written in Latin, a language accessible only to a small sector of lay society. Medieval laywomen's knowledge of Latin was even rarer than that of laymen, who were often taught Latin in preparation for a possible career in the church. Since women were expected to read devotional literature, it is not surprising that they played an important role as instigators of vernacular translations from the Latin and of vernacular literature in general. Nor is it surprising that an upsurge of such translations occurred in the twelfth and thirteenth centuries together with the development of Books of Hours.

Throughout the later Middle Ages, girls educated to remain outside the cloister did not learn a great deal of Latin.[60] The twelfth-century Abbess Herrad's *Garden of Delights,* with its captions in German and Latin, was intended to teach Latin to her novices who had been taught to read German at home.[61] Christine de Pizan, one of the most scholarly laywomen of the late fourteenth century, knew a minimum of Latin. She always read her sources in French or Italian translations and did not even advocate Latin for girls in her educational treatise for women, *The Book of Three Virtues.*[62] Bishop John Fisher, the confessor of Margaret Beaufort, mother of Henry VII, wrote soon after her death that although she was a woman who was always interested in scholarship, "ful often she complayned that in her youthe she had not gyven her to the understondynge of latyn wherein she had a lytell perceyvynge."[63] Latin "Instructions" written for an English layman of the early fifteenth century commanded him to "expound something in the vernacular which may edify your wife."[64] Knowledge of Latin also declined in English

60. Exceptions to this rule have been discussed in James Westfall Thompson, *The Literacy of the Laity in the Middle Ages* (Berkeley: University of California Press, 1920); and W. Wattenbach, *Das Schriftwesen im Mittelalter* (Leipzig: S. Hirzel, 1871).

61. On Herrad, see Eckenstein, pp. 238–55; and A. Straub and G. Keller, *Herrade de Landsberg, Hortus Deliciarum* (Strassburg: Trübner, 1901).

62. Susan Groag Bell, "Christine de Pizan (1364–1430): Humanism and the Problem of a Studious Woman," *Feminist Studies* 3, no. 3/4 (1976): 173–84, esp. n. 8.

63. Mayor, ed., p. 292.

64. William A. Pantin, "Instructions for a Devout and Literate Layman," in *Medieval Learning and Literature, Essays Presented to Richard William Hunt,* ed. J. J. G. Alexander and M. T. Gibson (Oxford: Clarendon Press, 1976), p. 400.

nunneries in the fourteenth and fifteenth centuries; thus girls sent to them for education were unlikely to learn the language. Similar evidence from the Netherlands demonstrates that the nuns in Dutch and Flemish convents read mostly in the vernacular.[65]

Other evidence of medieval women's lack of proficiency in Latin comes from the first rank of fifteenth- and sixteenth-century humanists. Exceptional male humanists, men like Leonardo Bruni, Vittorino de Feltre, Erasmus, Vives, Ascham, and Thomas More, all wanted girls to be as proficient in Latin as boys and advocated teaching Latin to girls as a new departure from the medieval norm.[66] It is clear that the first rank of humanists did not have their way, however. Walter Ong suggested that the grammar schools and institutions that proliferated from the six-teenth century onward used the study of Latin as a kind of male puberty rite that would make boys independent of women.[67] Clearly the pro-fessional institutions that required knowledge of Latin were disinclined to allow women the preparation needed to enter the professional occu-pations in the church, in academia, and in law and medicine.[68] Thus the aim of Renaissance teachers and humanists to revolutionize primary education by taking boys into institutions and by teaching girls Latin at home was frustrated.

Indeed, women had developed a vernacular home culture during the last four medieval centuries. By the mid-twelfth century, highborn women, still following patristic recommendations, had begun to commis-sion biblical and saintly themes in vernacular translations. An early example is Maud, first wife of Henry I of England, who commissioned the *Voyage of Saint Brendan* in Latin and later in a vernacular Anglo-Norman translation "for her ladies and maidens."[69] Also in the twelfth century, Eleanor of Aquitaine's daughter Marie of Champagne commis-sioned a French translation of Genesis from Evratt.[70] In 1328 Margaret

65. Eileen Power, *Medieval English Nunneries, 1275–1535* (Cambridge: Cambridge University Press, 1922); and Deanesly, *Lollard Bible,* p. 166.

66. W. H. Woodward, *Vittorino de Feltre and Other Humanist Educators* (Cambridge: Cambridge University Press, 1897), and *Studies in Education during the Age of the Renaissance, 1400–1600* (Cambridge: Cambridge University Press, 1906); Foster Watson, *Vives and the Renaissance Education of Women* (London: Edward Arnold, 1912); Ruth Kelso, *Doctrine for the Lady of the Renaissance* (Urbana: University of Illinois Press, 1956).

67. See Walter Ong, "Latin Language Study as a Renaissance Puberty Rite," *Studies in Philology* 56 (April 1959): 103–24.

68. Alison Klairmont Lingo, "The Rise of Medical Practitioners in Sixteenth Century France" (Ph.D. diss., University of California, Berkeley, 1980); and see Joan Kelly, "Did Women Have a Renaissance?" in *Becoming Visible: Women in European History,* ed. Renate Bridenthal and Claudia Koonz (Boston: Houghton Mifflin Co., 1977), pp. 137–64.

69. Mary Dominica Legge, *Anglo-Norman Literature and Its Background* (Oxford: Clarendon Press, 1963), p. 10.

70. Thompson, *Literacy of the Laity,* p. 144. In the same century, Aliz de Condé asked Sanson de Nanteuil to translate the "Proverbs of Solomon" into French (MS Harley, 4388, British Library, London); see also Karl Holzknecht, *Literary Patronage in the Middle Ages* (Philadelphia: University of Pennsylvania Press, 1923), p. 92. The Byzantine princess

of Provence commissioned John de Vignai to translate Vincent de Beauvais's *Speculum Historiale* (Mirror of History) almost as soon as her husband had commissioned the Latin composition of this work (pl. 6).[71] In
1382 Anne of Bohemia arrived in England to marry King Richard II,
bringing with her a New Testament written in Latin, Czech, and German.[72] Soon after her arrival she ordered an English translation of the
Gospels, presumably to learn English.[73]

Of the 186 laywomen who are known to have owned books between
1300 and 1500, 125 (or 67 percent) definitely owned vernacular translations. The actual percentage must have been higher; it is difficult to be
more precise because some of the books were described in inventories or
wills without indicating their contents: "a little book," "a bible,"
"Heures," or "a little book bound in green velvet." It is clear, however,
that by the mid-fifteenth century translations proliferated and, aided by
cheaper production, made reading and book owning a reasonable prop-
osition for a less wealthy segment of society, one not proficient in Latin.
This segment included a good proportion of women.[74]

Women, Books, and Cultural Influence

The significance of medieval women's book owning is apparent in
two other areas. First, women influenced the shaping of iconography in
books, thereby offering new images of womanhood. Second, women

---

Theodora Comnena (niece of the famous author Anna Comnena), who married the German Henry Jasomirgott and with him established an important literary court in Vienna,
ordered a German translation of the *Song of Roland* in about 1170, perhaps with the
intention of learning the German language. See William C. McDonald, *German Medieval
Literary Patronage from Charlemagne to Maximilian I* (Amsterdam: Rodopi, 1973), pp. 98–100.
In the 1290s, Jeanne de Navarre commissioned a French translation of the *Speculum
Dominarum*, which described ethics for women and was written by her confessor. See Karl
Wenck, *Philip der Schöne von Frankreich, Seine Persönlichkeit und das Urteil der Zeitgenossen*
(Marburg: Koch, 1905), p. 19. Mahaut, Countess of Artois, ordered the *Lives of the Saints*
and a Bible translated into French in 1328 (see Richard, p. 239). Clemence of Hungary, the
second wife of King Louix X, left thirty-nine books at her death in 1328; twenty-four were
written in French and one of them in both English and French. See *Bulletin du bibliophile*, 2d
ser., no. 18 (1836–37): 561–63.

71. See L. Delisle, "Exemplaires royaux et princiers du Miroir historial," *Gazette ar-
chéologique*, vol. 11 (1886), pl. 16.

72. Deanesly, *Lollard Bible*, p. 248.

73. Ibid., pp. 278–79, and p. 20; Anne's sister Margaret, having benefited from
Anne's experience in a foreign land, left home as a child bride in 1388 to marry the king of
Poland, carrying with her a Psalter in Latin, German, and Polish.

74. Margaret Deanesly stressed the increasing ownership of vernacular books in England in the late fourteenth and the fifteenth centuries. She is not explicitly concerned
about women's book owning, but it is significant that twenty-nine of her examples are
women book owners. See Deanesly, "Vernacular Books," pp. 349–58.

acted as international ambassadors of cultural change through their distribution of books over a broad geographic area.[75]

Medieval devotional manuscripts offer innumerable iconographic portraits of reading women. The woman book owner herself may be shown in a variety of poses with her book: kneeling before the Virgin and Child; standing by the side of the Cross; or kneeling at a prie-dieu, like the Duchess de Berry in her husband's famous *Belles Heures*. Or the new owner might be portrayed in the margin of a manuscript received as a wedding gift long after it was first produced, so that the difference in artistic style and fashion of her dress indicate the years gone by since the manuscript was written (pl. 7).[76] A most delightful portrait of a woman book owner is that of Mary of Burgundy reading her book while surrounded by her lapdog and her jewels. She sits in the window overlooking a magnificent gothic church, in which another replica of herself adores a majestic Virgin and Child (pl. 12).

Portraits of the Virgin Mary herself surrounded by books provide yet another ingenious artistic confirmation of women's close involvement with devotional literature. Uncountable paintings and sculptures of the Annunciation depict Mary as an avid reader. Mary had been portrayed with a book as early as the eleventh century, but by the fourteenth and fifteenth centuries books were common in Annunciation iconography (pl. 7).[77] The Master of Vissi Brod in a fourteenth-century Bohemian Annunciation piece represented two books on the Virgin's delicate desk (pl. 9). Robert Campin's Virgin in the *Merode Altarpiece* sits in a comfortable Flemish interior against a fireplace, near a table with two books (pl. 2). The Virgin in the *Belles Heures* of the Duc de Berry kneels by a lectern that harbors three books (pl. 10). The altarpiece of Sainte Marie Madeleine in Aix-en-Provence shows the Virgin kneeling beside a circular stand holding five books, and the Virgin in Catherine of Cleves's manuscript is also surrounded by five books.[78]

The scene is, of course, based on the common literature of the era—the Gospels, the "Golden Legend" of Jacobus de Varagine, and the apocryphal gospel of Pseudo-Matthew. Yet in none of these is there any

75. A third area for discussion might be women as patrons of new genres of literature—e.g., twelfth-century love poetry and romances, and books praising women that developed in the mid-fourteenth century. These important developments, however, are outside the scope of this study, which concentrates on women's role in the development of lay piety and the transmission of religious culture. See Herbert Grundmann, "Die Frauen und die Literatur im Mittelalter," *Archiv für Kulturgeschichte* 26 (1936): 129–61.

76. Millard Meiss, *French Painting in the Time of Jean de Berry* (New York: George Braziller, 1975), p. 109.

77. Gertrud Schiller, *Iconography of Christian Art,* trans. Janet Seligman, 2 vols. (Greenwich, Conn.: New York Graphic Society, 1971), 1:42.

78. Hans H. Hofstatter, *Art of the Late Middle Ages* (New York: Harry N. Abrams, 1968), p. 182; and Plummer, ed., no. 10.

reference to reading or even to prayer at the time of the Annunciation.[79] Mary is described as fetching water from the well or weaving, if any activity is described at all. Clearly, the artists themselves conceived Mary with books, without benefit of written tradition. Nor did they confine themselves to the scene of the Annunciation. The Virgin reads while two midwives prepare for her confinement at Bethlehem (pl. 11); she reads while recuperating from childbirth, relegating Joseph to rocking the baby (pl. 1); or while sitting in the garden watching the children at play.[80] She reads on the donkey while Joseph carries the babe during their flight into Egypt (pl. 8). She is even shown as the woman in Revelations who escapes the seven-headed monster by flying into the wilderness clutching her book, and then peacefully settles with her book in sanctuary (pl. 13).

Students of iconography suggest that the book in Christian art symbolizes the Word (that is, Christ);[81] that at the time of the Annunciation Mary was reading the Old Testament prophesy in Isaiah, "Behold a virgin shall conceive and bear a son, and shall call his name Emmanuel";[82] or that Mary was seen as a symbol of wisdom, learned in the law of God, because only such a woman would be worthy to bear His son.[83] These views may explain the symbolism involved, but artists' insistence on portraying the most significant medieval female ideal, the Virgin Mary, as a constant reader was surely based on the reality of their patrons' lives. It suggests that women were not only acquiring books but spending much of their time perusing them. The developing association of the Virgin with books in fact coincides with the rise in numbers of women book owners during the fourteenth and fifteenth centuries. Saint Anne teaching the Virgin to read, a symbol of the mother as her daughter's teacher, is also more frequently depicted in fourteenth- and fifteenth-century Books of Hours (pl. 5).[84] Artists using the circumstances of their patrons' involvement with books to change iconography

79. See, e.g., Caxton's translation of the *Golden Legend*, reprinted as *The Golden Legend, or Lives of the Saints by William Caxton* (London: J. M. Dent, 1900), 3:97–101; or M. R. James, *The Apocryphal New Testament* (Oxford: Clarendon Press, 1924), p. 74.

80. *Virgin in the Garden of Paradise*, Städesches Kunstinstitut, Frankfurt (reproduced in Hofstatter, p. 163); and Plummer, ed., no. 97.

81. André Grabar, *Christian Iconography: A Study of Its Origins* (Princeton, N.J.: Princeton University Press, 1968).

82. Isaiah 7:14.

83. Schiller, 1:42.

84. The Bodleian collection in Oxford has at least twenty such examples: MS Douce, 237, fol. 9v; MS Liturg., 401, fol. 30v; MS Rawl., D. 939; MS Astor, A. 18, fol. 82, (i) and (ii); MS Astor, A. 17, fol. 154v; MS Keble, fol. 148v; MS 311, fol. 100; MS Douce, 268, fol. 31; MS Rawl. Liturg., d. 1., fol. 100v; MS Add., A. 185, fol. 65v; MS Buchanan, E. 8, fol. 144v; MS Lat. Liturg., fol. 2, fol. 104v; MS Auct., D. Inf. 2.13, fol. 41v; MS Canon. Liturg., 178, fol. 101v; MS Auct., D. Inf. 2.11, fol. 51v. In an article on miniatures representing reading in late medieval manuscripts, Frank Olaf Büttner points out that the act of reading represents transmission of religious ideas, and that the user of the manuscript recognized "a mirror image of himself" in the reading motif. It is interesting, however, that while

thus produced a new symbolism. This symbolism showing the Virgin as a constant reader in turn added respectability to laywomen occupying themselves with books.

The most general significance of women's book owning emerges in conjunction with medieval marriage customs, which forced women to move from their native land to their husbands' domains. Medieval marriage bestowed upon women a role of cultural ambassador that it did not bestow upon men who remained on their native soil. It would have been pointless in this analysis to consider, for example, only Frenchwomen's books, or Italian or German women's books. Medieval noblewomen, more often than not, changed their cultural milieu with marriage. Their books are evidence of the influential role these women played as international disseminators of literary, artistic, and religious ideas. Arranged marriages, which forced young girls—indeed, child brides—to travel widely to foreign countries, underscore the importance of a familiar book. The accustomed devotional volumes could teach a new language, minimize the strangeness of new experiences, and comfort the homesick. In addition, the radius of a book's exposure was fairly wide. Noble households were extensive and included many members. Books were often borrowed and sometimes were lost, finding their way to new owners.

There are numerous examples of women book owners who functioned as cultural ambassadors throughout medieval centuries. In 1051 Judith of Flanders married Tostig, Earl of Northumbria. As a widow she later married the German Welf of Bavaria. She brought at least two large English Gospels, illustrated for her in Winchester, to her German marriage.[85] Their style was adopted in the Bavarian scriptorium at Weingarten Abbey where Judith retired in her old age. One of these Gospels, bound in thick wooden boards, covered with plates of silver, and encrusted with jewels, is now a treasure of the Morgan Library in New York.[86] Another became Judith's wedding gift to her new daughter-in-law, Countess Matilda of Tuscany, in 1086.[87] Thus, the "Winchester style" traveled from England, to Bavaria, and thence to Tuscany. The "Melissenda Psalter," one of the prized possessions of the British Library, was also an eleventh-century wedding gift.[88] Melissenda, heiress of the king of Jerusalem, married the crusader Fulk the Young,

---

every one of Büttner's many examples portrays either a reading Virgin Mary or a real medieval woman book owner, he does not develop the connection between his examples and females as actual readers and owners of books. See Frank Olaf Büttner, "Mens divina liber grandis est: Zu einigen Darstellungen des Lesens in Spätmittelalterlichen Handschriften," *Philobiblion* 16 (1972): 92–126, and "Noch Einmal: Darstellungen des Lesens in Spätmittelalterlichen Handschriften," *Scriptorium* 27 (1973): 60–63.

85. Meta Harrsen, "The Countess Judith of Flanders and the Library at Weingarten Abbey," *Papers of the Bibliographic Society of America* 24, pts. 1/2 (1930): 1–13.

86. MS 708, Pierpont Morgan Library, New York.

87. MS BB 437, Monte Cassino Library; and see Harrsen.

88. MS Egerton, 1139, British Library, London.

thereby bringing him the kingdom of Jerusalem. The carved ivory binding and Byzantine figures of her Psalter are part of the artistic heritage that returned with the crusaders from east to west.

By the end of the fourteenth century, women carried manuscripts of diverse languages and subject matter in their trousseaux. Anne of Bohemia brought Czech and German Gospels to England.[89] Isabelle of France, sister of book collectors Charles V and Jean de Berry, was married off to the rich Jean Galeazzo Visconti in 1360 in order to raise the ransom for her captive father. Isabelle carried her French books to Milan. A generation later she sent her daughter Valentina Visconti back to France to marry Louis d'Orléans, sending with her a trousseau containing twelve books, many of Italian origin. All but one of Valentina's books were prayerbooks and Psalters.[90] In the second half of the fifteenth century, Yolande of France brought three coffers of books when she married Amadeo of Savoy.[91] By the end of the fifteenth century brides brought romances, grammars, and educational treatises as well, but devotional works remained a part of the literary trousseau. Giovanna di Medici took a Mass book decorated with miniatures and silver clasps when she married Bernardo Rucellai in 1466.[92] Anna Sforza, who married Alphonso d'Este as the predecessor of Lucrezia Borgia, brought the De Sphaera, a fashionable humanist treasure of the Sforza library, to Ferrara, but she also brought a missal.[93] When Hyppolita Sforza married the son of the king of Naples in 1465, her trousseau contained twelve books. She carried Cicero's treatise on old age, De Senectute, which she had copied herself as an exercise in writing, together with a variety of other Latin books. The nucleus of her library, however, consisted of the obligatory books of piety: the lives of saints, in Italian translation; a luxurious copy of Augustine's City of God; and a New Testament in Greek, demonstrating Hyppolita's fashionable humanist education.[94] As an eager book collector she stopped to buy manuscripts on her wedding journey from Milan to Naples.[95]

89. Deanesly, Lollard Bible, p. 20.

90. "Inventaire des Livres Apportés en France par Valentine de Milan et Compris dans sa Dot (1388)," in Pierre Champion, La Librairie de Charles d'Orleans (Paris: Honoré Champion, 1910), pp. lxix–lxx.

91. A. Cim, Le Livre, 2 vols. (Paris: E. Flammarion, 1923), 2:372.

92. From the reminiscences of Giovanni Rucellai, cited in Yvonne Maguire, The Women of the Medici (New York: Dial Press, 1955), p. 69.

93. Elisabeth Pellegrin, La Bibliothèque des Visconti et des Sforza, Ducs de Milan, au XVe Siècle (Paris: Institut de recherche et d'histoire des textes, 1955), p. 69.

94. Ibid., p. 67.

95. Ibid. Hyppolita Sforza's books are now divided among Valencia, Milan, Paris, and London. Another member of the family, Bianca Maria Sforza, became Maximilian I's second wife in 1494, and brought eight books in her trousseau from Milan to Austria. At least five of these were devotional volumes. See Pellegrin, p. 69.

Anne of Bohemia exemplifies not only the relationship of these ambassadorial brides to their books, but also to the cultural pursuits of those living on her husband's domain. Anne married Richard II of England in 1382—in the age of Chaucer and Wycliffe. She arrived in England not only with her books but with Bohemian book illustrators. The influence of Anne's books and illustrators on English art is clearly established.[96] The *Liber Regalis* which documents the coronation of Richard and Anne, and which was used for English coronation ceremonies until the time of Elizabeth I, exemplifies the artistic influence Anne brought from Bohemia. The book is illustrated in the style of Bohemian art and is quite different from any previous English work (pl. 14, and compare pls. 9 and 11).

While Bohemian painters revitalized English art in the late fourteenth century, Anne herself influenced English literature. Critical of Chaucer's *Troilus and Criseyde,* in which he emphasized female infidelity, she inspired the poet by her patronage, which resulted in *The Legend of Good Women:* "And when this book is made / Give it the Queen, on my behalf / at Eltham or at Sheene," Chaucer wrote in the prologue.[97]

But it was in religious matters that the Anglo-Bohemian connection had the greatest impact. Anne came from the *Sachsenspiegel* domain. Her mother was the fourth of her father's wives, three of whom had come from areas served by *Sachsenspiegel* law. Anne's father, the Emperor Charles IV, had founded Prague University and encouraged a free circle of preachers and an impressive production of religious literature written in both local vernaculars, Czech (Bohemian) and German. His daughter clearly took this freedom of reading vernacular biblical texts for granted. When she arrived in London the English reformer John Wycliffe pointed to her in his pleas to legitimize the English translation of the Bible.

Wycliffe's aim was considered heretical by church officials. They objected to translations from the Latin, claiming that untrained minds would misinterpret the Bible and damage Christian principles; no doubt they feared that their own authority would be undermined. In a tract of 1383, a year after Anne had arrived in London, Wycliffe wrote:

> It is lawful for the noble queen of England [Anne] the sister of the Emperor, to have the gospel written in three languages, that is in Czech and in German and in Latin; and it would savor of the pride

96. See Margaret Rickert, *Painting in Britain: The Middle Ages* (London: Penguin Books, 1954), p. 152; and Sabrina Mitchell, *Medieval Manuscript Painting* (New York: Viking Press, 1965), p. 37. Note, however, that many historians still cite Anne as importing only fashions in clothing from Bohemia to England.

97. Samuel Moore, "The Prologue of Chaucer's 'Legend of Good Women' in Relation to Anne and Richard," *Modern Language Review* 7 (June–October 1912): 488–93, esp. 490.

of Lucifer to call her a heretic for such a reason as this! And since the Germans wish in this matter reasonably to defend their own tongue, so ought the English to defend theirs.[98]

Anne's uninhibited ownership of multilingual Gospels in England was remarked on even in her funeral oration at Westminster, in 1394. Archbishop Arundel spoke to hundreds who mourned the popular queen; she had died of a fever after only twelve years of marriage at the age of twenty-eight. He praised Anne for her biblical studies, and for requesting that he critically examine the text of her new English translation and commentaries on the Gospels. He commended her as a woman who was "so great a lady, and also an alien, and would so lowlily study in virtuous books."[99] Moreover, the cultural exchange that Anne initiated from Prague to London also encouraged the reverse: the influence of Wycliffe and other English reformers on Hussite Bohemia accelerated.[100]

Writing of the sixteenth-century Reformation, Roland Bainton states: "The Reformation had a profound influence on women and they in turn upon the church. The translation of the Scriptures into the vernaculars and their dissemination through the printing press stimulated literacy and the will to read."[101] I would suggest that we may find it was women who had a profound influence in bringing about the Reformation by their collective involvement in heresies and by their individual involvement with religious literature in the preceding centuries. Scholars agree that one of the key issues in reformist movements throughout the late Middle Ages was the public's greater familiarity with the teaching of the New Testament—a familiarity obviously deepened by the spread of literacy and the invention of printing, but first and foremost by the translation of scriptural texts into the vernacular. Women played an important role in teaching, in translating, and in loosening the hierarchical bonds of church control through their close and private relationship to religious books.

Medieval laywomen's ownership of devotional books, encouraged by legal convention and marriage customs, increased proportionately with the advent of technical aids to literacy, with the growth of dependence on the written word, and with the disintegration of Christian unity in this period. Because women were not able to take part in the ecclesiastical authority structure of spiritual life, they depended more heavily on

98. John Wycliffe, "De triplici vinculo amors," cited in Deanesly, *Lollard Bible*, p. 248.

99. MS 333, fols. 26–30b, Trinity College Library, Cambridge, England; reprinted in Deanesly, *Lollard Bible*, pp. 278–91. Deanesly also cites the 1405 text in the English. See *Lollard Bible*, p. 445.

100. Ottocar Odlozilik, "Wycliffe's Influence on Central Europe," *Slavonic and East European Review* 7, no. 21 (March 1929): 634–48.

101. Roland H. Bainton, *Women of the Reformation: In Germany and Italy* (Minneapolis: Augsburg Publishing House, 1971), p. 14.

books, especially vernacular books. In turn, in their choice of books used as teaching aids, mothers could influence the lives of their daughters. In times when a single book was often the only literary possession, such a choice was indeed of paramount importance.[102]

Medieval women's book ownership reveals a linear transmission of Christian culture and the development of a mother-daughter or matrilineal literary tradition that may also have influenced later generations. The evidence of books chosen by mothers and brought across Europe by their daughters reveals a geographically widespread transmission of culture. These young brides (and widows on remarriage) brought their books across regional and national boundaries, often transmitting artistic style, specific content, and ideas. Economic, political, and diplomatic pressures forcing young girls and widows to traverse the Christian world for arranged marriages may have propelled women's books haphazardly from one cultural milieu to another. But the content of these books was surely not arbitrary; rather, it reflects conscious choice on the part of mothers in shaping their daughters' futures. It would repay us to look more closely at the contents of pre-Reformation devotional books, especially the Books of Hours. These books express something of the medieval mother-child relationship—particularly the mother-daughter relationship—and of the values and ideals dispersed throughout Europe by medieval women.

Center for Research on Women
Stanford University

Acknowledgments and Details of Illustrations

Plate 1. Virgin reading while Joseph rocks the Babe. *Book of Hours.* Walters Art Gallery, Baltimore. MS 10.290, fol. 69.

Plate 2. The *Merode Altarpiece.* Metropolitan Museum of Art, New York.

Plate 3. The "Gerade," *Sachsenspiegel.* Sächsische Landbibliothek, Dresden. MS 32.

Plate 4. Margaret of York, receiving manuscript. Boethius, *Consolatione.* Universitätsbibliothek, Jena. MS El. f. 85; fol. 13v.

102. These medieval developments foreshadow the close involvement of women in the Reformation. See Nancy L. Roelker, "The Role of Noblewomen in the French Reformation," *Archive for Reformation History* 63, no. 2 (1972): 168–95; Bainton (ibid.), and Roland H. Bainton, *Women of the Reformation: In France and England* (Boston: Beacon Press, 1973); Patrick Collinson, "The Role of Women in the English Reformation Illustrated by the Life and Friendships of Anne Locke," *Studies in Church History* 2 (1965): 258–72; Charmarie Jenkins-Blaisdell, "Renée de France between Reform and Counter-Reform," *Archive for Reformation History* 63, no. 2 (1972): 196–226; Miriam V. Chrisman, "Women of the Reformation in Strasburg 1490–1530," *Archive for Reformation History* 63, no. 2 (1972): 143–67; and Natalie Zemon Davis, *Society and Culture in Early Modern France* (Stanford, Calif.: Stanford University Press, 1975), esp. chap. 3, p. 76.

PLATE 1.—The Virgin reads while Joseph rocks the swaddled Babe. Northern French. Early fifteenth century.

PLATE 3. — The "Gerade" in the *Sachenspiegel* Law.
German, ca. 1350.

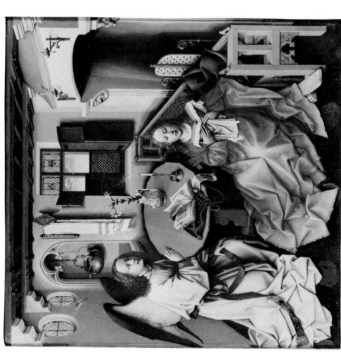

PLATE 2.—"Annunciation" with two books in a Flemish interior,
showing chimney fireplace, windows. Flemish, ca. 1425–28.

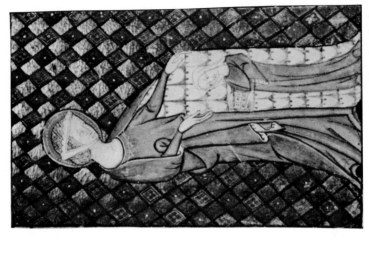

PLATE 5.—Saint Anne teaching the Virgin, who is holding an alphabet book, to read. English, ca. 1300.

PLATE 4.—Scribe presenting *Consolations of Philosophy* to Margaret of York. Flemish, 1476.

PLATE 7.—"Annunciation" with one book. French, ca. 1382. Later owner reading in margin painted into manuscript in 1438.

PLATE 6.—King Louis IX commissioning the *Mirror of History* in Latin, while his queen, Margaret of Provence, commissions a French translation of the same work. French, ca. 1333.

PLATE 8.—The Virgin reads on the donkey, while Joseph carries the Babe on their flight into Egypt. Flemish, ca. 1475.

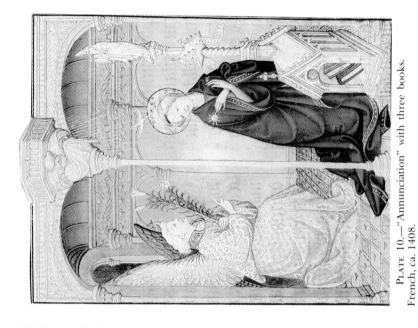

PLATE 10.—"Annunciation" with three books. French, ca. 1408.

PLATE 9.—"Annunciation" with two books. Bohemian, ca. 1350

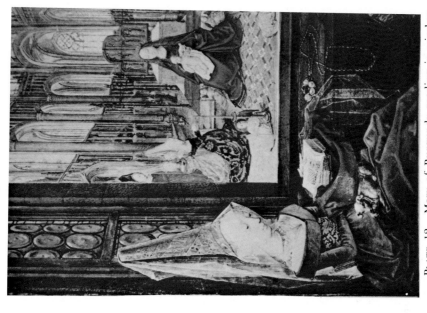

PLATE 12.—Mary of Burgundy reading in window overlooking gothic church. Flemish, ca. 1467–80.

PLATE 11.—The Virgin reads while midwives prepare for her delivery. East German or Bohemian, 1406.

PLATE 14.—Coronation of Richard II of England and Anne of Bohemia. English, ca. 1382.

PLATE 13.—The woman escaping a seven-headed monster carrying her book to read in sanctuary. "Revelations," Rhenish, ca. 1320.

Plate 5. Saint Anne teaching the Virgin to read from an alphabet book. *Psalter*. Bodleian Library, Oxford. MS Douce 231, fol. 3.

Plate 6. King Louis IX and Queen Margaret commission the *Mirror of History* and its French translation. *Mirroir Historial*. Bibliothèque nationale, Paris. MS Fr. 316, fol. 1.

Plate 7. "Annunciation" and later owner painted into margin. *Très Belles Heures de Notre Dame*. Bibliothèque nationale, Paris. MS Nouveau Acquisition Latin 3093, fol. 2.

Plate 8. Virgin reading on donkey. *Book of Hours*. Bibliothèque Royale Albert 1er, Brussels. MS IV 315, fol. 105v.

Plate 9. "Annunciation," Master of Vissi Brod. National Gallery, Prague.

Plate 10. "Annunciation" in *Belles Heures of Jean de Berry*. Metropolitan Museum of Art, New York. Fol. 30.

Plate 11. Virgin preparing for childbirth. *Missal*. Bayerische Staatsbibliothek, Munich. MS clm 14.045, fol. 41v.

Plate 12. Mary of Burgundy at the window of a Gothic church. *Book of Hours*. Bildarchiv der Oesterreichischen Nationalbibliothek, Wien. Cod. 1857, fol. 14v.

Plate 13. Woman escaping monster. *Apocalypse of St. John the Apostle*. Metropolitan Museum of Art, New York. Fol. 21v.

Plate 14. Coronation of Richard II and Anne of Bohemia. *The Liber Regalis*, Westminster Abbey Library, London. MS 38, fol. 20. By permission of the Dean and Chapter of Westminster.

THE LADIES' TOURNAMENT:
MARRIAGE, SEX, AND HONOR IN THIRTEENTH-CENTURY GERMANY

SARAH WESTPHAL-WIHL

Courtly literature rarely portrays women celebrating community
with one another. The erotic lyric displays the affects of a single
subject who is usually male. In the Arthurian romance, communities
are peripheral to the narrative that focuses on the hero. They generally arise through extraordinary or sorrowful circumstances: they
are neither desired by nor beneficial to the women who inhabit
them. The ladies of Chrétien de Troyes's "Pesme Avanture," for
example, are prisoners, exchanged as tribute for the life of their
young king. They live in poverty and starvation, producing fabrics
of silk and gold for their masters' profit. Their wretched community
of suffering is dissolved by the hero Yvain, who frees them from
their stockade and returns them to their lands. In an adaption of
another story by Chrétien, *Erec et Enide*, the German poet Hartmann von Aue describes a community of eighty mourning widows
wearing identical black gowns and sharing a common grief. Their

A Research Time Stipend during 1986–87 from the Social Sciences and Humanities Research Council of Canada enabled me to write this article. It was greatly
improved by the thoughtful comments of the associate editors and two anonymous
readers at *Signs*. Thank you to all of them.

This essay originally appeared in *Signs*, vol. 14, no. 2, Winter 1989.

community of suffering is dissolved through hero Êrec's courage and King Arthur's tact and munificence. Similarly, Wolfram von Eschenbach includes an episode in *Parzival* about four queens and four hundred ladies who are imprisoned by the vindictive enchantments of a castrated sorcerer. The sorrow of their condition lies not only in their loss of freedom but also in their total isolation from the four hundred knights held captive at the same place. Like those in the other stories, these women are liberated by a hero, Gâwân, who reunites all of the now freed knights and ladies by arranging a dance. The women's community of suffering quickly dissolves once they are no longer isolated from men.[1]

The Ladies' Tournament depicts a community of women who sustain their bond with one another. As in the romance, this community comes into existence because extraordinary events have called the men away; but the men's absence elicits pleasure rather than sorrow. As in the previous examples, there is an injustice, a fault in the social fabric, that needs to be corrected, but here the women themselves initiate the change, not a heroic knight like Yvain, Êrec, or Wolfram's Gâwân. In fact, the women refuse the gender roles assigned to them by their society, thus creating a site of social tension within patriarchal norms.

Das Frauenturnier or *The Ladies' Tournament* was composed by an anonymous author in Eastern Franconia shortly before 1300.[2] It is included among the medieval German *Mären* or short, secular tales in couplets that resemble the French fabliaux. Although there are three similar stories in the fabliau corpus, none is obviously related to *The Ladies' Tournament*.[3] The *Mären* flourished from the mid-thirteenth century until about 1500. As a genre, they are distinguished by a rigid standardization of plot and character: many *Mären* comically depict a power struggle between husband and

---

[1] Chrétien de Troyes, *Yvain*, in *Arthurian Romances*, trans. W. W. Comfort (New York and London: Everyman's Library, 1975), 248–49 and 255–56; Hartmann von Aue, *Erec: Mittelhochdeutscher Text und Übertragung*, trans. Thomas Cramer (Frankfurt: Fischer Taschenbuch Verlag, 1972), 356–65 and 426–33; Wolfram von Eschenbach, *Parzival*, trans. A. T. Hatto (New York: Penguin, 1980), 319–21.

[2] See Friedrich Heinrich von der Hagen, ed., "Der vrouwen turnei," in *Gesamtabenteuer: Hundert altdeutsche Erzählungen*, 3 vols. (1850; reprint, Darmstadt: Wissenschaftliche Buchgesellschaft, 1961), 1:371–82; all quotes are taken from the second edition unless otherwise stated. The text has not been translated into modern English or German. The translations from von der Hagen's edition are my own. Date and provenance according to Hans-Friedrich Rosenfeld, "Das Frauenturnier," in *Die deutsche Literatur des Mittelalters: Verfasserlexicon*, ed. Kurt Ruh, 2d fully rev. ed. (Berlin and New York: Walter de Gruyter, 1978–81), 2:882–83, esp. 882.

[3] "Le tournoi des dames" by Hue d'Oisy, "Li tournoiment as dames," and "Tournoiement as dames de Paris" by Pierre Gentien (cited in Rosenfeld, 2:883).

wife in a setting that is often rich in the detail of everyday life. Power is often expressed as the husband's attempt to control the wife's sexuality, which she asserts outside the bonds of marriage, although the genre also includes tales of wives who dominate their husbands through psychological manipulation.[4]

The Ladies' Tournament is an unusual story that does not fully reproduce the standard plots and characters that define the genre's core of texts. Although Hanns Fischer enumerates it among the Mären for formal reasons, he singles it out as one of several unique or experimental texts. These he believes to be the works of authors who borrowed elements from other genres such as the historical chronicles, or who produced Mären with an unusual degree of artistic self-awareness and independence.[5] The unusualness of The Ladies' Tournament from the perspective of genre taxonomy in no way reduces its literary or historical significance. In fact, I will show that its author made the most of the genre's structural conventions, especially the expectation of a moral, for political purposes. She or he was able to do so precisely because in the late thirteenth century the genre was in an experimental stage and open to multiple discourses.

Although it is difficult or impossible to produce exact data about the primary audience of any single Märe, Hanns Fischer's observations of the genre as a whole suggest some working assumptions.[6] Mären, he finds, were intended for a cultured readership and au-

---

[4] Peter Ketsch notes that "a good third of all Mären are comic tales of adultery. Significantly, seventy depict the adultery of the wife but only nine that of the husband" (Frauen im Mittelalter, Band 2: Frauenbild und Frauenrechte in Kirche und Gesellschaft; Quellen und Materialien, Studien Materialien Band 19: Geschichtsdidaktik, ed. Annette Kuhn [Düsseldorf: Schwann, 1984], 125). Ketsch's chapter on "Das Frauenbild der Märendichtung" (chap. 3.3) has many interesting perspectives on the genre.

[5] My brief characterization of the Mären genre and the place within it of The Ladies' Tournament follows the standard reference work by Hanns Fischer, Studien zur deutschen Märendichtung, ed. Johannes Janota, 2d rev. ed. (Tübingen: Max Niemeyer, 1983), 93–101, esp. 100. Fischer does not mean that The Ladies' Tournament and similar Mären describe the historical events or reflect historical reality as it might be defined by the standards of today. Rather, they resemble the narratives that medieval people regarded as history and transmitted in the chronicles of the period.

[6] See ibid., 244–45. Fischer advanced his ideas about the sociology of the Mären with extreme hesitation, "not so much as a firm result, but rather as a point of departure for developing research and discussion." His caution about information that is "full of holes" and "obscured by coincidences" of history and transmission (244) is particularly relevant when dealing with the reception of a single text, although The Ladies' Tournament is slightly more informative about its own audience than many other Mären.

dience who understood a sophisticated range of literary or historical references.[7] *The Ladies' Tournament* addressed such an audience by referring to the events of classical antiquity. One of the company of women invokes the fame of Hector and Paris, showing that its author assumed the primary audience would be familiar, through whatever channels, with the history of Troy.

Fischer relies on sophisticated references and other evidence to determine the probable social status of such audiences. He concludes that the *Mären* public consisted of the nobility exclusively, including earls and princes and highly placed churchmen of noble family. The circle eventually was extended to include "das arrivierte Bürgertum" (the urban citizenry who were socially successful). The urban elite of Basil and Strasbourg clearly are among the people who supported the work of Konrad von Würzburg, one of the best known and most innovative proponents of the *Mären* in the thirteenth century.[8] It is not as clear that *The Ladies' Tournament* was written for such an audience. As a literature-consuming public, the urban citizenry and the more traditional feudal elite had very similar tastes. Distinctly urban genres do not appear, at least in written transmission, until the later fourteenth century. In other words, it is very difficult without external evidence to determine the origin of any *Märe* composed before about 1350 (and many later ones as well) in an urban or nonurban elite milieu.

The earliest manuscript to transmit a complete copy of *The Ladies' Tournament*—that is, its first historically tangible context—is a monumental parchment codex now preserved in the library of Heidelberg University. Recent assessments have confirmed the view of earlier scholarship that this manuscript probably arose during the first third of the thirteenth century at the instigation of a member of a mighty Bohemian household, the Michelsberg family. Evidence includes the fact that the chivalric deeds of one of their scions are celebrated in another couplet poem in the manuscript.[9] About a

---

[7] Many *Mären* refer to the Germanic epic. Fischer points out that both genres served as "elevated entertainment" (ibid.).

[8] Ibid., 165; Fischer also notes that Konrad produced only courtly or gallant *Mären* for his urban and highly placed clerical patrons.

[9] Fischer lists the manuscripts transmitting *The Ladies' Tournament* on 339. He also discusses (232) the probable role of the Michelsberg dynasty in the production of the Heidelberg manuscript, Cpg 341, with references to the older scholarship. Ingeborg Glier affirms this connection, citing Karin Schneider, in *Die deutsche Literatur im späten Mittelalter: 1250–1370; Reimpaargedichte, Drama, Prosa*, ed. Ingeborg Glier, vol. 3, pt. 2 of *Geschichte der deutschen Literatur*, ed. Helmut De Boor and Richard Newald (Munich: C. H. Beck, 1987), 22.

generation after the text was composed, then, *The Ladies' Tournament* probably was read by the landed feudal elite whom Fischer counts among the genre's earliest proponents.

The characters in the story itself are elite, although their exact place in the feudal hierarchy is never revealed. The first seventy-nine lines of the tale present an unusually detailed description of their modus vivendi. The story is set in a fortress or perhaps even a fortified city (Middle High German *burk*) "across the Rhine."[10] Its inhabitants constitute an exemplary society whose ideals are embodied by the male residents who, in the words of the text, number forty or more. As knights, these forty are distinguished by their outstanding chivalry, understood solely as military prowess. No reference is made to an ethical obligation to protect the weak, although their exclusively military goals carry no negative meaning. The social function of their chivalry lies in the regulation of external affairs in a world of conflict and aggression. When they are not fighting in earnest, the forty attend tournaments where they engage in military sport. Thus their strength is based in their dedication to corporate action. Their participation in battle and tournament is always en masse. Any injury suffered by a member of the community becomes the affair of all, so his capacity for vengeance is magnified by a function of forty. Their form of government reflects their corporate identity. The forty may disagree among themselves, but they never allow this dissension to divide their community. Authority to resolve internal disputes is vested in a *houb(e)tman*, a "leader" with powers of arbitration who is elected from their number. The aspiration of the group is to "please courtly society" in the pursuit of honor. Famed and feared for their military might and their ability to cooperate, the knights enjoy "the highest honor (*prîs*) from the leading members of society."[11]

The characters in the story, then, represent the ranks of those who fight. Their exemplary cooperation and demonstration of group solidarity as a basis of power seem like the best indication of who, in the world beyond the text, the knights represent. Yet there were many social groupings in late thirteenth-century German society

---

[10] Lines 1–6: "Ich hôrte sagen, sunder wân, / daʒ mugt ir gerne verstân, / Ein seltsæneʒ mære, / wie ein burk wære / Verre über jenen Rîn." The expression "über jenen Rîn" can mean simply "far away," but Rosenfeld (n. 2 above) is inclined to read it more literally as evidence of low German or Rhenish backgrounds in the composition of the text. The primary evidence, though, is the role of Walraben von Limburk, without whose entrance at the end of the tale the phrase would convey little geographic specificity.

[11] Lines 8–9: "darumbe habent si groʒen pîn, / Wie sie der werlde wol behagen" and lines 32–33: "sô daʒ in der hœhste prîs / Von den besten wart gegeben."

whose political efficacy lay in the affirmation of a communal identity. The knights might reflect the emergence of an urban patriciate[12]
whose values, to please courtly society in the pursuit of honor, differ
little from those of the more traditional knighthood. They could also
suggest the ranks of vassals or lesser nobility on whose military
might the power and prestige of the territorial rulers, "the leading
members of society," rested.

One such ruler appears in *The Ladies' Tournament* as Duke
Walraben von Limburk and is presumed by modern scholars to be
Walram (or Walberan) IV, Duke of Limburg from 1247 to 1279 and
a participant in imperial politics on the side of Richard of Cornwall
during the interregnum.[13] It is unusual for a historical personage to
appear as a character in a *Märe*. Konrad von Würzburg's short, descriptive narrative, *The Tournament of Nantes*, is a good text for
comparison since Richard of Cornwall himself plays a central role.[14]
The blending of fiction and reality in the figure of Duke Walraben
suggests that those who read or heard *The Ladies' Tournament* were
as interested in the fame of a contemporary warrior, perhaps for
partisan reasons, as they were in the deeds of Hector and Paris.
This interest adds another detail to the portrait of the elite *Mären*

---

[12] Rosenfeld is confident that the forty proud men who follow the call of chivalry
reflect "the development of an urban patriciate" (2:882). It is perhaps significant
that Hector and Paris, the two heroes named in the story, both fought on the Trojan
side in defense of the walled city. If Rosenfeld is correct, then *burk* in line 4 might
well be translated as "city" rather than "castle" or "fortification." Recent literary-
historical scholarship in Germany has focused on the literature created by and/or
for such elite urban groups (see, e.g., Kurt Ruh, "Versuch einer Begriffsbestimmung
von 'städtischer Literatur' im deutschen Spätmittelalter," in *Über Bürger, Stadt und
städtische Literatur im Spätmittelalter: Bericht über Kolloquien der Kommission
zur Erforschung der Kultur des Spätmittelalters 1975–1977*, ed. Josef Fleckenstein
and Karl Stackman [Göttingen: Vandenhoeck & Ruprecht, 1980], 311–28). Still, Rosenfeld's assertion that this text belongs to an urban patriciate needs to be examined
critically.

[13] Walram IV's biographical sketch appears in the *Allgemeine Deutsche Biogra-
phie* (1896; reprint, Berlin: Duncker & Humblot, 1971), 40:775–76. He is believed
to have been among the princes who offered the imperial crown to Richard in 1257.
His second marriage was to the niece of King Otakar II of Bohemia, for whom Walram
went to war against the Hungarians in 1271 when Otakar was at the apex of his
power. Walram's Bohemian connections might suggest why *The Ladies' Tournament*
was received in the circle of the Michelsberg dynasty and preserved in Cpg 341.
Walram's appearance in this story provides a clue to the date of its composition,
which in all likelihood occurred before his death in 1279.

[14] The identification of King Richard in Konrad's *Turnier von Nantes* as Richard
of Cornwall is made by Helmut De Boor, *Die deutsche Literatur im späten Mittelalter: Zerfall und Neubeginn*, vol. 3, pt. 1 of *Geschichte der deutschen Literatur*,
ed. Helmut De Boor and Richard Newald (Munich: C. H. Beck, 1962), 44–45.

public as Fischer paints it—those who heard or read *The Ladies'
Tournament* were perhaps politically empowered themselves.

The action begins when the lands of the forty are attacked by a
brutal aggressor. Rather than meeting him with force, they decide
to negotiate a settlement. On the day of the peace talks the forty
set out from the city to meet their opponent, taking only their swords.
They leave behind their lances, armor, horses, and womenfolk.

The women form a community, but it is neither an imitation of
the men's nor an entirely independent social creation. Since under
ordinary circumstances they do not use weapons, the women are
excluded from the regulation of external conflict through military
action and negotiation. According to one of the city's male residents,
the women are responsible for maintaining the households. He
encodes this sexual division of labor by rhyming *turnieren varn*
(attending tournaments) with *hûs bewarn* (supervising the household) in lines 291–92, but the women are never actually depicted
in the context of the household. They congregate instead on a pleas-
ant meadow outside the fortifications, a conventional setting of
medieval narrative associated with festivity and relaxation. The goal
of their community is pleasure and the social and psychological
freedom that relaxation allows. Their autonomy from the male community on the day of the peace negotiation, and from the households
that, in the male perspective, they occupy, is temporary but re-
peatable; the women are together in the meadow on the subsequent
day when the problem at the heart of the story is happily resolved.

Like the male community, the women are committed to living
in harmony, although they do not follow the formal procedure of
electing a leader vested with the power to arbitrate disputes. The
women settle their disputes by "talking among themselves." The
language of the text actually emphasizes group process in the res-
olution of differences.[15] Leadership in the community is ad hoc and
based on one's rhetorical skills. The woman who, later in the story,
becomes mistress of the tournament earns her position by prevailing
in a spontaneous but well-structured debate.

The women value honor, but the relationship between honor
and gender, or, more precisely, women's share in men's honor, is
the topic that the women debate during their sojourn on the meadow.

[15] Lines 34–38: "ir vrouwen sazten ouch ir leben, / Swen(ne) sie zuo brâchen, /
daʒ sie dar zwischen sprâchen / Unde ebenten'ʒ ze hant, / daʒ man niht zornes
under in vant." *Zorn* or "anger" tends to be associated with domineering housewives
and shrews in the *Mären*, e.g., Sibote's *Frauenerziehung*, in which a man tames his
shrewish wife and mother-in-law by convincing them that he has amputated the
body part that produces their *zorn*. For editions, see Fischer, 401 (n. 5 above), entry
no. 121.

The interlocutors who open the debate are described only as the wise woman and the daring woman.[16] The daring woman begins with the thesis that there is no difference between women's and men's honor. The women benefit from the military success and high reputation of the men's community; therefore, they should enhance their own reputation for the sake of honor. Although she does not specify how, the substance of her suggestion becomes clear as the plot unfolds: the women should carry weapons and follow the time-honored path to fame reserved until now for men. Her choice of verbs—to hunt down praise, to win fame—clearly signifies the active pursuit of public acclaim in battle and military sport.[17] The wise woman rebuts by dissociating honor from public acclaim. She links it instead to womanhood, with the admonition that secular fame is fleeting: "What use is reputation to us in this transient existence? Rather we should preserve our honor with our womanhood."[18] She introduces the only pious note in an otherwise secular text. Women accomplish this, she continues, by loving their husbands and remaining faithful to them. She attempts to outflank her interlocutor rhetorically, making the statement that sets the literary horizons of the audience itself: the faithful wife's honor transcends the heroic honor of either Hector or Paris.

The daring woman responds with action rather than words. She takes an oath from all who are present, binding the company more

---

[16] Line 85: "ein vrouwe, diu was balt"; line 97: "Ein ander vrouwe, diu was wîs." The descriptive adjectives bear the full weight of character differentiation and provide the only indication of the narrator's own views. "Wise" is clearly a laudatory tag for a character who embodies conventional views on female honor. More interesting is the semantic range of the Middle High German *balt*, "daring," which runs from strongly positive (audacious, especially in battle) to decidedly negative (overly bold, fresh). The most appropriate translation depends on context, as well as the age of the document. Grimm and Grimm note that the adjective begins to fade in High German in the fourteenth century, so its use in *The Ladies' Tournament* is relatively late (Jacob Grimm and Wilhelm Grimm, *Deutsches Wörterbuch* [Leipzig: S. Hirzel, 1854], 1:1081). Here, the dissonance between the more archaic meanings, which are often bellicose and generally positive, and the newer ones implying impropriety inhibits the medieval reader's ability to judge the character's opinions and actions. The use of the ambiguous adjective *balt* is consistent with other evidence of the suspension of judgment, e.g., the fact that the narrator never criticizes or even comments on the character's unorthodox behavior.

[17] Line 93: "prîs bejagen"; line 116: "dâ mite gewinnen wir lobes vil." The daring woman elides the role of love in men's pursuit of honor and with it the role of the lady in courtly romance. The issue of courtly love is also evaded elsewhere in the poem.

[18] Lines 98–101: "diu sprach: 'waʒ sol uns hôher prîs / Ze dirre werlde mêre, / wan daʒ mir [*sic*] unser êre / Behalden und unser wîpheit.' "

tightly by committing them to a game. After they have sworn their allegiance, the game is explained. The women are to put on the men's armor, mount the men's warhorses, and joust against each other in the pursuit of honor. Each woman must assume the name of a male knight by whose deeds she cares to be known. At this point a third woman, described only as well bred, objects to the plan. Her dissent, never answered in the text, is silenced by the binding power of the oath.[19]

Most women assume the names of their husbands or male kin. One young woman, though, who is introduced here with a short panegyric, must cope with the painful fact that her father does not engage in chivalry because he is too poor. Nor can he provide her with a dowry, so she herself has no husband although she is long past the age of marriage. She chooses instead the name of Duke Walraben of Limburk, "the best knight under the sun."[20] Her high aspirations correspond to her own skill at warfare since she emerges the winner of the hard-fought tournament.

Upon their return the knights hear of the tournament from the young chamberlains and grant the women the praise they deserve, but they forbid the women from ever jousting again. Yet news of the joust spreads throughout the land, causing knights to laugh wherever they sit together with food and drink. Eventually the news reaches the ears of Duke Walraben himself. One day he is passing by the city when he encounters the women who are once again assembled in the meadow. He requests to meet the heroine who has increased the honor of his name. Her modesty and beauty, and the wise words of her father who is summoned to explain her marriage plight, move him to generosity. He dowers the young heroine with a hundred marks and two horses and marries her to a rich man. Like most *Mären, The Ladies' Tournament* has an ending that resembles a moral, at least formally: the narrator assures the audience that in the future, the young bride will engage only in the "tournament" that brings women "honor" in the conjugal bed.

* * *

The stated goal of the community of jousters is to put women's honor on a par with men's. Their actual accomplishment, to secure

---

[19] The legal scholar Hans Fehr notes that "in the orbit of the knightly classes breaking an oath was worse than death" (see "Das Recht in Iwein," in *Festschrift Ernst Mayer zum 70. Geburtstage* [Weimar: Verlag Hermann Böhlaus Nachfolger, 1932], 93–110, esp. 105).

[20] Lines 223–24: "Der ist der besten ritter ein, / den diu sunne ie beschein."

an honorable marriage for their most impoverished member, differs radically from their expressed intention, for the subject of marriage never enters the debate that initiates the joust. The narrative relays between intention and outcome may actually indicate tensions in the marriage system of thirteenth-century German society.

In the late Middle Ages, marriage was the social destiny of elite women who did not have a religious calling. Ann Haskell's observation about the lives of the Paston women in fifteenth-century Norfolk probably describes the general situation of elite women in thirteenth-century Germany: "Girlhood was merely a prelude to matrimony, and the adult years were spent as wife or widow. Some women adjusted to as many husbands as were necessary to fill out their life spans, one marriage following another within weeks of the death of a spouse." "Life for women of the gentry," Haskell concludes, "was synonymous with marriage."[21] Other options, when they did exist, were so few or so extraordinary that they hold little place in twentieth-century historical work.[22] Against this background, the marriageable woman who is not married emerges as a complex anomaly who challenges her society's deeply embedded assumptions about her gender role. The winner of *The Ladies' Tournament* is such a figure.

The text supplies a good deal of information about the marriage system and why it has failed to provide a husband for this young woman. Marriage in *The Ladies' Tournament* is characterized by a feature that is well known not only in the Middle Ages but also in later European and non-European cultures. In accordance with the kinship systems analyzed by Gayle Rubin in her exegesis of Lévi-Strauss, men have rights in women that women do not have in themselves, namely, the right to bestow women on other men through marriage.[23] When the marriage in *The Ladies' Tournament* is finally formed, it is through the agency of the males who stand in close relationship to the bride herself. Normally, the woman's father would enjoy this prerogative, but here it is exercised by a powerful outsider, Duke Walraben of Limburk, after consultation with the bride's father. The duke supplies the bridegroom as well as the material

[21] Ann S. Haskell, "The Paston Women on Marriage in Fifteenth-Century England," *Viator: Medieval and Renaissance Studies* 4 (1973): 459–71, esp. 459.

[22] Margaret Wade Labarge's chapter "Women Who Ruled: Noble Ladies" begins with women's responsibilities in marriage. The inevitability of marriage itself is not even discussed (see her *A Small Sound of the Trumpet: Women in Medieval Life* [Boston: Beacon, 1986], 72–97).

[23] Gayle Rubin, "The Traffic in Women: Notes on the 'Political Economy' of Sex," in *Toward an Anthropology of Women*, ed. Rayna Rapp Reiter (New York: Monthly Review Press, 1975), 157–210, esp. 177.

basis for the marriage, the dowry. The bride herself has little part in these proceedings.[24]

By the thirteenth century the right to bestow a woman in marriage was no longer, in theory at least, an exclusively male prerogative. Canon law, for example, tended to recognize the validity of marriages contracted by the partners alone, without the knowledge of their families or guardians.[25] Among the vernacular law codes in thirteenth-century Germany, the *Schwabenspiegel* explicitly upholds the right of a single woman to betrothe herself, although if she were under twenty-five she did so at the risk of losing her inheritance. In view of this restriction, Peter Ketsch concludes that the right articulated in the *Schwabenspiegel* represented a demand rather than a reality.[26] If he is correct, then the passive position of the woman in *The Ladies' Tournament,* who utters not a word as her marriage is negotiated, may be closer to social practice than legal theory.

Furthermore, the only marital assignment mentioned in the text is the dowry, or the transfer of wealth from the bride's side. There is no hint of a contribution from the groom's side, or of any informal exchange of gifts, despite a great deal of historical evidence that cultural traditions would have required both.[27] The dowry consists

[24] The bride's participation is indicated in lines 391–92: "Diu meit liez sich an in gar, / der herre gab sin gelübde dar." The first line might be translated, "The maiden trusted him" or even "Let him make the decision," and the second, "The lord gave his promise." An implication of the statement, which would be strengthened by knowing if the diction were legal, is that the woman made the duke her *Vormund* or "legal guardian." According to the *Schwabenspiegel,* an unmarried woman had the right to choose her legal guardian. Peter Ketsch, who includes this passage from the *Schwabenspiegel* in his source book, makes the additional point that by the thirteenth century, *Muntschaft* or "guardianship" in the German territories had become more a relation of protection than of power ([n. 4 above] 163). This form of guardianship would describe the duke's role fairly well.

[25] John T. Noonan, Jr., "Power to Choose," *Viator: Medieval and Renaissance Studies* 4 (1973): 419–34, esp. 430.

[26] Ketsch, 162.

[27] Property exchange customs for marriage were both diverse and complex, and constantly changing, if the historiography presents an accurate record. Still essential for an overview of how the issue of property in marriage was fixed in medieval private law, the legal corpus most relevant to the question is Andreas Heusler, *Institutionen des deutschen Privatrechts,* 2 vols. (Leipzig: Duncker & Humblot, 1885–86). I will refer only to his general discussion of marital assignments in 2:364–79. Heusler begins this discussion with a proviso: the complexities of property exchange in marriage can be understood only with reference to property ownership *within* marriage (common property versus principles of separation) as well as inheritance practices (365). This is the context in which they are presented in the law codes themselves and also in other legal instruments such as marriage contracts. But Heusler also allows for the influence of custom and tradition, or those aspects

of a large amount of cash (100 marks), plus two horses, which, beyond their considerable material value, symbolize the knightly standing of the nuptial pair.[28]

With the emergence of the dowry by 1200, fathers were not legally bound to dower their daughters, but "everywhere in all of Germany dowry was deeply embedded in custom and counted as a duty of honor which no father shirked without exposing his daughter to shame."[29] Such would have been the social pressures and expectations that informed the audience for *The Ladies' Tournament.*

---

of marital property exchange that are not fixed in the law codes or other legal sources and that recent feminist scholars find so provocative for understanding women's position (see Christiane Klapisch-Zuber, *Women, Family and Ritual in Renaissance Italy,* trans. Lydia Cochrane [Chicago and London: University of Chicago Press, 1985], particularly her chapter "The Griselda Complex: Dowry and Marriage Gifts in the Quattrocento," 213–46).

[28] The emergence of dowry by 1200 after the long domination of the Germanic custom of brideprice has been the subject of recent historical research, in particular, David Herlihy, *Medieval Households* (Cambridge, Mass., and London: Harvard University Press, 1985), 98–103. Herlihy gives a more detailed account of his demographic theories in "The Medieval Marriage Market," in *Medieval and Renaissance Studies: Proceedings of the Southeastern Institute of Medieval and Renaissance Studies Summer, 1974,* ed. Dale B. J. Randall (Durham, N.C.: Duke University Press, 1976), 3–27; see also Jack Goody and S. J. Tambiah, *Bridewealth and Dowry,* Cambridge Papers in Social Anthropology no. 7 (Cambridge: Cambridge University Press, 1973). In an important article, Diane Owen Hughes traces the emergence of dowry against the background of earlier customs and speculates about its causes (see her "From Brideprice to Dowry in Mediterranean Europe," *Journal of Family History* 3 [1978]: 262–96; reprinted in *The Marriage Bargain: Women and Dowries in European History,* ed. Marion A. Kaplan [New York and Binghamton: Harrington Park Press, 1985], 13–58). Quotes are taken from the latter source. Unfortunately Hughes's data for the period after 1200 is drawn mainly from the Mediterranean littoral. For information about Germany, one may turn to Heusler, 367–70. He explains that dowry in the later Middle Ages was not an exclusively legal transaction, nor can it be defined as the woman's inheritance portion, since in many German territories and cities women had asserted inheritance rights. For a more recent overview of women's right to inherit in urban and nonurban settings, see Edith Ennen, *Frauen im Mittelalter* (Munich: C. H. Beck, 1984), 94, 133. Ennen emphasizes women's "equal rights" with respect to inheritance in the cities and points out that in the feudal territories, women had to constantly reassert their position throughout the thirteenth century. The erosion of inheritance rights is intimately connected to the issue of dowry, although Ennen, who is a historian of cities, does not follow this line of reasoning. The content of the dowry differed according to place and the bride's social standing. According to Heusler, noble women were dowered more richly than the peasantry, and in the higher ranks of the nobility, dowry could include feudal rents and properties ("Renten" and "Liegenschaften"). In southern Germany, dowry was prominent among the elite and could consist of cash as well as rents and property.

[29] Heusler, 369.

But the thirteenth-century German audience would also have been familiar with the *Widerlegung* (countergift)—the items that the wife could expect to receive from her husband.[30] Rooted in Germanic brideprice, the countergift was not simply a substitute for the dowry, a conversion of its substance from one kind of wealth to another. Instead, it supplemented the dowry, since on the death of the husband, the wife would inherit both intact. Yet its worth was determined by the size of the dowry, and in many regions *Widerlegung* matched the dowry in kind as well as worth, "plot of land for plot of land, and capital for capital."[31] It appears in the nobility's marriage contracts, especially in those of the highest ranks.

Another traditional contribution from the husband's side is called *Wittum*.[32] Basically it is the husband's provision for his wife's widowhood. Unlike *Widerlegung*, its worth is not linked to the dowry. In the vernacular law codes *Wittum* assured the woman some income for her lifetime, whether or not she should remarry, in a way that suggests her enjoyment of it during marriage. Although more typical in economically advantaged segments of the society, the way that it is discussed in the *Sachsenspiegel* shows that *Wittum* was "deeply grounded in custom."[33]

Finally, there was also the morning gift.[34] The content of the morning gift was as varied by region and class as were the other contributions from the husband's side, with which it tended to merge. Where it remained separate, it often consisted of movable goods or capital, although rents and properties could also have been included in the higher social echelons. The morning gift may have been particularly common among the feudal landed gentry.[35]

---

[30] Ibid., 370–72.

[31] Ibid., 371.

[32] Ibid., 372–74.

[33] Heusler's comment on the customary nature of the *Wittum* is on 374. The *Sachsenspiegel*, to which I will refer below, was composed between 1220 and 1235 by Eike von Repgowe in the circle of Graf Heinrich I von Anhalt. Its importance lies not only in its use of the vernacular, for it also served as a model for numerous subsequent law codes, in the cities as well as the territories. On the origin and influence of the *Sachsenspiegel*, see Peter Johanek, "Rechtsschrifttum," in De Boor and Newald, eds. (n. 9 above), 402–31, esp. 403–5.

[34] Heusler, 374–79.

[35] Ketsch (n. 4 above) prints the sections of the *Sachsenspiegel* that deal with women's property rights. It would exceed the scope of the present argument to discuss them at length, except to mention that dowry is named along with the husband's morning gift. The content of the latter is modest and limited according to class. The wife's *Leibgedinge*, which, in 1:21, sec. 2, consists of land she may use in her own lifetime but not pass on to heirs, is also mentioned and seems to correspond to Heusler's *Wittum*. Also mentioned are the woman's own *Grundeigen*,

What this survey shows is that *The Ladies' Tournament* was produced and received at a time when marriage in the knightly classes usually involved property transfer in both directions. The text, though, depicts only the woman's contribution and focuses attention on a father-daughter relationship in which the father cannot meet his obligations.

According to Diane Owen Hughes, "dowry must inevitably have centered attention on the father-daughter bond; for daughters would live all their lives in the light of their father's generosity or in the shadow of its absence."[36] The only family unit in *The Ladies' Tournament* consists of a father and a daughter. No other women are linked to this nucleus, nor are there any males in the second generation. The father has male kinsmen, but like him they fail to participate in the rites of chivalric honor, and their narrative function is simply to amplify the father's disability.[37] Duke Walraben himself is not related to the family, but he assumes a father's duties. His contribution to the story elaborates the central, familial bond between father and daughter by supplying a positive paternal model. Thus both parsimony and generosity are represented in *The Ladies' Tournament:* by the father, whose poverty—an exonerated form of parsimony—bars his daughter from marriage, and by the duke, whose munificence secures her future. The daughter's dependence was complete, but once dowered her economic status became more complex.

Hughes's understanding of dowry as part of a status system is an important innovation over earlier economic discussions.[38] She provides a fuller analysis of the rearrangement of the terms of marriage in Europe after 1200, when "demographic growth, land shortage, and unprecedented commercial development were creating in both cities and countryside a crisis of status."[39] However, her illus-

---

or properties she owns outright and may pass on to her heirs, and her *Lehn* or fiefs (Ketsch, 166–72).

[36] Hughes (n. 28 above), 38.

[37] The medieval reader's fascination with the knight who is so impoverished that he cannot provide his daughter a dowry is evinced not only by *The Ladies' Tournament* but also by Ênîte's father, Koralus, in Hartmann's romance of *Êrec*. Bernhard von Jacobi, "Rechts- und Hausaltertümer in Hartmanns Erec" (Ph.D. diss., University of Göttingen, 1903), 38–39, looks upon Êrec's offer to let Ênîte share the sovereignty over his kingdom as "Brautgabe" and points out that Êrec rejects Koralus's counter offer of "Mitgift" or dowry. Koralus does not actually make a counter offer but, rather, regrets that he is too poor to do so in lines 547–54 in Cramer's edition (n. 1 above).

[38] Hughes, 45.

[39] Ibid., 42.

trations of the relation between dowry and status, especially in the lives of medieval women, only begin to chart the complexity of the problem. Klapisch-Zuber summarizes more fully the social and personal meanings of dowry: "The dowry penetrated to the very heart of the social ideology of the time. It was what guaranteed honor and the share of respect due each individual: it ensured the nubile girl and the widow a marriage that respected the taboos concerning feminine purity; it conferred and proclaimed before all the social rank of the marrying couple and of their families. It was therefore a regulating force in society."[40]

* * *

The European crisis in status after about 1200 was imprinted in literature. Concerns about status, in fact, are central in those genres associated with the German elite. In *The Ladies' Tournament*, status refers to both social standing (class or estate) and honor. These are interrelated concepts, although their exact relationship varies by gender. The social standing and honor of the woman depend on the smooth functioning of the marriage system. During the debate in the meadow, the wise woman defines female honor as love and fidelity to one's spouse: "This honor one demands of a woman: let her love her husband and cherish him faithfully."[41] Her emphasis on fidelity equates women's honor with women's acceptance of male control of female sexuality. Work in literary history confirms that in late medieval German society, specifically, female honor was defined as premarital chastity and marital fidelity.[42] More generally, others document and expand this concept as a prevalent social norm elsewhere in Europe during the late Middle Ages and early Renaissance.[43]

The idea that wives should obey their husbands is ubiquitous in medieval culture but the root of this concept is the Pauline code of marriage as stated in Ephesians 5:22–33. The Pauline code enjoins the wife to fear and respect her husband (5:33), but the husband is commanded three times over (5:25, 28, 33) to love his wife on the model of Christ's love for the Church. As Elisabeth Schüssler

[40] Klapisch-Zuber (n. 27 above), 214.

[41] Lines 106–8: "Sie minne iren lieben man, / Und habe in mit triuwen wert, / des prîses man von vrouwen gert."

[42] George Fenwick Jones, *Honor in German Literature*, University of North Carolina Studies in the Germanic Languages and Literatures no. 25 (Chapel Hill: University of North Carolina Press, 1959), 126.

[43] Julius Kirshner, *Pursuing Honor while Avoiding Sin: The Monte delle doti of Florence*, Quaderni di *Studi Senesi* 41 (Milan: Dott. A. Giuffrè Editore, 1978), 7.

Fiorenza concludes, "the exhortations to the husbands spell out what it means to live a marriage relationship as a Christian, while those to the wives insist on the proper social behavior of women."[44]

The wise woman's definition of woman's honor conforms to these aspects of social and sexual control. But she also supplements such traditional notions by expanding the Pauline injunction on husbands to include wives as well. Loving becomes the wife's duty, with the further implication that husbands should be lovable. Women's honor emerges as an affective value that affirms the mutuality of sentiment between spouses. Had she invoked exemplary figures to illustrate her concept of woman's honor as love, they would have included not only the obedient wives Griselda and Marcia but also the romance heroines who achieve a marital utopia of mutual affect, Ênîte and Condwîrâmûrs.

The wise woman's definition of honor thus embeds a contradiction. She affirms male control of female sexuality, but behind her injunction to love is the requirement that women must be obedient voluntarily. She does not mention maiden's chastity or widow's renunciation, the other paths to honor available to women in late medieval society. Her exclusive focus on the wife's relationship to her husband indicates a social reality wherein women are ambivalent and anxious about their relations with men.

The valorization of dowry as the centerpiece of marriage formation thus becomes a site of tension, evinced in *The Ladies' Tournament* by the story of the young woman who prevails in the joust. Not surprisingly, she is introduced with reference to her qualifications as a bride. She has been a maiden for too long and now she may be too old to marry.[45] The panegyric passage that follows assures the reader that there are no physical or mental reasons why the woman should not marry. "She knew how to be prudent," a virtue she will display later when the duke offers to manage her affairs; "She was beautiful and full of spirit" affirms her desirability as a wife; and "She was well inclined" establishes her intent to

<hr>

[44] Elisabeth Schüssler Fiorenza, *In Memory of Her: A Feminist Theological Reconstruction of Christian Origins* (New York: Crossroad, 1983), 269–70, esp. 270.

[45] In F (= Freiberg i. S., Bibliothek des Gymnasiums Albertinum, no signature) the heroine is "zen iar oder me," that is, ten years or more beyond marriageable age. The crisis has been amplified. This parchment fragment is transcribed by Eduard Heydenreich, "Ueber ein neugefundenes mittelhochdeutsches Handschriftenbruchstück der Freiberger Gymnasialbibliothek und über das Gedicht von der vrouwen turnei," *Archiv für Literaturgeschichte* 13 (1885): 145–75, esp. 147, line 90.

marry.[46] Her father's inability to provide her with a dowry appears
to be the primary reason for her failure to find a husband.

In medieval Germany, marriage alliances, like the rules of inheritance, operated within a grid of custom and expectation by
which social groups and classes "project forwards provisions and
(as they hope) guarantees of security for their children."[47] For women,
provisions and security both were determined by the dowry. The
value of one's dowry determined whom one could marry. Under
ideal circumstances an adequate dowry assured that a woman would
marry someone of equivalent or even superior social standing. But
in the world represented by *The Ladies' Tournament,* a woman
with a small dowry must marry down the social scale. This threat
of slippage is articulated by the father of the maiden jouster in his
interview with Duke Walraben. When asked how much he would
need for his daughter's dowry, the father explains: "She would be
satisfied / even if the amount were small / and her husband were
not her social equal / she would do as ordered."[48] He exposes the
link between the size of the dowry and his daughter's options in
marriage. By accepting a modest amount he barters her status away
since he can rely on her obedience. As Hughes puts it, a "daughter's
status came to be defined by the dowry she bore."[49] The repercus-
sion of a misalliance is expressed in legal discourse in the *Sachsenspiegel,* which states that a woman who marries beneath her rank
loses her own natal standing and assumes that of her husband.[50] In
Germany, in a society where elite marriages were formed in a complex nexus of property exchanges in both directions, the author of
The Ladies' Tournament seems to apprehend and fear this translation of a woman's social identity into a cash equivalent.

Not only does dowry in this provocatively selective text guarantee a woman's status in marriage, it is also the sine qua non of

[46] Lines 192–94: "si kunde sich vil wol verstên, / Si was schœne und hôch gemuot.
/ ir wille was ouch vil guot."

[47] E. P. Thompson, "The Grid of Inheritance: A Comment," in *Family and Inheritance: Rural Society in Western Europe, 1200–1800,* ed. Jack Goody, Joan Thirsk,
and E. P. Thompson (Cambridge: Cambridge University Press, 1976), 328–60, esp.
358.

[48] Lines 378–81: "sie liez' ir wol genuegen, / Wær(e) der schaz niht gar grôz; /
und wurde ir niht ir genôz', / Sie tæte, swaz man sie hiez'tuon."

[49] Hughes (n. 28 above), 42.

[50] Ketsch (n. 4 above), 163; Ketsch quotes *Sachsenspiegel* 1:45, sec. 1, which
states that "even if a man is not equal in birth to his wife he is still her guardian
and she is his social equal and becomes subject to the laws of his class when she
occupies his bed" (168); he presents another confirmation of this relationship from
the *Sachsenspiegel* on 171.

her social existence since in its absence no marriage can take place. This meaning of dowry is the most ominous. *The Ladies' Tournament* gives no hint of the fate of women who do not marry, although as the silent emergency behind the decision to joust such a fate is clearly undesirable. Historians have little to say about the undowered woman, although there is a hint of what this text refuses to state in fourteenth- and fifteenth-century Florentine memoirs. There, the absence of a dowry is associated with concubinage and prostitution, that is, total loss of a woman's social standing and honor.[51] In medieval Europe, "society recognized in the undowered woman a threat to its moral stability."[52] In the German context, the *Schwabenspiegel* permits an unmarried woman who is over twenty-five years old to "lie with a man" without her father's consent, and without loss of her inheritance.[53] This freedom must have appeared to some to be a license for unbridled sexuality. To others, perhaps, it meant freedom from male control.

In contrast to the meeting between the father and the duke, the meeting between the heroine and Duke Walraben contains elements of an alternate social code in which women's status is subject to wholly different considerations. According to historian Joan Kelly, the courtly conventions in twelfth- and thirteenth-century European literature signify the "ideological liberation of [women's] sexual and affective powers," particularly in the possibilities of choice and mutuality.[54] I would argue that the daughter's choice of the duke's identity in the joust as a reflection of her own high chivalric aspirations is conditioned by the freedom of the courtly lady to choose or reject a lover. In their meeting, the duke himself uses the language of the courtly servitor, saying to the heroine: "Young lady, what you have done on my account demands my service." Yet *The Ladies' Tournament* shows not so much an ideological liber-

[51] Kirshner (n. 43 above), 11; Kirshner also refers to the life of Saint Nicholas, Bishop of Myra, contained in the *Legenda aurea*. It relates how an impoverished father intended to turn his three dowerless daughters into prostitutes in order to gain enough money to live (11–12). Composed by Iacopo de Voragine at the end of the thirteenth century and widely circulated, the fate of the daughters in this vita perhaps suggests the attitudes of the society that produced and read *The Ladies' Tournament*.

[52] Hughes, 39; it would be helpful to know what historical conditions lay behind the threat of prostitution and concubinage. Hughes also seems somewhat puzzled about the fate of undowered girls and refers, by way of analogy, to Herodotus's Lydian prostitutes who converted their profits into dowries.

[53] Ketsch, 172, for *Schwabenspiegel* sec. 15.

[54] Joan Kelly, "Did Women Have a Renaissance?" in *Women, History and Theory: The Essays of Joan Kelly* (Chicago and London: University of Chicago Press, 1984), 19–50, esp. 26.

ation as an ideological tension between courtly conventions and those that are encoded by the dowry system of marriage. This tension is present in the same dialogue when the duke commands an authority over the heroine that no lover would dare to claim: "I would like to meet the young woman / who named herself after me / You should show her to me / I will praise her forever / and always reward her for it [taking him as her guardian]."[55] While the duke's offer of service and praise belongs to courtly discourse, the substance of his offer, to provide a dowry so that she may marry someone else, does not. The woman's complete silence in his presence shows that courtly convention cannot displace the investiture of power in class and gender that is enjoyed by the duke. The temptation to see the duke as a lover in a Cinderella-style ending fades into the economic reality of the dowry system.

I have shown that women's honor in *The Ladies' Tournament* is a quality tightly intertwined with a particular woman's status as an object of property. As a wife she must establish a mutually respectful relationship with her husband even within the constraints of the dowry system of marriage. The definition of male honor in this text represents an entirely different set of concerns. For men, honor is the reward of chivalry. Thus *The Ladies' Tournament* uses key aspects of the value system of the Arthurian romance with respect to male honor.[56] The problem that scholars of the romance have long debated is also applicable to this text: Is male chivalric honor equal to the reputation that society bestows on the successful knight, or is there also an ethical content internalized by the individual? This debate, though androcentric, supplies well-honed concepts. One advocate of the former or extrinsic view defines male honor in a way that works especially well for *The Ladies' Tournament* as "the recognition, respect, reverence, or reputation which a person enjoyed among men, or else physical tokens thereof."[57] In the following discussion I will show how the physical tokens of male honor are important for the women in this text. Yet *The Ladies' Tournament* does not choose one alternative over the other but,

[55] Lines 351–56: "Die junk vrouwe(n) het ich gern erkant, / diu sich nâch mir hât genant, / Die sult ir mir wîsen, / die wil ich immer prîsen, / Und wil eȥ verdienen immer mê"; lines 362–63: "junk vrouw', hie hœrt dien(e)st nach, / Daȥ ir durch mînen willen habt getân."

[56] Hugo Kuhn sees the rise and fall of the hero's honor as the key to romance structure in his article "Erec," reprinted in *Hartmann von Aue*, ed. Hugo Kuhn and Christoph Cormeau, Wege der Froschung 359 (Darmstadt: Wissenschaftliche Buchgesellschaft, 1973), 17–48.

[57] Jones (n. 42 above), 6; he cites the most important publications in the debate on the meaning of honor on 114, esp. nn. 4–7.

rather, constructs an ever shifting balance between the two. For the intrinsic construction of male honor that centers on the merit of the individual plays a role in the characterization of the father.

The father in *The Ladies' Tournament* is too poor to endow his daughter, so his rights over her in the marriage system are curtailed. But neither his social standing nor his honor are compromised by poverty. The narrator is quick to point out that he has maintained his valuable horse and weaponry ("not a strap was missing")[58] despite his financial ruin. These objects are tokens of an ideology of honor upheld by elite males. Historically, access to the order of fighting men was open to anyone who could acquire and use these expensive items. Here, the father remains a knight simply because he possesses the accoutrements of chivalry. In the *Sachsenspiegel* and other German law codes special provisions are made for the inheritance of these items in the male line, indicating their immense significance in late medieval society.[59] Even the fact that neither the father nor his kinsmen engage in tournaments "from which they could be known"[60] does not compromise their status, but in *The Ladies' Tournament* the young woman's feelings of shame at their inactivity suggest that this tokenism has strained the social system to its utmost.

The father's restraint and subtle speech in his interview with Duke Walraben suggests that the father's honor rests in his own inner qualities rather than in the public acclaim of chivalric military rites. When the duke inquires about why the father has failed to provide a dowry, the father explains, with precise insight into the differential link between gender and status, that although poverty has been harmful to him, it is his daughter who "has been made to pay."[61] In the ensuing interview his modest yet grateful response to the duke's generosity, along with his affirmation of paternal authority over his jousting daughter, recommend him to the powerful patron.

In response the duke provides a huge cash dowry, plus the two horses, and promises to arrange a marriage for the daughter. The right to bestow the woman in marriage is transferred to the duke through the power of a verbal agreement, apparently with the woman's prudent consent. This transfer of male authority entails no loss of honor for the father. The duke's generosity is not so much an act of charity (the horizon of this narrative is rigorously secular) as it

---

[58] Line 205: "Da gebrach niht eines riemen an."
[59] Ketsch (n. 4 above), 164, 165, 167, 173, 181, 193; Ennen (n. 28 above), 103.
[60] Line 213: "Turneis, nach dem si sich nente."
[61] Line 373: "Herre, des engildet sie."

is a commitment to the impoverished gentleman in the interests of class.[62]

* * *

The marriage system in *The Ladies' Tournament* has failed to function for the impoverished heroine, condemning her to an ambiguous social exile. The daring woman uses her rhetorical skill and physical energy to impose an alternate system by which she can reclaim her honor and elite standing. In so doing, she does not create a new system but rather adapts and adopts the chivalric path to public recognition and esteem that is open to men. The central gesture of this bold act is the seizing of the armor and weaponry that guarantee men's status and honor, powerful tokens that have no equivalent in the women's status system.

The narrative never makes these connections explicit, proceeding instead in an elliptical, almost dream-like manner that suggests meaning through the juxtapositions of various narrative elements. Yet the precise selection of these elements (dowry, e.g., but not *Wittum* or morning gift), and the narrator's economy of substitution also signify what is not stated: that the women's assumption of male gender roles in the performance of the joust is motivated by the injustice of a marriage system in which a woman's status is given an exchange value in the form of dowry. This invisible narrative economizes the social symbolic representation of a woman who is disadvantaged in the marriage system by reason of poverty so that she emerges as the most deserving of honor in the military rite.[63] Her military honor is then converted by the duke into dowry, the form of exchange demanded by the marriage system.

The women's seizure of the tokens of male honor and their assumption of male gender roles does not take place without resis-

---

[62] The endowment of poor or orphaned women was recognized as an act of charity in Genoese wills of the thirteenth century according to Steven Epstein, *Wills and Wealth in Medieval Genoa, 1150–1250* (Cambridge, Mass., and London: Harvard University Press, 1984), 185–86.

[63] Joachim Suchomski interprets the exchange of gender roles in *The Ladies' Tournament* as an instance of comic adynaton, or the trope of "the world upside down." Such exchanges of male and female roles are indeed common in medieval adynaton poetry. But in limiting his interpretation to this rhetorical point he overlooks the relationship between the women's joust and the malfunction of the marriage system (see *'Delectatio' und 'Utilitas': Ein Beitrag zum Verständnis mittelalterlicher komischer Literatur*, Bibliotheca Germanica 18 [Bern and Munich: Francke, 1975], 303, n. 514). Natalie Zemon Davis explores the social meanings of "the world upside down" in her essay "Women on Top," in her *Society and Culture in Early Modern France* (Stanford, Calif.: Stanford University Press, 1975), 124–51.

tance. Before the joust can occur, the daring woman must bind the community on a formal and legalistic basis through an oath. By swearing the oath, the women unite themselves in *triuwe* that is the equivalent of feudal fealty, except that it does not establish a hierarchical relationship of service and expectation. The oath also serves to commit them to an unspecified future plan of action and to silence dissent during its implementation. The seriousness of the oath is evident when the well-bred woman raises her objections; she is silenced with the threat of expulsion from the oath-bound community, the force that medieval society could bring against a perjurer.[64] Through their community the women create honor by establishing their own internal code of behavior and expectation.

The well-bred woman resists the joust with three objections: that good wives do not joust; that she herself cannot "ride like a man" since she has never done it before; and that no woman has ever jousted.[65] Her lines fall immediately after the daring woman has ordered the horses and armor to be brought out. The timing here is significant from the perspective of characterization, since the lines suggest eleventh-hour qualms. Her lines also retard the progress of the narrative just when it is reaching its climax in the joust itself, creating dramatic tension. But their content is important because the well-bred woman expresses modes of resistance that the audience or reader may have shared. Her first objection trans- forms the wise woman's construction of female honor as marital love and fidelity into prescriptive and androcentric imperative: wives should not usurp the prerogatives of their husbands.[66] She never receives a direct rebuttal on this point. Her objection is simply overridden by the higher priority of communal honor, established by oath. The second objection, that she herself cannot "ride like a man" since she has never done it before, seems to be directed at an audience well aware that jousting requires strength and skill. It is refuted by the turn of events; the women joust splendidly despite their lack of training. The third objection is the most subtle, for it

---

[64] The daring woman utters the threat in the following words: "Swer hie wider sprich(e)t / und sîn triuwe brich(e)t, / Den künde ich mein eide / unde triu lôs, beide; / Des enmak kein rât (ge) sîn" (lines 153–57). A translation is, "Whoever dissents and breaches their fidelity, from that person I withdraw both my oath and my loyalty; there is no remedy." The diction seems legalistic.

[65] Lines 143–50: "Dô sprach ein vrouwe wol gezogen: / 'des ist selten mêr gep- flogen; / Lâʒt den turnei blîben; / eʒ zimt niht quoten wîben. / Wie begünd' ich, des ich nie began? / sold' ich rîten als ein man? / Wir sullen von der rede lân, / daʒ ist vroulîch getân.' "

[66] Her prescriptive turn anticipates the instructions to good wives preserved in didactic texts of the late Middle Ages.

raises the interesting question of precedents. The well-bred woman's belief that no woman has ever jousted is a thin veil for the complex presence of armed women in medieval culture and literature.[67]

After dealing with these objections, the women choose male names by which they may be known. This act, consistent with the assumption of male gender roles, is more than a playful disguise. The women assume honor in the form of reputation and fame that accrues to the male names they select. By assuming male names, the women avoid a treasonous breach with the patriarchy that identification with female forbearers such as the amazons, whose contact with male society was primarily violent, would imply. But there is also an innovation in their act: although the bold woman suggests that the jousters assume the names of their husbands, they need not do so. Their choice is open. The patronymic is the logical but not the inevitable choice. Thus the young heroine who is ashamed at her kinsmen's lack of chivalry is able to select the name of Duke Walraben of Limburk, "one of the best knights under the sun." Her choice sets the high honor to which she herself aspires and quickly accedes on the strength of her deeds. The disability of her agnatic family has no consequences for her own standing in the eyes of the female community.

At the conclusion of the tournament the women wash and consign themselves to secrecy, but the other traces of their joust—the

[67] In making this claim I am situating *The Ladies' Tournament* against the background of women's participation in all forms of armed combat, whether in serious warfare or, like the market women at Dollenstein in bk. 8 of *Parzival* (n. 1 above), for pleasure or frivolity during shrovetide (210). I have come across many references to women directing (if not actually engaged in) combat during the Middle Ages, especially in defense of towns, castles, or other fortifications. See Pauline Stafford, *Queens, Concubines, and Dowagers: The King's Wife in the Early Middle Ages* (Athens: University of Georgia Press, 1983), 117–20; and Labarge (n. 22 above), 79–80, for references to Ermengarde of Narbonne and Nicolaa de la Haye. An important literary reference is in Wolfram von Eschenbach's *Willehalm*, where Gîburc, wearing armor, defends the city of Orange by shooting with the crossbow and casting missiles. Wolfram emphatically distinguishes between her defensive warfare and the offensive jousting of the amazons, since Gîburc did not fight on horseback (see *The Middle High German Poem of Willehalm by Wolfram von Eschenbach*, trans. Charles E. Passage [New York: Frederick Ungar, 1977], 135). Even if one focuses specifically on the question of jousting, there is still an obvious literary precedent. The amazons in Heinrich von Veldeke's late twelfth-century German retelling of the *Aeneid* are shown jousting against the Trojans in defense of the city of Laurentum. The silence surrounding the precedent of the amazons is especially eloquent in a text where reference is made to the fame of Hector and Paris (see *Heinrich von Veldeke: Eneit*, trans. J. W. Thomas, Garland Library of Medieval Literature Series B, vol. 38 [New York and London: Garland, 1985], 99). It is, of course, impossible to determine exactly which tale of the amazons served as precedent for *The Ladies' Tournament*.

lathered horses and battered physical condition of many of the participants—rouse the men's suspicion. Once they have heard the chamberlains' eye-witness account, the knights assemble to decide on a course of action. Although other *Mären* ratify the notion that each husband wields ultimate authority in his own household, *The Ladies' Tournament* makes marital discipline a community issue. The husbands treat the incident as a communal matter, as they treat the military invasion with which the story opens. Even though individuals may differ in their response, the course of action, once decided, is followed by all. The regulation of marriage is ultimately open to public debate and communal control.

The male community is divided about how to respond. One spokesman proposes that the men beat their wives, with the justification that "if women elect to go jousting / men will have to run the household."[68] His anxiety comes remarkably close to the realization that the division of labor by sex is not a biological specialization but a social convention dividing men and women into two reversible categories that merely assures that the smallest viable economic unit will contain one housekeeper and one jouster.[69] This spokesman's proposal that the men beat their wives attempts to reestablish a physical basis for the sexual division of labor. For if men can master their wives physically, then they have a superior right to bear arms, pursue military fame, rule as lords of the household, and even assure the continuation of the species.[70] Like the battering husbands of other *Mären*, the first spokesman regards violence as a prerequisite for preserving men's dominance in the gender hierarchy.

The proposal of a second spokesman is more complex. His position accommodates the men's pleasure at the incident, which is signified by their laughter. He attributes the women's joust to their youth, intending to exonerate them in direct response to the first speaker's suspicion that the devil has led them astray. Beatings, he continues, would simply add to their already considerable injuries. Finally, he recommends that the men affirm the women's accomplishments since they jousted well but forbid the women ever to joust

---

[68] Lines 291–94: "Wellen sie turnieren varn, / sô mueʒe wir daʒ hûs bewarn. / Hât sie der tiuvel daʒ gelêrt? / wie sich diu werlt hât verkêrt!"

[69] Rubin (n. 23 above), 178.

[70] According to Isidore of Seville, women's physical weakness was necessary for procreation, for "if a man easily could be repelled by a woman, his lust might lead him to turn to his own sex for satisfaction" (Vern L. Bullough, "Medieval Medical and Scientific Views of Women," *Viator: Medieval and Renaissance Studies* 4 [1973]: 485–501, esp. 489). In addition to Isidore, Bullough discusses other medieval authorities.

again since their actions were evil. This view, with its equivocal but
reconciling emphasis, wins the male community's approval.[71]

The second spokesman's proposal assures the men that they
need not be threatened by a single act of role reversal and even
allows them to celebrate the women for their jousting skill. For he
assumes that men will continue to rule over women. Again, the text
seems to distinguish between the notion of men's physical supe-
riority, which the women challenge successfully without sanction,
and men's superior social power, which the women are told never
to challenge again. Once this distinction is made, male power can
be restored and the story of the joust becomes a tale to be enjoyed.
The pleasure of the returning men is amplified as the story escapes
into the public domain: "Knights laughed at the story wherever
they sat together eating and drinking."[72] Even Duke Walraben, who
now crosses the border between reality and fiction to enter the tale
as one of its characters, takes pleasure in the story when it finally
reaches his ears. This laughter does not seem to be directed against
the community of forty knights for their failure to control their
wives; they are not scorned like the henpecked husbands in other
Mären. Rather, it is an aesthetic response to a narration that stages
its own reception.

With honor as their motivation, the jousters perform a task that
can be interpreted in literary terms as an audacious reversal of the
romance topoi. When the male Arthurian hero sets out on an ad-
venture he frequently finds himself in the service of a woman or a
community of women who are the victims of blatant social injustice.
Often a liberated lady-in-distress becomes his bride. Here the community of women plays the heroic role for the benefit of one of its
own rank. They convert martial honor into marital honor. However,
although they can joust like men, they do not possess what Gayle
Rubin would call the phallic power of exchange to complete the
marriage.[73] Their ability to cross over into men's gender roles has
a limit. Their lack necessitates the arrival of the male personage

---

[71] His motivation of mercy and reconciliation is reminiscent of the husband who
binds his wife's burned hand at the end of Stricker's *Das heisse Eisen, The Glowing
Iron.* For bibliography and editions of Stricker's *Märe,* see Fischer (n. 5 above),
409–10, entry 127f. I am referring to lines 177 through 180 in the text that appears
in *Der Stricker: Verserzählungen I,* 2d rev. ed. by Hanns Fischer (Tübingen: Max
Niemeyer, 1967), 48.

[72] Lines 325–27: "Die ritter swâ sie sâzen, / trunken oder âzen, / Sie lachten der
mære jô."

[73] Rubin, 191–92; phallus, in her usage, carries many meanings, including the
difference between exchanger and exchanged, or giver and gift, in a marriage system
where men have rights in women that women do not have in themselves.

with the social and material means to effect the marriage. "The maiden put herself in his power. / Duke Walraben gave his promise, / and married her to a rich man."[74] The poem ends when the heroine achieves honor by becoming the marriage partner of a male of appropriate status.

The final lines of the poem make a lewd joke by transforming the ladies' joust into a figure for conjugal intercourse. This ending may seem discordant in a text probably composed for a feudal or urban elite. But the joke, which comes at the point in the text where the audience would expect a moral, serves the serious purpose of reestablishing male dominance in frankly sexual terms that collapse social and biological categories. The humor resides in the phallic meaning of "hard lances," and in a pun on the Middle High German word *underligen,* which means to be vanquished militarily and to lie on the bottom: "This tale is called *The Ladies' Tournament.* They were able to break hard lances. It is a miracle: with young men or old they are always vanquished in battle [or, they always lie on the bottom], but they still preserve their honor."[75] The women's jousting skill is translated into phallic terms in the battle of the bed, where they are always "on the bottom" beneath their husbands. The wider implication of these lines is that the missionary position guarantees a woman's place beneath the authority of her husband in the marital hierarchy.

These final lines, however, may not have been written by the author of *The Ladies' Tournament* but instead added by a scribe.[76] The ending that the author apparently intended conveys a similar message but with a different emphasis: "He gave her to a rich man with whom she frequently initiated the tournament of honor. She preserved her honor at all times. Her pleasure [or, her sport] was great and varied in that tournament of honor. At the same time the lady won so much fame that no man in the world will acquire honor

---

[74] Lines 391–93: "Diu meit lieʒ sich an in gar, / der herre gab sin gelübde dar, / Er gab sie einem rîchen man."

[75] Lines 407–12: "Der vrouwen turnei heiʒt diz mær.' / sie kunnen brechen herte sper, / Daʒ ist ein michel wunder: / sie ligent stæte under, / Und behaldent doch den prîs, / der man sî junk oder grîs."

[76] Edward Schröder, "Der Frauen Turnei," *Zeitschrift für deutsches Altertum* 59 (1922): 160. Schröder contrasts "die zierliche hindeutung" ("the delicate suggestion of sex") with the "zwiefache grobe zote" ("doubly coarse and smutty joke") of the scribe. Later in the same issue, Schröder doubts the originality of lines 396–99 as well, which assert the young wife's great and varied pleasures (327). The thematic integration of these lines with the body of the text, however, argues for their authenticity.

now or in the future such as she won with her beloved husband."[77] The author of these lines is also making a joke about sex. However, what is striking in this ending is that the ideological tensions rehearsed in the poem disappear into the complicated mediations that are retrieved within marriage. Both concepts of female honor seem to reemerge. The lady *wins fame*—the active diction is borrowed from the speech of the daring woman—but in loving fidelity to her husband. At the same time, the lady *preserves her honor*—the passive notion of preservation is chosen by the wise woman in her panegyric of wifely loyalty—in the "tournament" that gives her "great and varied pleasure." These phrases are also euphemisms for sex, but here the "tournament" suggests a mutual exchange of sexual skill. The decisively active conjugal tournament, a recuperation of the heroine's jousting skill, gives full credence to her heterosexual pleasure.

The tensions between patriarchal constructs are not resolved but, rather, converted into sexual tensions that are released in the joke. The joke's heterosexual assumptions show that the foundations of patriarchy remain intact. Yet the laughter of the medieval audience—the male audience that is constructed in the text itself—arises from an ambiguity that cuts across the entire genre. One of the earliest *Mären, Der Liebhaber im Bade* or *The Lover in the Bath* opens with these lines: "Women who never do things for the pleasure they engender, and by which they can be remembered for a long time, lack gumption and spirit. One should always be grateful to her who arranges her affairs so that she is remembered whenever one speaks of ingenious women."[78] The affairs under consideration in *The Lover in the Bath*, as in most *Mären*, are amorous and usually adulterous. Female ingenuity consists in transgressing the moral

[77] Lines 393–406: "Er gab sie einem rîchen man, / mit dem sie ofte began / Turneis, des man ze êren pflît, / und behielt den prîs z'aller zît. / Ir spil was mangerleye / mit dem turneye, / Des man zuo den êren pflît. / diu vrouwe zuo der selben zît / Alsô grôzen prîs gewan, / daz in der werlde kein man / Nû, noch nimmer mêre / erwirbet grôzer êre, / Sô diu junk vrouw(e) gewan / mit irem vil lieben man." This ending appears in the most important manuscript, Heidelberg, University Library, Cpg 341. Another complete version of the text is transmitted in Genève-Cologny, Bibliotheca Bodmeriana, Cod. Bodmer 72 (olim Kálocsa, Library of the Archbishop, MS 1), although von der Hagen's apparatus shows that lines 403–406 are missing.
[78] Lines 1–9: "Ez ist ein swacher wibes muot, / diu niemer solhes niht entuot / daz ze gamene getuge, / dabi man ir gedenken muge / unz darnach vil überlanc. / man sol irs iemer wizzen danc, / diu ir dinc so hat vollebraht / daz ir muoz werden gedaht, / so man von kluogen vrouwen seit" (in Heinrich Niewöhner, ed., "Der Liebhaber im Bade," *Neues Gesamtabenteuer*, vol. 1, 2d ed. by Werner Simon [Dublin and Zürich: Weidmann, 1967], 1:170–71). For bibliography, see Fischer (n. 5 above), 372, entry 79.

laws of marriage; and although they are often condemned in moral terms, the narrative transformation of women's (im)morality into aesthetic delight is invariably applauded as the source of pleasure and, as in this passage, the source of women's fame. *The Ladies' Tournament* does not deal with adultery or related *Märe* topics, but it makes a similar transformation. Like adultery, jousting is condemned, but tales of women's challenges to patriarchal power change the psychic and social surplus of laughter into literature itself.

Comparative Literature Program
McGill University

A FEMALE UNIVERSITY STUDENT IN LATE MEDIEVAL KRAKÓW

MICHAEL H. SHANK

Although the patron saint of the medieval faculty of arts was Saint Katherine,[1] women in the Middle Ages were not permitted to enroll in institutions of higher education. Their presence was acknowledged only at the fringes of university life, when a clerk married or divorced, for example, or when the faculty of medicine condemned the illicit practice of medicine.[2] Occasional references also appear in allusions to university

For constructive criticism, advice, and assistance in various forms, I thank Klara Antosiewicz, Caroline Walker Bynum, Stanisław Kłoczowski, Londa Schiebinger, Carol Troyer-Shank, George Williams, and two anonymous referees for this journal.

[1] See, e.g., Albert Lang, "Die Katharinenpredigt Heinrichs von Langenstein," *Divus Thomas* 26 (1948): 123–59, 233–49. On Saint Katherine, see D. Balboni, "Caterina di Alessandria," in *Bibliotheca sanctorum*, ed. F. Caraffa and G. Morelli, 12 vols. (Vatican City: Istituto Giovanni XXIII, 1961–70), 3:954–63; and the Benedictines of Paris, eds., *Vies des saints et des bienheureux selon l'ordre du calendrier* (Paris: Letouzey et Ané, 1954), 2:854 ff., esp. 863.

[2] See Lynn Thorndike, ed. and trans., *University Records and Life in the Middle Ages* (New York: Columbia University Press, 1944), 119, 235 ff.; E. Denifle and J. Chatelain, eds., *Chartularium Universitatis Parisiensis* (Paris: Delalain, 1889–97), 1:488; 2:39, 149–53, 255–67; 3:16–17; 4:198-99. On the problems of married students, see Paul Uiblein, ed., *Acta Facultatis Artium Universitatis Vindobonensis, 1385–1416* (Vienna: Böhlau, 1968), 1:150, lines 32–38; and the remarks by Rudolf Kink, *Geschichte der kaiserlichen Universität zu Wien* (Vienna: C. Gerold, 1859), 1:133, n. 149.

This essay originally appeared in *Signs*, vol. 12, no. 2, Winter 1987.

social life, usually with considerable ambivalence.[3] Women who wished to acquire an education faced a narrow range of possibilities. Some studied at home with a tutor, as in the notorious case of Héloïse and Abelard.[4] The convent provided another avenue, but its primary purpose was ostensibly not education. Although its goals and standards differed significantly from those of the university, the convent nevertheless offered more educational opportunities than society at large.[5]

Another option, one that required much stamina, resourcefulness, and determination, was to circumvent university rules altogether. In his autobiography, Martin of Leibitz (died 1464),[6] the elderly abbot of the Benedictine Schottenstift in Vienna, tells this remarkable story:

> *Youth:* Tell me some unusual event that occurred in Kraków if you know one.
>
> *Elder:* When I was there, a young woman who claimed to be a virgin attended the university for two years in male dress, and came close to the baccalaureate in arts. She lived in a student hostel, behaved properly toward others, did not frequent the baths, and attended the lectures diligently. In Magna Polonia[7] she had had a teacher [*pater scholasticus*], under whom she had studied with

[3] See Robert Seybolt, trans., *Manuale scholarium* (MS dated 1481) (Cambridge, Mass.: Harvard University Press, 1921), esp. 88–97.

[4] Peter Abelard, *Historia Calamitatum: The Story of My Misfortunes*, trans. H. A. Bellows (St. Paul, Minn.: T. H. Boyd, 1922), chap. 6, 16 ff.

[5] Lina Eckenstein, *Women under Monasticism: Chapters on Saint-Lore and Convent Life between AD 500 and AD 1500* (1896; reprint, New York: Russell & Russell, 1963), esp. 356. Nuns made up the single largest group of readers for the didactic literature surveyed by Rolf Engelsing, *Analphabetentum und Lektüre: Zur Sozialgeschichte des Lesens in Deutschland zwischen feudaler und industrieller Gesellschaft* (Stuttgart: Metzler, 1973), 10 ff. See also Joan Ferrante, "The Education of Women in the Middle Ages in Theory, Fact, and Fantasy," in *Beyond Their Sex: Learned Women of the European Past*, ed. Patricia Labalme (New York: New York University Press, 1980), 9–42; Eileen Power, *Medieval Women*, ed. M. M. Postan (Cambridge: Cambridge University Press, 1975), chap. 4; and Sara Lehrman, "The Education of Women in the Middle Ages," in *The Roles and Images of Women in the Middle Ages and Renaissance*, ed. Douglas Radcliff-Umstead, University of Pittsburgh Publications on the Middle Ages and Renaissance, vol. 3 (Pittsburgh: Center for Medieval and Renaissance Studies, ca. 1975), 133–44. On the social and moral education of women in the late fourteenth century, see Anatole de Montaiglon, ed., *Le livre du Chevalier de la Tour Landry pour l'enseignement de ses filles* (Paris: Jannet, 1854). The fifteenth-century English translation by William Caxton has recently been republished as *The Book of the Knight of the Tower*, ed. M. Y. Offord, Early English Text Society, suppl. ser., no. 2 (London and Oxford: Oxford University Press, 1971).

[6] See Ernst Hauswirth, *Abriss einer Geschichte der Benediktiner Abtei U. L. F. zu den Schotten in Wien* (Vienna: Mechitaristen-Congregationsbuchdruckerei, 1858), 37–41.

[7] This designation covers present-day northwest Poland, bounded by East and West Prussia, Silesia, Brandenburg, and the Pilica and Bug rivers. See J. G. Th. Graesse, F. Benedict, and H. Plechl, eds., *Orbis Latinus* (Braunschweig: Klinkhardt & Biermann, 1972), 3:176.

other children. When her parents died, she came into an inheritance and, after dressing in male clothing, she went to the university.

Youth: How was she discovered? And what happened to her thereafter?

Elder: Upon seeing her walk through the city, a soldier in the house of a burgher named Kaltherbrig said to his companions: "If that person walking about in the guise of a student is not a girl, I will pay you so much. If she is, you will pay me." They agreed. Later, as she approached the entrance of the house, the soldier called her as if to talk to her, and he set her on a table before his companions. Once she was undressed, it became clear what she was. She was taken before the judge. When asked why she had disguised her sex, she answered: "For the love of learning." The head of her hostel was questioned under oath, and her colleagues as well. They could find nothing improper to say about her. She chose to be taken to the convent, where she was made Mistress [*Magistra*] and Abbess over all the others. And I think she still lives there, for I recently heard news about her from someone who stayed in Kraków.[8]

[8] My translation. The text was published in the early eighteenth century as "Senatorium sive Dialogus Historicus Martini Abbatis Scotorum Viennae Austriae," in *Scriptores rerum Austriacarum veteres ac genuini* . . . , ed. Hieronymus Pez, 2 vols. (Leipzig: Gleditsch, 1725), 2, col. 629 ff. Pez transcribed the work from a Melk manuscript (currently no. 139, 187ra–187va; the earlier call numbers are 632, L 59, and C 19). I have checked Pez's transcription against a microfilm of the original available at the Hill Monastic Manuscript Library (St. John's University, Collegeville, Minn.). The variant manuscript readings appear in brackets: "*Juvenis*: . . . Dic aliqua rara, si nosti, ibidem Cracoviae facta. *Senex*: Accidit cum ibidem moram facerem, quod prodita fuit quaedam puella, quae Virginem se affirmavit, quae per duos annos in veste virili et Studentis studium [*ms.*: studii] frequentavit, et vicina fuit ad Baccalariatum in Artibus. In bursa stetit, cum aliis honeste se rexit, balnea non frequentavit, lectiones diligenter visitavit. Patrem habuit in Magna Polonia scholasticum, circa quem cum aliis pueris rudimenta puerorum didicit; et mortuis parentibus, patrimonium suum recepit, et latenter veste virili [*ms.*: virila] induta ad Studium venit. *Juvenis*: Quomodo fuit deprehensa, et quid postea de ea actum est? *Senex*: Quidam miles videns eam transire in civitate, in domo civis qui dicebatur Kaltherbrig, dixit ad socios suos: Si persona illa in specie Studentis vadens non est puella, dabo vobis tantum; si est, dabitis michi. Placuit illis. Postea cum prope portam domus veniret, vocavit eam quasi [*ms. add.* sibi] locuturus, et coram sociis posuit eam ad mensam, et nudata ea, apparuit cujus sexus esset. Deinde tradita fuit Judici. Interrogata, cur sexum occultasset, respondit: amore Studii. Interrogatus conventor bursae sub juramento et socii, nichil inhonestum de ea dicere potuerunt. Optavit tradi ad Monasterium Monialium, et ita factum est. Et facta est Magistra et Abbatissa omnium aliarum, et puto quod adhuc vivit: quia noviter habui scrutinium de ea a quodam, qui Cracoviae moratus fuit." A recent popular history (P. Jasienica, *Polska Jagiellonów* [Warsaw: Państwowy Instytut Wydawniczy, 1963]) parallels the account above. Martin is mentioned and the student is said to come from Wielkopolska (Magna Polonia), where her father was a school teacher (perhaps a misunderstanding of *pater scholasticus*, which clearly is used here not in the familial but in the technical sense). Regrettably, no references are provided, either in the original or in the translation by Alexander Jordan (*Jagiellonian Poland* [Miami: American Institute of Polish Culture, 1978]), 88.

This tale raises a number of literary and historical issues. After examining it first as a narrative, I shall consider the likelihood that it also reflects a historical event. Since the theme of female transvestism has a long tradition in patristic and medieval literature, this short story sounds like another variation on a familiar topos. One need only read the lives of Saint Margaret (Saint Pelagia) and Saint Hildegund, for example, or skim Caesarius of Heisterbach's *Dialogue on Miracles* to be convinced that the theme was well known.[9] Since the Kraków story is recounted in the context of male monastic life, it is tempting to see this account as the creative transposition of a familiar monastic motif into the academic context.[10]

This presumption is especially alluring because the structure of the story fits smoothly into the pattern of narratives that anthropologists such as Victor Turner have outlined. Like Turner's "social dramas," the story involves the breach of a norm (the female student in male disguise), a crisis (the discovery of her identity), an adjustment or redress (her appearance in court), and a reintegration of the anomalous into the social structure (her appointment as *magistra* and abbess, accepted roles for an educated woman). It also conforms strikingly to Caroline Walker Bynum's critique of Turner from the perspective of her work on medieval spirituality. Whereas Turner sees the social drama as a fundamental unit of human experience, Bynum argues that his model accounts for only a portion of the material she has studied. Although Turner's scheme provides a useful tool for understanding the stories of male narrators, it does not do justice to those of females, who rarely—if ever—hinge their stories on the crisis that characterizes the social drama.[11]

[9] See John Anson, "The Female Transvestite in Early Monasticism: The Origin and Development of a Motif," *Viator* 5 (1974): 1–32; Vern Bullough, *Sexual Variance in Society and History* (Chicago: University of Chicago Press, 1976), chaps. 13–14, esp. 393–95, and "Transvestites in the Middle Ages," *American Journal of Sociology* 79 (1973): 1381–94; Michael Goodich, "Contours of Female Piety in Later Medieval Hagiography," *Church History* 50 (1981): 25; and Caesarius of Heisterbach, *The Dialogue on Miracles*, trans. H. von E. Scott and C. C. Swinton Bland (London: Routledge & Kegan Paul, 1929), e.g., bk. 1, chaps. 40, 41.

[10] The literary possibilities of the motif have been exploited to the fullest in Isaac Bashevis Singer's short story "Yentl the Yeshiva Boy," in his *Short Friday and Other Stories* (New York: Farrar, Straus & Giroux, 1964), 131 ff. Like her Christian counterpart, Yentl realizes her inheritance at her father's death and sets on to study in the male environment of a yeshiva, disguised as a boy. She, too, avoids bathing and eventually undresses—voluntarily in this case—so that her identity may be revealed. It is perhaps not a coincidence that both stories take place in Poland; as the Latin story is known there (see the works by Jasienica and Morawski in n. 8 above and n. 16 below), the connection between them may be more than thematic.

[11] Victor Turner, "Social Dramas and Stories about Them," in *On Narrative*, ed. W. J. T. Mitchell (Chicago: University of Chicago Press, 1981), 137–65, esp. 145–46; and Caroline Walker Bynum, "Women's Stories, Women's Symbols: A Critique of Victor Turner's Theory of Liminality," in *Anthropology and the Study of Religion*, ed. Frank Reynolds and Robert Moore (Chicago: Center for the Scientific Study of Religion, 1984), 105–25.

Alerted by this insight, it becomes possible to see both how much of the story the narrator devotes to the crisis, and how extensively he has oriented it to males. All of the other protagonists are male—the *pater scholasticus*, the soldier and his companions, the head of the hostel, the fellow students, and the judge. In contrast to these men, the woman protagonist utters only two words. Whereas her successful disguise and her academic career for two years required much activity (mentioned in the preamble), the student's attitude in the body of the story is largely passive, as are the verbs used to recount it: she was undressed, taken to the judge, and so on. The very elements that the narrator identifies as the locus of the crisis betray a male outlook. The discovery of the student's identity casually glosses over the distressing features of the event, both in the short term (her humiliation) and in the long term (the end of her academic aspirations).

Although "male" in outlook and form, the account is nevertheless far from hostile. The narrator portrays the student as unimpeachable in character. She behaves properly and studies diligently. In this context, even her avoidance of the public baths is given a moral connotation, presumably because of the promiscuity associated with them,[12] even though this behavior was a necessary prerequisite for the success of her disguise. Indeed her subsequent elevation to the head of a convent not only brings the story to a proper conclusion but also places it in a positive light.

Informative though they are, these structural and archetypal considerations ultimately avoid the obvious historical questions. How ought one to evaluate the narrator's claim to be recounting an event? What is the connection, if any, between this narrative and the transvestite motif in earlier saints' lives? Rephrased in the blunt language of a child, is this a true story?

The narrator's intentions are certainly not in doubt. The reader is to understand that the story takes place in historical time. Martin claims that the incident occurred during his youth and that the chief protagonist is still alive, as he has recently heard. Can the narrator be believed? At the outset, it is important to note that the archetypal or legendary character of material from one era need not necessarily undermine the historicity of similar accounts at a later date. Particularly when the legendary material serves a hortatory purpose, one ought not rule out the possibility that saints' lives inspired action. Although the details of this story are too meager to infer complex motivations from them, they offer good grounds for believing that a historical event undergirds the striking literary qualities of the narrative.

The strongest case for the historicity of the narrative rests on the allusion to the "house of a burgher named Kaltherbrig." From a literary or typological point of view, this incidental reference to the man's name is

---

[12] For a contemporary description of the customs in Germany, see Poggio Bracciolini's letter to Nicholius, written from Baden in 1417: Poggius Bracciolini, *Opera omnia*, ed. Thomas de Tonellis (Florence, 1832), 3:4–10.

curious. It contains the only personal proper name in the story. Yet the owner of the house plays no role in the narrative. At best, his name adds nothing to the tale; at worst, it detracts from the story line by drawing attention to a trivial and irrelevant detail. Indeed, this reference makes sense only if one shifts to a historical mode: the name "Kaltherbrig" is then either a conscious attempt on Martin's part to enhance the credibility of his account or a trivial detail that he unthinkingly inserted into the story while remembering his youth. The first alternative is highly implausible on internal grounds. If Martin deliberately had sought to substantiate his story, surely he would have chosen to name one of the main protagonists or the informant who had recently heard from the abbess—not the man in whose house the disguise was discovered.

In this instance, however, it is not necessary to rely on internal considerations alone, for this proper name finds an echo in city and university documents. The matriculation registers of Kraków list a *dominus Keldeherberg* among the benefactors of the university.[13] He is probably identical to the "Petrus Kaldherberg" whose name appears in town and university records between 1392 and 1421. A prominent merchant and citizen of Kraków, he served on the town council and was frequently involved in real-estate transactions. A document of August 13, 1400, even mentions him in connection with the purchase of a house for the university.[14] This item suggests a plausible explanation not only for Martin's recollection of the name (which presumably remained associated with the building after the owner gave it to the university), but also for the student's presence in the neighborhood. The surprisingly thorough corroboration of this passing allusion to Kaldherberg's name gives the account a credibility that is difficult to impugn. Under these circumstances there is little reason to distrust Martin's story or his claim to have heard news about the abbess from a recent traveler.

[13] See the *Album studiosorum Universitatis Cracoviensis*, vol. 1, *1400–1489* (Kraków: University of Kraków Press, 1887), 9.

[14] See the *Codex Diplomaticus Universitatis Studii Generalis Cracoviensis*, 5 vols. (Kraków: University of Kraków Press, 1870–1900), 1, no. 17, 30. Kaldherberg served as a town official on several occasions. His name last appears in a document of 1421. For the reference from 1392, see Stanisław Krzyżanowski, ed., *Acta Scabinalia Cracoviensia, 1365–1376 et 1390–1397* (Kraków: University of Kraków Press, 1904), 174, passim. A document of June 17, 1410, lists him among the *seniores mercatorum*, presumably the leaders of the merchants' guild; see Jan Ptaśnik, ed., *Cracovia Artificium, 1300–1500* (Kraków: Nakładem Akademii Umiejetności, 1917), 49–50. Between 1401 and 1416, he vouched for several individuals when they became citizens of Kraków. He also served on the militia for his quarter of the city in 1404; see Kazimierz Kaczmarczyk, ed., *Libri iuris civilis Cracoviensis, 1392–1506*, Wydawnictwa archiwum, vol. 5 (Kraków: University of Kraków Press, 1913), 1156, 1497, 2441, 2442, 2897, 2963, 9503c. It is important to note that the spelling of proper names is notoriously erratic in medieval documents; these variants are strikingly consistent by comparison with those on "Heytesbury" or "Swineshead."

If the event is rooted in historical rather than imaginary time, it ought in principle to be datable. Although the chronological limits of the story are difficult to determine with precision, the narrative and its protagonists offer enough clues to date it within twenty years. The upper limit is 1420, the date of Martin's matriculation at the University of Vienna, where he witnessed the destruction of the Jewish community the following year.[15] The lower limit is not so tidy. The oldest matriculation lists for Kraków mention neither Martin of Leibitz, nor Martin of Zips (as he is also known), nor an incident involving a female student.[16] The dialogue implies, however, that the event took place during the author's adolescence. Since Martin of Leibitz died in 1464, the early years of the fifteenth century suggest themselves as an approximate date. Before its revival in 1400, the University of Kraków was not a significant institution. It is unlikely that student hostels [bursae] existed in Kraków prior to this date. Since 1400 is also the year of Kaldherberg's gift to the university, a likely chronological frame for the event extends from 1400 to 1420, which is consistent with the meager biographical data available for both Kaldherberg and Martin of Leibitz.

Unfortunately the student herself remains shrouded in mystery. The reference to her *pater scholasticus* and her successful matriculation at the university suggest that she had first attended a coeducational grammar school, where she had met the prerequisites for study in a faculty of arts.[17] Her social origins are difficult to determine with certainty. The fact that her parents sent her to grammar school does suggest roots in the burgher class rather than the peasantry (where academic prospects for a girl would have been bleak) or the nobility (where tutoring or the convent were the norm).[18] Thanks to her inheritance, she was in a position to support herself.

---

[15] Martinus de Lewbicz matriculated as a member of the Hungarian nation during the winter semester of 1420 (*Die Matrikel der Universität Wien* [Graz-Cologne: H. Böhlaus Nachfolger, 1954], 1:130, line 24). His brief account of Jewish executions in 1420 also occurs in his autobiography (see Pez, ed., 2, col. 631).

[16] Heinrich Zeissberg, ed., *Das älteste Matrikel-Buch der Universität Krakau* (Innsbruck: Wagner'sche Universitäts-Buchhandlung, 1872). The *Acta rectoralia* of the University of Kraków begin only in 1469. In his *Histoire de l'Université de Cracovie* (Paris: Picard, 1900–1905), Casimir Morawski mentions the incident and conjectures without further explanation that it should be dated before 1400 (1:49, n. 2).

[17] Coeducation was not unusual during this period. For parallel cases, see Denifle and Chatelain, eds. (n. 2 above), 3:51–52 (the English translation is in Lynn Thorndike [n. 2 above], 239–40); and Caesarius of Heisterbach (n. 9 above), bk. 4, chap. 25 (about two girls with a very competitive zeal for learning).

[18] The story is consistent with E. Ennen's generalizations about city life in the later fourteenth century. Before ca. 1350, she sees little difference between the educational patterns of boys and girls in the towns. After that date, when burgher sons begin to attend the university in larger numbers, asymmetries in educational opportunity begin to correlate with gender; see Edith Ennen, *Frauen im Mittelalter* (Munich: Beck, 1984), 193–94.

Her irrepressible enthusiasm for learning pervades her brief but very moving answer to the judge (presumably a civilian authority since, as a fraudulent member of the university, she could scarcely appeal to scholarly immunity from civil prosecution).

The ecclesiastical authorities acquiesced both to the former student's wish to join a convent and to her subsequent elevation to the leadership of that institution. Hence they evidently did not think that her action placed a permanent blemish on her character but in the end recognized it as an achievement. In any case, it is unlikely that the student immediately assumed a position of responsibility at the convent. Her youth, compounded by her lack of experience with monasticism, would have made her a most improbable abbess, especially since the office was usually filled by election. Thus far, the convent that she eventually administered remains unidentified, and the student-turned-abbess is still anonymous. Some day, it is hoped, her name will transpire from the ongoing research on the religious orders of medieval Kraków.[19]

The literary and typological features of the narrative stand out so prominently that the temptation to interpret it as an artistic creation is at first glance difficult to resist. The archetypal characters of both the narrative structure and the woman's strategy seem to cast a shadow on the reliability of the account. The evidence for its historicity, however, places the entire episode in a new light by shifting the locus of creativity from the narrator to the anonymous fifteenth-century woman. Evidently it was she who transposed a familiar religious motif into an academic setting and—most remarkable of all—acted on it.

Department of the History of Science
Harvard University

[19] Of the three local convents, one was Premonstratensian, one Clarist, and one Benedictine (in Staniatki, outside Kraków). A will written in February 1394 mentions gifts "pro duobus conventibus monialium, in ipsorum uno morantur Wartinberginne et alio Langekete acto mrc." (Krzyżanowski, ed., no. 1866, p. 242) and also names the "sisters of Saint Andrew's" ("Sororum sancti Andreae"). See also no. 1035, p. 120; and no. 1893, p. 247, where the will is revised. I thank Professor Kłoczowski (Lublin) and Sister Klara Antosiewicz (Kraków) for their help in trying to trace the identity of the abbess.

THE CONVERSION OF WOMEN TO ASCETIC FORMS OF CHRISTIANITY

ROSS S. KRAEMER

Accounts of the conversion of women to ascetic forms of Christianity abound in a collection of texts known as the Apocryphal Acts of the Apostles. Extant in numerous languages, including Greek, Latin, Syriac, Coptic, and Arabic, these Acts often seem to be composite works containing diverse legends associated with the apostles of Jesus. Most scholars doubt that the apocryphal Acts reflect the actual histories of the apostles, or that they relate to the actual conversion experiences of historical women or men: Paul of Tarsus may never have converted Thecla of Iconium; nor Andrew, Maximilla of Patrae; nor Thomas, Mygdonia of India. Nonetheless, these Acts are important sources of information about the postapostolic churches in which they circulated. Analogously, the conversion accounts, in my view, illuminate a significant aspect of women's religion in the Greco-Roman world, namely, the appeal of Christian asceticism, which was particularly strong in the eastern provinces of the Roman Empire.[1]

Kraemer's essay was an early contribution to the now-abundant feminist scholarship on the Apocryphal Acts. Whether or not the stories in the Acts reflect the historical reality of women's lives in the first three or four Christian centuries, their broad dissemination undoubtedly testifies to an audience interested in stories of women's conversions. The powerful attraction of asceticism for Christian women can, however, be documented from historical sources, and formed the basis for the development of communal monasticism for women in the fourth century.

1. The rise of asceticism in early Christianity apparently dates from the earliest communities (see the so-called undoubted epistles of Paul), but the degree to which it prevailed, either in theory or in practice, varied from community to community, from region to region, and from time to time. On asceticism in the eastern provinces of the Roman Empire, see S. P. Brock, "Early Syrian Asceticism," *Numen* 20 (April 1973): 1–19, and Arthur Voobus, *A History of Asceticism in the Syrian Orient,* Corpus Scriptorum Christianorum Orientalium Subsidia 14 (1958). Asceticism also features prominently in many Gnostic Christian writings, and many, if not most, of the apocryphal Acts of the Apostles are considered to have Gnostic or related provenances.

This essay originally appeared in *Signs*, vol. 6, no. 2, Winter 1980.

The problematic nature of these texts, however, makes the endeavor to examine the appeal of ascetic Christianity to women admittedly and consciously speculative. Like much of early Christian literature, both the conversion legends and the collections in which they occur are pseudonymous or anonymous. We do not know whether these legends had their origins in oral or written form, who first circulated them, or who first incorporated them into the various and composite Acts of the Apostles. Frequently, fragments and whole works are lumped under the name Acts of such-and-such-an-apostle, although the relationship between these disparate parts remains unclear. This is especially true of the Acts of Andrew and of John, in contrast to the legends of Thomas which are more tightly woven into single literary entities. Many sections of the Acts appear to have circulated independently at one time or another, such as the Acts of Thecla, which are now embedded within the larger Acts of Paul, and which are usually referred to as the Acts of Paul and Thecla. The story of Paul and Thecla was clearly known to the North African Christian apologist Tertullian by about 200 C.E.,[2] but the dates of the other legends are more difficult to determine. The various apocryphal Acts are attributed by most scholars to the late second and/or early third centuries, whereas the individual legends may date from considerably earlier. Further, since the apocryphal Acts themselves consist of discrete elements thought by many scholars to antedate the composition of the Acts by later author-editors, important questions remain about the audience and the function of both the discrete legends and the various composite Acts. In the absence of explicit dedications and declarations, we may hypothesize that the legends initially arose in Christian circles and functioned both to reinforce the beliefs of the Christian community and to serve as conversion propaganda. Probably, the Acts were intended primarily for Christian audiences, and secondarily as conversion literature for interested non-Christians. In either case, Christians would have viewed such stories as confirmation of their own faith, whether they heard them recounted or read them. Because of the enigmatic nature of these texts,[3] my primary concern is to illuminate the dynamic of conversion depicted in these legends, on the explicitly stated assumption that they accurately describe the patterns of ancient conversions if not the conversions of specific historical persons.

2. Tertullian *De Baptismo* 17.

3. For a more thorough discussion of this complex literature, see the introductions in E. Hennecke, *New Testament Apocrypha*, ed. W. Schneemelcher, 2 vols. (Philadelphia: Westminster Press, 1965) (hereafter cited as Hennecke-Schneemelcher). The majority of Acts may be found in the Greek collection *Acta Apostolorum Apocrypha*, ed. M. Bonnet and R. A. Lipsius (Darmstadt: Wissenschaftliche Buchgesellschaft, 1959). Syriac texts with English translations may be found in W. Wright, *The Apocryphal Acts of the Apostles* (London: William & Margate, 1871). English translations of the Greek texts, with lengthy introductions, may be found in Hennecke-Schneemelcher. See also M. R. James, *Apocryphal New Testament* (Oxford: Clarendon Press, 1924).

All of these conversion stories follow a similar literary pattern. Each relates the conversion of a woman whose husband, fiancé, lord, or father is of relatively high social status in a community which an apostle has recently entered. Persuaded by the apostle's teachings to accept Jesus, the woman adopts a sexually continent way of life, which is the principal feature of her conversion. If already married, she withdraws from her husband; if unmarried, she vows to remain a virgin. A ritual induction of the woman into the Christian community often takes place, although this does not always follow the conversion immediately. Thecla, for instance, baptizes herself a considerable time after she converts to Christian asceticism, and this is also true of Tertia in the Acts of Thomas.[4] The practice of continence does not seem to depend upon formal ritual induction, which thus cannot be considered an integral element of the legend.

The principal male in the woman's life invariably opposes her new-found asceticism,[5] and frequently threatens the woman, the apostle, or both. Such threats are never successful: the woman continues her association with the apostle and her practice of chastity. As a result, both apostle and woman are imprisoned, scourged, or otherwise punished. Frequently, as in the martyrdons of Thomas, Andrew, and Peter, the angered husband is the direct cause of the apostle's death; only rarely does the husband convert.[6] The woman does not denounce asceticism in any of the accounts;[7] rather, she lives chastely outside her husband's home, and in some cases, such as those of Thecla and Charitine, she even joins a band of wandering Christian apostles. Maximilla in the Acts of Andrew continues to live a celibate life within her husband's household, despite his vigorous protestations. Drusiana in the Acts of John, however, lives chastely and harmoniously with her husband, Andronicus, an instance of the "virgin marriage" apparently practiced by some early Christians. But most of the women in these conversion legends do not enter into such chaste partnerships, since chastity is desired only by one partner. Spouses who do convert to an ascetic form of Christianity naturally acquiesce to the chaste marriage, as does, for example, the couple in the wedding episode and Prince Vaisan and his wife in the Acts of Thomas.[8]

4. See the Acts of Paul and Thecla 34; Acts of Thomas 137, 157.

5. Only Charitine's father, in the Acts of Philip, converts with her (Acts of Philip 44).

6. See, e.g., Andronicus in the Acts of John 63, and Misdaeus in the Acts of Thomas 170.

7. However, the tale of Artimilla in the Acts of Paul (Hamburg Papyrus, p. 3) hints at such a possibility when Paul, having baptized Artimilla, sends her back to her husband Hieronymus.

8. See the Acts of Thomas (8–16, 150). How widespread was the custom of "virgin marriage" in early Christian communities is not clear. Two passages in Paul's first letter to the church at Corinth have been interpreted as evidence for very early Christian chaste marriages; 1 Cor. 7:29 advocates that "from now on, let those who have wives live as

In the apocryphal Acts, Christianity is essentially defined as the acceptance of an ascetic way of life. In the Acts of Thomas the basic assumptions of ascetic Christianity and the specific aspects of secular life to be renounced are forcefully articulated:

> Look upon us Lord, since for your sake we have left our homes and our father's goods, and . . . have gladly and willingly become strangers. . . . we have left our own possessions for your sake, that we may obtain you, the possession that cannot be taken away . . . we have left those who belong to us by race, that we may be united with your kindred. . . . we have left our fathers and mothers, and fosterers, that we may behold your Father and be satisfied with his divine nourishment . . . for your sake we have left our bodily consorts and our earthly fruits, that we may share in that abiding and true fellowship and bring forth true fruits.[9]

Similar attitudes are reflected in the beatitudes attributed to Paul in the Acts of Paul: "Blessed are they who have kept the flesh pure, for they shall become a temple of God. Blessed are the continent, for to them will God speak. Blessed are they who have renounced this world, for they shall be well pleasing unto God. Blessed are they who have wives as if they had them not, for they shall inherit God. . . . Blessed are the bodies of the virgins, for they shall be well pleasing to God, and shall not lose the reward of their purity."[10]

The Christianity of the apocryphal Acts demands of its adherents both chastity and severance from family. This had substantial implications, especially for women. Ascetic Christianity, in fact, offered women a new measure of worth which involved a rejection of their traditional sociosexual roles.[11] As do most societies, the larger Greco-

---

though they had none." But it is unclear whether this passage means living together in an asexual relationship, or abandoning the familial household altogether. An enigmatic passage over which there has been much debate, 1 Cor. 7:38, is translated in the Revised Standard Version as "he who marries his betrothed does well, and he who refrains from marriage does better." More important, perhaps, there are significant differences between circumstances of the early churches which Paul addressed and those of the second and third centuries with which this paper is primarily concerned. I agree with Walter Schmithals's judgment that first-century Christian asceticism is rooted in a pragmatic response to the imminent demise of the present world which only later develops into asceticism for the sake of asceticism. Most scholars are in accord that the early evidence for such "virgin marriages" is insubstantial, while the later evidence is more convincing. For an introduction to this debate, see Hans Lietzmann, *An die Korinther, Handbuch zum Neuen Testament 9* (with revisions by W. G. Kümmel) (Tübingen: J. C. B. Mohr, 1949); Hans Conzelmann, *1 Corinthians: A Commentary on the First Epistle to the Corinthians*, trans. James W. Leitch (Philadelphia: Fortress Press, 1975); and Walter Schmithals, *Gnosticism in Corinth*, trans. John E. Steely (Nashville, Tenn.: Abingdon Press, 1971).

9. Acts of Thomas 61 (translation adapted from Hennecke-Schneemelcher).
10. Acts of Paul 5–6 (translation from Hennecke-Schneemelcher).
11. The notion I will pursue in the following pages relies to some extent on a

Roman communities in which ascetic women lived clearly propounded different measures of worth for women than for men. While men were valued by and large for their public achievements in varying realms— hunting or military prowess, financial success, intellectual capability, etc.—women were to derive their worth from the ascribed roles of wife, mother, and household mistress.[12] The texts of the apocryphal Acts provide evidence that women in the Greco-Roman communities from which ascetic Christianity drew its members were defined in terms of traditional sociosexual roles and their relationship to men. In the Acts of Thecla, for instance, the heroine is sentenced to burn to death because she will not marry Thamyris, her fiancé, and because she will not be a bride, not because she has listened to the words of a sorcerer. Paul, on the other hand, is only scourged and exiled.[13] Indeed, Theocleia, Thecla's mother, cries out at her trial, "Burn the lawless one! Burn her that is no bride in the midst of the theatre, that all women who have been taught by this man may be afraid."[14] Thus, to be a woman is to be a wife; she who refuses has committed sacrilege—she is *anomos*.

The predominant definition of women as sexual beings in the conversion legends may also be found in two episodes from the Acts of Peter. In the first,[15] Peter explains that his daughter, who at age ten strongly tempted Ptolemaeus, became paralyzed through a miracle and

---

deprivation-compensation theory of religion. While such a model has many contemporary advocates and critics, they are often particularly anathema to scholars who study antiquity, especially religion in general and Christianity in particular. Criticism of the application of social science theories and models derived from the twentieth-century research to study of early Christianity usually focuses on the internal inconsistencies of deprivation theory, but it often disguises hidden theological agenda. Since deprivation theory may be interpreted to mean that religions express no external ultimate truth because they function to alleviate certain social conditions, scholars with theological interests have an a priori stake in its refutation. In my view, however, a model which sheds light on data should be considered, and data which reveal the inaccuracy of a model should prompt reconsideration, refinement, or rejection of the theory. For excellent discussions and examples of the fruitfulness of such applications, see John G. Gager, *Kingdom and Community: The Social World of Early Christianity* (Englewood Cliffs, N.J.: Prentice-Hall, Inc., 1975), and Gerd Theissen, *Sociology of Earliest Palestinian Christianity*, trans. John Bowden (Philadelphia: Fortress Press, 1978).

12. There is a substantial literature on the roles and status of women in Greco-Roman antiquity. See J. Leipoldt, *Die Frau in der antiken Welt und im Urchrisentum* (Gutersloh: G. Mohn, 1962); Maurice Bardèche, *Histoire des femmes* (Paris: Stock, 1968); Vern Bullough, *The Subordinate Sex: A History of Attitudes toward Women* (Urbana: University of Illinois Press, 1973); Sarah B. Pomeroy, *Goddesses, Wives, Whores and Slaves: Women in Classical Antiquity* (New York: Schocken Books, 1975). For additional references and reviews, see Marilyn B. Arthur, "Review Essay: Classics," *Signs: Journal of Women in Culture and Society* 2, no. 2 (1976): 382–403.

13. Acts of Paul and Thecla 20, 21. Schneemelcher, in Hennecke-Schneemelcher (2:332), attributes this disparity to the fact that the emphasis of the story is Thecla, not Paul, but this seems to me to miss the whole point.

14. Acts of Paul and Thecla 20, translation from Hennecke-Schneemelcher.

15. From a Coptic fragment attributed to a larger Acts of Peter. See Hennecke-Schneemelcher, 2:300–302.

thus ceased to be attractive. Peter argues that it is better for her to be a cripple than to be the subject of further temptation. In the episode entitled "The Gardener's Daughter," an old man asks Peter to pray for his virgin daughter, whereupon she drops dead. The next comments: "O reward worthy and everpleasing to God, to escape the shamelessness of the flesh and to break the pride of the blood."[16] The distressed old man beseeches Peter to resurrect her, which he does, whereupon she is seduced and disappears. The alternatives available to women are here defined as sexuality or death, with death clearly preferable to sexuality. The two stories suggest that these limited alternatives are accepted by both Christians and non-Christians, but that Christian asceticism has reversed the values normally attached to these alternatives.

Even within the ascetic Christian framework of the Acts, the definition of woman in terms of men and marriage persists. In the opening sections of the Acts of Thomas, for example, when Thomas prevents a newlywed couple from consummating their marriage and converts them instead to a spiritual union, the bride speaks of receiving marriage with "the true man," whereas the bridegroom interprets his conversion as receiving knowledge.[17] Indeed, virtually all of the conversion stories contain a motif of erotic substitution. In the Acts of Thecla, the heroine seeks Paul out at every opportunity, but the erotic nature of her attraction is particularly evident in the narration of their encounter in prison: Thecla is discovered with the apostle late at night in his cell, "bound with him, so to speak, in affection."[18] In the Acts of Thomas, Mygdonia explicitly states her preference for Jesus/Thomas to her husband Charisius: "He whom I love is better than you." To which Charisius replies: "Look upon me, for I am [far better and more handsome—Syriac] than that sorcerer . . . you are my family and kinship, and behold he is taking you away from me."[19] Likewise, in the Acts of Paul, Hieronymus is distressed by the rumors that his wife has left him for Paul; and in the Acts of Philip, Nicanora's husband says categorically: "It is better for you to be destroyed by the sword than for me to see you fornicating with such strangers and sorcerers."[20] The repeated presence of the motif of erotic substitution derives in part from the theme of divine marriage. In the Acts of Thomas, for example, Mygdonia says to Charisius: "You are a bridegroom who passes away and is destroyed, but Jesus is a true bridegroom, abiding immortal forever. . . ."[21] However, this erotic motif also suggests that when women are represented as re-

16. Pseudo-Titus *De Dispositione Sanctimonii* 83 ff. (in Hennecke-Schneemelcher, 2:298–99).

17. Acts of Thomas 14, 15.

18. Acts of Paul and Thecla 18–19.

19. Acts of Thomas 116, 117; translation adopted from Hennecke-Schneemelcher.

20. The Hamburg Papyrus fragment of the Acts of Paul, p. 4; Acts of Philip 120.

21. Acts of Thomas 4 ff., esp. 6–7, 124 (translation adapted from Hennecke-Schneemelcher).

jecting their traditional sexual roles in the legends of ascetic Christianity, they are nonetheless still defined in terms of men, namely, the male divinity and his agent, the male apostle.[22]

Since the Acts provide ample evidence that women in the Greco-Roman communities in which ascetic Christianity flourished were defined primarily in terms of traditional roles, we may now investigate the appeal of ascetic Christian theology for its female adherents, while recognizing that these texts do not permit us to reconstruct the psychological states of individual women. Here the insights of contemporary anthropological studies of women's religious activities may enable us to grasp the significance of the specific characteristics attributed to women converts. I. M. Lewis, for example, suggested in *Ecstatic Religion* that among Sar and Bori cults in Africa and the Caribbean, women are particularly vulnerable to peripheral spirit possession when their status is in a state of flux—pubescent girls, women on the verge of marriage, newly married women, women whose polygamous husbands are about to take on a new wife, divorced women, and widows. By that token, very young girls and married women raising children and running households are less disposed toward such cultic activities.[23] A high proportion of the Christian women in the Apocryphal conversion legends fall into Lewis's categories. Thecla is a virgin about to be married, Mygdonia in the Acts of Thomas and Xanthippe in the acts which bear her name are newly married women who have no children, and Drusiana in the Acts of John has been married for an indeterminate amount of time and has no children.[24] Only Maximilla in the Acts of Andrew may possibly have borne children during her marriage to Aegeates.[25] Moreover, a number of women in the conversion legends are of inferior sociosexual status. Agrippina, Nicaria, Euphemia, and Doris in the Acts of Peter are all the concubines of Agrippa, and Trophima in the Acts of Andrew is an ex-concubine.[26] It is not surprising that these marginal women who had

22. The erotic triangle also figures prominently in the Greco-Roman romances, a literary form to which the acts are closely related. For various treatments of Greco-Roman romance literature, see Martin Braun, *History and Romance in Greco-Oriental Literature* (Oxford: Basil Blackwell, 1938); T. R. Glover, *Life and Letters in the Fourth Century* (Cambridge: Cambridge University Press, 1901): E. H. Haight, *Essays on the Greek Romances* (New York: Longmans, Green & Co., 1943) and *More Essays on Greek Romances* (New York: Longmans, Green & Co., 1945); B. E. Perry, *The Ancient Romances: A Literary-historical Account of Their Origins*, Sather Classical Lectures 37 (Berkeley: University of California Press, 1967).

23. I. M. Lewis, *Ecstatic Religion* (Harmondsworth, Middlesex: Penguin Books, 1971), pp. 66–69, 191.

24. Acts of Paul and Thecla 7–8; Acts of Thomas 100; Acts of Xanthippe 6. The tale of Drusiana, continent wife of a now-consenting husband, Andronicus, relates the attempt of one Callimachus to fulfill his sexual desire for her, even to the point of raping her entombed corpse. The tale (Acts of John 62–86) makes no mention of any children of the marriage of Andronicus and Drusiana.

25. Acts of Andrew (Vaticanus Gr. 808 4).

26. Vercelli Acts of Peter 33; the Latin *Liber de Miraculos Beati Andreae Apostoli*, compiled by Gregory of Tours in the twelfth century.

no way of gaining prestige in the established social hierarchy would be attracted to cultic activities which offered validating mechanisms and a new measure of worth.

Whether their status is marginal or transitional, all the women in these conversion legends reject traditional female sociosexual roles by rejecting their husbands or fiancés, often leaving their homes and towns and becoming members of the wandering Christian band, if not explicitly teachers themselves.[27] Often, role rejection is expressed as role reversal. Mygdonia, the convert of Thomas, cuts short her hair, as does Thecla, the disciple of Paul.[28] Thecla also dons male clothing when she sets out to follow Paul, as does Charitine in the Acts of Philip.[29]

That the conversion of women to ascetic Christianity constituted a break with the traditional expectations of women is also evident in the sanctions which are taken against them and the labels which are applied to them by their antagonists. The motif of women's madness, for example, occurs to a significant extent in the conversion stories. Thecla's mother several times describes her as mad, or possessed,[30] and in the Acts of Thomas, Charisius emphasizes the insanity of Mygdonia's actions. "Noble lady as she is, whom none of her house ever charged [with impropriety—Syriac] she has fled naked from her chamber and run outside, and I know not where she has gone. And perhaps, maddened by that sorcerer, she has in her frenzy gone to the market-place in search of him. For indeed, nothing seems loveable to her but that man and the things said by him."[31] Later, Mygdonia's friend, Tertia, also suspects her of being mad: "why do you do the deeds of madmen?" she asks.[32] After Mygdonia has won Tertia over to Christianity, both women are described as being possessed. This designation of insanity expresses a judgment, but, as I have emphasized elsewhere, it also serves as a form of social control. Women who defy traditional expectations are ostracized through the label of insanity.[33]

The tale of Trophima in the Acts of Andrew, compiled by Gregory of Tours in the twelfth century, illustrates more clearly the sanctions

27. For example, Acts of Paul and Thecla 23, 26, 40; Acts of John 105.
28. Acts of Thomas 114; Acts of Paul and Thecla 25.
29. Acts of Philip 44; Acts of Paul and Thecla 25.
30. Acts of Paul and Thecla 8–9.
31. Acts of Thomas 99. The element of madness is played down in the Syriac.
32. Acts of Thomas 135. The Syriac text claims that Mygdonia was "like a madwoman because of Judas [Thomas]" (114).
33. For provocative discussions of the social functions of the label of insanity, see Phyllis Chesler, *Women and Madness* (Garden City, N.Y.: Doubleday & Co., 1972); Thomas Szasz, *The Manufacture of Madness* (New York: Harper & Row, 1970); and Thomas Scheff, *Being Mentally Ill: A Sociological Theory* (Chicago: Aldine Publishing Co., 1966). For a study of the function of women's ritual madness in ancient Greece, see R. Kraemer, "Ecstasy and Possession: The Attraction of Women to the Cult of Dionysus," *Harvard Theological Review* 72 (1979): 55–80. See also R. Kraemer, "Ecstasy and Possession: Women of Ancient Greece and the Cult of Dionysus," in *Unspoken Worlds: Women and Religion in Cross-cultural Perspectives*, ed. R. Gross and N. Falk (New York: Harper & Row, 1980), pp. 53–69.

taken against women who reject their traditional roles. For her refusal to have marital relations with her husband, Trophima is suspected of infidelity[34] and condemned to prostitution. Although she escapes through divine intervention, the fact remains that the woman who renounces acceptable forms of sexual behavior in favor of celibacy is doomed to the most degrading form of the very sociosexual identity she has rejected—prostitution. Against such vehement opposition, the language of the ascetic forms of Christianity must have provided a strong set of validating mechanisms, particularly for women. Indeed, the justification of sexual purity preached by the apostle in the Acts of Thomas constitutes a promise of the ultimate rewards for rejecting women's traditional sexual function: "Know this, that if you abandon this filthy intercourse . . . you will not be girt about with cares for life and for children, the end of which is destruction. . . . But if you obey and keep your souls pure unto God, you shall have living children whom these hurts do not touch, and shall be without care, leading an undisturbed life without grief or anxiety, waiting to receive that incorruptible and true marriage, as befitting for you."[35] The notion that women who refrain from bearing children will be rewarded with the gift of divine children[36] contains a deeper message: women who do not fulfill their traditional sociosexual roles can find in ascetic Christianity a new standard of worth by which they are superior to all other sexually bound women.

The conversion stories of the Apocryphal Acts of the Apostles reveal elements of the attraction which ascetic Christianity may have held for certain women in the Greco-Roman world—either women who found the traditional roles of wife and mother inadequate measures of their worth, or women who could not participate in the rewards guaranteed by adherence to those standards—socially marginal women, widows, or barren women. Although the Acts of the Apostles are replete with the conversion accounts of men, the renunciation of sexuality and sociosexual roles, as we have seen, had far greater implications for women than it did for men. Religious systems which legitimize the rejection of the established sociosexual standards, as did ascetic Christianity,

34. This is true of most of the converted women, although the lover is usually believed to be an apostle; in Trophima's case it is her former lover, the now Christian, chaste Lesbius.

35. Acts of Thomas 12.

36. A similar motif appears in the description of the women of a mixed-sex monastic Jewish community outside Alexandria, Egypt, in the first century c.e., called the Therapeutae by Philo Judaeus (*On the Contemplative Life*). Since Philo is the only source for this group, some scholars have suggested that he invented the group as an example of the perfect life; the current scholarly consensus is against this view. For a more detailed discussion of the women of Therapeutae, see R. Kraemer, "Ecstatics and Ascetics: Studies in the Functions of Religious Activities for Women in the Greco-Roman World" (Ph.D. diss., Princeton University, 1976), pp. 203–19.

are likely to attract large numbers of discontented and marginal women and to propound standards of worth and redemption more consonant with their circumstances.

Office of the President
Stockton State College

WOMEN'S MONASTIC COMMUNITIES, 500–1100: PATTERNS OF EXPANSION AND DECLINE

JANE TIBBETTS SCHULENBURG

The great founding mothers of Frankish and Anglo-Saxon monasticism—among them Saints Caesaria of Arles, Radegund of Poitiers, Burgundofara of Faremoutiers-en-Brie, Salaberga of Laon, Gertrude of Nivelles, Balthild of Chelles, Ethelburga of Barking, Etheldreda of Ely, Hilda of Whitby, and Cuthburga of Wimborne—are familiar to most scholars of the Middle Ages. As founders of monastic communities for women and (with the exception of Radegund and Balthild) the first abbesses of their monasteries, they achieved great visibility in the early Church and in society and were rewarded for their contributions by recognition of sanctity. However, the prominence of women in the early Church and the appreciation of women's contributions to monastic life seem to have been relatively short-lived. Although scholars have singled out for study this formative period in which women religious flourished, their research has not focused on subsequent changes in women's opportunities and status within the Church. In general, the study of change in

An earlier version of this paper was presented at the fourteenth International Congress on Medieval Studies, Western Michigan University, Kalamazoo, Michigan, May 1979.

This essay originally appeared in *Signs*, vol. 14, no. 2, Winter 1989.

women's religious communities across time has received scant critical attention. Scholars have only recently become interested in this area of research.[1]

This study explores the growth and decline of communities of female religious from approximately 500 to 1100 in Britain and the areas of modern-day France and Belgium. This comparative survey of the number of new foundations of women's communities relative

[1] While there has been a proliferation of scholarship on women and the late medieval church, the early history of women in monasticism has not received adequate attention from scholars. See, e.g., the classic studies by Lina Eckenstein, *Woman under Monasticism: Chapters on Saint-lore and Convent Life between* A.D. *500 and* A.D. *1500* (Cambridge: Cambridge University Press, 1896); Philibert Schmitz, *Histoire de l'ordre de Saint Benoît*, 7 vols. (Liège: Maredsous, 1942–56), vol. 1, *Origines, diffusion et constitution jusqu'au XIIe siècle*, and vol. 7, *Les Moniales*; and Michel Parisse, *Les nonnes au moyen age* (Le Puy: C. Bonneton, 1983). For an excellent study of women in the Frankish Church, see Suzanne Fonay Wemple, *Women in Frankish Society: Marriage and the Cloister, 500–900* (Philadelphia: University of Pennsylvania Press, 1981), 127–97. For a discussion of the recent literature, see Wemple, 4–5. For the Merovingian period, see Jean-Marie Guillaume, "Les abbayes de femmes en pays franc, des origines à la fin du VIIe siècle," in *Remirement, l'abbaye et la ville: Actes des journées d'études vosgiennes Remiremont 17–20 avril, 1980*, ed. M. Parisse (Nancy: Service des publications de l'université de Nancy II, 1980), 29–46. See also Jean Verdon's pioneering articles on female monasticism in medieval France (ninth through eleventh centuries): "Notes sur le rôle économique de monastères feminins en France dans la second moitié du IXe et au debut du Xe siècle," *Revue Mabillon* 58 (1975): 329–43, "Recherches sur les monastères feminins dans la France du sud aux IXe–XIe siècles," *Annales du Midi* 88 (1976): 117–38, "Les Moniales dans la France de l'ouest aux XIe et XIIe siècles: Etude d'histoire sociale," *Cahiers de civilisation médiévale* 19 (1976): 247–64, and "Recherches sur les monastères feminins dans la France du nord aux IXe–XIe siècles," *Revue Mabillon* 59 (1976): 49–96. See also the very useful collection of essays on women and the Church by John A. Nichols and Lillian Thomas Shank, eds., *Medieval Religious Women* (Kalamazoo, Mich.: Cistercian, 1984 and 1987), vol. 1, *Distant Echoes*, and vol. 2, *Peaceweavers*. For Anglo-Saxon women, see the classic studies by Sr. Mary Byrne, *The Tradition of the Nun in Medieval England* (Washington, D.C.: Catholic University of America, 1932); and M. Bateson, *Origin and Early History of Double Monasteries*, Transactions of the Royal Historical Society, n.s. 13 (1899), 137–98. For more recent studies, see Barbara Kanner, ed., *The Women of England from Anglo-Saxon Times to the Present: Interpretive Bibliographical Essays* (Hamden, Conn.: Archon, 1979); Pauline Stafford, *Queens, Concubines, and Dowagers: The King's Wife in the Early Middle Ages* (Athens: University of Georgia Press, 1983), 175–97; Christine E. Fell, Cecily Clark, and Elizabeth Williams, *Women in Anglo-Saxon England and the Impact of 1066* (Oxford: Basil Blackwell, 1986), 108–28; Joan Nicholson, "*Feminae Gloriosae*: Women in the Age of Bede," in *Medieval Women*, Studies in Church History, Subsidia 1, ed. Derek Baker (Oxford: Basil Blackwell, 1978), 15–29. For Ireland, see also Kathleen Hughes, *The Church in Early Irish Society* (London: Methuen, 1966), and *Early Christian Ireland: An Introduction to the Sources* (Ithaca, N.Y.: Cornell University Press, 1972); and Lisa M. Bitel, "Women's Monastic Enclosures in Early Ireland: A Study of Female Spirituality and Male Monastic Mentalities," *Journal of Medieval History* 12, no. 1 (1986): 15–36.

to the number of men's foundations underscores the fact that women's presence and influence in the Church were neither assured nor stable. The early expansion of the Church into Europe; the relative peace and stability of society; the Viking, Saracen, and Hungarian invasions; the subsequent reform efforts of church leaders; and the economic relations between the Church and the lay aristocracy all shaped the prevalence of women's religious communities. Over the course of six centuries, these factors contributed to a marked increase and an equally striking decline in the number of women's monasteries relative to that of men. This study, then, will attempt to explore through a comparative approach some of the antecedents of change. It will offer a few tentative explanations for the shifting disparity, or the growing asymmetrical patterns, that emerged between the communities for men and women during this formative period in monastic history.

A statistical overview of new foundations

Despite the paucity and unevenness of documentation for this era, through the collective use of a wide variety of sources a wealth of information is available. Primary source material, such as the thousands of Latin saints' lives, monastic charters, chronicles, correspondence, ecclesiastical and royal legislation, as well as archeological evidence, enables historians to reconstruct this early period. The rough statistical data for this survey are provided by the following collections: *Répertoire topo-bibliographique des abbayes et prieurés* by Dom L. Cottineau, *Histoire de l'église en Belgique: Circonscriptions ecclésiastiques, chapitres, abbayes, couvents en Belgique avant 1559* by E. de Moreau, *Medieval Religious Houses: England and Wales* by Dom David Knowles and R. N. Hadcock, and the Ordnance Survey's *Monastic Britain.*[2] Although these sources are somewhat limited and provide only an incomplete statistical distribution for these

---

[2] L. H. Cottineau, *Répertoire topo-bibliographique des abbayes et prieurés*, 2 vols. (Mâcon: Protat frères, 1935–37); E. de Moreau, *Histoire de léglise en Belgique: Circonscriptions ecclésiastiques, chapitres, abbayes, couvents en Belgique avant 1559* (Brussels: L'édition Universelle, 1948); David Knowles and R. Neville Hadcock, *Medieval Religious Houses: England and Wales* (London: Longman, 1971); Ordnance Survey, *Monastic Britain* (Southampton: Director General of the Ordnance Survey, 1978). At the moment there is no convenient reference collection that catalogs information on female monastic communities in the Middle Ages. The computer-assisted project, "Women's Religious Life and Communities," founded at Barnard and coordinated by Suzanne Wemple, Mary Martin McLaughlin, and Heath Dillard, is preparing the much needed, comprehensive repertory of female religious communities in existence before 1500 in Latin Christendom.

early centuries, collectively they furnish enough information to form a rather crude yet accurate evaluation of the changing importance of monastic communities for women. Furthermore, these data provide an indirect index of shifts in family strategies to maintain wealth and social status and, thus, women's opportunities to initiate new foundations, as well as changes, in women's attraction to monastic life. These patterns also reflect fluctuating attitudes toward women on the part of the Church and society.

The first monasteries founded in France and Britain were established exclusively for men. However, affiliated communities for women, which maintained close ties to the male founders and their monasteries, were soon established. In France, the earliest men's communities appear to have developed under the inspiration of Saint Martin of Tours (d. 397) with monastic centers at Ligugé (near Poitiers) (363) and Marmoutier (on the banks of the Loire) (371). Although the extant sources are limited and somewhat difficult to interpret, there may have been a few small women's settlements associated with this early movement.[3] In the south of France, the origins of cenobitic life can be traced to Saint Honoratus and his famous community of Lerins. Founded at the end of the fourth or beginning of the fifth century on a small island off Cannes, Lerins provided monastic foundations for both male and female religious.[4] About the year 410, John Cassian established affiliated or twin monasteries in Marseilles: one of these communities was for men and the other for women.[5] Influenced by the foundations at Lerins and Marseilles, Caesarius, Bishop of Arles, at the beginning of the sixth century, built a convent for his sister, Caesaria, within the walls of the city of Arles.[6]

The early monastic development in Britain is perhaps more complex. The first monasteries in Britain appear to have been founded in the fifth century, specifically in Wales, Cornwall, and western England. The south of England was converted to Christianity by a group of monks sent by Pope Gregory the Great (590–604) from his own monastery in Rome. Under the leadership of Saint Augustine,

[3] Schmitz, *Histoire de l'ordre de Saint Benoît*, 7:7; David Knowles, *Christian Monasticism* (New York: McGraw-Hill, 1969), 25–27.

[4] C. H. Lawrence, *Medieval Monasticism: Forms of Religious Life in Western Europe in the Middle Ages* (London and New York: Longman, 1984), 14; Schmitz, 7:7.

[5] Lawrence, 14–15.

[6] Mother Maria Caritas McCarthy, *The Rule for Nuns of St. Caesarius of Arles: A Translation with a Critical Introduction*, Catholic University of America Studies in Mediaeval History, n.s. 16 (Washington, D.C.: Catholic University of America Press, 1960), 13–14.

a monastery of monks (later known as St. Augustine's Abbey) was established at Canterbury. The first religious communities for women were founded several decades later by Eanswith (daughter of King Eadbald of Kent) at Folkestone sometime between 630 and 640 and by Queen Ethelburga at Lyminge around 633.[7]

Another important center of early monastic activity was located in the north of Britain and owed its existence to Saint Aidan's Celtic mission to Northumbria. Recruited by King Oswald, Aidan came from the great Celtic monastic center of Iona to establish his monastery and missionary see on the tiny island of Lindisfarne in 635. In the wake of this mission, new monastic communities, for male and female religious recruited from the first generation of enthusiastic converts, were established in the north of Britain.[8]

A rough index of the popularity and early development of monastic life, as reflected by the foundation of new religious houses in France, Belgium, and Britain, is provided in tables 1 and 2, which indicate the number of monasteries founded for men and for women in each fifty-year increment from 500 to 1099 and the percentages of women's houses relative to those of men. It should be noted from the outset that the numbers in these tables are neither precise nor absolute; rather, they are only approximate due to the problematic nature of the sources. For example, the lists of foundations are incomplete. Historians possess specific details about only a fraction of the monastic communities that were known to have existed in this early period. Also, it is not always clear whether some of the monasteries noted in these catalogs had a "real" existence since they are known only through later documentation, such as charters and saints' lives. In some cases it is difficult to affix a precise foundation date, for only the century or fifty-year period in which a community was said to have been established is known. In addition, the exact locations of a few of the original communities are uncertain.[9]

For the period under consideration, approximately 3,178 new religious houses were established for men and women; of these settlements, roughly 2,822 were situated in France and Belgium, and 356 in Britain. Of the total, fewer than 300 foundations were established for women: approximately 223 houses in France and

[7] Knowles and Hadcock, 66, 473, 477.

[8] Bede, *A History of the English Church and People*, trans. Leo Sherley-Price (Harmondsworth: Penguin, 1955, 1968), bk. 3, chap. 3, 144–45. Lawrence, 50–53; Knowles, *Christian Monasticism*, 40–41.

[9] Charles Higounet, "Le problème économique: L'église et la vie rurale pendant le très haut moyen age," in *Le chiese nei regni dell'Europa occidentale* (Spoleto: Presso la sede del centro, 1960), 775–804, esp. 781–82.

TABLE I **NEW RELIGIOUS FOUNDATIONS: FRANCE/BELGIUM**

Years	New Foundations (Total)	Men's Houses	Women's Houses Number	Percentage[a]
500–549.	108	100	8	7.4
550–99.	156	137	19	12.2
600–649.	102	77	25	24.5
650–99.	159	107	52	32.7
700–749.	63	55	8	12.7
750–99.	91	80	11	12.1
800–849.	146	134	12	8.2
850–99.	107	99	8	7.5
900–949.	136	130	6	4.4
950–99.	232	219	13	5.6
1000–1049	543	515	28	5.2
1050–99.	979	946	33	3.4
Total	2,822	2,599	223	. . .

SOURCE.— Based on the monastic foundations listed in L. H. Cottineau, *Répertoire topo-bibliographique des abbayes et prieurés*, 2 vols. (Mâcon: Protat frères, 1935–37); and E. de Moreau, *Histoire de l'église en Belgique: Circonscriptions ecclésiastiques, chapitres, abbayes, couvents en Belgique avant 1559* (Brussels: L'édition Universelle, 1948).
Reprinted by permission of the University of Georgia Press from *Women and Power in the Middle Ages*, ed. Mary Erler and Maryanne Kowaleski. © 1988 by The University of Georgia Press.
[a]Average = 7.9 percent.

TABLE 2 **NEW RELIGIOUS FOUNDATIONS: BRITAIN**

Years	New Foundations (Total)	Men's Houses	Women's Houses Number	Percentage[a]
500–549	8	8	0	0
550–99	39	39	0	0
600–649	29	20	9	31.0
650–99	94	56	38	40.4
700–749	26	19	7	26.9
750–99	16	15	1	6.3
800–849	12	8	4	33.3
850–99	11	9	2	18.2
900–949	22	19	3	13.6
950–99	26	21	5	19.2
1000–1049	16	15	1	6.3
1050–99	57	51	6	10.5
Total	356	280	76	. . .

SOURCE.—Based on the monastic foundations listed in David Knowles and R. Neville Hadcock, *Medieval Religious Houses: England and Wales* (London: Longman, 1971); and Ordnance Survey, *Monastic Britain* (Southampton: Director General of the Ordnance Survey, 1978).
Reprinted by permission of the University of Georgia Press from *Women and Power in the Middle Ages*, ed. Mary Erler and Maryanne Kowaleski. © 1988 by The University of Georgia Press.
[a]Average = 21.3 percent.

Belgium and 76 in Britain. That is, during this formative period in
monasticism, only 9.4 percent of the total number of new houses
were founded for female religious. Although the total number of
new communities in Britain is small relative to that in France and
Belgium (in several cases less than thirty per fifty-year increment),
the percentage of new houses in Britain that were founded for
women is nearly three times that in France and Belgium.

Certain periods during these centuries also seem to have been
more open than others to providing new opportunities for women
to exercise active roles in the Church. These same periods proved
to be especially conducive to the establishment of new women's
communities. The era of most intense activity for women in monastic life (as reflected by the founding of new women's houses) in
both France/Belgium and Britain was the seventh century. During
the first half of the seventh century, 24.5 percent of the religious
communities established in France/Belgium were women's communities. For the years 650–99, this increased to 32.7 percent. Although the earliest houses for women were located in the south of
France, the majority of the communities established in the seventh
century were founded in the north of France and modern Belgium.
Many of these settlements were associated with the new wave of
missionary activity, including the Celtic missions under the leadership of Saint Columban (540–615) and his followers Saints Eloi,
Ouen, and Philibert, and the Aquitainian mission under Saint Amand
(d. ca. 679).[10]

During these formative years, many English women with religious leanings, having few religious communities of their own,
crossed the channel and took vows in the established cloisters of
France. Bede notes that "for as yet there were few monasteries built
in English territory, and many who wished to enter conventual life
went from Britain to the Frankish realm or Gaul for the purpose.
Girls of noble family were also sent there for their education, or to
be betrothed to their heavenly Bridegroom, especially to the houses
of Brie, Chelles, and Andelys."[11] Although the development of wom-
en's houses in Britain began several decades later than the devel-

[10] Lawrence, 43–48; *Vitae Columbani Abbatis Discipulorumque eius libri duo
auctore Iona, Monumenta Germaniae Historica* [hereafter cited as *MGH*]: *Scriptorum Rerum Merovingicarum,* ed. Bruno Krush (Hanover: Impensis Bibliopolii
Hahniani, 1902), 4:1–152; L. Van der Essen, *Étude critique et littéraire sur les vitae
des saints merovingiens de l'ancienne Belgique* (Louvain: Bureaux du recueil, 1907);
Robert Folz, "Remiremont dans le mouvement colombanien," in Parisse, ed. (n. 1
above), 15–27; Marquise de Maille, "Les monastères colombaniens de femmes," in
Les cryptes de jouarre (Paris: Picard, 1971), 13–57; Wemple (n. 1 above), 158–60.
[11] Bede, bk. 3, chap. 8, 153–54.

opment in France, the popularity of monasticism in Britain remained relatively strong into the first half of the eighth century, well after the number of women's religious communities in France had begun to decrease. During the years 600–649, approximately 31 percent of the new foundations in Britain were established for women. During the second half of the seventh century this percentage increased and peaked at 40.4 percent. As was the case in France, the proliferation of new houses in Britain was closely related to missionary activities; for example, a number of women's communities founded in the north of England were promoted by the missionary bishop-saints Aiden, Cuthbert, and Wilfrid.[12]

Beginning early in the eighth century there appears to have been an overall decline in the number of new monasteries established for both men and for women in France/Belgium. Documents of the period reveal an apparent waning of the early enthusiasm for monastic life, as well as perhaps the saturation of some areas with a surplus of small proprietary houses. However, coinciding with these general shifts in monasticism, there occurs an especially sharp fluctuation in the percentages of newly founded female communities. The percentage of new foundations in France/Belgium established for women dropped from 32.7 percent for the years 650 to 699 to 12.7 percent for the period 700 to 749. This was the beginning of a drastic decline in new foundations for women, which continued in France and Belgium through the late eleventh century.

Beginning in about 750, Britain witnessed a similar decline in the total number of new communities as well as in the percentage of new foundations established for women. The percentage of new monasteries founded for female religious declined to approximately 27 percent for the years 700 to 749, and to 6.3 percent for the period 750–99.[13] Moreover, the total number of new foundations established in Britain after the year 700 (and prior to the eleventh century) was indeed very small. The percentage of these houses established for women for this period must therefore be interpreted

---

[12] Ibid., bk. 4, chap. 19, 239; bk. 4, chap. 23, 246.

[13] C. H. Talbot, trans. and ed., *The Anglo-Saxon Missionaries in Germany* (New York: Sheed & Ward, 1954), vii–xvii, 25–62, 205–26; Wilhelm Levison, *England and the Continent in the Eighth Century* (Oxford: Clarendon, 1946). The number of new foundations and the percentages of houses for women in the first half of the eighth century would no doubt have been greater if one considered the missionary efforts of the Englishwomen in Germany during this time. Under the auspices of the missionary-saints Boniface and Lioba, a number of English nuns were recruited to spread the new faith in Germany. There they established several religious communities for women, or double houses, which became centers of missionary activity and education.

with caution; since each of the fifty-year increments has fewer than thirty new foundations, a change of one would substantially skew the percentage of these houses that were founded for women.

In contrast to the eighth, ninth, and tenth centuries, the eleventh century, in general, witnessed a great effervescence and revitalization of monastic life. It was an age of reform and renewed religiosity, in which there was a heightened enthusiasm for the cenobitic as well as the eremitic life.[14] Nevertheless, the number of new foundations for women and the percentage of these in the aggregate of new communities continued to decline.

For the years 1000 to 1049 some 543 new monasteries and priories were established in France and Belgium. (This is more than twice the number of monasteries founded in any fifty-year period between 500 and 1000.) However, out of this rather impressive total, approximately 28 or only 5.2 percent of the monasteries were established for women. Between 1050 and 1099, this growing disparity became even more exaggerated. Some 946 houses were founded for men and only about 33 (3.4 percent) were founded specifically for women. For the entire eleventh century in France and Belgium, only 4.0 percent of the new foundations were established for female religious.

Similarly, in Britain the number of new foundations for women relative to those for men declined. For the years 1000 to 1049, only 6.3 percent of the new monasteries were founded for women; while during the years 1050 to 1099 the number increased to approximately 10.5 percent.[15] Although the Norman Conquest facilitated the foundation of numerous new communities for men, only a few women's communities were founded in its wake. In comparison to the scores of new houses commissioned for men after the Norman Conquest, it appears that only two or three small foundations for

[14] Knowles, *Christian Monasticism* (n. 3 above), 62–82; R. W. Southern, *Western Society and the Church in the Middle Ages* (Harmondsworth: Penguin, 1970), 214–30.

[15] Immediately after the Norman Conquest in 1066, many noble Englishwomen joined monastic communities. As daughters and wives of Harold Godwinson's loyal supporters, they were particularly afraid of being raped by the Norman invaders. They therefore took the veil for protection and sought asylum in the English monasteries. As noted by Eadmer (d. ca. 1124) in his *History of Recent Events in England,* "Thereupon a number of women anticipating this and fearing for their own virtue betook themselves to convents of Sisters and taking the veil protected themselves in their company from such infamy" (Geoffrey Bosanquet, trans., *Eadmer's History of Recent Events in England: Historia Novorum in Anglia* [London: Cresset, 1964], 129). See also David Knowles, *The Monastic Order in England: A History of Its Development from the Times of St. Dunstan to the Fourth Lateran Council: 943–1216* (Cambridge: Cambridge University Press, 1940), 137–38.

women were established, these during the reigns of William the Conqueror and his son, Rufus. Also beginning in the eleventh century, communities for religious women were generally founded as "secondary foundations" or priories, rather than as independent, primary abbeys.[16]

Consequently, although the eleventh century offered new choices and opportunities to men in monasticism (as reflected in the multiplicity of new monastic movements and new foundations), this does not seem to have been the case for women. In fact, the founding of new monasteries for men frequently appears to have occurred only at the *expense* of women. During this period of reform and renewed monastic activity, women's options within the Church and expectations were narrowed: they began to diverge substantially from those of their male contemporaries.

The first period of expansion

What then are some of the factors that might explain the growing gender-based pattern of monastic asymmetry? What special conditions initially coalesced to create an atmosphere of enthusiasm, high expectations, and popular support for a rather fragile "Golden Age" of female monasticism? How did these conditions change to bring about the dramatic decline in the formation of monastic communities for women? And why, by the end of this period, did the opportunities and expectations for female religious appear to differ significantly from those of their contemporary male religious?

These rough statistics of new religious foundations indicate that during the seventh century, a particular set of conditions prevalent in Frankish Gaul and Anglo-Saxon England fostered the development of monastic life for women. Much of this monastic activity occurred in the essentially rural frontier areas, which were in the process of being converted to the new faith. In this milieu of necessity, the survival of the Church depended on the contribution and cooperation of every member of society. The missionaries needed to recruit workers from among the newly converted church members for their missionary and educational centers. Recognizing from the start the receptivity of noblewomen to the new faith, as well as the crucial role women would assume as domestic proselytizers (in the conversion of their families to Christianity), churchmen actively recruited women with power and property into the

---

[16] Knowles and Hadcock (n. 2 above), 17.

monastic movement.[17] They encouraged the wives and daughters of the nobility to use their landed wealth to establish churches and endow monastic communities. These women's foundations became the focus of religious and social activity and the center of organization for the region. They fulfilled the missionary and educational functions of the Church through the establishment of monastic schools. They also served as the bases of operation for churchmen who were converting the region, by providing them with supplies and other support. In addition, these early women's communities assumed all of the local rights and functions of the parish church.

Many of these early monasteries were essentially "family houses" or proprietary foundations. They were established and endowed by the aristocracy on their own family estates. In addition to responding to the very real spiritual or religious aspirations or needs of the period, these communities also alleviated the "practical" concerns of the noble households by providing a proper place of security or refuge for daughters who did not wish to marry or for whom marriages were perhaps politically or economically inexpedient in light of family strategies. These monasteries also provided sanctuary as well as convenient places of retirement for widows or repudiated wives.[18]

The eagerness of the upwardly mobile nobility to endow family monasteries seems to have been prompted largely by the rapid influx of landed wealth, the spoils of pillage and war, and the augmentation of power and lordship, coupled with the early enthusiasm of these new converts to Christianity. In part, as Karl J. Leyser has noted with regard to Germany, this initial desire to establish new foundations for women seems to have been a fulfillment of the self-protective aristocratic caste's present needs.[19] The aristocracy regarded family monasteries established on their villas as an integral part of their own extensive estates. The founders of these new houses saw their endowments (which frequently consisted of newly won lands) as a temporary family investment in the Church rather than a permanent alienation of their patrimony. In some cases, the monastery and its properties even reverted back to the original

[17] Jane T. Schulenburg, "Female Sanctity: Public and Private Roles, ca. 500–1100," in *Women and Power in the Middle Ages*, ed. Mary Erler and Maryanne Kowaleski (Athens: University of Georgia Press, 1988), 102–25, esp. 105–6; Jo Ann McNamara, "Living Sermons: Consecrated Women and the Conversion of Gaul," in Nichols and Shank, eds. (n. 1 above), 2:19–37.

[18] Stafford (n. 1 above), 175–90; Wemple (n. 1 above), 158–65; Karl J. Leyser, *Rule and Conflict in an Early Medieval Society: Ottonian Saxony* (London: E. Arnold, 1979), 63–73.

[19] Leyser, 63–73.

donor's heirs after the death of the founding abbess. As part of the general strategy to maintain control over their proprietary foundations, the founders installed family members as abbesses, guardians, or advocates of the monasteries and required that in the future these positions be held by their heirs.[20] Also greatly concerned about safeguarding their own future "lives" beyond the grave, the aristocracy established family mausolea within their new religious foundations, so that the nuns could provide perpetual prayers for the "safety of their souls."

Although many of these family houses were created for daughters of the aristocracy or, frequently, sisters of bishops or abbots, some of them were in fact established by women acting in their own names, who had either separated from their husbands or were widows. They liberally endowed these religious foundations with their own dower lands and inherited properties. For some this may have been a strategy to maintain direct control over their estates as well as to gain the added protection of the Church.

Frequently, successful family monasteries serving as missionary and parochial centers required the collaborative efforts of both monks and nuns. They therefore adopted the popular ad hoc arrangement of the double monastery, or the affiliated house.[21] The double monastery was a pragmatic arrangement especially suited to women who wished to live a religious life in the countryside. Away from the protection provided by the city walls and the surveillance or assistance of the local bishop and his clerics, the double house provided nuns with the priests required to administer the sacra-

[20] Ibid.

[21] Double monasteries or coeducational communities varied in organization and composition. Many of the double foundations were initiated primarily for female religious. They then supported a supplementary community of monks or priests and male servants who provided the necessary sacerdotal functions and performed manual labor. Sometimes the male component was relatively large, other times it consisted of only a few male religious and servants. In this type of arrangement, the abbess usually held jurisdiction over the entire community of both monks and nuns. Other double communities established primarily for monks or canons later accepted an added component of nuns. This type of foundation was usually under the authority of an abbot, or sometimes an abbot and abbess. A third variation, although not technically a double monastery, was the affiliated house or twin foundation. Here, two distinct houses were established (often by the same founder) in the vicinity of one another. Although they remained autonomous communities, each electing its own abbess or abbot, they provided mutual support by maintaining close ties and assuming special privileges, rights, and obligations toward one another. See Wemple, 159–62, 170; Guillaume (n. 1 above), 38–39; Bateson (n. 1 above), 137–98; Schmitz, *Histoire de l'ordre de Saint Benoît* (n. 1 above), 1:321 ff., 7:45–53; and Lawrence (n. 4 above), 46–47, 51–52.

ments, men to perform hard manual labor in the fields and forests, as well as the male protection thought necessary by the Church.

Women's houses in fifth- and sixth-century France traditionally had been founded within the walls (*intra muros*) or the protective confines of the city and had been grouped within episcopal cities; by the seventh century, many of the new communities were located in rural areas.[22] According to a study by Higounet, at least three-fourths of all of the Merovingian monasteries for both men and women were established in the countryside.[23] In her study of early women's abbeys of France, Jean-Marie Guillaume discusses the great flowering of women's communities in the seventh century. She notes that although the seventh century remained an epoch of urban foundations for women, for the first time women's houses were established in great numbers in the countryside, primarily on the villas of the powerful Frankish aristocracy.[24] In contrast to many of the women's houses located within the cities, these rural double monasteries or affiliated houses were free from the close monitoring or scrutiny of the local bishops. Within this environment, abbesses were provided with greater opportunities to assume authority and to act autonomously as independent heads of their communities. The double monastery provided a symbiotic relationship wherein both nuns and monks aided one another in their religious and material lives.[25] Moreover, in this environment, where monks and nuns lived, worked, and worshipped in close proximity, both frequently came to know and respect members of the opposite sex.

The climate of relative peace and security found in Frankish Gaul and Britain during this early period also encouraged the expansion of monastic life. This atmosphere allowed missionaries to travel freely. Monastic life appeared to be a positive option, a safe sanctuary for aristocratic women. Free from the imminent danger and destruction caused by constant warfare or invasion, the nobility and churchmen and -women could focus on something other than wartime measures and defense: they could use their resources, time, and energy to establish new religious foundations. This auspicious beginning, however, was very soon cut short; for with the coming of the invasions, this positive environment would be shattered.

[22] Guillaume, 38–42; Wemple, 156.

[23] Higounet (n. 9 above), 785.

[24] Guillaume, 38–42.

[25] According to the *vita* of Saint Gertrude of Nivelles (d. 659), the abbess, as head of the community, delegated the care of the monastery's external, temporal affairs to its monks; she assigned responsibility for concerns within the monastic enclosure to a group of her nuns (*Vita Sanctae Gertrudis*, chap. 3 in *MGH: Scriptorum Rerum Merovingicarum* [n. 10 above], 2:457).

Patterns of decline and reform

Despite favorable conditions that initially encouraged the proliferation of new monasteries, a survey of more than three thousand
religious houses of this early period reveals the extremely precarious and frequently ephemeral nature of many of these new foundations. Some survived only a decade or so, others only a generation
or two. As Kathleen Hughes has noted with regard to the development of women's monastic communities in early Christian Ireland, some aristocratic women established religious houses on their
family lands with, it seems, the intention that their foundations
would endure for only the length of their own lifetimes. These small
"family houses" attracted female relatives and friends of the founder, as well as a few women from the local area. Thus, when the
founder died, the community was dispersed (its members joined
other houses or returned to secular life), and the land reverted to
the founder's family.[26] In any case, the initial or short-term survival
of many houses seems to have been directly related to the personal
power, charisma, wealth, and connections of their founding abbesses.

A number of other factors also contributed to the untimely demise of many of these early communities. Some of the monastic
foundations suffered from what in hindsight appears to have been
faulty planning on the part of their generous benefactors. Several
saints' lives describe cases in which new convents were either
under construction or had actually been completed on property
outside of the city walls (*extra muros*) only to have the founder or
community members realize the potential danger of the site. The
nuns were then moved within the protective city walls (*intra muros*), where their foundations were rebuilt.[27] Other monasteries were
established on land without a water supply, or situated too close to
the sea, only to be lost to the tides. There are several instances in
which noblewomen—sisters or friends—established separate communities in very close proximity to one another.[28] While the insti-

[26] Hughes, *Early Christian Ireland* (n. 1 above), 234–35.

[27] In regard to the moving of Caesarius of Arles' monastery for nuns from the
city's suburbs, or outside the city walls, to within the city walls, see *MGH: Scriptorum Rerum Merovingicarum*, 3:467; and McCarthy (n. 6 above), 13–14. For reference to the transfer of Saint Salaberga's monastery from a site outside of the city
of Langres to within the walls of Laon, see *Vita Sadalbergae, MGH: Scriptorum
Rerum Merovingicarum*, 5:56–57. A similar shift in sites can be noted for an early
convent built outside the walls of Soissons (see Verdon, "Recherches sur les monastères feminins dans la France du nord" [n. 1 above], 55).

[28] See the case of Ermengitha and her sister Domneva, who established two
monasteries in Kent located one mile from one another, in Knowles and Hadcock
(n. 2 above), 478.

tution of proprietary houses encouraged a proliferation of new foundations, in the long run this duplication of communities dependent on or competing for essentially the same support base seems to have led to a certain redundancy, decline, and, in some cases, the eventual abandonment of these houses.

A case that further illustrates the eagerness and haste with which many new monasteries were built (perhaps at the expense of careful planning) can be found in the *vita* of Saint Bertha, founding abbess of Blagny in Artois (d. ca. 725/35). On one occasion, while Bertha visited with Saint Rictrud, Abbess of Marchiennes, at Marchiennes (located about thirty miles from Blagny), they allegedly heard a loud crash off in the distance. According to the *vita*, this was the sound of the collapse of Bertha's church at Blagny. It had just been completed and was ready to be consecrated. The Life also notes that shortly before this the monastery's first church had fallen down while it was under construction.[29]

Other monastic foundations succumbed to disasters such as flood and, especially, fire. Some fell victim to pestilence. For example, Bede describes the virulence of the plague of 686, which nearly decimated several monastic communities in Britain.[30] Sources also attest to the plundering and burning of monasteries by local lords.

However, the greatest external threat to monastic security and longevity during the eighth through the eleventh centuries came from the invasions of the Vikings, Saracens, and Hungarians. The chronicles and charters provide especially lugubrious accounts of the invasions and their heavy toll on monastic life. Although these ecclesiastical sources may exaggerate the extent of the damage, in reality a great number of religious communities fell victim to the invaders. In England alone it appears that at least forty-one houses for women (including double foundations) were destroyed by the Danes. Very few of the English women's communities survived these repeated onslaughts by the Vikings; in fact, by the time of the Norman Conquest, only nine houses for women in Britain remained.[31] The chronicles and saints' lives are particularly descriptive of the destruction wrought by the invaders, including the murder of entire communities of nuns. Barking Abbey was destroyed by the Danes in 870, and all of the nuns of the community were burned alive inside the monastery.[32] In the same year, the monastery of Ely

[29] *Vita S. Bertae Abbatissae Blangiacensis, Acta Sanctorum*, ed. Socii Bollandiani (Paris: V. Palme, 1867), Iulii, vol. 2, chap. 1, 50–51.
[30] Bede (n. 8 above), bk. 3, chap. 27, 195–96; bk. 4, chap. 7, 218–19; bk. 4, chap. 14, 229–30.
[31] Knowles, *The Monastic Order in England* (n. 15 above), 101.
[32] Knowles and Hadcock, 256.

was destroyed and its nuns were killed by the Danes.[33] The nuns of Whitby fled from the devastations of the Vikings, first to Hartlepool and then, as the invaders approached, on to the strongly fortified monastery of Tynemouth. It, too, fell to the Danes, who plundered and destroyed the church and monastic buildings. The nuns of Whitby who had sought refuge there were all massacred.[34] The community of Coldingham was also attacked and destroyed by the Vikings. Although the nuns heroically attempted to protect their virginity by mutilating themselves (cutting off their noses and lips) and thus discouraging rape, they were burned alive inside their monastery.[35]

Some of the communities that were destroyed by the invaders were unfortunately located near the sea or on routes frequented by the invaders. Saint Sexburga's house at Minister-in-Sheppey, for example, was a frequent landing place for the Danes and was therefore repeatedly devastated by the invaders.[36] The nearby monastery of Saint Mildred in Thanet was plundered and burned by the invaders in 980. In 1011 the Danes returned. This time they took the abbess hostage, after which the community was dispersed.[37]

Thus, the invasions destroyed many of the defenseless monastic communities, and the killing of nuns and monks and the rape or kidnapping of abbesses and female religious by the "pagan" invaders took a toll in human suffering and psychological trauma. In so doing, they threatened the continued prosperity or even existence of many monastic communities, and consequently numerous houses were temporarily deserted or permanently abandoned. Church leaders' recruitment for monastic life and promotion of new monasteries also suffered.

Churchmen of the period became increasingly alarmed at the immense destruction and disruption of religious life caused by the

[33] E. O. Blake, ed., *Liber Eliensis*, Camden 3d ser., vol. 92 (London: Offices of the Royal Historical Society, 1962), bk. 1, chaps. 39–41, 53–56.

[34] Knowles and Hadcock, 80; Debra Shipley and Mary Peplow, *England's Undiscovered Heritage: A Guide to 100 Unusual Sites and Monuments* (New York: Henry Holt, 1988), 116.

[35] Roger of Wendover, *Flowers of History: Comprising the History of England from the Descent of the Saxons to A.D. 1235*, trans. J. A. Giles, 2 vols. (London: H. G. Bohn, 1849), 1:191–92. See also Jane T. Schulenburg, "The Heroics of Virginity: Brides of Christ and Sacrificial Mutilation," in *Women in the Middle Ages and the Renaissance: Literary and Historical Perspectives*, ed. Mary Beth Rose (Syracuse, N.Y.: Syracuse University Press, 1986), 29–72, esp. 41–62.

[36] Knowles and Hadcock, 261. See also William Page, ed., *Kent*, vol. 2 of *The Victoria History of the Counties of England: Kent* (London: St. Catherine Press, 1926), 2:149.

[37] Knowles and Hadcock, 70.

invasions, along with the secularization of religious landholdings and the proliferation of lay abbacies, all of which contributed to indigency and decline in monastic life. During the tenth and eleventh centuries, several different reform movements—including the famous Cluniac reform, the reforms of Gerard of Brogne, Gorze, and Richard of St.-Vanne, and the English and Papal or Gregorian reforms—attempted to abolish these abuses in the Church. Recognizing the dangers inherent in continued lay control over monasteries and over the offices of abbess and abbot, they stressed the need to free monastic life, to extricate it totally from its involvement with the "worldly" or secular. That is, the reformers advocated that the property and administration of monasteries be removed from lay control and placed completely under the control of the Church.

The reform councils and synods of the period painted an especially bleak and perhaps somewhat exaggerated picture of the decline of monastic life. The Council of Trosley in 909 described the destruction of many monasteries and the complete disorder of others. Monks, canons, and nuns were no longer under the supervision of their own superiors but, rather, obeyed churchmen from the outside. Laymen carried the title of abbot and ruled over houses in which they lived with their wives, children, soldiers, and dogs. Their morals were corrupt and they squandered monastic revenues. Enclosure was no longer observed, and many religious inmates of the monasteries, reduced to indigency, were forced to work at secular trades.[38]

Church leaders were rather articulate in their descriptions of the general level of moral decadence that they found in the monasteries of the period. Their reform policies, therefore, aimed to eradicate the corruption, abuse, and irregularities of practice among male and female religious. The institution of the double monastery caused growing suspicion among churchmen. Already in the seventh century, Archbishop Theodore had questioned the propriety of the double community, contending that it was unseemly for men to rule women in religion or women, men. Nevertheless, he at that time decided on a policy of toleration for this established custom.[39] Later, in the Anglo-Saxon councils of the eighth century, various decrees required all monks and nuns to adhere to the austere regular life. These canons were probably intended to enforce the observ-

---

[38] Charles J. Hefele and H. LeClercq, *Histoire des conciles d'après les documents originaux* (Paris: Letouzey et Ané, 1911), vol. 4, pt. 2, 722–25.

[39] Arthur West Haddan and William Stubbs, *Councils and Ecclesiastical Documents Relating to Great Britain and Ireland* (1871; reprint, Oxford: Clarendon, 1964), 3:195, chap. 6, no. 8: "Non licet viris feminas habere monachas neque feminis viros; tamen nos non destruamus illud quod consuetudo est in hac terra."

ance of the Benedictine Rule in England. One of the results seems to have been that mixed communities of monks and secular clerks were separated into distinct houses of monks and canons. These decrees may have had a similar effect on the double communities, encouraging segregation of their inmates into separate houses for men and women.[40] On the continent, reformers of the Carolingian period and of the tenth and eleventh centuries, motivated by their exaggerated emphasis on celibacy, attacked the "morally suspect" double monastery. Sternly set against this concept, in the reestablishment and creation of new monastic communities, they chose not to reintroduce the earlier cooperative arrangement of the double monastery.

The demise of the double monastery was paralleled by the Carolingian reformers' increased efforts to regulate and enforce strict cloistering for female religious. This gender-specific measure was necessary, they claimed, to insure stability and to maintain the high moral and spiritual standards required for women in monastic life. In reality, this reform policy was used to control female religious and to supervise more closely women's communities. Women's participation in monastic life became circumscribed. Enclosure severely restricted the influence and movements of abbesses, and many women's houses were denied their significant function as primary educational centers. Moreover, this policy of strict enclosure hampered the economic activities of women's communities. In so doing it made them increasingly dependent on outside secular or ecclesiastical male "protectors." Strict cloistering or enclosure thus insured that women's communities would become less autonomous and, frequently, burdens on or liabilities of the Church and society.[41]

Also during the Carolingian period, efforts were made to make monastic life more efficient and viable through the consolidation of women's communities. Thus, perhaps in response to the proliferation of small proprietary houses, the Carolingian reformers established a policy requiring that small women's houses either be eliminated or consolidated into larger communities.[42]

[40] Knowles and Hadcock (n. 2 above), 464.

[41] See Jane T. Schulenburg, "Strict Active Enclosure and Its Effects on the Female Monastic Experience (ca. 500-1100)," in Nichols and Shank, eds. (n. 1 above), 1:51–86. Wemple (n. 1 above), 187–88. Wemple has also observed for the Carolingian period: "The strict cloistering of nuns and canonesses on the one hand and the shrinking economic resources of monasteries on the other considerably tempered women's enthusiasm for monastic life in the ninth century" (165–74, esp. 171).

[42] *MGH: Capitularia, Duplex legationis edictum*, no. 19, I:69; Hefele and LeClercq (n. 38 above), vol. 4, pt. 2, 685. See Schulenburg, "Strict Active Enclosure," 72, 75–76; Wemple, 167–68.

However, the immediate priorities of the tenth- and eleventh-century reforms included the reconstruction of destroyed monastic foundations, the restoration of despoiled lands, the regularization of monastic practices, and the much needed renewal of the moral fiber of monastic life. In their battle for asceticism and clerical celibacy, the reformers regarded contact with women as a definite hazard to their souls. They fostered an exaggerated fear of women that frequently took the form of full-blown misogyny. In his *Collationum*, the reformer Saint Odo of Cluny (d. 940) contends that the prime instrument of the devil is *luxuria*, the unchaste woman. He bemoans the fact that two lapsed nuns of the area left their monasteries and returned to the secular life, and he notes pessimistically that he would like to be able to convert to chastity at least the women of his own region. However, despite these claims to support female reform, he restored only one convent for nuns, at Bauxières, circa 930, in contrast to the scores of male houses that he refounded and established.[43]

Only in 1055, after Cluny's foundation of hundreds of monasteries for men, did the reformer Abbot Hugh establish the first house of Cluniac nuns at Marcigny. Hugh notes in his writing the clear need at this time for new monasteries for women and his contemporaries' low regard for women's monasticism. Nevertheless, the primary motivation for the establishment of the Cluniac foundation at Marcigny seems to have been pragmatic and based on moral compulsion or guilt: Marcigny was constructed to provide a refuge, a "glorious prison," for the wives of men who had become monks at Cluny.[44]

The Cluniac reformers' exclusionary policies toward women and their initial disinterest in women's monastic life was shared, al-

---

[43] Odo of Cluny, "*Collationum*," in *Bibliotheca Cluniacensis*, ed. Martinus Marrier and Andreas Quercetanus (Brussels: Librairie nationale d'art et histoire, 1915), bk. 2, 194; bk. 3, 234–35. In his writings, Odo is careful to emphasize that women are forbidden to enter the great reform monastery at Cluny. However, in his *Chronicle*, Hugh of Flavigny mentions the eleventh-century case of Ava, abbess of the monastery of Saint Maur of Verdun. Apparently Ava desired to learn more about the regular, reform practices of monasticism. Out of friendship for Abbot Richard, founder of Saint Maur, Saint Odilo was said to have allowed Ava to come to the great reform center of Cluny to observe monastic life (see *Chronicon Hugonis, Patrologia Latina*, ed. Jacques Paul Migne, 221 vols. [Paris: Bibliothecae cleri universae, 1844–64], 154:239). In contrast to the general pattern of decline or neglect in female monastic life, Mary Skinner has noted a rather localized "boomlet" or religious revival for women in central France in the tenth and eleventh centuries (see "Benedictine Life for Women in Central France, 850–1100: A Feminist Revival," in Nichols and Shank, eds. [n. 1 above], 1:87–113).

[44] Southern (n. 14 above), 310–11.

though to a much lesser degree, by Saints Dunstan, Ethelwold, and Oswald in the tenth-century English religious revival. Both Dunstan and Ethelwold had been strongly influenced by continental reform ideas, and Saint Oswald of Worcester had spent his formative years as a monk at the great French abbey of Fleury, where he was introduced to Cluniac ideas of reform.[45] However, in marked contrast to the situation in France, English noblewomen and abbesses were allowed a certain formal involvement in the early stages of the reform movement. Abbesses, nuns, and Queen Aelfthryth attended the synodal council at Winchester (ca. 970) and were involved in the acceptance of the reform customary, which was called the *Regularis concordia anglicae nationis monachorum sanctimonialiumque*. This monastic code, as its title denotes, recognized the roles of both monks and nuns in England. The customary specifically designated King Edgar as guardian of the rule of monks, and Queen Aelfthryth as "the protectress and fearless guardian of the communities of nuns; so that he himself helping the men and his consort helping the women there should be no cause for any breath of scandal."[46] Despite the early involvement of the queen and abbesses in this ecclesiastical revival, the actual number of new houses for women created or reformed during this period remained relatively modest in comparison to those for men. Knowles, for example, has attributed approximately forty new and reestablished monasteries to the half century between the reestablishment of Glastonbury in 940 and Dunstan's death in 988. Of these houses, only six or seven appear to have been principal convents of nuns.[47]

Although the English reform, backed by the king and queen, supported the founding or restoration of houses for nuns, the monastic movement itself was controlled by the church reform leaders Dunstan, Ethelwold, and Oswald. These churchmen set the priorities and agenda for the actual restoration of monasteries in Britain during this period. Thus, it became nearly a formula for the destroyed and abandoned women's foundations to be reestablished by the reformers as houses for monks or canons. The unwritten policy of reestablishing monasteries that had formerly belonged to communities of female religious is exemplified by a 963 entry in the *Anglo-Saxon Chronicle*. Saint Ethelwold asked King Edgar "to

[45] Knowles, *The Monastic Order in England* (n. 15 above), 28–56.

[46] Saint Aethelwold, *Regularis Concordia: The Monastic Agreement of the Monks and Nuns of the English Nation,* ed. Thomas Symons (London: Thomas Nelson, 1953), 1–2.

[47] Knowles, *Christian Monasticism* (n. 3 above), 54; Aethelwold, xxiii. (Here the figures in table 1 are perhaps misleading, for they do not reflect the English houses for women that were refounded or restored.)

give him *all* the monasteries which the heathen had destroyed, because he wished to restore them: and the king cheerfully granted it." According to the *Chronicle*, "The bishop [Ethelwold] went first to Ely [which had been a double community founded by Saint Etheldreda], where St. Ethelthryth [Etheldreda] is buried, and had the monastery built, giving it to one of his monks. . . . He consecrated him abbot and peopled it with monks to serve God, *where formerly there had been nuns*."[48]

The following is only a partial listing of some of the famous early houses for women or double monasteries ruled by abbesses that were destroyed or abandoned during the invasions, only to be restored as exclusively male settlements: in Britain—Whitby, Coventry, Gloucester, Folkestone, Leominster, Minster-in-Thanet, St. Milburga of Wenloch, Tynemouth, St. Frideswide, Oxford, Repton, Bath, Carlisle, Exeter, Berkeley, Wimborne, Winchcombe, and Chichester. In France and Belgium the list includes: Vézelay, les Andelys, Auchy, Blangy, St. Pierre-le-Pullier in Poitiers and Bourges, St. Vincent of Laon, Marchiennes, Alden-Eyck, Mouzon, St. Enimie, Tuffé, and St. Trinité of Fecamp.[49] This short catalog underscores the rather clear priorities and direction of the reformers in their reestablishment of monastic life. Providing new opportunities for women was no longer a primary concern. And, as noted in the case

[48] *The Anglo-Saxon Chronicle*, trans. and ed. G. N. Garmonsway (London: Dent; New York: Dutton, 1972), 115 (emphasis mine).

[49] Brief references to each of these monasteries with the dates of destruction or abandonment (as well as restorations as male foundations) appear in the repertories of Knowles and Hadcock and of Cottineau (n. 2 above). See Knowles and Hadcock: Whitby (destroyed ca. 867), 58, 80; Coventry (destroyed in 1016), 53, 63; Gloucester (deserted after 767), 54, 66, 473; Folkestone (destroyed before 947), 54, 66; Leominster (deserted around 1046), 55, 69; Minster-in-Thanet (nuns dispersed in 1011), 55, 70; St. Milburga of Wenloch (suppressed before 1050), 97, 101; Tynemouth (destroyed ca. 865–75), 57, 78–79; St. Frideswide, Oxford (dispersed during Danish invasion), 142, 169–70; Repton (destroyed 874), 480; Bath (destroyed before 758), 467; Carlisle (destroyed ca. 875), 469–70; Exeter (destroyed before or during Danish invasion), 473; Berkeley (dissolved before 1051), 421, 467; Wimborne (destroyed ca. 998), 443, 485; Winchcombe (turned over to secular clerks in ninth century), 80, 485; Chichester (nuns replaced by canons in 1075), 422. See Cottineau: Vézelay 2:3354–56 (destroyed by the Vikings), 3354–56; les Andelys (destroyed ca. 900), 1:96; Auchy (destroyed by the Vikings in 881), 1:193–94; Blangy (destroyed by the Vikings in the ninth century), 1:389; St. Pierre-le-Pullier in Poitiers (occupied by monks by 980), 2:2311–12; in Bourges (occupied by monks before ninth century) 1:463; St. Vincent of Laon (destroyed in ninth century), 1:1560; Marchiennes (reformed by Benedictine monks in 1028), 2:1738–39; Alden-Eyck (destroyed by the Vikings in 881), 1:51–52; Mouzon (destroyed in 882) 2:2007–8; St. Enimie (destroyed in eighth century) 2:2663; Tuffé (destroyed by the Vikings), 2:3229; St. Trinité of Fecamp (destroyed by Vikings ca. 876), 1:1116–20.

of Ely, the original prominence of women in monasticism had become only a faint memory.

Moreover, the few women's houses that survived the invasions and secularizations became the objects of increasing disfavor by churchmen of the reform period. The activities of nuns were looked on with suspicion and were closely monitored. Moral abuses and scandals in the convents became a source of concern for the reform councils.[50] A number of these cases underscore the close relationship of indigency and "moral lapse" to the reformers' gender-specific requirement of strict enclosure. In fact, in some places, where nuns were forced to break enclosure because of economic hardship, those convents were described as *lupanaria* or brothels.[51] Monk-ecclesiastics were then sent to examine the situations and reform these communities. Frequently, the end result of these investigations was the harsh evictions of nuns from their monasteries and their replacement by reformed monks. In this age of strict reform ideals, no compromise seemed possible. This must have been especially frustrating for the communities of nuns, for, with the exception of the tenth-century reform in England and the issuing of the *Regularis concordia*, it appears that abbesses and nuns were unable to participate in the reform councils that formulated the policies that affected them; nor had they any real recourse in appealing decisions—some of which determined their very existence or survival.

One example of expulsion is the case of the great Merovingian foundation for women of Saint Salaberga and Saint Jean of Laon. Here, in 1060, the local bishop accused the members of the house of moral and material decadence and, without even a hearing, removed the abbess. Despite appeals by the pope and Archbishop of Reims on behalf of the female community, the bishop refused to rescind his decision. These "recalcitrant" nuns were then forcefully vacated from their house in order to accommodate a group of re-

---

[50] A fascinating case of monastic moral decline is documented in the records of the Council of Douzy, held in 874. A nun named Duda, after allegedly plotting with a priest to become abbess, later accused him of being the father of her child. An investigation took place, including an interrogation of the nuns of Duda's convent. The document then describes in detail the various "appropriate" punishments to which Duda and the priest were to be submitted if guilt was established (Hefele and Leclercq [n. 38 above], vol. 4, pt. 2, 638–39).

[51] Concilium Aquisgranense A. 836, in *MGH* (n. 10 above): *Legum Sectio III, Concilia*, vol. 2, pt. 2, *Concilia aevi Karolini*, vol. 1, pt. 2 (no. 36), chap. 12, 713: "In some places the monasteries seem to be brothels (*lupanaria*) rather than monasteries; and this because of neglect of revenues or, indeed the negligence of superiors. And so it is demanded that men with proved piety [monk-ecclesiastics] make an initial survey of the situation after which they are to strive to reform such things according to [the norms of] monastic observance."

formed Benedictine monks from the community of St. Nicaise of Reims.[52]

A number of letters written by the reformer Ivo of Chartres and dating to the end of the eleventh century also describe cases in which nuns were evicted from their convents. In one letter, Ivo describes the nuns of Faremoutiers as "female demoniacs" (*mulierum daemonialium*), who were "prostituting their bodies for lewd use by every sort of male." His condemnation of their behavior was based on a written complaint from Countess Adelaide and oral reports from the monks of Tours. Based on these complaints, Ivo urged the local bishop to reform the convent and restore its moral order. However, if reform proved impossible, he recommended replacing the nuns with reformed monks. This transfer did, in fact, occur in the early twelfth century.[53] The monastery of Homblières experienced a similar fate. In the tenth century, the Archbishop of Reims sent the holy widow Bertha to reform the house. However, the nuns did not satisfactorily modify their behavior and were therefore expelled from their monastery.[54] The nuns of Marchiennes similarly were evicted in the first quarter of the eleventh century by the reformer Leduin for their secular activities. They were then replaced by reformed monks.[55]

Walter Map, in his *De Nugis Curialium* (written ca. 1181–82), provides a detailed description of the eleventh-century destruction of the female community of Berkeley Abbey. This rather remarkable episode underscores the special vulnerability of communities of female religious at that time. According to Map's account, Earl Godwine devised a ruse in order to dissolve the convent and reappropriate its properties to himself. Map notes: "Berkeley by Severn, a vill of £500 value, belonged to certain nuns who dwelt there and had a noble and comely abbess. Now the man of whom I tell [Godwine] took stock of all with subtle craft, and conceived desire not of the abbess but of her property, and as he passed by the place left in her care his nephew, a very handsome lad, on pretense of

[52] "Letter of Pope Alexander II to the Archbishop of Reims, Gervais," in Migne, ed. (n. 43 above), 146:1319. See also Verdon, "Recherches sur les monastères feminins dans la France du nord" (n. 1 above), 66.

[53] J. O'Carrol, *Sainte Fare et Faremoutiers: Treize siècles de vie monastique* (S.-et-M: Abbaye de Faremoutiers: 1956), 40.

[54] P. Lauer, ed., *Recueil des Actes de Louis IV, roi de France (936–954)*, no. 32 (Octobre 1, 949), 76–77, cited by Verdon, "Recherches sur les monastères feminins dans la France du nord," 53.

[55] *Miracula sanctae Rictrudis*, bk. 1, chap. 3, *Acta Sanctorum Belgii* (Brussels: Typis Mattaei Lemaire, 1783–94), 4:509–510. See also de Moreau (n. 2 above), 2:164. In all fairness it should be noted that during this same period canons also fell out of favor with the Church; they were similarly singled out and evicted by the reformers.

his illness, till he should return, and enjoined the invalid not to recover completely until he had made a conquest of the abbess and as many of the nuns as he could, and to give the youth the means of finding favour with them he supplied him with rings, girdles, and fawnskins, starry with gems, to be presented to the nuns in traitorous wise. . . . [He] made a church sacred to the Saviour and the saints a cursed Pantheon, and a sanctuary into a brothel, and the ewe-lambs into she-wolves [or prostitutes (*et delubrum lupanar, et sic agnas euertit in lupas*)]. So, when the swelling wombs of the abbess and many of the nuns were past concealment, their seducer fled, and speedily brought to his lord the conquering eagles that had earned the reward of iniquity. Godwine at once approached the king, made public the news that the abbess and nuns were pregnant wantons (*abbatissam et suas publicas pregnantes et prostitutas omnibus edocet*), sent men to investigate, and on their return proved the truth of all he had said." Thus, as Map relates, the ultimate result of this deceitful stratagem was that "the nuns were cast out, and he [Godwine] asked for and received Berkeley from his lord, who might better be called his fool."[56]

Although historians believe this account to be somewhat distorted and are reluctant to accept Map's rendition of the incident in full, other sources verify that there once existed a flourishing community of nuns at Berkeley and that the house was suppressed in the reign of Edward the Confessor.[57] An entry in the Domesday Book (1086) provides further evidence in support of these events. According to this source, when Godwine and his wife Gytha visited Berkeley, Gytha refused to eat anything that had been produced on the lands belonging to this estate "because of a pious scruple arising out of the destruction of the Abbey." Godwine therefore was forced to buy land at Woodchester for Gytha's maintenance while they stayed on their properties in Gloucestershire. From this entry it appears that Godwine was somehow implicated in the destruction of the abbey and his immoral behavior had alienated his wife. Gytha, apparently disapproving of his conduct, subtly registered her indignation by refusing to eat from the fruits of the tainted estate.[58]

Edward Freeman and other scholars have noted that Map's description of the suppression of Berkeley has probably confused some

[56] Walter Map, *De Nugis Curialium: Courtiers' Trifles*, ed. and trans. M. R. James, rev. C. N. L. Brooke and R. A. B. Mynors (Oxford: Clarendon; New York: Oxford University Press, 1983), 417–19.

[57] Edward A. Freeman, *The History of the Norman Conquest of England: Its Causes and Its Results*, 2d rev. ed. (Oxford: Clarendon, 1870), 2:544; Map, 416, n. 1; Knowles and Hadcock (n. 2 above), 476.

[58] Freeman, 545.

of the details with the events of the destruction of the Monastery of Leominster.[59] The community of Leominster also seems to have been dissolved or vacated during the reign of Edward the Confessor. Godwin's son, Swein (rather than the nephew mentioned in the case of Berkeley), was instrumental in the destruction and dissolution of this foundation. On his return from a foray into Wales, Swein carried off the Abbess of Leominster whom he "debauched" and held captive for a while before allowing her to return home. Soon after this, apparently, the monastery was dissolved and the nuns dispersed.[60] In 1123, Leominster was refounded as a Benedictine house for men.[61]

These two eleventh-century cases underscore the special vulnerability of communities of women to the lawlessness and violence of the age. The added need for physical protection of their communities, the reliance on their "protectors"—who sometimes appear instead as predators—as well as the prerequisite defense of their virginity, placed the nuns in an especially disadvantageous position. Within this context, church reformers or the aristocracy could use any kind of irregular activity as an excuse or rationale for the necessary reform or dissolution of a women's community. Invariably, the nuns were replaced by communities of monks or canons: there are only a few exceptions in which "lapsed" houses of monks or canons were replaced by communities of women.

Donors and their changing patterns of support

Although the aristocracy resisted some of the ideology and policies that the reformers attempted to impose on them, it was receptive to many of the values and basic priorities of the reforms. Kings and queens, along with the nobility, supported the various reform movements with generous donations and endowments of monasteries. However, beginning with the Carolingian reforms of the ninth century and increasingly with the tenth- and eleventh-century reforms, a number of significant shifts occurred in the primary allegiances of donors of monastic foundations and in their general patterns of giving.

[59] Ibid., 545; Map, 416, n. 1.
[60] *The Anglo-Saxon Chronicle* (n. 48 above), 164; Freeman, 592–93. See also M. W. Campbell, "Aelfgyva: The Mysterious Lady," *Annales de Normandie* 34, no. 2 (1984): 127–45; and Jane Schulenburg, "Women as *miserabiles personae* in the Bayeux Tapestry" (paper presented at the Fifteenth International Congress on Medieval Studies, Western Michigan University, Kalamazoo, May 1, 1980).
[61] Knowles and Hadcock, 47.

During the seventh century, the majority of women's communities were founded by queens and noblewomen or they were established by the fathers or brothers of these women in response to their requests. However, women donors initiated the greatest number by far of new women's communities, which were generally established for the donors' immediate benefit or profession. During this period of early enthusiasm for women in the Church, churchmen actively promoted monastic life for women, allowing and even encouraging them to establish their own houses or double communities. Furthermore, abbots and bishops instituted with their own resources and on their own properties a sizable number of new houses for women.

Although many of the monasteries established for monks during the seventh century were also royal or aristocratic foundations, the majority of houses for men instituted during this early period appear to have been founded by bishops and abbots.

With the reform movements of the ninth century, these patterns began to change. Although queens and noblewomen continued to be the primary initiators of new women's foundations, particularly in France, the number of both women's and men's houses that they endowed declined in comparison to the number they endowed in the seventh century. The number of women's communities founded by bishops and abbots also decreased dramatically in the reform period. In contrast, during this same period, bishops and abbots played an increasingly critical role in the establishment and restoration of men's communities. In the decades of disorder and chaos following the invasions, many houses that had been deserted, along with their properties, were appropriated by kings or local lords. During the ensuing period of reform, these estates were frequently turned over to or reclaimed by the Church, which invariably restored them as communities for monks or canons.

The ideology of church reformers, which advocated a strong preference for monks and their spiritual efficacy over and against that of nuns, seems to have been accepted and supported by both male *and female* patrons (especially in France). Although some noblewomen continued (on noticeably reduced levels in France) to be generous benefactors of monasteries for both monks and nuns from the ninth through the late eleventh centuries, many designated their bequests solely for the establishment of men's communities at the expense of women's houses. This important shift in the pattern of donations by women of the aristocracy can in part be attributed to changes brought about by the reform movement. It was also no doubt influenced by shifts in family strategies. For example, it became much more prevalent in this later period than in the seventh century for new foundations to be endowed in a collective manner. Perhaps in an attempt to stem seemingly impulsive and excessive donations, endowments increasingly involved the approval and consent of donors' family members.[62] Thus in this later period, many new foundations were endowed jointly by women and their husbands along with other family members. This practice may have influenced women's choices in regard to which communities to support. Also during this period, changes occurred that seem to have affected the freedom of widows to alienate their property. It appears that some of the royal and aristocratic families now viewed their female relatives as more valuable for political purposes, territorial consolidation, and marriage alliances. They were no longer convinced of their special value as religious propitiatory offerings, or as abbesses acting as administrative heads of the family's landed investments in the Church. Karl Leyser has suggested that the rapid decline in the number of foundations for women in early eleventh-century Saxony and the decay of many of the existing houses was based in part on the fact that "Saxon princes became somewhat less tolerant of wealthy widows disposing of great inheritances." These widows were instead forced into marriages and forced to use their possessions to build up great territorial lordships.[63] These shifts in family strategies seem to have contributed to the decline in the number of houses for women in France and, to a lesser degree, in England during this period.

In the early stages of research for this study, my initial supposition was that the increasing gender-based discrepancy in the number of monasteries over the centuries might be explained by the

[62] Georges Duby, *La société aux XIᵉ et XIIᵉ siècles dans la region mâconnaise* (Paris: A. Colin, 1953), 272.

[63] Leyser (n. 18 above), 70–71. Wemple (n. 1 above) also notes in regard to the motivation of women joining monastic communities: "Undoubtedly, the improved legal position of married women (as a result of the Carolingian marriage reforms) also contributed to the waning of women's interest in ascetic life. In the highest echelons of society, fewer ladies preferred the convent to marriage. We do not hear of ninth-century princesses running away from eager suitors or ardent husbands and clamoring for admittance to convents" (171, see also 150–54). Also beginning with the Carolingian period, the French queens and royal princesses appear to have established new monastic communities as essentially acts of piety, rather than for their own immediate benefit or profession. Again, as Wemple has observed, "They chose the convent as a place of dwelling only when they needed shelter in old age or adversity" (171). In contrast to this situation on the continent, monastic life remained popular among the queens and princesses in Britain. There were, e.g., several instances of royal women who endowed convents and took the veil in tenth- and eleventh-century England (Knowles, *The Monastic Order in England* [n. 15 above], 137).

general lack of or loss of control over property and property rights by noblewomen during this period.[64] However, as is frequently the case, it appears that the growing imbalance between men's and women's institutions is far more complex than I had originally assumed. While female patrons continued to be the major force behind the new communities established for women during the ninth through eleventh centuries, a substantial number of women during this period chose to financially support the foundation of men's monastic communities. Moreover, a few aristocratic women initiated the eviction of communities of nuns, only to reestablish these foundations for monks. The eleventh-century community, Saint Pierre-sur-Dives, for example, appears to have suffered this fate. Established in 1040 as a Benedictine monastery for women, it was shortly thereafter appropriated for Benedictine monks by the noblewoman, Lesceline, Countess d'Exmes and wife of Guillaume d'Exmes.[65]

Unlike their sisters on the continent, royal and noblewomen in Britain continued to exercise an active role in the Church and in monasticism. Their impressive level of participation in the development of women's monasticism was sustained through the tenth century.[66] Their continuing commitment to women's communities (along with that of their families and, to a lesser degree, churchmen) is exemplified by the consistently higher percentages in Britain than in France of new women's houses relative to those for men. However, during the eleventh century, female aristocratic donors in Britain, like their contemporaries in France, often chose to endow men's communities and parish churches rather than women's houses with their land and money. A rather famous example is that of Countess Godiva, recorded by the fourteenth-century chronicler, Matthew of Westminster. In his entry for the year 1057, he notes that Count Leofric (Godiva's husband) had been buried in the Monastery of Coventry

which he and his wife . . . had built from its foundations out of her own patrimony; and having established monks in it, they endowed it so abundantly with estates, and treasure of

[64] See Wemple, 106–23.

[65] Cottineau (n. 2 above), 2:2851–52. See also the initiatory role of Countess Adelaide in the reform of Faremoutiers, 24.

[66] Marc A. Meyer, "Women and the Tenth-Century English Monastic Reform," *Revue Benedictine* 87 (1977): 34–61. In this article, Meyer underscores the importance of the generosity of royal and noblewomen to the monastic revival of this period. See also Susan Millinger, "Humility and Power in Anglo-Saxon Nuns in Anglo-Norman Hagiography," in Nichols and Shank (n. 1 above), 1:115–29.

various kinds, that there was not found such a quantity of gold, and silver, and precious stones in any monastery in all England as there was in that monastery at that time. . . . They also magnificently endowed with estates, and houses, and various ornamental gifts, the churches of Worcester, Evesham, Wenlock, and Leominster, and some other convents [monasteries], especially that of Saint John the Baptist, and Saint Wereburga the Virgin, situated in Leicester, and the church of Saint Mary of Stowe, which Eadmot, bishop of Dorchester, had built.[67]

Thus, as is true of their primary endowment, which provided for the foundation of the great monastery of Coventry, the majority of Countess Godiva and Count Leofric's diversified endowments were directed to men's foundations and churches.

Christopher Brooke and C. H. Lawrence have each noted briefly in their studies of medieval monasticism the importance of lay patrons' attitudes and the prejudices of monastic reformers in circumscribing the active participation of women in the religious movements of the tenth through twelfth centuries.[68] While endowments were provided for monasteries as perhaps never before or since, they were provided, as noted by Brooke, "chiefly by male patrons for men."[69] Lawrence observes for the revivals of the tenth and eleventh centuries:

These were movements initiated and led by men and sponsored by patrons who were interested in creating male monasteries. Those women's houses that were founded in their wake were few and undistinguished by comparison with the plethora of important foundations for monks. . . . The lay do-

---

[67] Matthew of Westminster, *The Flowers of History*, trans. C. D. Yonge, 2 vols. (London: H. G. Bohn, 1853), 1:543–44. This account is based on that of Roger of Wendover in *Chronica sive Flores Historiarum*, ed. Henry O. Coxe, 4 vols. (London: English Historical Society, 1841–42), 1:497–98. He describes the donation to Coventry: "Quod monasterium cum per consilium nobilis comitissae Godivae uxoris suae in proprio fundasset territorio, mediante foemina religiosa, monachos imposuit, quibus sufficienter in terris, silvis et ornamentis ditatis, ita providit, quod in tota Anglia non inventum fuit coenobium adeo abundans in auro et argento, in gemmis vel vestibus. . . . Wigornensem praeterea et sanctae Mariae de Stone, sanctaeque Wereburgae virginis, In Legecestria, ecclesias cum coenobiis de Hevesham, de Weneloac et de Lentana terris, aedificiis ac variis ornamentis idem comes instinctu comitissae magnifice ditavit."

[68] Christopher Brooke, *The Monastic World* (New York: Random House, 1974), 168; Lawrence (n. 4 above), 178.

[69] Brooke, 168.

nor who endowed a monastery hoped to reap spiritual benefits from his gift, and the most highly valued of these was
one that women could not provide: women could not celebrate mass. Medieval piety increasingly emphasized the ex-
piatory value of the mass. And as it became the normal practice
to ordain professed monks to the priesthood and the institution of the private mass enabled all to offer mass daily,
patrons were increasingly eager to sponsor communities of
monks.[70]

Conclusion

The seventh and early eighth centuries in France, Belgium, and
England experienced a burgeoning of women's religious communities, an early "Golden Age" in women's monastic life. During
this period, France and Belgium witnessed for the first time the
phenomenon of women's communities established in great numbers in the countryside. These rural monasteries were promoted by
the Columbanian and other missionary movements and the upwardly mobile aristocracy; they were made possible by the institution of the double monastery or the affiliated house. Once these
special conditions that had encouraged rural houses for women
were no longer present, the number of new houses for women
rapidly declined. With the growing success and organization of the
Church, women's houses no longer served as missionary centers;
in many cases they lost the important functions of parish churches
that they had previously assumed. Moreover, with the increased
requirements of security for women's communities (brought about
by the invasions), a growing suspicion of double houses, the reformers' insistence on enclosure, and the consolidation of women's
communities, fewer new women's monasteries were established in
the countryside. At the same time, the majority of new foundations
for men were located in rural areas. (The significance of this rural/
urban dichotomy of men's and women's houses needs to be studied
in much greater detail.) The tradition of restricting, to a great extent,
women's houses to the cities or suburbs during this period of invasion and urban decline seemed to work against the proliferation
of nunneries and may help to explain, in part, a growing discrepancy
in the number of men's and women's foundations. Suzanne Wemple
notes, "Because feminine communities were not organized in the

[70] Lawrence, 178.

countryside, their number remained relatively low in comparison to male communities."[71] However, the urban tradition of women's monasticism was perhaps not as strong in Britain as it was in France. Throughout this period, rural locations remained popular for many of the prominent English monasteries for both women and men. It is tempting to suggest that the greater flexibility in location and the rural tradition of women's houses and double monasteries in England might shed further light on the difference in the percentage of new women's foundations in Britain relative to those in France.

This study has attempted to provide a survey of a number of aspects of change in the development of women's religious communities over some six centuries. It is by no means an exhaustive study of this period; rather it attempts to provide an overview of some of the important patterns that emerged. During this period, a growing disparity in women's and men's foundations arose. This pattern became especially exaggerated in France. In general, according to the statistics on new foundations, women's greatest activity in monasticism occurred during the seventh century. In contrast, the eleventh century, an age of aggressive church reform, appears from the data as one of the true nadirs in the development of monastic life for religious women. It should be noted, however, that this nadir was relatively short-lived. For in the twelfth century, there occurred a heightened interest in women's religious life and again a great proliferation of new women's communities.

This early period in Frankish Gaul and Anglo-Saxon England was an especially positive age in the development of women's monasticism. It was a time when royal and ecclesiastical authority was weak and decentralized. Political and economic power was situated within royal and aristocratic households and easily accessible to women. Society was essentially "open" and fluid. It was an era of relative peace and prosperity. It was also an age of new beginnings—a time of necessity during which the Church was becoming established and was not yet highly organized, reformed, or right-minded. In this milieu, women's practical assistance was especially valued. Female religious were accepted as partners, friends, sisters, and collaborators in the faith. In the original enthusiasm for monasticism, there appeared to have been a supportive atmosphere, a healthy view of women in religion. Perhaps one of the best examples of this positive attitude was the experiment of the double monastery, which proved to be especially popular and successful in rural areas. Unfortunately, with the reform movements and their emphasis on ascetic piety and clerical celibacy, the initial appreciation of women's active partici-

---

[71] Wemple (n. 1 above), 156.

pation in the Church was lost and replaced by an atmosphere of heightened fear and suspicion of female sexuality. In their attempts to avoid women, monastic reformers were reluctant to undertake the responsibility of directing nuns. Similarly, aristocratic donors increasingly preferred to sponsor communities of monks rather than communities of nuns. The periods of invasion and reform, then, witnessed a great deal of change in the popularity and viability of monastic life for women; these crises also served as catalysts that hastened change and gave rise to a pronounced gender-based disparity in religious communities.

Department of Liberal Studies—History
University of Wisconsin—Madison

THE ORIGINS OF THE BEGUINES

CAROL NEEL

Francis of Assisi, the preeminent holy man of the thirteenth century, belonged to a generation that explored many pathways to sanctity. His own route, leading away from traditional monastic walls and into mendicancy in secular society, proved accessible only to men. Francis's friars grudgingly accepted female participation in their order but restricted their sisters to the cloisters they refused for themselves. Eventually, the Franciscans came to allow tertiaries, a kind of lay shadow-order in which both sexes were uncloistered, to adhere to their establishments.[1] In the meantime, many women

This essay has grown out of a paper entitled "Women's Roles in Monastic Life: Double Monasteries in the Twelfth-Century Reform" presented at the sixth Berkshire Conference of Women Historians, Smith College, Northampton, Mass., June 1984. It was initially conceived on a short-term fellowship at the Newberry Library, Chicago, in February of 1983, and recast at the Newberry in February 1987. In the lengthy interim, it has benefited from the comments of Lester Little, Caroline Bynum, and Penny Gold, to whom thanks are due.

[1] Rosalind B. Brooke and Christopher N. L. Brooke, "St. Clare," in *Medieval Women*, ed. Derek Baker, Studies in Church History, Subsidia (Oxford: Basil Blackwell, 1978), 1:275–87. See also Brigitte Degler-Spengler, "Die religiöse Frauenbewegung des Mittelalters: Konversen—Nonnen—Beginen," *Rottenburger Jahrbuch für Kirchengeschichte* 3 (1984): 85.

This essay originally appeared in *Signs*, vol. 14, no. 2, Winter 1989.

had come on their own to a pious life more radical than the Franciscans' in both its involvement in the world and its separation from ecclesiastical structures.

The number of these women, called beguines, increased rapidly throughout the thirteenth century, especially in the Low Countries and the Rhine valley.[2] Their history is less well documented than that of Francis's followers or many other movements in medieval religious life, in part because they lacked a specific founder and never received papal sanction. Moreover, the beguines' experience frequently was recorded by great men of the Church, outsiders to their way of life, whose descriptions are muddled with tendentiousness. Although recent scholarship on the beguine life has established the importance of these women's contribution to the changing religious practice of the later Middle Ages, their origins and their relation to earlier communities of pious women remain poorly understood.[3]

Modern historians have generally responded to the thinness of evidence about the earliest beguines by accepting their early thirteenth-century emergence as spontaneous.[4] This essay will chal-

---

[2] The basic English work on the beguine life is Ernest W. McDonnell, *The Beguines and Beghards in Medieval Culture, with Special Emphasis on the Belgian Scene* (New Brunswick, N.J.: Rutgers University Press, 1954). Of recent studies, one in particular emphasizes the large numbers of thirteenth- and early fourteenth-century women who chose the beguine life: Bernard Delmaire, "Les beguines dans le Nord de la France au premièr siècle de leur histoire (vers 1230–vers 1350)," in *Les religieuses en France au XIIIe siècle,* ed. Michel Parisse (Nancy: Presses Universitaires, 1985), 121–62, esp. 131. The most influential discussion of the beguines and of medieval women's religious practice generally remains Herbert Grundmann's: *Religiöse Bewegungen im Mittelalter* (1935), in *Ausgewählte Aufsätze,* vol. 1, Schriften der Monumenta Germaniae Historica, vol. 25 (Stuttgart: Hiersemann, 1976).

[3] Of recent scholarship, see especially Caroline Walker Bynum, *Jesus as Mother: Studies in the Spirituality of the High Middle Ages* (Berkeley and Los Angeles: University of California Press, 1982), 235–47; Frederic M. Stein, "The Religious Women of Cologne: 1120–1320" (Ph.D. diss., Yale University, 1977), esp. 55–100, 171–83. This reassessment of the beguines' importance has already found its way into broad interpretive essays on medieval and early modern religion (see, e.g., Stephen Ozment, *The Age of Reform 1250–1550: An Intellectual and Religious History of Late Medieval and Reformation Europe* [New Haven, Conn.: Yale University Press, 1980], 93–95).

[4] Herbert Grundmann's argument that the beguines appeared quite suddenly (esp. 204–5) has cast a long shadow over subsequent scholarship. McDonnell's survey of the beguines' appearance thus repeatedly characterizes their movement as "spontaneous" (120). Although Grundmann's magisterial work remains fundamental for this inquiry and, indeed, for most investigation of medieval women's religious lives, his larger thesis that the thirteenth century brought radical change in women's spirituality seems, at least in regard to the beguines, to have minimized

lenge that interpretation, instead seeking the beguines' antecedents. It will compare their movement with aspects of women's monasticism in the twelfth century, proposing that the beguine life appears more novel than it was because twentieth-century scholars have perpetuated fundamental misrepresentations about pious women's tradition in medieval commentary. The beguine way of life, contrary to its description in much modern historiography, followed the road opened by sisters of earlier monastic communities in regard to both its spiritual and social directions.

The elusiveness of those pious women who adhered, in the thirteenth century, to the beguine movement extends beyond their earliest appearance to the years of their widest efflorescence in the late 1200s. Even after their existence was abundantly evident and remarked in contemporaneous documents, the beguines remained difficult for other medieval people to characterize. Tracing their roots backward into the twelfth century is therefore, for the modern historian dependent on medieval records, a subtle undertaking. Although there is no question that the beguines represented a distinctly feminine expression of popular piety, little else about them is immediately clear. Thirteenth-century description of their lives often centers on what they were not, rather than what they were. The Franciscan Gilbert of Tournai remarked in 1274, for instance, that "there are among us women whom we have no idea what to call, ordinary women or nuns, because they live neither in the world nor out of it."[5]

The beguines' awkward, middling posture produced a constant and finally destructive tension between themselves and thirteenth-century society, which had little sympathy for anomalous persons.[6]

---

thirteenth-century women's connectedness to earlier movements. This point, central for the present article, has at least been broached in some prior treatments of the beguines' appearance. Stein, e.g., reviews scholarship on the beguines' origins (3–9), rightly pointing out that Joseph Greven long ago noted a connection between the patterns of beguine life and the spirituality and careers of twelfth-century religious (Greven, *Die Anfänge der Beginen: Ein Beitrag zur Geschichte der Volksfrömmigkeit und des Ordenswesens im Hochmittelalter* [Münster: Aschendorff, 1912], 115). Greven's suggestion has, however, met with little response. A notable exception is the work of Degler-Spengler, whose assertion that the similarity of monastic lay sisters and beguines bears investigation ("Die religiöse Frauenbewegung des Mittelalters," 83) has in part motivated the present study.

[5] Gilbert of Tournai, in *Collectio de scandalis ecclesiae*, ed. Ignaz von Döllinger, Beiträge zur politischen, kirchlichen und Culturgeschichte, vol. 3 (Vienna: Manz, 1882), 3:197.

[6] See Monique Paulmier-Foucart, "Les religieuses dans une encyclopédie du XIIIe siècle: Le *Speculum historiale* de Vincent de Beauvais," in Parisse, ed., 199–213, esp. 205.

Communities of laywomen whose lives centered on pious activity violated the venerable frontier between religious and secular individuals in a fashion so objectionable to the ecclesiastical hierarchy that the beguines were finally condemned on suspicion of heresy by the Council of Vienne in 1312; subsequently their communities all but disappeared, forced out of existence by ecclesiastical reprobation.[7] More important for the present inquiry, the beguines' separateness from recognized categories of spiritual and social activity tended to preoccupy medieval commentators as they described these women's roles.

Despite the frequent pejorativeness of the sources, among which Gilbert's negative remarks about the beguines are typical, an array of positive traits emerge as common to many adherents of this women's movement.[8] Women known as beguines generally came from the middle class and lived in urban contexts. They embraced mystical piety and pursued their spiritual goals while they lived singly or in groups; their households excluded males.[9] Beguine communities were only informally connected with each other, and clerical authorities oversaw them only informally. Although the earliest beguines served the poor and sick, their successors in the movement performed a variety of worldly tasks, often participating in the textile production typical of the towns in which they chiefly lived. As

---

[7] Jean-Claude Schmitt's study focusing on the beguines' dissolution in Strasbourg describes the interplay of social and institutional forces working against them (*Mort d'une hérésie: L'église et les clercs face aux béguines et aux beghards du Rhin supérieur du XIVe au XVe siècle*, Civilisations et sociétés, vol. 56 [Paris: Mouton, 1978]). He notes that, already in 1250, the women's group met with the reprobation of the faculty of theology at Paris (50). The beguines managed to survive their official suppression in the fourteenth century, although in greatly reduced numbers, through the intervention of friendly prelates and secular authorities. In the fifteenth and sixteenth centuries, most of their houses had generally become charitable institutions that only minimally reflected their original religious intentions. The beguine life was suppressed again during the French Revolution but reemerged in the second decade of the nineteenth century to attract, by 1825, more than 1,700 Belgian women. Beguine foundations continue to exist in Belgium, although they involve fewer women than in their nineteenth-century revival. For a survey and bibliography of these modern developments, see *Oxford Dictionary of the Christian Church*, ed. F. L. Cross and F. A. Livingstone, 2d ed. (London: Oxford University Press, 1974), 150; J. van Mierlo, "Béguines," in *Dictionnaire d'histoire et de géographie ecclésiastique*, ed. Alfred Baudrillart (Paris: Letouzey et Ané, 1934), 7:457–73.

[8] McDonnell surveys the origins of hostility toward beguine communities (439–44). Delmaire points out the connection between the beguines' failure to enter recognized social categories and the difficulty of identifying further archival sources cataloged according to those categories (122–26).

[9] The beguines' male counterparts, beghards, lived separately. There is no question that they followed, rather than led, their sisters (see Ozment, 98).

beguines, these medieval women were independent of male authority in marriage and in the church to a degree otherwise unknown in their culture.[10]

The beguine life is therefore of clear interest in a growing body of feminist scholarship about the ways in which religious activity empowered medieval women.[11] The wide variety of ways in which beguines led their lives of piety, however, initially frustrates any attempt to identify prior groups of women who shared their broad range of behavior. Beguine experience nevertheless did have a few common denominators; these are keys to exploring their movement's origins.

Chastity and extraregular status, or freedom from governance by a monastic *regula,* or rule, were the twin traits that underlay the diverse manifestations of the beguine movement and were recognized by thirteenth-century commentators as distinguishing beguines. Chastity and extraregular identity separated beguines from, on the one hand, ordinary secular females and, on the other, nuns.[12] Gilbert of Tournai was in this sense right in his negative description of these pious women: they were and are known by their separation from males, both as bodily mates and as spiritual fathers. Although by the end of the thirteenth century the many females embracing the path of chastity outside monasticism had made their movement a powerful force in the European economy as well as religion, the fundamental shape of beguine experience—chaste and extraregular—is the standard according to which its indebtedness to prior women's activity must be assessed. If earlier pious women can be shown to have linked chastity to a breaking down of monastic regulation approaching extraregular status, then those women may be identified as the beguines' antecedents.

The first clear documentation of the beguine experience comes from the second decade of the thirteenth century when James of Vitry, an important ecclesiastical administrator and analyst of the state of contemporary religion, recorded the life of Mary of Oignies. James claimed that his recently dead friend and counselor Mary, a holy woman of the diocese of Liège, had been the model for a new variety of lay piety.[13] His account has been as influential among modern historians as it was among medieval readers. In praising to

---

[10] Bynum, *Jesus as Mother,* 14–15; Stein, 182. See also Delmaire, 141.

[11] The outstanding recent example is Caroline Walker Bynum's book, *Holy Feast and Holy Fast: The Religious Significance of Food to Medieval Women* (Berkeley and Los Angeles: University of California Press, 1987), esp. 6.

[12] Stein (n. 3 above), 57–67.

[13] James of Vitry, *Vita Mariae Oignacensis* (hereafter *VMO*); Acta Sanctorum, ed. J. Bolland et al. (Paris: V. Palme, 1863–), June, 5:542–88.

its thirteenth-century audience the ostensible novelty of Mary's way of life, James's work has convinced twentieth-century medievalists that the beguine experience was unique to his own times. Attention to James's objectives in the composition of his life of Mary of Oignies, however, calls the medieval author's presentation and its modern interpretation into doubt.

James undertook to memorialize Mary two years after her death in 1213. His ambitious intention was to compose a hagiographical text for use against a variety of heresies rife in southern France and northern Italy. Chief among these heterodox cults was Catharism, or Albigensianism, a revival of the Manichee dualism of late antiquity. Catharism, in admitting women to the ranks of its elite—the *perfecti* and *perfectae*, whose lives demonstrated rejection of the evil forces and substances in the created world—was especially appealing to the female population of the Midi. Cathar women were recognized for their holiness and authority beyond what would have been possible within the exclusive fraternity of the Catholic hierarchy.[14] James of Vitry, in combatting the Cathar heresy, portrayed the beguine life as an orthodox option for women that offered similar advantages in terms of independence from male direction. Mary of Oignies, although befriended and supported by James and other prelates, is never represented as their subordinate in his account of her life, as a thirteenth-century nun necessarily would have been. On the contrary, Mary, an extraregular and a lay holy woman, appears in his text as the spiritual superior of the Church's male hierarchs.[15]

By using his life of Mary to develop the possibility for women to have authority outside of the traditional male-dominated institutions of the Church, James of Vitry hoped that his version of the beguine's life would recover for Catholicism many females drifting toward suspect beliefs.[16] The papacy was less enthusiastic about these pious laywomen. The cutting edge of orthodoxy in the south of Europe, among women as well as men, was to lie instead with the mendicant orders.[17] Honorius III, the pope to whom James of

---

[14] Ozment (n. 3 above), 92–93.

[15] *VMO*, 5:562–63.

[16] Brenda Bolton, "*Vitae matrum:* A Further Aspect of the *Frauenfrage,*" in Brooke and Brooke, eds. (n. 1 above), esp. 264–67; for a summary of the bibliography on James's and Mary's relationship, see ibid., 253, n. 1. Compare Brenda Bolton, *The Medieval Reformation* (New York: Holmes & Meier, 1983), 83, 93–94, and "*Mulieres sanctae,*" in *Women in Medieval Society,* ed. Susan Mosher Stuard (Philadelphia: University of Pennsylvania Press, 1976), 141–58.

[17] For a survey of the mendicants' changing attitudes toward women, see Bolton, "*Mulieres sanctae,*" 149–52.

Vitry praised Mary, informally approved the beguine movement, but in the aftermath of the Fourth Lateran Council's prohibition of new orders he was unwilling to institutionalize it.[18]

James of Vitry's hagiographical account sought to make of Mary of Oignies the paradigm of a newly vigorous lay spirituality. The heresies he combatted were new, and he represented the beguine life as an appropriately new weapon for their extirpation. It would hardly have served James's intent to depict Mary as the daughter of monastic forebears or to have legitimated her way of life according to historical patterns. The Cathar threat in the south demanded a fresh Catholic response. James took the essential features of Mary's experience and described them as a new, exciting form of piety even though, if he had had other motives, the woman saint he portrayed might have seemed far more familiar, especially to the inhabitants of his or her Brabantine homeland.

James's literary recreation of the life of Mary of Oignies thus did not achieve the result he intended. It did not convince a retrenching ecclesiastical hierarchy that the beguine life merited establishment as a formal sorority along the lines of the mendicant orders. In the long run, however, James's account has persuaded its readers of the novelty of Mary's experience. The newness he imputed to Mary's pursuit of chastity in the secular world, however, was so exactly in harmony with his own rhetorical purposes that its accuracy should be suspect. James's record must therefore be read critically, especially with respect to the beguines' origins. Because his work is uniquely informative about the early beguines, it remains the necessary point of departure for study of their beginnings. If it is considered for the specific information it offers about the beguine life rather than for its author's presentation of that life's uniqueness, James's eulogy of Mary suggests not disjuncture but connection between her experience and the work and worship of monastic women of earlier generations.

James's text records that Mary was born in Nivelles. As a child, she showed such desire to achieve holiness that she set out from her wealthy parents' house in admiring pursuit of pilgrim monks. Her mother and father, wishing her to lead a secular life, decided to stop her precocious saintliness by marrying her at the age of fourteen. They did not anticipate, however, that Mary would find marriage no obstacle to holiness. According to James, she quickly convinced her young husband John that the two should dedicate themselves to chastity and charity. Toward this end, the young cou-

---

[18] See Bolton, "*Vitae matrum*," 264–67, and *The Medieval Reformation*, 92–93.

ple converted their house at Willambrouk into a hospital and tended the sick and leprous with their own hands.[19]

Mary eventually left this enterprise to join a small community of Augustinian canons at Oignies, where James himself was drawn by her fame as a holy woman. She never submitted to the obedience governing the lives of her hagiographer and his confreres, who were not strictly monks but were nevertheless bound by a rule for common life and spiritual activity. Living outside the walls of the Augustinian house, Mary became an inspiration for single and widowed laywomen as well as for those who, like herself, maintained celibacy in marriage.

Meanwhile, she subjected herself to harsh physical abuse in order to enhance her mystical imagination. She never wore warm clothes, her rough rope girdle chafed her to bleeding, she wept constantly, and she almost continually was subject to visitation by a variety of divine and angelic presences. Mary was so devoted to the Eucharist that she often said she could find no rest outside its presence. During her painful final illness, her ecstasy took the form of a kind of "singing," probably utterance in musically rhythmical prose.[20]

Thus, Mary of Oignies was, in James's presentation, a chaste townswoman, dedicated to charitable activity and participating in a highly individual mystical spirituality outside the bonds of monastic governance. The features James chose to emphasize as most important in Mary's experience, chastity and extraregular status, would subsequently be the defining characteristics of the beguine life. There is no question that Mary transformed marriage into virginity and lay life into imitation of apostolic poverty. Nor is there doubt that James—who, venerating her as a saint, carried a relic of her finger as protection against temptation and shipwreck—believed her model important in the history of lay piety.[21] Whether she was, as he represented her, the epitome of a new religious phenomenon is another matter.

Although the term "beguine" was first used in Mary's time, the way of life to which it was applied represented a social reality and a spiritual stance whose pasts may have been less truncated.[22] Al-

[19] *VMO*, 5:550.

[20] Ibid., 568–72.

[21] James of Vitry, *Lettres de Jacques de Vitry*, ed. R. B. C. Huygens (Leiden: Brill, 1960), 72.

[22] On the origin of the term "beguine," see Grundmann (n. 2 above), 201–2, including n. 2. The lengthy discussion over the beguines' name has generated little insight into their activity or influence. Schmitt's suggestion (n. 7 above) that their name came from the French word for "chatter" (19) is at least more amusing than other proposed etymologies.

though the number of women seeking pious lives increased rapidly at the beginning of the thirteenth century, there had been much religious activity among women of all social classes since the late eleventh-century origins of monastic reform.[23] In a general sense, then, Mary's fervor grew from a century of tradition. The richly complex development of earlier women's piety presents many institutions in which Mary and her sisters may have found inspiration. Two among these have immediately obvious similarities to beguine life.

Among the most important elements in the one hundred years of intensifying spiritual activity before Mary's career were the orders of Cîteaux and Prémontré, founded in 1098 and 1124, respectively. The Cistercian and the Premonstratensian orders expanded rapidly through the twelfth century, attracting many sisters. The nature of women's participation in the maturing Cistercian and Premonstratensian communities remains a topic of lively debate. At least in Cologne, the medieval city for which women's religious life has been most fully studied, both orders by the thirteenth century received only cloistered choir nuns into heavily endowed foundations. The women of both thirteenth-century Cîteaux and Prémontré thus came exclusively from the urban patriciate and higher social groups.[24] These nuns' contemplative path differed radically from the life of their beguine contemporaries, who lived and worked uncloistered among secular folk. Thirteenth-century sisters' experience did not, however, exactly mirror that of their twelfth-century monastic predecessors. The beguines of the 1200s may have looked to historical women, rather than their own contemporaries, for models for their pious lives.

Cistercian women have long been recognized to have embraced a mystical piety similar to the beguine movement.[25] The worldly

[23] See Stein's persuasive account (n. 3 above) of women's religious activity in Cologne, which seems to have been typical of northern European towns (120, 175–76). Compare Ludger Horstkötter's remarks on the social origins of Premonstratensian men and women in "Die Prämonstratenser und ihre Klöster am Niederrhein und in Westfalen," in *Norbert von Xanten: Adliger, Ordensstifter, Kirchenfürst*, ed. Kaspar Elm (Cologne: Weinand, 1984), 247–65, esp. 250.

[24] Stein, 238–40.

[25] Simone Roisin's investigation of thirteenth-century Cistercian hagiography devotes a long section to "le milieu Cistercien-béguinal," emphasizing that spirituality crossed institutional boundaries (*L'hagiographie cistercienne dans le diocèse de Liège au XIIIe siècle*, Recueil de travaux des conférences d'histoire et de philologie, ser. 3, fasc. 27 [Louvain: Bibliothèque de l'université, 1947], esp. 145–50). See also Brigitte Degler-Spengler, "Zisterzienserorden und Frauenklöster: Anmerkungen zur Forschungsproblematik," in *Die Zisterzienser: Ordensleben zwischen Ideal und Wirklichkeit*, Ergänzungsband, ed. Kaspar Elm (Aachen: Rhineland-Verlag, 1982), 214–15.

experience of the twelfth-century Cistercian nuns seems, however, to have had less in common with that of subsequent beguines than their similar devotion to mysticism might suggest. Although recent scholarship demonstrates that—contrary to the statements of the hierarchs of the twelfth-century Order of Cîteaux—the Cistercians' early sisters were not strictly enclosed, twelfth-century evidence shows that their activity outside the cloister was agricultural rather than eleemosynary, and thus differed fundamentally from the work of early beguines.[26] Moreover, although at least some Cistercian abbeys for women embraced lay sisters, the order as a whole never did so as devotedly as it nurtured its lay brotherhood.[27] Because beguine life was uncloistered and because its extraregular nature makes it more similar to the experience of laywomen attached to monastic communities than to such cloistered aristocratic nuns as seem to have been typical of even twelfth-century Cistercianism,[28] the link between women of the first century of the Order of Cîteaux and thirteenth-century beguines seems weak, at least in respect to the two groups' social origins and social functions.

Medievalists' understanding of women's religious life in the twelfth and thirteenth centuries has, however, changed much in the last decade, particularly in regard to Cîteaux. The Cistercians, long thought profoundly misogynist, are now recognized to have fostered nuns' informal involvement in their order from its origins, while decrying the formal acceptance of women.[29] Close regional investigation of Cistercian life in the late twelfth century may eventually reveal closer similarities than are now apparent between the many sisters among the Cistercians and beguine communities of the following century. One study of Cistercian nuns has, nevertheless, already suggested that the Order of Prémontré, rather than Cîteaux, dominated women's religious imagination at the moment

---

[26] On the enclosure of the Cistercians' early sisters, see Janet I. Summers, "The Violent Shall Take It by Force: The First Century of Cistercian Nuns, 1125–1228" (Ph.D. diss., University of Chicago, 1986), 125–26. Regarding the work of early beguines, see Hermann of Tournai, *De miraculis D. Mariae Laudunensis*, Patrologia Latina, ed. J.-P. Migne (Paris: Garnier, 1844–), vol. 156, cols. 1001–2.

[27] Summers cites only one French or Belgian Cistercian abbey of women that included lay sisters, Argensolles (79). This house was established for ninety choir nuns and ten lay sisters. This ratio suggests that the latter were servants to the cloistered ladies rather than participants in work outside the abbey. Compare Baudrillart, ed. (n. 7 above), 2:16.

[28] Degler-Spengler, "Die religiöse Frauenbewegung des Mittelalters" (n. 1 above), 81.

[29] Compare R. W. Southern, *Western Society and the Church in the Middle Ages* (Harmondsworth: Penguin, 1970), 314–15; Summers, 312.

and in the region where Mary of Oignies and the first beguines came to their own form of religious life.[30]

Unlike the Cistercians, the Order of Prémontré initially welcomed women enthusiastically. Its founder, Norbert of Gennep, was himself a member of the higher nobility. The order of regular canons that he established was generally aristocratic, but the Premonstratensians were noted for encouraging the piety of women from many levels of society. Later beguine communities would include women of similarly diverse social origins.[31] Moreover, the experience of Mary at Oignies was, at least in the sense that she was closely associated with canons, like the experience of women among the early Premonstratensians; the men who tended the spiritual needs of Premonstratensian women were living under the rule of Saint Augustine rather than under the rule of Saint Benedict.

Most important, the geographical concentration of beguine activity in the Flemish and Brabantine epicenter of the Order of Prémontré suggests more than coincidental connection.[32] Although the Cistercians had little presence among women in the area of Liège —later to become Mary and James of Vitry's home—until the last years of the twelfth century, the Order of Prémontré in the same period established many women's houses there, effectively absorbing local women's religious enthusiasm until the emergence of the beguines.[33] Nevertheless, scant scholarly attention has been paid to the lives of women adhering to the Order of Prémontré in the twelfth century and to the ways in which they may have been like or unlike Mary of Oignies's. The public posture of the medieval order has discouraged and misled modern historians' efforts to investigate the experience of Premonstratensian sisters.

Although Norbert and his earliest companions received women warmly, their successors in the governing body of the established Order of Prémontré, its General Chapter, adopted a misogynist of-

[30] Summers, 235–40.

[31] Bernold of Constance attests the breadth of the Premonstratensians' appeal (L. F. Hesse, ed., *Chronicon*, Monumenta Germaniae Historica, Scriptorum [Hanover: Hahn, 1846], 5:452–53). On the beguines, see John B. Freed, "Urban Development and the 'Cura monialium' in Thirteenth-Century Germany," *Viator* 3 (1972): 311–27, esp. 324; Dayton Phillips, *Beguines in Medieval Strasburg: A Study in the Social Aspect of Beguine Life* (Stanford, Calif.: Stanford University Press, 1941), 8–9. Stein concurs with Bolton ("*Mulieres*" [n. 16 above], 146–48) that, although some beguines were of high social origins, most were from the urban middle class (221).

[32] Compare the concentration of the beguines in the Netherlands, Rhineland, and France with the distribution of Premonstratensian houses. The map in *Grosser Historischer Weltatlas* (ed. Josef Engel [Munich: Bayerischer Schulbuch-Verlag, 1970], 2:81) clearly marks Premonstratensian women's establishments.

[33] Summers, 238.

ficial stance. Much of the hierarchical commentary on the status of
women within the order suggests that females were effectively expelled from Premonstratensian houses after 1198.[34] The widely accepted scholarly interpretation of the order's position on women
has been that the only connection between Premonstratensian sisters and beguines lay in the Order of Prémontré's rejection of its
nuns, who were then forced into other roles such as beguine life.[35]
Recent research, however, demonstrates that the Premonstratensians' ostentatious, papally sanctioned attempt to eliminate nuns in
the last decade of the twelfth century failed. Instead the order,
founded as communities for both men and women with many double monasteries, continued in the thirteenth century to receive both
sexes, frequently still in double abbeys.[36]

The roles of Premonstratensian women within the order, as well
as their social origins, may indeed have changed through the last
years of the twelfth and the early years of the thirteenth century,
but women's participation in Premonstratensian life had taken firm
root since the order's inception more than three-quarters of a century before.[37] The many Premonstratensian double monasteries of

[34] A. Erens outlined the order's official policies toward women in its first centuries
("Les soeurs dans l'ordre de Prémontré," *Analecta Praemonstratensia* 5 [1929]: 5–
260). His interpretation retains currency; compare Brooke and Brooke (n. 1 above),
279. Erens's work was, however, undercut by exclusive dependence on the order's
official sources. For a more broadly based interpretation, see Penny Schine Gold,
who offers a lucid overview of the Premonstratensians' difficulty in deciding how
to manage their double monasteries and the sisters of the order (*The Lady and the
Virgin: Image, Attitude and Experience in Twelfth-Century France* [Chicago: University of Chicago Press, 1985], 86–88). For further bibliography, see Rainer Rommens, "Gebhard, Propst und erster Abt von Windberg (ob. 1191): Skizzen zur
Frühgeschichte einer Prämonstratenser-Abtei," in *Secundam regulam vivere:
Festschrift für Norbert Backmund, O. Praem.*, ed. Gert Melville (Windberg: Poppe,
1978), 192.

[35] Greven (n. 4 above), 115. McDonnell echoes Greven's point of view ([n. 2
above], 101–5).

[36] Stein (n. 3 above) moves beyond the General Chapter's pronouncements against
nuns (see n. 38 below), which only imply women's continued eagerness to join the
Premonstratensians, to document the foundation of double houses even in the early
1200s (132–33). Degler-Spengler argues persuasively that the Premonstratensians
were consistently trying to regulate, not eliminate women ("Die religiöse Frauenbewegung des Mittelalters" [n. 1 above], 79–81). See also Horstkötter (n. 23 above),
264–65. Horstkötter's listing of Premonstratensian houses in the lower Rhine valley
and Westphalia shows that, of thirty-two founded in the twelfth or thirteenth centuries, twenty-two were predominantly female and only ten predominantly male.
All but two, one women's and one men's, continued to be active into the fourteenth
century.

[37] Regarding changing roles and social origins of Premonstratensian women, see
Degler-Spengler's remark on the interest in this question ("Die religiöse Frauenbewegung des Mittelalters," 81, n. 6).

the region in which Mary of Oignies grew up were important elements in her religious landscape. It is therefore not surprising that
the experience of Premonstratensian women, when it is clarified,
is markedly similar to the way of life James of Vitry described as
novel with Mary of Oignies.

James's flawed historiographical legacy has yielded among later
commentators on the beguine life a search for discontinuity over
time and in institutions rather than a search for the continuity of
pious affect and its social expression. This investigation has, in turn,
produced a flawed historical reconstruction: because the beguines
proliferated outside monastic regulation in the thirteenth century,
their antecedents cannot have belonged to the established orders.
On the contrary, women who strained definition as nuns, and so
occupied a historical position between traditional female monasticism and the extraregulars of the thirteenth century, participated
in at least the twelfth-century Order of Prémontré, and perhaps in
other monastic groups as well. These nuns' lives stood as a model
for the beguines of the early 1200s, as they articulated their lives
of lay devotion.

Like the beguines, uncloistered sisters among twelfth-century
religious communities were sparsely documented, in part because
of the precariousness of ecclesiastical toleration of their activity. A
succession of statute collections promulgated by the Premonstratensian General Chapter punctuated the first two centuries of the
order's life, and these administrative regulations alternated between careful commentary on women and failure to mention their
participation. The first formal statutes, issued in 1140 in imitation
of the Cistercians' organizational charter, presented a picture of
Premonstratensian women as choir nuns or, more properly, canonesses living a cloistered, contemplative life—a picture in basic con-
tradistinction to the subsequent beguines' care of the poor and sick,
manual labor, and employment outside the monastic enclosure.[38]
The lives of women saints among Premonstratensian communities,
however, demonstrate convincingly that this picture of the order's
nuns is distorted.

[38] For the statutes of circa 1140 regarding women, see R. van Waefelghem, "Les
premiers statuts de l'ordre de Prémontré: Le Clm. 17.174 (XIIe siècle)," *Analecta
praemonstratensia*, vol. 9, separatum (1913), 63–66. Micheline Pontenay de Fontette
discusses these early strictures concerning women in *Les religieuses a l'age classique
du droit canon: Recherches sur les structures juridiques des branches féminines
des ordres* (Paris: J. Vrin, 1967), 15–16. For a recent discussion of the relationships
between this and other collections of the order's statutes, see A. H. Thomas, "Une
version des statuts de Prémontré au debut du XIIIe siècle," *Analecta praemonstratensia* 55 (1979): 153.

The contrast between official regulation of Premonstratensian women and hagiographical evidence about them can be understood in light of the twelfth-century order's confusion about its worldly mission. Norbert's and the earliest Premonstratensians' original active apostolate had been quickly replaced, in the first generation of their followers, by a contemplative commitment imitating the Cistercian pattern.[39] This change had specific consequences for women associated with Prémontré and its daughter houses. The founder's successor as abbot of Prémontré, Hugh of Fosses, was the principal advocate of contemplative practice. Hugh's was the most important voice in the General Chapter that first promulgated statutes describing the role of Premonstratensian women as parallel to the strict enclosure of other orders' nuns.[40] Advocating that the canons of Prémontré should retreat from the world rather than bring their religion into it, Hugh saw no need for the women associated with his order to step outside the cloister.

Premonstratensian sisters were thus caught between an initial commitment to hospital and hospice work, with which Norbert had charged them and which necessitated their exemption from strict enclosure, and Hugh's determination that religious women's good government precluded their contact with secular folk.[41] The hagio-

[39] H. M. Colvin's discussion of variations in the Premonstratensians' sense of their mission is especially well developed (*The White Canons in England* [Oxford: Oxford University Press, 1951], 7–24). See also Stefan Weinfürter, who emphasizes the importance of Norbert's personal model as obviating legislation in the order's early years ("Norbert von Xanten als Reformkanoniker und Stifter des Prämonstratenserordens," in Elm, ed., *Norbert von Xanten* [n. 23 above], 159–87, esp. 172). Like Colvin, Weinfürter argues that Norbert's continued active involvement in German houses after he assumed his episcopacy at Magdeburg left the eastern order differently shaped from the more traditionally monastic western houses (174).

[40] Placidius F. Lefevre argues for Hugh's agency in the promulgation of the first statutes (introduction to *Les statuts de Prémontré réformés sur les ordres de Gregoire IX et d'Innocent IV au XIIIe siècle*, ed. Placidius F. Lefevre, Bibliothèque de la Revue d'histoire ecclésiastique, vol. 23 [Louvain: Bibliothèque de l'université, 1946], viii–x).

[41] Horstkötter, while affirming Premonstratensian involvement in the care of the sick, neglects sisters' participation (254). Pontenay, however, acknowledges that the hospice work of Premonstratensian women distinguished them from cloistered nuns (14–17). Hugues Lamy supports the notion that Premonstratensian women were heavily involved in hospital work (*L'abbaye de Tongerloo depuis sa fondation jusqu'en 1263*, Recueil de travaux des conférences d'histoire et de philologie, fasc. 44 [Louvain: Bibliothèque de l'université, 1914], 93–102). Compare Lamy's perspective with Gréven's; the latter noticed the similarity of Premonstratensian leprosaria to later beguine hospices (36, n. 1). Karl H. Schäfer long ago argued for the indebtedness of thirteenth-century beguines and earlier canonesses who were also committed to hospital service (*Die Kanonissenstifter im deutschen Mittelalter*, Kirchenrechtliche Abhandlungen, vols. 43–44 [1907; reprint, Amsterdam: P. Schip-

graphical memorials of individual sisters of Prémontré, however, reveal that Hugh's attempt to redirect the activities of the order's nuns was only partly successful.

The first recorded woman Premonstratensian was a noblewoman called Rycwer. Evidence of her career is so late and vestigial that even the great Jesuit collection of saints' lives, Acta Sanctorum, offers only a few repetitive remarks about her from seventeenth-century publications based on manuscripts now lost. Born in Vermand, married to Bernard of Clastres, the mother of one child, Rycwer joined Norbert's group with her husband's consent. She entered the new abbey of Prémontré, then a monastery for both sexes, in 1121. She died fifteen years later. Beyond this, sources for her life mention only that she was of such great piety that she was able to extinguish a raging fire by making the sign of the cross and that she was in charge of Prémontré's hospital or hospice facility.[42] The latter piece of information, while brief, suggests that although Rycwer was not a poor woman, she served the poor. In that capacity, she necessarily left the closed company of her sisters. The model that Rycwer provided for her sucessors was therefore incompatible with the order's statutes regarding nuns' strict enclosure.

The lives of sisters of Prémontré of the following generation are reflected in greater detail in the vita of Oda of Rivreulle, who died in 1157 and was memorialized by her prior, the prominent Premonstratensian scholar and eventual abbot, Philip of Harvengt.[43] In its theological and rhetorical sophistication and in the major features of its protagonist's experience, Philip's account of Oda offers a striking parallel to James of Vitry's life of Mary of Oignies.

Oda of Rivreulle, like Mary, came from a highly placed family; her father was a noble whose holdings were near Mary's birthplace.

---

pers, 1965], 254–55). Other studies have argued or assumed that Premonstratensian women were uncloistered lay sisters without tracing the implications of this assumption for later forms of religious life. See, for instance, Ursmer Berlière, *Les monastères doubles aux XIIe et XIIIe siècles*, Mémoires de l'Académie royale de Belgique, classe des lettres et des sciences morales et politiques 18, fasc. 3 (Brussels: M. Lamertin, 1923), 27; Greven, 113–14; Simone Roisin, "L'efflorescence cistercienne et le courant féminin de piété au XIIIe siècle," *Revue d'histoire ecclesiastique* 39 (1943): 350, including n. 1. Like Roisin, Bolton has developed the beguines' connection to the habits and spirituality of contemporary, not earlier regular religious ("*Vitae matrum*" [n. 16 above], 260); she has, however, argued for the possibility of establishing links to earlier religious women as well (*The Medieval Reformation* [n. 16 above], 81).

[42] Acta Sanctorum (n. 13 above), October, 13:51–53.

[43] Philip of Harvengt, *Vita beatae Odae* (hereafter VO), in Migne, ed. (n. 26 above), vol. 203, cols. 1359–74.

Like Mary's parents half a century later, Oda's father wished to cure his young daughter of her religious enthusiasm. When he arranged Oda's marriage to a young man named Simon, the girl waited until the ceremony and then refused to go through with it, citing her desire to join a local abbey of the Premonstratensian order. Simon and his retinue rode off in indignation. Oda's father with great difficulty persuaded the groom to return, but Oda made sure on this occasion that there would be no other attempted marriage. She shut herself in her mother's bedchamber and mutilated her face. At first failing "through feminine weakness" to cut off her entire nose with a dagger, she finally succeeded in gouging out her nostrils. Simon was duly repelled, and Oda's family reluctantly acceded to her desire to join the Premonstratensians.[44]

The abbot of the order's nearby house of Bonne-Espérance, to which Oda was then sent, was coincidentally named Odo. "Odor obedientiae," the scent of humble virtue, surrounded his and Oda's subsequent happy cooperation. Philip of Harvengt, Odo's assistant and eventual successor, filled his account of the abbot's and the nun's activities with variations on the olfactory pun to which Oda's christening and self-mutilation had exposed her.[45] Philip's humor in the course of a saint's life stands in refreshing contrast to James of Vitry's unrelieved sobriety in his memorial to Mary of Oignies. In the content of his presentation more than in its style, however, Philip of Harvengt's description of Oda's spirituality, charitable work, and relationship to ecclesiastical authority forms a point of reference for the career of the beguine Mary.

After Oda took refuge at Bonne-Espérance, she was sent to its women's house not far away at Rivreulle.[46] There she met with further difficulties. Her self-mutilation caused her health and, specifically, her skin to deteriorate. Her sisters, who were experts in

[44] VO, cols. 1361–68. See Jane Tibbetts Schulenburg, "The Heroics of Virginity: Brides of Christ and Sacrificial Mutilation," in *Women in the Middle Ages and the Renaissance: Literary and Historical Perspectives*, ed. Mary Beth Rose (Syracuse, N.Y.: Syracuse University Press, 1986), 29–72, esp. 46–49. Schulenburg sees Oda, to whom she refers as Oda of Hainault, after her birthplace, in the context of several medieval women saints who cut off their noses. She points out that, while occasional descriptions of such behavior in saints' lives may indeed be topoi, they are not improbable. Especially in Oda's case, the story seems well founded (56–61).

[45] For instance, VO, col. 1372: "In domo obedientiae optimum nominis eius unguentum tanto circumquaque diffusum est odore, ut multos utriusque sexus ad currendum viam bonam in odore unguentorum suorum invitaret."

[46] See Ursmer Berlière for a discussion of Rivreulle's hospital and its status as typical of Premonstratensian women's houses attached to men's abbeys ("L'ancien monastère des Norbertines de Rivreulle," *Messager des sciences historiques de Belgique* 67 [1893]: 381–91).

skin diseases since their chief activity was the administration of a leprosarium, diagnosed her as unclean and forced her to live apart from their community. After Oda was later found to be disease-free, she was made prioress at Rivreulle. As such she was the abbot's subordinate, but in practice she had independent charge of all of the house's sisters as well as the inmates of their hospice. For the remainder of her life, Oda's holiness inspired the women's company and that of their brothers at Bonne-Espérance. As her death approached, she abandoned ordinary activity, even eating, for constant prayer and tears.[47]

Philip of Harvengt, who came to know Oda well into her career at Rivreulle, was as inspired by her worship and her work as James of Vitry would later be by the beguine Mary. In his life of Oda, however, Philip was describing a female member of his own established religious order rather than encouraging laywomen's orthodoxy as a defense against growing heresy. He made no effort to characterize Oda's activities as novel or archetypal because they were for him exemplary of Premonstratensian life. Apart from traits common to many saints, the similarities between Oda's experience and Mary's were many: both were chaste, both chose poverty, both were leper nurses, and both mutilated and starved themselves for the sake of holiness.

The salient difference between Oda and Mary was that the former was attached to a religious order, while the latter—although she always lived near and interacted with ecclesiastical foundations and was particularly close to Augustinian canons—never submitted to a monastic or canonical rule. Mary of Oignies was a lay holy woman, strictly speaking, and therefore differed from earlier nuns with a similarly ascetic orientation and similar social engagement. Oda was a nun; Mary was not quite a nun. The question remains how significant that distinction really was.

While early beguine life transgressed the boundary between laypersons and religious in an especially obvious fashion, that boundary had for a hundred years been eroded by the participation of lay brothers as well as lay sisters in reformed monasticism.[48] Women's religious activity was defined with increasing subtlety as the new orders of the twelfth century became established. Choir nun, canoness, lay sister: all of these labels were variously applied to women of the Order of Prémontré.[49]

[47] VO, cols. 1370–74.

[48] See Southern's (n. 29 above) graph stressing the proliferation of Cistercian lay brothers (266).

[49] The early thirteenth-century redaction of the order's statutes made the emphatic point that only choir nuns were to be received: "Nulla mulier in ordine nostro

Oda herself seems, like most early Premonstratensian women, to have been a lay sister. If she were considered a choir nun, then that category had been bent from the strict enclosure typical of other orders' choir nuns to permit work among the secular poor and infirm as well as lively contact with male religious. Lay sisters such as Oda were difficult for the Premonstratensians to maintain, as they were for monasticism generally, because women's work outside the cloister presented both moral and administrative difficulties. It allowed nuns to perform socially useful tasks and to provide for themselves economically, enabling persons whose families could not dower them to adopt religious lives. At the same time, however, outside work made possible sexual activity that might embarrass the monks responsible for these women's behavior.[50] The Order of Prémontré dreaded such embarrassment, and for this reason it attempted throughout the late twelfth century, although with incomplete success, to eliminate lay sisters in favor of more easily managed choir nuns—who were dowered to preclude the necessity of their working in the secular world and cloistered in order to control their sexuality.

The kind of religious life known to Oda of Rivreulle and adopted by her many Premonstratensian sisters began with the support of the order's male hierarchy and was immediately, firmly established. The same male prelates, however, soon judged this women's activity harmful to the prestige of their order. Even though Premonstratensian sisters accepted the authority of priors and abbots when they submitted to the obedience of the rule of Saint Augustine, their involvement outside the cloister gave them real economic and moral independence. The order soon recognized that this freedom was inimical to its interests, but before the men of the Order of Prémontré succeeded in confining women's activity to cloistered contemplation, the beguine movement began.

---

recipiatur de cetero in sororem nisi in locis illis qui sunt ab antiquo recipiendis cantantibus sororibus in perpetuum deputata" (Lefevre, ed. [n. 40 above], 114). Yet the same constitution acknowledged that there were still lay sisters among the Premonstratensians: "Et ubi sorores cantantes habentur, scapularibus albis sine caputis uti poterunt . . . et etiam non cantantes si velint habere" (ibid., 113). Innocent III, in his 1198 confirmation of the Chapter General's recent and, as it turned out, unsuccessful attempt to eliminate women from the order, referred to both *sorores cantantes* and *conversae:* "ut nulam de caetero in sororem recipere teneamini vel conversam" (Migne, ed. [n. 26 above], vol. 214, cols. 173–74).

[50] Jane Tibbets Schulenburg, "Strict Active Enclosure and Its Effects on the Female Monastic Experience (ca. 500–1100)," in *Distant Echoes: Medieval Religious Women,* ed. John A. Nichols and Lillian Thomas Shank (Kalamazoo, Mich.: Cistercian, 1984), 1:69–79.

The beguines, a constituency not of a single monastic order but of the Church in general and towns of northern Europe, eventually posed the same challenge on a much larger scale as had their Premonstratensian predecessors. Both the Premonstratensians and medieval society at large were fundamentally intolerant of women who eluded men's direct control. Yet women still managed to express their piety in roles of chastity and charity throughout the High Middle Ages. Twelfth-century lay sisters of the Order of Prémontré moved outside of the cloister in ways that would be typical of later extraregulars. Beguines, including Mary, created a new sphere of religious activity in their explicit departure from submission to monastic obedience, but they did so in imitation of generations of religious women who had pioneered similar social and spiritual pathways. The novelty of Mary and her followers therefore was in their phenomenal numbers, not in the originality of their roles as leper nurses and hospice administrators or their chastity outside the cloister.

Even the beguines' successful avoidance of ecclesiastical repression throughout the thirteenth century may be evidence of their indebtedness to prior monastic models. The male hierarchy of the Church tolerated beguine communities exactly as the Cistercians had tolerated the participation of women before they officially recognized nuns as part of the order, and as the Premonstratensians had tolerated women in their houses even after they had officially banned them. Cistercian women had effectively forced their way into the order's approbation only after first gathering on its fringes under the informal patronage of friendly abbots.[51] Premonstratensian sisters resisted suppression by continuing their religious work unsanctioned by the order but supported by local custom and abbatial encouragement.[52] Similarly, beguines of the thirteenth century sought the security of association with and spiritual counsel from secular, monastic, and mendicant clergy.[53] To acquire and retain such ecclesiastical support was perhaps easier for beguines, for in their refusal even to pretend submission to established orders they also reduced the possibility of prelates' financial or moral embarrassment for their actions.

The beguines' relations with the Church's hierarchy were informal, even further distanced from the ecclesiastical establishment than twelfth-century nuns had been. Their lack of direct governance

[51] Summers (n. 26 above), 312–13.
[52] Rommens (n. 34 above).
[53] Phillips (n. 31 above), 219–22; Stein (n. 3 above), 31.

opened the way for a century of expanded opportunities for pious women to live religious lives. The eventual suppression of their communities in the early fourteenth century demonstrates not only the fragility of medieval women's efforts to express their religious devotion in new roles but also the Church's recognition of their efforts' dynamism.

Sisters of other orders may, like Premonstratensian and Cistercian women, have provided models for the beguines. Further study, based on a careful reevaluation of the sources on which prior interpretations have depended, may indeed reveal an even richer ancestry for Mary of Oignies than this article suggests. Just as the Order of Prémontré's official pronouncements on women members' status were more corrective than descriptive, and Cistercian statutes and Cistercian realities diverged, so the legislation of other orders is likely to have distorted religious women's actual experience. Yet scholarship on medieval religious women has heretofore heavily depended on such sources. Determination of the accuracy of these documents, and thus modern historians' conclusions, calls for a new reading of other varieties of evidence—cartularies, municipal records, and hagiographical materials—with a view to the ways in which their presentations of women's roles differ from those offered in the official legislation of ecclesiastical fraternities.

Hagiography is of special interest in this reevaluation. As lively recent scholarly discussion has affirmed, saints' lives are a difficult but uniquely valuable genre of historical evidence.[54] At once normative and descriptive, they shape the culture from which they emerge as well as document its existing features. Frequently, they skew historical detail, but they nevertheless resonate with their audiences' religious values and social contexts in order successfully to engage and persuade them. Paradoxically, the ideals that saints' lives present must reflect the importance of these ideals to readers and listeners of their times.

The memorials of Oda of Rivreulle and Mary of Oignies thus suggest a continuity with many more medieval women. Although

---

[54] Donald Weinstein and Rudolf M. Bell, *Saints and Society: The Two Worlds of Western Christendom, 1000–1700* (Chicago: University of Chicago Press, 1982), 220–24. See also Caroline Bynum, review of *Saints and Society,* by Weinstein and Bell, *Speculum* 59 (1984): 457–60. Weinstein and Bell, like Bynum, are heavily indebted to two important works that together rescue hagiography from solely antiquarian or spiritual uses: Pierre Delooz, *Sociologie et canonisations* (Liège: Faculté de droit, 1969); and Andre Vauchez, *La sainteté en Occident aux derniers siècles du moyen âge: D'après les procès de canonisation et les documents hagiographiques,* Bibliotheque des écoles francaises d' Athènes et de Rome, vol. 241 (Rome: Ecole francaise de Rome, 1981).

these saints' lives were recorded by men, their texts reflect their
women subjects' experience and aspirations more accurately than
do the rules composed for sisters by male ecclesiastics. Other saints'
lives may eventually reveal that women of still earlier or more
distant institutional situations were also like Oda and Mary and that
the beguines' past extends back further than the twelfth-century
efflorescence of Cîteaux and Prémontré. At least, it is clear that the
generation of Francis of Assisi witnessed not the first appearance
but a great increase of communities of uncloistered pious women.
In ignoring the beguines' past, the men of the medieval Church
and, in turn, modern historians have minimized the coherence and
vitality of the tradition of women's piety.

Department of History
Colorado College

CREATING AND RECREATING COMMUNITIES OF WOMEN: THE CASE OF CORPUS DOMINI, FERRARA, 1406–1452

MARY MARTIN MC LAUGHLIN

Corpus Domini: The significance of its early history

In April 1452, the abbess and nuns of the monastery of Corpus Domini in Ferrara received a letter from Pope Nicholas V confirming their rights and privileges as members of the "order of Saint Clare" and resolving a difficulty that had plagued the community for more than twenty years.[1] The problem was the claim on the monastery and its property tenaciously defended by a pious laywoman, Lucia Mascheroni. The designated heir of Corpus Domini's founder, she had been its head during the last years of its existence as a lay community. Definitively releasing Lucia from the commitment that had long dominated her life, the papal letter succinctly reviewed the troubled history of this now flourishing monastery of

---

[1] Archivio del monastero del Corpus Domini, Ferrara (hereafter ACD), Cartella B, n. 13, n. 14, April 15, 1452. This letter can also be found in Antonio Samaritani, "Ailisia de Baldo e le correnti reformatrici femminili di Ferrara nella prima meta del sec. XV," *Atti e memorie della Deputazione provinciale Ferrarese di Storia Patria*, ser. 3, 13 (1973): 91–157, esp. 154–56. The letter is also published, along with other papal documents relating to Corpus Domini, in the seventeenth-century collection by Luke Wadding, *Annales Minorum*, ed. J. M. Fonseca, 3d ed., 31 vols. (Quaracchi: Quaracchi, 1931–88), 12:562–63.

This essay originally appeared in *Signs*, vol. 14, no. 2, Winter 1989.

Clarisse, whose ninety-nine members included Caterina Vegri, who would later become known as Saint Catherine of Bologna.

The story began about forty-five years earlier, when a Ferrarese woman, Bernardina Sedazzari, founded a community of devout lay-women, which she dedicated to the "Body of Christ and the Visitation of the Blessed Virgin Mary." Bernardina died in 1425 and within a few years after her death, there had emerged from her small community not one but two permanent and distinguished monasteries, Corpus Domini and Sant'Agostino. Among the women whose visions of the communal and spiritual life had become, during and after its founder's lifetime, strongly attached to the community called Corpus Domini, there had also appeared several remarkable personalities whose initiatives contributed fundamentally to its creation and reshaping.

The history of Corpus Domini during this relatively brief period is significant for a number of reasons, first of all for what it reveals about the fortunes of a community of laywomen. Although scholars have long been aware of the numerous lay communities that appeared spontaneously and informally in various parts of Europe during the late Middle Ages, recent research has led to illuminating discoveries about the origins and early history of these communities. Exemplifying such finds for Italian communities is a document of circa 1322, recording the entrance of five women in a very small town near Spoleto into a house that all of them (*tutte cinque noi*) had bought with the intention of establishing their religious life there.[2] Like Corpus Domini, this community eventually adopted the rule of Saint Clare, thus attaining the canonical status and the permanent identity that would give many communities of this kind in Italy and elsewhere a traceable history.

[2] Monteleone di Spoleto, Archivio Parrocchiale, Registro degli atti de monastero di S. Caterina, 1r. There is no comprehensive study of Italian lay communities of women or of Italian religious women in general. Valuable insights are offered in two collections of essays by Roberto Rusconi, ed., *Il movimento religioso femminile e francescanesimo nel secolo XIII*, Atti del Convegno internazionale, Assisi, 11–13 ottobre 1979 (Assisi: Società internazionale di studi francescani, 1980), and *Il movimento religioso femminile in Umbria nei secoli XIII–XIV*, Atti del Convegno internazionale di studio nel ambito delle celebrazione per L'VIII centenario della nascità di S. Francesco d'Assisi, Città di Castello, 27–29 ottobre 1982, Quaderni de Centro per il Collegamento degli Studi Medievali e Umanistici nell'Università di Perugia, vol. 12 (Florence and Perugia: Regione dell'Umbria e La Nuova Editrice, 1984). Recent studies of northern cities and regions include Frederick Stein, "The Religious Women of Cologne, 1200–1320" (Ph.D. diss., Yale University, 1977); and Bernard Delmaire, "Les beguines dans le Nord de la France au premièr siècle de leur histoire (vers 1230–vers 1350)," in *Les religieuses en France au XIIIe siècle*, ed. Michel Parisse (Nancy: Presses Universitaires, 1985), 121–62.

Rarely, however, can we follow in precise and revealing detail the experience of a community of women actively engaged in creating their history as we can in the documents that record the early years of Corpus Domini in Ferrara and the power struggles through which it evolved. Here we see in sharp focus the not uncommon but too often obscure process by which a small, informal community of women institutionalized itself, in this instance by division as well as by association with recognized religious orders. Here are revealed with truly exceptional clarity the initiatives of individuals at work in the creation of new communities as well as the personality conflicts and reforming ideals that shaped the destiny of a late medieval community of women.

Corpus Domini is still an active community today and its substantial body of records has held an unusual attraction for scholars during the last two decades. Two circumstances help to explain a concern that has fostered studies valuable in themselves and also for their publication of important early documents. One is scholarly interest in the lively religious environment of early fifteenth-century Ferrara.[3] The other is a growing attention to the life and work of Corpus Domini's most celebrated member, Caterina Vegri, by scholars intent on removing this exceptionally interesting woman from the embrace of pious hagiography to the light of critical history.[4]

Drawing on this research and my own work, this essay is meant to be suggestive rather than exhaustive. I offer it as an *exemplum* with a twofold purpose. It is concerned, first of all, with the initiatives of women in creating and recreating a religious community,

[3] In an appendix to his article, "Ailisia de Baldo," Antonio Samaritani published important documents from the archives of Corpus Domini, Ferrara, dating from 1402–52 and pertaining to the foundation and early history of the community (131–57). For Samaritani's earlier studies of religious movements in late medieval Ferrara, see his *Medievalia e altri studi* (Codigoro: Giari, 1970). Other documents, discovered by Teodosio Lombardi, are among those published in Lombardi's study of Corpus Domini in *I Francescani a Ferrara*, vol. 4, *I Monasteri delle Clarisse: San Guglielmo, Corpus Domini, S. Bernardino, S. Chiara* (Bologna: Antoniano, 1974–75), 4:63–95. See also G. Ferraresi, *Il b. Giovanni Tavelli da Tossignano e la riforma de Ferrara nel Quattrocento*, 4 vols. (Brescia, 1969–70).

[4] Further important documentation from unpublished and printed sources, pertaining to Caterina Vegri, her family, and her relationship with Corpus Domini, accompanies Santa Caterina Vegri, *Le sette armi spirituali*, ed. Cecilia Foletti (Padua: Antenore, 1985); for Ferrarese sources and perspectives on Caterina, see ibid., esp. 16–76; 165–77. An indispensable guide, especially to Bolognese sources, is Serena Spanò (Martinelli), "Per un studio su Caterina da Bologna," *Studi Medievali*, ser. 3, 12 (1971): 713–59. See also G. Alberigo, "Caterina da Bologna dall'agiografia alla storia religiosa," *Atti e Memorie della Deputazione di Storia Patria per le Province di Romagna*, n.s., 15–16 (1967): 5–23.

with their varied conceptions of its meaning, and with the religious and social opportunities it offered. Focused on the leaders, the ideals, and the inner struggles depicted in the early records of a particularly well documented community, this "case study" also proposes some larger themes and questions pertaining to power and community in the history of women. Exemplifying at the same time a modern quest for medieval communities of women, my essay has another purpose: to illustrate the goals and possibilities of the research project that led to my own "discovery" of Corpus Domini, among a multitude of other communities created and recreated by medieval religious women.

The project to which I refer is intended, in fact, to "recreate" these communities and to identify their notable members in their historical dimensions. At present the most comprehensive enter-prise of its kind pertaining to the history of medieval women and religious life, this computer-assisted project aims to produce three coordinated research instruments encompassing women's religious life and communities in the Latin West between 500 and 1500. I have described these works in detail elsewhere, along with the research procedures designed to produce them.[5] Here the kinds of inquiry that this project will assist, and initiate, are suggested in a case study of the early history of Corpus Domini, Ferrara, illus-trating in expanded form the character of the sources and the data record on which it is based.

The founder and her intentions

Beginning with what we know of the remarkable woman who was its founder, the story of Corpus Domini also begins, in a special sense, with her dowry of a hundred gold ducats. Bernardina Sed-azzari was the daughter of a merchant of Ferrara, Gregorio Sedaz-zari, and his wife, Lucia Zumignani de Tamisaris, whose father was

[5] The format and content of our data records and other aspects of our project are discussed in Mary M. McLaughlin, "Looking for Medieval Women: An Interim Report on the Project 'Women's Religious Life and Communities, A.D. 500–1500,' " *Medieval Prosopography* 8 (Spring 1987): 61–91. This project and the research for this article have been supported by the National Endowment for the Humanities and sponsored by Barnard College. Members of our research group since 1982 have included Suzanne F. Wemple, Mary M. McLaughlin, Heath P. Dillard, Eleanor S. Riemer, and Constance H. Berman. Our long-term purpose is to produce a repertory of female religious communities in the Latin West before 1500; a biobibliography of noteworthy women associated with these communities as founders, heads, and other administrators or members distinguished as spiritual leaders, teachers, writers,

a Venetian merchant.[6] In 1375, as a child and probably after the death of her mother, Bernardina was entrusted to the nuns of San Silvestro, the oldest Benedictine abbey of women in Ferrara, with a dowry of a hundred ducats provided by her maternal aunt, the Venetian Caterina Zumignani. Perhaps already showing signs of a characteristic independence, Bernardina left San Silvestro after some years, apparently to marry, taking her dowry with her. Still later— the time is not known—she returned with her dowry to San Silvestro where, according to a document of 1398, she was living as a widow and perhaps as a candidate for the monastic life.[7] But four years later, in 1402, she departed once more, now officially emancipated by her father and again in possession of her dowry, which would play a crucial part in her future plans.[8]

The reasons for her second departure are not clear. She may have been expelled; a restless spirit, she was apparently dissatisfied with the quality of religious life in this ancient and declining abbey, and she may already have been dreaming of a community of her own. During the years after she left San Silvestro, she had spent some time in Venice, where she had family connections. Perhaps inspired by the reform movements then active in Venice and the Veneto, she was certainly in close touch with a group of devout women, with whom she discussed her strong desire to found a new community. These friends—among them, possibly, her aunt and original benefactor—not only encouraged her in this plan but actively supported it as well, sending her, after she returned to Ferrara, another hundred ducats to add to those she already possessed.[9] Women thus provided all of the funds initially invested in Bernardina's venture, including her dowry.

and artists (included here also are important religious women, anchoresses, and others, who were not members of communities); and an international bibliography of modern studies of women's religious life in the Middle Ages. The first two works will be produced ultimately as a series of fascicles devoted to major European regions, each accompanied by appropriate maps and tables. The third, based on the other two, will be published as a single volume, organized chronologically, topically, and geographically.

[6] Lombardi, 60–64.

[7] Archivio di Stato, Ferrara, Archivio Notarile Antico: a notarial act dated December 8, 1398, recording a gift of money to Bernardina Sedazzari, "living as a widow in the monastery of San Silvestro," also in Lombardi, 61.

[8] The emancipation of Bernardina is recorded in a document dated May 5, 1402, in ACD, Cartella B, n. 1, and in Lombardi, 61–62.

[9] ACD, Cartella A, n. 2, July 13, 1407, and in Samaritani, "Ailisia de Baldo" (n. 1 above), 131–34, esp. 131.

With these funds in hand, and with the help of a male friend, Ser Giacomo de Caligis, in 1406 Bernardina bought a house and two plots of land in the quarter of San Salvatore in Ferrara, with the intention of building a monastery dedicated to "the Body of Christ and the Visitation of the Virgin Mary."[10] In a document of 1407 recording this purchase and her arrangements with Ser Giacomo, her plans for her new foundation, which may be dated in this or the preceding year, are described in some detail.[11] The projected "monastery" was to house twelve or more nuns professing the rule of Saint Augustine and wearing the customary habit of Augustinian nuns, the "gonella," or gown, the scapular, the mantle of black cloth, the white veil and the black veil. These nuns would also be subject to perpetual enclosure. Bernardina's original intentions are worth noting because, as later events would show, she seems to have made every effort to avoid realizing them.

During the nearly two decades of her leadership, her new community did not formally adopt the Augustinian rule. Nor were its members strictly enclosed, although a letter of Pope Martin V in 1420 had authorized the bishop of Bologna to establish the Augustinian rule there or, alternatively, to oblige these women to accept the status of "veiled virgins."[12] Apparently ignoring these directives of ecclesiastical authority, Bernardina and her companions continued, instead, as a community of pious laywomen, of the kind called *penitente* or *pinzochere,* living a common religious life of Augustinian inspiration but taking no vows and lacking precisely defined ecclesiastical status.[13] In communities of this sort, usually small groups of congenial companions, women might continue the informal household and family patterns of ordinary life, more appealing and accessible to many of them than formal monastic structures. Lay communities offered a way of life and a security especially attractive to widows and unmarried women of respectable, if sometimes modest, social status, who often invested in them their small "capital" in the form of dowries, inheritances, and gifts. These women may also have shared Bernardina's desire to live independently of male authority, which did not prevent their turning at times to the assistance of male friends and relatives.

Members of these communities led a simple life of religious devotions, domestic activity, and "good works," often serving the

[10] Samaritani, "Ailisia de Baldo," 132–34.

[11] Ibid., 131.

[12] ACD, Cartella A, n. 6, May 31, 1420.

[13] On these women and their communities, see Romana Guarnieri, "Pinzochere," in *Dizionario degli Istituti di Perfezione* (Rome: Edizioni Paoline, 1980), 6:1721–49.

poor and sick and sometimes, as was apparently the case in Bernardina's community, assuming the care of young girls, perhaps orphans or others who needed such provision and who might also become a source of future recruits. One such girl, among the earliest members of Corpus Domini and, it seems, the closest to its founder, was Lucia Mascheroni, who was later identified as one of two girls taken in and reared by Bernardina; by 1426 Lucia could say that she had lived in Corpus Domini for eighteen years or more.[14] Described in documents sometimes as a monastery but also as an "oratorio" or "ospizio" or "mansione," Bernardina's community, very small at first, with the original dwelling said to be suitable for no more than four persons, evidently took in new members during these early years. New construction began in 1415, with Bernardina's limited funds supplemented, perhaps substantially, by contributions from Lucia Mascheroni and her brother.[15] Its growing appeal attested by this expansion, Corpus Domini had become a modest but lively nursery of the devout life and also, it seems, of the reformist spirit then gaining strength in Ferrara and other north Italian cities.

On April 2, 1425, nearly twenty years after its founding, at a time when many were dying of pestilence and Bernardina herself was "ailing in body though sound in mind," she made her last testament, in which she named Lucia as her "universal heir."[16] On April 3, Bernardina granted Lucia all rights and powers over Corpus Domini and its property, having asked and received from her a sworn promise to "defend, maintain and improve" the community in the form in which it had existed since its foundation.[17] This legacy, and Lucia's solemn promise, would play a critical part both in her own later life and in the destiny of the community she inherited, a part, it is tempting to say, as critical in the ensuing history of Corpus Domini as Bernardina's dowry had been in its founding.

Though much that is known about the life of her community dates from events following Bernardina's death not long after her testament was written, the community's importance for Bernardina herself is suggested by the history just reviewed. Whatever may remain impenetrable concerning her life and her intentions, Bernardina was evidently a woman of remarkably independent character, whose early experience of traditional monastic life and later

---

[14] ACD, Cartella A, n. 9, April–May 1426, and in Samaritani, "Ailisia de Baldo," 137.

[15] Samaritani, "Ailisia de Baldo," 137, 140.

[16] The last testament of Bernardina Sedazzari in ACD, Cartella A, n. 7, April 2, 1425, and in Samaritani, "Ailisia de Baldo," 134–36.

[17] ACD, Cartella A, n. 8, April 3, 1425.

exposure to reformist ideals had inspired, or confirmed, her determination to found a community of her own. Underscoring this purpose, she had from the start given her community a distinctive identity, with a name and double dedication that were in themselves revealing: the name, Corpus Domini, signifying the devotion to the Body of Christ that was a major theme in late medieval female piety, and the Visitation of the Virgin by Saint Elizabeth, symbolizing women's companionship and association.

Never explaining why she had departed from her original plan without explicitly renouncing it, Bernardina herself contributed to the ambiguities that would encourage those with designs on her community to interpret her intentions diversely. According to one self-serving view, for example, she had always intended to found an Augustinian monastery and had failed to realize her plan only because Corpus Domini was in its early years too small and poor to permit her to carry it out. In the same account, however, she was contradictorily described as having followed a self-imposed rule, veiling herself and her companions and receiving their promises "between her own hands."[18] Whatever we may make of these statements, more reliable evidence strongly suggests that she preferred autonomy to authority and wished most of all to preserve the independence of the community she regarded as her creation and her property. Leaving her options open and her intentions unclear apparently made it easier to resist papal and episcopal attempts to impose the Augustinian rule officially on Corpus Domini and thus to draw it more closely within the net of ecclesiastical authority. Her efforts to ensure the continuity, and the autonomy, of Corpus Domini after her death are most clearly demonstrated in her testament and in the promise she extracted from Lucia Mascheroni, whose determination to preserve the lay character of this community affirms her own understanding of her friend's intention.

The legacy of Bernardina Sedazzari

If Bernardina's careful planning won the lasting loyalty of her chosen successor, it failed to prevent the dissension that arose soon after her death, when Lucia's control was challenged by another leading figure in the community. This was Ailisia de Baldo, who had brought with her to Corpus Domini, either before or after Ber-

---

[18] These remarks on Bernardina's community are those of Verde Pio da Carpi in a much later letter to Pope Eugene IV, published in Lombardi (n. 3 above), 78–79; for a notarial draft of her request, see also ACD Cartella B, n. 3.

nardina's death, her own following, including several young girls in her "care and custody."[19] Strongly resisted by Lucia and her supporters, who were determined to maintain the community as it had been during Bernardina's lifetime, Ailisia and her faction were intent on realizing their founder's original plan for Corpus Domini, by formally accepting the Augustinian rule and the institutional status that this action would bring. With the support of episcopal and secular authorities, perhaps as their instruments, Ailisia and her followers were able for a time to expel their rivals.[20]

This victory was soon reversed, however, when Lucia's appeals to the highest secular authority in Ferrara, the council of Marchese Niccolò III d'Este, won recognition of her legal rights and restored her control of the community.[21] Although she had insisted on its lay character and its independence of ecclesiastical jurisdiction, her appeal also invited the kind of intervention she wished to avoid. Among the officials participating in the decision of her case were three churchmen of high rank, including the archbishop of Ravenna, who appointed a commission of prominent local clerics to define more precisely the way of life of this lay community and, by reconciling the differences among its members, to help them to live "honorably, peacefully, harmoniously and quietly."[22]

Now describing Corpus Domini as an "oratory and hospice," the commission's decree attempted to achieve some compromise between Lucia and Ailisia, making concessions to both, yet still affirming the lay character of their community. Carefully reserving the proprietorial rights of Lucia Mascheroni, except in the matter of the "ecclesiastical goods" used in the chapel, the decree prescribed that no members of the community should be permitted to own any personal property or speak with outsiders without the permission of Lucia or Ailisia. These were probably concessions to Ailisia's desire for monastic poverty and enclosure. A similar concession to Lucia, very likely, was the provision that, according to the custom in lay communities, their "confessor" should be the parish priest of their "contrada" or quarter of the city, or another appointed by the bishop. Reflecting the informal structure of such communities, though difficult to reconcile with the apparent joint

[19] ACD, Cartella A, n. 10, May 11–June 19, 1426, also in Samaritani, "Ailisia de Baldo," 141.

[20] See the appeal of Lucia Mascheroni (a contemporary copy) in ACD, Cartella A, n. 9, April–May 1426, also in Samaritani, "Ailisia de Baldo," 136–38.

[21] See the decision in Lucia Mascheroni's favor in ACD, Cartella A, n. 10, May 11–June 19, 1426, also in Samaritani, "Ailisia de Baldo," 138–41.

[22] A record of the commission's decree follows the document in ACD, Cartella A, n. 9, April–May 1426, also in Samaritani, "Ailisia de Baldo," 141–45.

rule of Lucia and Ailisia, a final provision prescribed that each month members should elect one of their number as the person in charge of community affairs.

Despite the commission's efforts, whatever peace had been made between the two rivals was short-lived. Although they and their adherents appear to have been irremediably divided in their goals for their community, clearly the conflict here was not between the supporters and opponents of spiritual reform but between two different visions of the religious life. This was a community torn between the desire of some to preserve its autonomous and familiar way of life, even at the cost of instability, and the wish of others to ensure its permanence through more formal structures, even if this meant a loss of independence. The nature of the conflict became evident when, two months after Lucia's restoration, Ailisia de Baldo departed with her following, those sisters who agreed with her notion of the proper direction for Corpus Domini and shared her vision of a monastery of professed nuns following the rule of Saint Augustine.[23]

Having lost her battle for control of one community, Ailisia won a kind of victory by making the inner division permanent in the founding of another, which could be perceived as implementing Bernardina's original intention. A woman of respectable though otherwise unknown family—she is called *domina* in the documents—Ailisia evidently had strong ties to certain groups of reformers in early fifteenth-century Ferrara.[24] She may also have been inspired by the ideals of the *devotio moderna,* which was influential in Italian circles at this time.[25] Clearly, what this determined and resourceful woman wanted was a cloistered, disciplined community, reformist in spirit, and this she achieved in her new foundation, Sant'Agostino, which became the first of the two permanent and formally organized monasteries that would emerge from the lay community founded by Bernardina Sedazzari. From the "success story" of Ailisia's Sant'Agostino we learn something about her own gifts as an administrator and reformer; we learn, too, how much more attractive to lay patronage and ecclesiastical favor monasteries of this kind were likely to be than were lay communities such as Lucia's Corpus Domini.

---

[23] Samaritani, "Ailisia de Baldo," 99–102.

[24] Ibid., 142–43, for references to "domina Aylisia filia ser Johannis Aldi."

[25] On the influence of the *devotio moderna* in Ferrara and north Italy, see Antonio Samaritani, "Biagio Novelli (1388–1475) nella riforma cattolica ferrarese dei secoli XIV–XV," in his *Medievalia e altri studi* (n. 3 above). See also Massimo Petrocchi, *Una "devotio moderna" nel Quattrocento italiano ed altri studi* (Firenze: Le Monnier, 1961).

By July 1426, Ailisia de Baldo had acquired a house with a well and two courtyards, where she established herself with her original companions and other honest "women" and "ladies" who wished to live chastely. Finding financial support among local devotees of religious reform, she obtained her first benefaction from the legacy of a Ferrarese layman, distributed for the benefit of various reformist communities. Two years later her acquisitions of property were confirmed in a document signed by Ailisia and the members of her community, at that time thirteen in number. In February 1429, a letter of Pope Martin V authorized her to take the Augustinian habit; this was confirmed by a diploma of Cardinal Nicolò Albergati, delegating to the celebrated reformer, Ludovico Barbo, abbot of Santa Giustina in Padua and later bishop of Treviso, the authority to receive the vows of Ailisia and her sisters, who by this time numbered fifteen.

A year later, Abbot Barbo came to Ferrara and accepted the profession of Ailisia and eleven other sisters, who assumed the Augustinian habit and veil after the fashion of San Ludovico in Venice and Santa Maria degli Angeli in Murano. With the recognition of Sant'Agostino as a community exempt from episcopal jurisdiction and subject directly to the Holy See, Ailisia had also achieved some autonomy, along with the stability she greatly desired. During the next five years (1430–35) the new community gradually built up a modest patrimony through gifts and bequests; for example, a widow who became a nun at Sant'Agostino donated her inheritance to the "poor nuns" of a community "daily increasing in grace."[26]

Growing in prosperity and numbers during these early years, Ailisia's community won a considerable reputation as a center of Augustinian reform. In 1442, she was authorized by the bishop of Ferrara to go with four sisters to Verona to help establish a new Augustinian monastery there, and three years later she was entrusted with the reform of the oldest Augustinian monastery of women in Ferrara, San Vito, which later became temporarily a dependency of Sant'Agostino. Still later, Ailisia undertook the reform of another local Augustinian community, San Barnaba. By 1461, the year of her death, Ailisia's Sant'Agostino had achieved a prominent place among Ferrara's monasteries of women, including among its twenty-five choir nuns many who were members of Ferrara's patrician and noble families.[27]

[26] Samaritani, "Ailisia de Baldo," 112. This summary of the early history of Sant'Agostino is based on ibid., 101–25, 145–53.

[27] On the death of Ailisia in 1461, see Lombardi (n. 3 above), 77, referring to a document in the Archivio di Stato, Ferrara, which reports the election of her successor in this year.

The capture of Corpus Domini

Meanwhile, the community Ailisia had left behind more than thirty years earlier had become considerably larger and even more eminent than her own foundation, but it had attained this position only after enduring much internal travail and, ultimately, transformation. After Ailisia and her companions departed, Corpus Domini remained a community of pious laywomen under the direction of Lucia Mascheroni, apparently a woman of great dedication and personal appeal. Yet, apart from her obsessive fidelity to her promise to Bernardina Sedazzari, she was less resolute in character and less effective as a leader than either her friend or her former rival. These weaknesses left her ill-prepared for the next phase in the vicissitudes of her community, when the challenge of another powerful personality made it clear that Ailisia's departure had not solved the problems of Corpus Domini.

The new catalyst for change was a woman who, though not herself a member of the community, would by patronage and pressure determine its fate. This was the pious, well-born, and wealthy Ferrarese matron, Verde Pio da Carpi, who was the prime mover in the transformation of Corpus Domini, the lay community, into Corpus Domini, a monastery of Clarisse. Verde belonged to an ancient noble family with close ties to the dominant Este and with other important if more unstable political connections. Her sister, Taddea, had been married to the lord of Imola, who was expelled in 1424 and died soon afterward, and Verde herself may have been a widow when she began her intervention in the affairs of Corpus Domini.[28]

Why this *grande dame* of Ferrarese society should have fixed her attention on a modest community of middle-class women is a question perhaps best answered by suggesting that she saw in it an attractive investment opportunity. This is not to deny to Verde a genuine sympathy with Lucia and her companions and a sincere response to the piety of a community whose high reputation had been sustained for more than twenty years. It is, however, apparent that Verde's motives were complex; taking a realistic view of its limited means and prospects, she also perceived in Corpus Domini possibilities that might be realized by a firmer hand than Lucia's. With Verde Pio and her benefactions, worldly ambition and social power entered the simple life of this community and set in motion the process of transformation.

[28] Regarding the family of Verde Pio da Carpi, see Foletti, ed. (n. 4 above), 48–52; and Trevor Dean, *Land and Power in Late Medieval Ferrara: The Rule of the Este, 1350–1450*, Cambridge Studies in Medieval Life and Thought (Cambridge: Cambridge University Press, 1988), esp. 76, 86–87, 177–78.

Wishing only to lend these women a helping hand, as she would later say, Verde gradually increased her influence over them through her financial support, especially her substantial investment in rebuilding and enlarging their house in a fashion befitting a formally organized monastery. For such a monastery was Verde's vision of Corpus Domini. Like Ailisia before her, this forceful, some might say overbearing, woman proposed to stabilize the community by associating it with a recognized order and, perhaps, in the process to assume for herself the role of second founder. What she had in mind was more fully revealed by a letter written sometime between 1429 and 1431, requesting papal approval of her plans.[29] She began by offering the pope her own version of the early history of Bernardina's foundation, stressing its limitations in size and its lack of sufficient income to ensure continuing support. Ignoring the complex evolution recorded in other documents, she insisted on the founder's plan for a formally organized monastery and portrayed herself as its belated instrument, the generous benefactor who had come to the rescue of Lucia and her companions after Bernardina's death.

Pursuing Bernardina's intention, Verde had, she said, first considered the Augustinians and looked in vain for a suitable woman to instruct Lucia and her sisters in the requirements of this order. Only when this plan failed had she turned to the idea of a community of Clarisse, quite logically since her sister, Taddea, and Taddea's widowed daughter had by this time become nuns of Corpus Christi and Santa Paola in Mantua. Then the most distinguished center of reform among the Clarisse of north Italy, Corpus Christi had been founded some years earlier by Marchesa Paola Malatesta Gonzaga under the influence of San Bernardino of Siena, whose preaching made him a potent advocate of Franciscan reform.[30]

Why should Verde Pio, wishing to have her sister and niece near her in Ferrara, not dream also of gaining for herself and her family the prestige of establishing just such a prominent monastery of Clarisse in their own city?[31] Assuring the pope that a contingent of reformed Clarisse from Mantua was ready to join or take over Cor-

[29] For a notarial draft of her request to Pope Eugene IV, see ACD, Cartella B, n. 3, also in Lombardi, 78–79.

[30] See A. Fantozzi, "La riforma osservante dei monasteri delle clarisse nell'Italia centrale," *Archivum franciscanum historicum* 23 (1930): 361–82. In her plans for Corpus Domini, Verde Pio may have been imitating Paola Gonzaga quite directly, since the first members of Paola's foundation, dating from 1414, were said to have belonged to a community of pious women living together without a rule.

[31] There was already one long-established monastery of Clarisse in Ferrara, San Guglielmo, founded circa 1251, but in its acquisitions of property and its worldly life it had departed so alarmingly from its original ideals that strenuous reform was undertaken by papal command between 1437 and 1439 (see Lombardi, 33–34).

pus Domini, Verde requested his permission to introduce there the rule of Saint Clare in its less rigorous "Urbanist" version. At the same time she asked for Lucia Mascheroni's absolution from her earlier promise to Bernardina Sedazzari.[32] This absolution, and Lucia's renunciation of her rights to Corpus Domini and its property, would be essential steps in Verde's realization of her plan.

Whether or not Lucia ever agreed, even momentarily, to this high-handed capture of her community is not clear, though it seems unlikely in view of her reaction. For if Verde had thought to accomplish her goal without opposition, she had not sufficiently considered Lucia's obstinate and scrupulous adherence to her sworn promise or her support within her community. Just as Lucia had opposed the plans of Ailisia de Baldo, she now balked at the schemes of Verde Pio, which had matured while Lucia and other sisters were absent during the rebuilding of their house. When, sometime during the early months of 1431, Lucia and five companions, among them the young Caterina Vegri, returned "to restore the monastery to good order," they found Verde Pio's projected transformation well on the way to becoming an accomplished fact.[33] Her request to the pope regarding the introduction of the rule was granted in a papal decree of April 4, 1431, which also directed that an abbess should be elected from among the Clarisse who were to come from Mantua.[34] By October, Sister Taddea Pio and her companions were installed, and in 1432, an abbess, in all likelihood Taddea herself, was chosen for the now prescribed term of ten years.

So bald a summary of these critical events hardly does justice to the difficulties and distress that attended the institutionalizing of Corpus Domini. The traumatic effects of this experience would be assimilated and later recorded by Caterina Vegri, who had entered the community in 1426 at age thirteen. Although she ultimately accepted the new dispensation, she played an active part in this crisis despite her youth, not only as a loyal supporter of Lucia Mascheroni but also, according to her biographer, as an unwilling and unsuccessful candidate for the office of abbess.[35] During the

---

[32] Ibid., 79.

[33] *Le sette armi spirituali*, 7.31–32 in Foletti, ed., 128.

[34] See Lombardi, 82–83, for the decree of Pope Eugene IV, April 4, 1431, directed to the abbot of Gavello, giving him authority regarding the adoption of the rule of Saint Clare at Corpus Domini.

[35] According to her biographer, Illuminata Bembo, an attempt was made to elect Caterina, against her vigorous protests (see Bembo, *Specchio de Illuminatione*, fols. 29–30, cited from the autograph manuscript in the monastery of Corpus Domini, Bologna, in Foletti, ed., 52).

early years of the "new" Corpus Domini, she would also be threatened with severe ecclesiastical penalties as a member, perhaps the leader, of a group of nuns adamant in their insistence on the strictest version of the rule of Saint Clare, rather than the more relaxed version Verde had requested.[36]

The plight of Lucia Mascheroni

Soon after the arrival of the Mantuan Clarisse, Lucia Mascheroni, too, may have accepted the habit. Shortly afterward, however, she left "of her own will" the community of which she had been a member for twenty-five years and head from about 1425 to 1431 following the death of Bernardina and the departure of Ailisia de Baldo. She left, it seems clear, because, when finally faced with the decisive taking of vows, she could not renounce her promise to Bernardina. Though the nuns proposed that she return as a "private sister" or give up her rights in the community, she refused, believing herself forever bound by her sworn word. The sisters then embarked on a prolonged effort to free themselves, and her, from this impasse and to regularize their own de facto control of Corpus Domini. They eventually appealed to the bishop of Ferrara to liberate Lucia from her vow, with the condition that she renounce once and for all her rights over the monastery.[37] They explained that they had no confidence in her stability and firmness of purpose and were afraid that, even after she was absolved of her oath, she would refuse to make the desired renunciation. On this account they felt obliged to request that, her rights notwithstanding, the monastery and property of Corpus Domini should be freed and exempted from her control in perpetuity and belong in full right to the sisters living there.

Lucia did, in fact, make this formal renunciation, sometime between 1446 and 1452, accompanied by her relatives and heirs, in the presence of a notary and a certain unidentified venerable "nobildonna," no doubt the now elderly but still powerful Verde Pio da Carpi.[38] Even so, the bishop's absolution, which accompanied or followed her renunciation, did not relieve the scruples that still

---

[36] Foletti, ed., 59, n. 55, and 60–66, for the text, and Foletti's discussion, of an episcopal decree absolving Caterina and her companions of the sin of "apostasy" and the ecclesiastical penalties they had incurred on this account.

[37] ACD, Cartella B, n. 12, also in Lombardi (n. 3 above), 80–81, where it is incorrectly dated.

[38] ACD, Cartella B, n. 13, also in Lombardi, 81, where it is also incorrectly dated; see Foletti, ed. (n. 4 above), 54–55, regarding both of these documents.

tormented Lucia. Not until the papal letter of 1452 finally released her from her long fidelity to her promise did this obstinate and troubled woman attain peace of soul.

As a prisoner of her conscience and her promise to Bernardina, Lucia was undoubtedly a victim of the unhappy choices to which absolute loyalties sometimes lead. Deprived by Verde Pio's machinations of her control of Corpus Domini, she had, by refusing to abandon her commitment and accept the compromises offered by her former sisters, lost the opportunity to continue with them a life that had been hers since childhood. Her intransigent fidelity to her promise and defense of her rights to her community may indeed appear the more courageous in a woman so susceptible to the influence of personalities stronger than hers. Poignant or quixotic as it may seem, however, Lucia's plight also has a larger meaning, dramatizing the critical issues played out in the early history of Corpus Domini. For in the crises of her community's transformation, it was she who met most directly the problems and pressures facing late medieval women who wished to create for themselves congenial and autonomous forms of religious life and who sought to secure the continuity of their communities outside the formal structures of monasteries and orders. What made the community that Lucia inherited so revealing a mirror of these conflicts was that they were intrinsic to its founder's legacy, which encompassed, in Bernardini's original plan for a formally organized monastery and in the lay community she actually created, two distinctive visions of the religious life.

Although Lucia had won a victory for her community and her leadership in her conflict with Ailisia de Baldo, the economic survival of women who shared a commitment to her vision of a lay community was at best precarious. If Verde Pio or someone like her had not intervened in its affairs, the eventual fate of Corpus Domini would in all probability have been that of numerous groups of this kind, which often have left only the barest traces of their existence, usually in records of the donations that helped to sustain them while they lasted. Documents of the late fourteenth and early fifteenth centuries in Pisa, for example, record the existence of several groups of "good Christian women," along with the names of individual members, though these groups apparently lacked a distinctive identity of the kind significantly possessed by Corpus Domini.[39]

[39] I am indebted to Alessandra Veronese, Scuola Normale Superiore, Pisa, an Italian collaborator in our project, for information concerning these late medieval women and for references to unpublished documents in the State Archives of Pisa and Florence.

Yet for Corpus Domini, as for similar communities, economic support was from the first a major problem. Thanks to her dowry and the assistance of other women, Bernardina Sedazzari was able to provide a "house," a physical setting, for her community, and she invested later donations, including Lucia Mascheroni's inheritance, in its expansion. But the funds that individual urban women of merchant and artisan families could have contributed to sustain their community were rarely sufficient to support its needs. For this, a community would have required a steady flow of income or the kind of patronage that was more likely to be given to monastic houses, always more attractive to both members and donors from nobel and patrician families.

For lay communities like Lucia's, the social homogeneity that made them especially appealing to respectable middle-class women was also a disadvantage in the struggle for survival. A common solution to this problem for communities of women who aspired to live a religious life without becoming professed nuns was the adoption of a "third-order" Franciscan or Dominican rule, which would give them a recognized status along with greater security and stability. Whether or not Lucia and her companions ever considered this option, it would have been ruled out after Verde Pio appeared on the scene. Her social position and ambitions led naturally to the expansion of Corpus Domini as a heterogeneous monastic community encompassing women of middling and even, as lay sisters, lower social rank but dominated by its large numbers of noble and patrician women.

The pressures of ecclesiastical authorities on lay communities like Corpus Domini might be even more variable and complex than financial exigencies and social distinctions. Although popes and bishops were often uneasy about communities of religious women independent of their control, these authorities did not always act aggressively on their anxieties. Ailisia de Baldo and her companions may have been serving their interests in challenging the leadership of Lucia Mascheroni, but the ecclesiastical commission appointed to settle this conflict affirmed the existence of Corpus Domini as a lay community. Both Bernardina and Lucia, as we have seen, had in the main contrived to evade or exploit ecclesiastical initiatives until Verde Pio invited papal action in the affairs of Corpus Domini. Far more important, however, than the intervention of sometimes competing authorities in the life of this community was the influence of an environment enlivened by reformist movements in which religious orders like the Augustinians and Franciscans were polarized by conflicts between the advocates of reform and their opponents.

For it was the centralizing and polarizing forces of these reform movements that were apparently most threatening to the autonomy of a modest lay community like Lucia's, creating the tensions that divided its members. Religious women like Ailisia de Baldo, who were drawn to these movements and who wished to participate actively in them, were quick to perceive the importance of establishing a "power base" in a well-disciplined and well-endowed monastery. Franciscan ideals of reform would have a similar attraction for Caterina Vegri and perhaps others in Lucia's community. Within a decade or so after the introduction of the rule, Corpus Domini, as a focus of Clarist reform in north Italy, became an eminent center of social and religious power, rewarding Verde Pio's investment, it may be, even beyond her expectations.

In its reflection of larger issues, Lucia's plight also suggests that, quite apart from other influences, a community whose sense of commitment and cohesion had sustained its existence for several decades would find it hard to resist the institutional changes that could ensure its permanence. At least as much as other pressures, the strength of these communal bonds, and the desire for continuity, made institutionalization almost inevitable. The greater its vitality, it appears, the more likely a lay community was to invite this transformation. If the early history of Corpus Domini illumines the constellation of meanings a community might have for its makers and its members, Lucia's experience reveals most vividly the power of its affective ties. To her, the community she had promised to preserve was more than the place and property and legal rights on which, during her long ordeal, she based her claims. Emotional rather than proprietorial, Lucia's possessiveness embraced, above all, the "poor little family" (*questa povereta familiola*) of which she was the "mother."[40]

No words express this relationship more eloquently than those in which Caterina Vegri paid tribute to Lucia and her role in the life of Corpus Domini, testifying to her own lasting attachment to "our first mother, sister Lucia Mascheroni, who by God's will received me in this place and was the first to show me, with pure charity and maternal love, how to serve God." Declaring herself always indebted to Lucia's piety, she urged all of her sisters to remember "how truly you are all indebted to her, not only because of the many labors she bore during many years in this place, but also because its beginnings were hers and in the time of her humble rule she always preserved it in good fame, holy peace and honorable

---

[40] For this quotation, see Samaritani, "Ailisia de Baldo" (n. 1 above), 140. For the document from which it comes, see n. 21 above.

life." Praising Christ for this sister from whom they were now separated, Caterina ended with the hope that "in his presence we shall
at last find ourselves united with her most joyfully."[41]

Caterina Vegri, community saint

When in 1438, long before Lucia's ordeal had ended, Caterina wrote
the work in which this tribute appears, the events of the preceding
years were still vivid in her mind and the participants in them were
still living. Probably for this reason, she never permitted anyone
to read her little book, *Le sette armi spirituali*, keeping it completely secret for a quarter of a century. Then in 1463, as abbess of
another Corpus Domini in her native Bologna, on her deathbed she
entrusted her manuscript to the priest who attended her, along with
two brief letters explaining her intentions.[42] Asking that a copy be
sent, first of all, to the sisters of her former community in Ferrara,
she also suggested that her treatise might be circulated more widely,
as a help to all followers of Christ and especially her sister Clarisse.[43]
Whatever Caterina may have intended, her book and most notably
her vision of the Last Judgment in which she saw herself among
the saved were received by those close to her as displaying the
marks of divine favor.[44]

Immediately after her death, her sisters observed the physical
signs of sanctity—the pervasively sweet fragrance associated with
her body and its incorruption when it was disinterred after brief
burial—and one of them described these in a letter that accompanied the copy of her book sent to Corpus Domini in Ferrara.[45] To
this letter were soon added testimonies to her healing power and,
a few years later, a vita, the personal account of Illuminata Bembo,
who had shared Caterina's life in both Ferrara and Bologna.[46] With

---

[41] *Le sette armi spirituali*, 10.1 in Foletti, ed. 156–57.

[42] Ibid., 176. Caterina Vegri was chosen as abbess of the newly established monastery in the city of her birth by her community in Ferrara, which had been entrusted
by papal decree with direction of the new foundation. She departed for Bologna in
July 1456.

[43] Ibid., 162.

[44] For her vision of the Last Judgment, in 1431, see *Le sette armi spirituali*, 10.3–
7, in ibid., 157–58.

[45] See Lombardi (n. 3 above), 149–53.

[46] Illuminata Bembo, who entered Corpus Domini, Ferrara, in its early years as
a Clarist monastery, was a close friend of Caterina there and in Bologna, where
Bembo succeeded Caterina as abbess. Bembo wrote two versions of her vita of
Caterina: an earlier brief personal recollection, surviving in a Brussels manuscript

her incorrupt body as the icon of her Bolognese community and the focus of civic pride, Caterina Vegri would become a "community saint" in a double sense, inspiring her sisters and her fellow citizens to the long and dedicated campaign that finally achieved her canonization as the saint of Bologna in 1713.[47]

But the Caterina Vegri whom we come to know best in the "little book" she wrote as a young woman in Ferrara was also a "community saint" in a more existential sense. It is one that made especially fitting her last request to have a copy of her book sent to the "colegio" of her sisters in Ferrara, the community whose early crises, together with her own, it encompassed. Indeed, the meaning of this somewhat perplexing treatise on the "seven spiritual weapons" can hardly be understood except in the setting of the community in and for which it was composed.[48] Restored to this setting, Caterina's little book may be read with confidence as a personal testament of the young novice mistress, embedded and made exemplary in the record of her teaching.

For in the critical events of her early years in Corpus Domini lies the key to our understanding of the actual experience half hidden in the "temptations and visions" that fill the greater part of her work. Linking the "old" Corpus Domini and the "new," Caterina is the only witness to events otherwise recorded in official documents. Addressed to her "consorelle," especially her "beloved novices," and reflecting the instruction she gave them, her book offers us not only an unusual insight into the making of a gifted teacher but a still rarer glimpse of the adolescent girl whose experience would shape her teaching.

Why the choice of this lay community was made by or for her, Caterina never explained. Before entering Corpus Domini at the age of thirteen, she had, according to her biographer, just spent several years as a companion at court to the young Margherita d'Este.[49] For a girl with her high connections there would, it seems,

---

(see F. Van Ortroy, "Une vie italienne de S. Chaterine de Bologne," *Analecta Bollandiana* 41 [1923]: 386–416); and Bembo's longer *Specchio de Illuminatione* (n. 35 above), completed in 1469 but not printed until 1787.

[47] Serena Spanò Martinelli, "La canonizzazione di Caterina Vigri: Un problema cittadino nella Bologna dei Seicento," in *Culto dei santi, istituzioni e classi sociali in età preindustriale*, ed. Sofia Boesch Gajano and Lucia Sebastiani, Collana di studi storici (L'Aquila: L. U. Japadre Editore, 1984), 719–33.

[48] Foletti, ed. (n. 4 above), 77–78.

[49] Bembo, fol. 60, cited by Foletti, ed., 38–39. Possibly the timing of her departure was related to the court scandal arising from the adultery and execution of the second wife of Niccolò III d'Este.

have been more attractive options among the several prominent Ferrarese monasteries of women. Caterina belonged, after all, to a family of notaries, lawyers, and judges, who had risen to considerable prosperity and influence in Ferrara, and who enjoyed the favor of the ruling house.[50] About her immediate family, however, there are also some perplexities—among them the identity of her father—and more than a breath of scandal; one of her kinsmen, probably her grandfather, died an apostate in 1438, rejecting the sacraments, as he had done for some years, and explicitly refusing burial in the Church.[51]

There may, then, have been personal or familial reasons for entrusting this young girl, like others of respectable status whose futures might be uncertain or who might wish to test their vocations, to the care of the pious women of Corpus Domini, in a setting that required less formal commitment than a monastic community. Caterina clearly regarded Lucia Mascheroni as a maternal figure, though her own mother would live into her seventies, when she was granted permission to become a lay member of Caterina's monastery in Bologna.[52] In any case, family concerns and scandals have no explicit place in Caterina's "little book," which is centered entirely on her community, its members, and their religious life.

By 1438, at age twenty-five, she was writing in and for a Corpus Domini at peace after the years of change and dissension in which she herself had been actively involved. Fully committed, with a convert's zeal, to the ideals of Franciscan reform, she had held out for the most rigorous version of the rule of Saint Clare until she and her companions, absolved of charges of "apostasy," had at last achieved their goal in 1435.[53] In this reformist spirit, she recalled her own conversion to the religious life as a time of intense emotional and spiritual crisis, accompanied by the visionary experiences powerfully evoked in the last long chapters that are the heart of her book.[54]

---

[50] See Foletti, ed., 16–40, for the results of her research on the Vegri family.

[51] On the identity of Giovanni Vegri, who has traditionally been regarded as her father, following Bembo, fol. 61, see Foletti, ed., 27–34. He was probably a son of Bonaventura Vegri, regarding whose apostasy see Foletti, ed., 32–34. It is worth noting that the widow of Bonaventura Vegri, at her death in 1444, left among various bequests to local monasteries the largest of all to Corpus Domini (see Foletti, ed., 34, n. 61).

[52] For the text of the papal decree granting this permission, see Foletti, ed., 176–77.

[53] See Bembo (n. 35 above); for the papal decree of 1435 concerning the rule, see Wadding (n. 1 above), 10:546–47.

[54] *Le sette armi spirituali*, 7–10, in Foletti, ed., 122–61. Although, according to Caterina herself, this work was composed in 1438, internal evidence shows that her

Though she began *Le sette armi spirituali* by recommending to her sisters the weapons of their spiritual battle, it is only in these last chapters that she made clear the nature and meaning of this battle. Only when she arrived at her seventh weapon, the "memory of Scripture," with special reference to the episode of Christ's temptation by Satan, did she announce her intention to speak more fully, making the experience of a "certain religious," herself, an *exemplum* of the tests and temptations of the spiritual life.[55] Occasionally moved to speak out directly but usually referring to herself in the third person, she impersonalized her experiences in ways that obscure but do not really conceal the feelings of an embattled girl striving to realize her genuine spiritual aspirations amid the choices and temptations she faced.

She described herself, in what she saw as her first happy years under the guidance of Lucia Mascheroni, as a strong-willed and sensitive adolescent, over-confident in her own judgment, yet already troubled by doubts about her vocation and by her difficulties over obedience to her superiors. Even in these early years, she had felt herself drawn away from the piety of Lucia Mascheroni by the appeal of Franciscan teaching, to which she was introduced by a confessor of that order whom she had sought out. Doubting the rightness of her choice of Corpus Domini, she was strongly tempted at sixteen to adopt a solitary life, until this crisis was resolved by divine instruction to remain in the "place and life to which she had been called."[56]

Her troubles were intensified when the peace of this "place and life" was disturbed by what Caterina felt as a powerful malign force manifested in the diabolical apparitions and machinations that she described at length. These almost certainly, as Cecilia Foletti suggests, mask a devil of flesh and blood in the person of Verde Pio da Carpi, whom Caterina never mentioned by name.[57] Verde was probably the "highly placed person" who tempted her, unsuccessfully, to leave her community and become a companion to a young noblewoman; but Verde was also certainly responsible, through her plans for Corpus Domini, for a much more serious temptation. Torn

---

autograph copy was made between 1450 and 1456, when she left Ferrara. This copy contains numerous linguistic and orthographical revisions in Caterina's hand but no substantial changes (see Foletti, ed., 103). The autobiographical elements remain intact and attached to a more remote past.

[55] *Le sette armi spirituali*, 7.8, in Foletti, ed., 124.

[56] Ibid., 7.95, in Foletti, ed., 141, and regarding her choice of confessor, ibid., 9.2, in Foletti, ed., 151.

[57] Foletti, ed., 48.

between devotion to Lucia and the powerful appeal of Franciscan ideals, which Verde now proposed to implement, Caterina faced what seemed to her a devastating conflict of loyalties and obedience.

Interpreting visions that she believed to come from God as commands to continue in her loyal obedience to Lucia, she would later discover through what she regarded as genuinely divine inspiration that these visions were actually diabolical deceptions.[58] Rather than persisting in obedience to her superior and resistance to Verde Pio, she should have withdrawn her support of Lucia and accepted as God's will the transformation of her community, which she, too, deeply desired, though she mistrusted its agent. This was the "great error" of which she harshly accused herself, lamenting her long persistence in it and her part in the dissension in her community.[59] Worse still, while she was caught up in its troubles, she was plunged into a profound spiritual crisis by her doubts about such central teachings of faith as the Eucharist, the forgiveness of sins, and the salvation of souls. Although this crisis was resolved in 1431, by a series of "illuminations" culminating in her vision of the Last Judgment, even this consoling vision marked only a temporary victory in the spiritual battle on which she had embarked.[60]

In drawing for herself and others the lessons of her experience, Caterina Vegri was following a familiar path, as she was in making her visions the instruments of her teaching. She was following even more closely, she declared, the example of Saint Francis, "passing by the way of the Cross in true and humble obedience, through the way of temptation to the rewards of consolation."[61] Yet joined to this strong strain of Franciscan affective piety is a more austere and troubled spirituality of incessant inner striving. What gives her teaching a distinctive vitality and a larger significance is her own coming to terms with her experience in a community with which her ties can only be described as symbiotic.

Speaking of the mistakes and rewards of her own apprenticeship to the religious life, in a lively, eloquent vernacular, she offered in herself and in her teaching a model in some ways ideally suited to the guidance of other young novices. But the "way of perfection" on which she led them was beset by difficulties and it had no earthly end. For the dangers and temptations against which she repeatedly

---

[58] *Le sette armi spirituali*, 7.10–110, in Foletti, ed., 124–44, where Caterina describes and interprets these visions.

[59] Ibid., 10.15, in Foletti, ed., 159.

[60] For these visions, see ibid., 8–10, in Foletti, ed., 147–61, and for the date of the last, ibid., 10.3, in Foletti, ed., 157.

[61] Ibid., 7.88–89, in Foletti, ed., 139.

warned her sisters were not of the flesh and the world—the ascetic note is little stressed—but rather temptations of the mind and spirit. The spiritual battle for which she armed them was a lifelong inner struggle to subdue the will and the self, to attain conformity with Christ not in his physical suffering but in his obedience and humility. It was a battle whose earthly victories, though consoling, were only temporary—the outcome remained uncertain.

Although she strongly emphasized the inner spiritual striving of the individual, Caterina never lost sight of the communal life that was its setting. Indeed, in her insistence on the mutual obligations of its members, she showed most clearly the meaning of the community for the young teacher who would contribute greatly to its shaping. She was stern in her warnings to the abbess and other superiors never to place on those subject to them burdens too heavy to bear, urging them to watch constantly for those who might be afflicted in spirit, in order to sustain them with compassionate maternal love. Repeatedly, in the spirit of Saint Clare, she reminded her sisters of the "sweetness of charity" in which they should love the common good and "holy fraternity," obeying equals and inferiors as well as superiors while bearing the burdens and labors of community.[62]

If she seems mindful also of Lucia Mascheroni in her stress on these affective bonds, her thoughts may well have turned to Verde Pio when she vehemently condemned "the damnable and pestiferous striving of worldly ambition" in those "either within or outside the community" who would disturb the peace of communal love that was the mediator of divine grace.[63] Rather, she urged each of the sisters to be "the least and last in all things," acting always to make the community not only the center of their own religious life but also a "model of the Christian life for all Christian people."[64] Marking Caterina Vegri's place in the history of late medieval spirituality and monastic reform, her youthful book shows her clearly as the remarkably gifted teacher who made the lessons of Corpus Domini's early experience a shaping force in this community's later development.

Although she never held an office in Corpus Domini higher than that of novice mistress, for more than twenty years Caterina Vegri molded its religious life by the teaching that helped to make it also a vital center of Franciscan reform in north Italy. As her own rep-

[62] Ibid., 7.120, in Foletti, ed., 120; ibid., 7.120, in Foletti, ed., 146; ibid., 7.91, in Foletti, ed., 140.

[63] Ibid., 9.14–16, in Foletti, ed., 153–54.

[64] Ibid., 8.16, in Foletti, ed., 150.

utation for holiness grew, her community prospered in other ways, increasing dramatically in numbers from perhaps twenty to over one hundred in these two decades. It was this reputation, we are told, that led its members to choose her as abbess of the new Corpus Domini in Bologna, despite the efforts of Borso d'Este to prevent Ferrara's loss of this "holy woman," in whom her own abbess, as she assured the Bolognese authorities, saw nothing less than "a second Saint Clare."[65] Caterina's was a singular contribution to the religious eminence of Corpus Domini, but this community was surely indebted for its social prominence and its appeal to the great families of the city and their daughters, to the investment and influence of Verde Pio. Not least among the many ironies of its early history was the crucial and fortuitous collaboration of its ambitious benefactor and its saintly teacher.

A modern quest for medieval communities of women

Caterina Vegri's share in the shaping of Corpus Domini, along with its other distinctive features, may seem to underscore what is exceptional, even unique, in its story. But perhaps this is simply because its early history shows in high relief features that we often merely glimpse in the records of other communities. How exceptional Corpus Domini really is in its surviving documentation is a question that only more comprehensive research can answer. What can be said is that its early records exemplify most strikingly the character and diversity of the sources on which modern knowledge of medieval religious communities depends. Among these sources, documents pertaining to property, always a prolific generator of records, are commonly the most numerous, encompassing wills, bequests, and donations, as well as acts of purchase, sale, and litigation. Office books, calendars, obituaries, martyrologies, and, more rarely, customaries, histories, and annals all contribute to documenting the history and religious life of medieval communities. Sometimes, as in the case of Corpus Domini, more personal testimonies such as autobiographical, biographical, and religious writings are still extant. Records like these, together with official documents of ecclesiastical and secular authorities, will constitute by far the most substantial portion of the primary sources, both published and unpublished, incorporated in the bibliographies and community records of the Women's Religious Life and Communities project's data base.

[65] Bembo (n. 35 above), fol. 60. On Borso d'Este, see Lombardi (n. 3 above), 142.

From such sources, ranging from the plentiful to the extremely scanty, the participants in this project draw the profile of a community in the data records of the monastic repertory and, wherever possible, identify those members who were most important in its history. The rewards of the quest for individuals are, again, manifest in the case of Corpus Domini. For if Caterina Vegri represents those who are known to us through their own works and other sources, then Bernardina, Lucia, Ailisia, and Verde Pio are members of a much larger company who can be brought into the light of history only through the kinds of official records used in this study. What we can learn about these women from such documents may suggest something of the larger importance of these sources for our understanding not only of women's religious life but of many other aspects of their experience as well. The range of possibilities is, in fact, so extensive as to make the surviving records of women's religious communities and their members the most substantial and coherent body of sources available for the study of European women before 1500.

Focusing here on the initiatives and relationships of individuals has, I hope, shown their often critical importance in the history of women's communities and religious life. Yet this focus must inevitably foreshorten and sometimes distort, pointing out but leaving unexplored themes and questions that must be pursued in larger settings. To probe more deeply the significance of Bernardina Sedazzari's legacy would require anchoring a study much more firmly in the society with which it is concerned. It would mean exploring in depth the place of Corpus Domini and Sant'Agostino in their social and religious environment and their relationship to the other Ferrarese communities of women, which are also encompassed in our project's monastic repertory, as well as to the ecclesiastical authorities and religious orders and reforming movements briefly noted here. Further investigation of the economic problems and social issues examined in this essay would need to consider also the ties between women's communities and an urban and commercial society that was also, perhaps predominantly, courtly and aristocratic.

Pursued in these directions, a "microhistorical" study of this kind might end by making such communities a mirror not only of women's religious strivings but also of their larger social world. Indeed, if there is truth in the perhaps over pessimistic judgment that "we know little about what motivated women, what they experienced and thought, across the social and economic spectrum of late medieval Italy," such studies should contribute a good deal to recovering this history.[66] But our research project is also meant to generate and support the more broadly based "macrohistorical" inquiries demanded by the larger questions raised by the early history of Corpus Domini. I have stressed issues pertaining to late medieval lay communities and their fortunes, but equally important are the social and religious questions posed by a related expansion of monasteries associated with religious orders. In both cases these are questions of great significance for our understanding of what is often called the "women's religious movement" of the later Middle Ages, and they can be most fruitfully explored in the larger contexts, regional and institutional, to which the data base will eventually extend. Exploiting what is, in effect, another research instrument can provide quantitative information on a variety of subjects: for example, the numbers of women's communities in every province, town, or city of those major regions on which work is completed, in different monastic and religious orders, by location, urban or rural.

Eventually data will be retrievable on the relative size of communities in different times and places, about their origins and the circumstances of their foundation, their benefactors, female as well as male, including their relative numbers, their family ties, and the relationships between female and male communities. Other categories for which data can be provided include endowments and relative wealth or poverty, economic, caritative, and educational activities of women's communities, and other aspects of their functions and histories: for example, the numbers and locations of hospitals served by women and of communities of repentant prostitutes. With respect to individuals and groups, information can be supplied regarding those engaged in particular activities, such as teachers, writers, scribes, artists, musicians, or those who represent varieties of devotional practice and spiritual achievement, such as visionaries and mystics, saints and *beate,* including writings by or about these individuals.

Pointing to these possibilities is one of the major aims of this brief excursion into the early history of a single community. There is also the hope of enlisting the support and collaboration of other scholars on both sides of the Atlantic in producing the research

[66] Julius Kirshner, "Wives' Claims against Insolvent Husbands," in *Women of the Medieval World: Essays in Honor of John H. Mundy,* ed. Julius Kirshner and Suzanne F. Wemple (Oxford and New York: Basil Blackwell, 1985), 265.

instruments on which this project has embarked.[67] Only with this cooperation can we test and replace our fragile generalizations about women's religious life during the medieval centuries and open fresh lines of inquiry into the larger experience of medieval women, formulating and finding answers to questions that we have not yet imagined.

Millbrook, New York

[67] Since the initiation of this project in 1982, research has concentrated largely on Italy and the British Isles, with very substantial progress in both areas; work is also under way on Spain, France, Belgium, and Austria. To serve the needs of current scholarship, our computer data base will eventually be accessible to all scholars with interests in the areas of our concern; we hope to supply printouts of bibliography, data on specific communities and individuals, and topically selected lists. We invite the contributions of specialists on particular areas, communities, and individuals. We have prepared and will gladly provide forms for contributions to the repertory and biobibliography and for research in unpublished sources. Address inquiries and requests for printed forms to Mary M. McLaughlin, R.D. 3, Box 422, Valley Farm Road, Millbrook, N.Y. 12545.

ABOUT THE CONTRIBUTORS

SUSAN GROAG BELL   is an affiliated scholar and senior research associate at the Institute for Research on Women and Gender at Stanford University. She is coeditor, with Karen Offen, of *Women, the Family and Freedom: The Debate in Documents, 1750–1950*, 2 vols. (Stanford, Calif.: Stanford University Press, 1983) and the editor of *Women from the Greeks to the French Revolution* (Stanford, Calif.: Stanford University Press, 1980). Presently, she is researching women's relationship to the garden in Western history. She is also the codirector, with Barbara Kanner, of a National Endowment of the Humanities-sponsored project on British women's autobiographies.

JUDITH M. BENNETT   is associate professor of history at the University of North Carolina at Chapel Hill. The author of *Women in the Medieval English Countryside: Gender and Household in Brigstock before the Plague* (New York: Oxford University Press, 1987), she is now working on a study of women in the English brewing industry, ca. 1200–1700.

JAMES A. BRUNDAGE   is professor of history at the University of Wisconsin—Milwaukee. A medieval historian who specializes in the history of law, he is the author of *Law, Sex and Christian Society in Medieval Europe* (Chicago: University of Chicago Press, 1987).

ELIZABETH A. CLARK   is John Carlisle Kilgo Professor of Religion at Duke University. Her most recent books are *Ascetic Piety and Women's Faith: Essays on Late Ancient Christianity* (Lewiston, N.Y.: Edwin Mellen Press, 1986) and *The Life of Melania the Younger: Introduction, Translation, and Commentary* (Lewiston, N.Y.: Edwin Mellen Press, 1984). Currently she is working on a book about the Origenist controversy of the late fourth and early fifth centuries.

MONICA GREEN   is assistant professor of history at Duke University. She teaches medieval European history and the history of science and medicine. Currently, she is preparing a study of early medieval Latin gynecological literature and finishing a translation of the treatises attributed to Trotula.

RUTH MAZO KARRAS   is assistant professor of history at the University of Pennsylvania. Her current research focuses on the history of prostitution and female sexuality in the late Middle Ages, particularly in England. She is also interested in Scandinavian history and has written *Slavery and Society in Medieval Scandinavia* (New Haven, Conn.: Yale University Press, 1988).

MARYANNE KOWALESKI   is associate professor of history at Fordham University. Her research interests include the history of women, work, and the family in medieval towns. Among her recent publications are *Women and Power in the Middle Ages*, coedited with Mary Erler (Athens: University of Georgia Press, 1988), and *Local Markets and Regional Trade in Late Medieval Exeter* (Cambridge: Cambridge University Press, in press).

ROSS S. KRAEMER   is a visiting scholar in religious studies at the University of Pennsylvania. Her research focuses on women's religions in the Greco-Roman period, including Judaism and Christianity. She is the editor of *Maenads, Martyrs, Matrons, Monastics: A Sourcebook on Women's Religions in the Greco-Roman World* (Philadelphia: Fortress Press, 1988) and is presently completing a companion volume to this work with fellowship support from the National Endowment for the Humanities.

MARY MARTIN McLAUGHLIN   is an independent scholar in Millbrook, New York, who is research director of the project "Women's Religious Life and Communities, A.D. 500–1500," founded at Barnard College. The project is designed to collect and computerize data on women religious leaders and religious communities in the Latin West before 1500. Her book, *Powers of Their Own: Women in Western Society from Late Antiquity to the Fifteenth Century*, written in collaboration with J. B. Ross, is forthcoming from Harper & Row.

CAROL NEEL   is associate professor of history at Colorado College. Her research interests include women's roles in medieval society and historical writing in the Middle Ages. She is currently completing a translation, with commentary, of Dhuoda's *Liber Manualis*, a ninth-century Frankish noblewoman's handbook for her children.

JEAN F. O'BARR   is director of women's studies at Duke University where she teaches in the political science department. Her interests focus on contemporary feminism and women in higher education. She is the editor of *Feminist Theory in Practice and Process* (Chicago: University of Chicago Press, 1989), with Micheline Malson, Sarah Westphal-Wihl, and Mary Wyer; *Women and a New Academy: Gender and Cultural Contexts* (Madison: University of Wisconsin Press, 1989); *Reconstructing the Academy: Women's Education and Women's Studies* (Chicago: University of Chicago Press, 1988), with Elizabeth Minnich and Rachel Rosenfeld; and *Sex and Scientific Inquiry* (Chicago: University of Chicago Press, 1987), with Sandra Harding. She currently serves as the editor of *Signs*.

JANE TIBBETTS SCHULENBURG   is professor of history in the department of liberal studies at the University of Wisconsin—Madison. Her publications include "The Heroics of Virginity: Brides of Christ and Sacrificial Mutilation," in *Women in the Middle Ages and the Renaissance: Literary and Historical Perspectives*, ed. Mary Beth Rose (Syracuse, N.Y.: Syracuse University Press, 1986), 29–72; and "Female Sanctity: Public and Private Roles, ca. 500–1100," in *Women and Power in the Middle Ages*, ed. Mary Erler and Maryanne Kowaleski (Athens: University of Georgia Press, 1988), 102–25. She is currently completing a book on female sanctity and "deviancy."

MICHAEL H. SHANK   is associate professor of the history of science at the University of Wisconsin—Madison. His primary research interests are late medieval and early modern natural philosophy and astronomy. He is the author of *"Unless You Believe, You Shall Not Understand": Logic, University, and Society in Late Medieval Vienna* (Princeton, N.J.: Princeton University Press, 1988).

B. ANNE VILEN   is assistant editor of *Signs*.

SARAH WESTPHAL-WIHL   is assistant professor and Canada Research Fellow in the comparative literature program at McGill University. Her publications include "Power and Fantasy in Courtly Love" in *Women and a New Academy: Gender and Cultural Contexts*, ed. Jean F. O'Barr (Madison: University of Wisconsin Press, 1989); and *Feminist Theory in Practice and Process* (Chicago: University of Chicago Press, 1989), co-edited with Micheline R. Malson, Jean F. O'Barr, and Mary Wyer.

INDEX

Aelfthryth, Queen, 227
Affiliated house. *See* Double
  monastery
Agency: of ascetic women, 201,
  205–6; of Beguines, 244,
  258–59; of guildswomen, 20–21;
  of laywomen, 263, 266, 276; of
  married women, 186–89; of
  medieval women, 1, 6–7; of
  Premonstratensian sisters,
  258–59; of prostitutes, 106, 118
Aidan, Saint, 212
Albergati, Cardinal Nicolo, 271
Alderotti, Taddeo, 62
Alexander III, Pope (Rolandus), 97
Alexandria, Catherine of, 2
Andrea, Joannes, 82
Andrew, Acts of, 199–200, 205
Anglo-Saxon Chronicle, 227–28
Anne of Bohemia, 157–59
Anne of Brittany, 141–42
Anjou, Countess of, 140
Annunciation, 154
Anomos, 202
Apocrophyl Acts of the Apostles:
  audience for, 199; history of,
  198; marriage in, 200–204;
  religion in, 201; validity of, 199
Apprenticeship: of nuns, 283; in
  trades, 13, 27–28
Arthurian romance, 162, 180
Artois, Countess of (Mahaut), 140,
  143
Asceticism, 204, 226
Aue, Hartmann von, 162
Augustine, Saint, 84, 211–12, 263,
  266, 270–71
Augustinian reform, 271

Baptism, 200
Barbo, Ludovico, 271

Barking Abbey, 222
Bathhouses, 102, 194. *See also*
  Brothels
Bathild of Chelles, Saint, 208
Beguines: appeal to women, 145;
  attitude of church toward,
  245–46, 258; composition of,
  241–43; condemnation of, 243;
  historical record of, 241–42;
  impact of monastic reform on,
  247–48; life-style of, 249;
  participation in economy, 243;
  similarities to Cistercian nuns,
  248. *See also* Cistercian nuns,
  Mary of Oignies,
  Premonstratensian nuns
Bembo, Illuminata, 279–80
Benedictine Rule, 225
Benton, John, 47, 65
Bequeathals. *See* Inheritance
Berkeley Abbey, 230
Bertha, Saint, 222
Blagny in Artois, 222
Bologna, 279
Bolton, Brenda, 145
Book of Hours, 140, 142–43,
  146–47, 150
The Book of Three Virtues
  (Christine de Pizan), 151
Book owners: and class, 140, 147,
  153; and cultural influence, 136;
  and marriage, 156; numbers of,
  140, 147, 153
Books: collections of, 157; commis-
  sioning of, 150, 152; cost of, 140;
  decoration of, 146–48; inheritance
  of, 141–43; mothers' gifts to
  daughters, 142; religious, 139,
  142, 146; wedding gifts, 156–57
Brooke, Christopher, and C. H.
  Lawrence, 236

Brothel keepers: political power of, 125–26; regulation of, 104, 112–16

Brothels: clientele of, 105, 110–11, 121; establishment of, 94–95, 102; legally sanctioned, 111–12; terms for, 107–8

Brown, Judith, 22

Burgundofara of Faremoutiers-en-Brie, Saint, 208

Bynum, Caroline Walker, 193

Caesaria of Arles, Saint, 208

Cajetan, Cardinal, 91

Canoness, 256. See also Lay sisters

Carolingian reforms, 225, 232

Cassian, John, 211

Catharism, 245

Catherine of Bologna, Saint, 262. See also Vegri, Caterina

Catholic Church: attitude toward beguines, 243, 245–46, 258; attitude toward female sexuality, 239; attitude toward women's literacy, 145; and lay communities, 269–70; and vernacular literature, 158

Celibacy, 200, 206–7, 225, 247

Chastity, 177, 244

Chaucer, 158

Chauliac, Guy de, 61

Childbirth, 40, 73, 206

Choir nun, 256. See also Lay sisters

Cicely, Duchess of York, 145

Cistercian nuns: composition of, 248–49; participation in economy, 249. See also Beguines; Cîteaux, order of; Premonstratensian nuns

Cîteaux, order of, 248–49. See also Cistercian nuns

Clare, Countess of, 140

Clare, order of Saint, 261–62, 273–74

Class privilege: and book ownership, 140, 147; and educated women, 196; and guilds, 12; and marriage, 171, 178–79; and monastic patronage, 234–35. See also Dowry, Economic constraints on women, Economic opportunity for women

Cloister. See Enclosure

Cluniac reforms, 226–27

Communities of women: constraints on, 2–4, 24, 243, 276; creation of, 145, 263–64; economic autonomy of, 267–68; emotional support in, 268, 278, 284; documentation of, 285–87; and guilds, 12; homogeneity of, 277; honor in, 183–85; informality of, 4, 6, 106, 262–63, 266; institutionalization of, 278; internal dissension in, 270, 272–74, 282–83; in literature, 163, 168; and prostitution, 127

Concubinage, 82–83, 179, 204

Conversion legends, 200, 203–4, 206

Corpus Christi, 273

Corpus Domini: dissension in, 270, 274; institutionalization of, 274; leadership of, 268–69; as religious center, 278; significance of name, 268; transformation of, 272, 276

Council of Trosley, 224

Cross dressing, 184, 193–94, 205

Cultural ambassadors, 136–37, 139, 156, 158–59

Cultural influence, women's: and book ownership, 150; and marriage, 139, 160; in medieval society, 7, 136–37, 142, 154–56, 158

Cuthburga of Wimborne, Saint, 208

da Carpi, Verde Pio, 272–73

Dale, Marian K., 12, 17, 24. See also "The London Silkwomen of the Fifteenth Century"

Davis, Natalie Zemon, 21, 75

de Baldo, Ailisia, 268

Decretals, 97–98

Decretum, 81, 88–89, 96–98

dei Gandini, Alberto, 94

de la Tour, Gabrielle, 143

de Pizan, Christine, 147, 149, 151

Deschamps, Eustache, 147

d'Este, Isabella, 144

d'Este, Marchese Nicolò III, 269

d'Este, Margherita, 280

de Troyes, Chrétien, 162
de Villiers, Katherine, 143
de Vitry, Jacques, 95
Devotio moderna, 270
Disease, 40, 121
Divine children, 206
Divine intervention, 206
Divine marriage, 203
Domesday Book, 231
Donations, to monasteries. *See* Patronage: of monasticism
Double monastery: advantages of, 219; church's questioning of, 224; institution of, 211, 251
Dowry, 170–76, 178, 264, 277
Dress code, 94, 104, 122, 266
Dunstan, 227

Economic constraints on women, 2–3, 6, 16, 21, 101, 106, 175, 178, 276
Economic opportunity for women, 7, 12, 119–20, 266
Economy, household. *See* Household economy
Economy, trade. *See* Trade economy
Ecstatic Religion (I. M. Lewis), 204
Education: of boys, 152; of children, 7, 148; of girls, 148–50, 160; medical, 52, 64; of women, 136, 190
Edward the Confessor, 231
Egalitarianism, 53
Eleanor of Aquitaine, 2, 137
Enclosure, 225, 252–53, 257, 269. *See also* Monasticism, female; Sexuality, female: control of
Endowment of monasteries. *See* Patronage: of monasticism
Erec et Enide (Chrétien de Troyes), 162
Eschenbach, Wolfram von, 162
Ethelburga of Barking, Saint, 208
Etheldreda of Ely, Saint, 208
Ethelwold, 227
Eve, 8, 147

Familial obligation, 4, 175–76, 218, 234, 281
Father-daughter relationship, 141, 175. *See also* Dowry

Felicie, Jacoba (or Jacquéline), 52–53, 61, 74
Fiorenza, Elisabeth Schüssler, 177
Fischer, Hanns, 164
Francis of Assisi, 240
Franciscan reforms, 278, 281–84
Freeman, Edward, 231

Garcia Ballester, Luis, Michael McVaugh, and Augustin Rubio Vella, 48, 53
Garosi, Heide, 46
Gertrude of Nivelles, Saint, 208
Gilbert of Tournai, 242–44
Godiva, Countess, 235–36
Gonzaga at Mantua, Countess of, 144
Gottfried, Robert, 45
Gratian. *See Decretum*
Gregory IX, Pope, 96
Gregory of Tours, 205
Gregory the Great, Pope, 211
Guainerius, Anthonious, 62–63, 67
Guilds: access to, 18, 24, 38; in Cologne, 18, 22; formation of, 13, 22, 52; hierarchy in, 12–15; and marriage, 14–15; membership in, 11–12, 15; in Paris, 19, 22–23; political power of, 11, 20; in Rouen, 18. *See also* Class privilege, Communities of women, Economic opportunity for women
Guillaume, Jean-Marie, 220
Gynecological illnesses, 40, 58, 66

Hagiography, 259
Haimo of Halberstadt, 140
Hallaert, M. -R., transcription of Middle English texts, 68–72
Hector and Paris, 167, 169
Heidelberg University, 165
Héloïse and Abelard, 191
Henry VIII, 112
Higounet, 220
Hilda of Whitby, Saint, 208
Hildegard of Bingen, 2, 72
Hildegund, Saint, 193
Historical record: of medicine, 49, 51, 77; paucity of, 2, 24; of religious communities, 185–89, 210–11
Historiography, 8, 137, 194

Honor, female, 168–71, 176–78
Honor, male, 166, 180–81
Honoratus, Saint, 211
Honorius III, Pope, 245
Horsley, Richard, and Ritta Jo
  Horsley, 56
Hostiensis, Cardinal, 81, 91–93
Household economy, 16, 20
Howell, Martha, 21
Hugh, Abbot, 226
Hugh of Fosses, 253
Hughes, Diane Owen, 175
Hughes, Kathleen, 221
Huguccio, 83–85, 93

Iconography, 153, 155, 280
Ideology of women's proper role,
  5, 8, 73, 124–26, 145–47, 153–55,
  179–80, 202, 233, 243
Inheritance, 141–43, 178, 261, 267,
  271, 277
Innocent III, Pope, 97
Insanity, 205
Invasions, 222–24, 228–29
Isabeau of Bavaria, 143, 150
Ivo of Chartres, 230

Jacobsen, Grethe, 21
James of Vitry, and his account of
  Mary of Oignies, 244–47, 252,
  254–56
Jerome, Saint, 81, 85
Jews, 49, 57, 105
John, Acts of, 199–200

Katherine, Saint, 190
Kealey, Edward, 45
Kelly, Joan, 179
Ketsch, Peter, 172
Klapisch-Zuber, Christiane, 176
Kraków, University of, 196

The Ladies Tournament: audience
  of, 165; as experimental text,
  164; origins of, 163–65; women's
  community in, 168
Lateran Council, Fourth, 246
Lay piety, 135–36
Lay sisters: church's attitude
  toward, 256–57, 277–78; and
  class, 277; in community, 263,
  266; in Italy, 262
Lemay, Helen, 62

Leofric, Count, 236
Le sette armi spirituali (Caterina
  Vegri), 279–82
Lévi-Strauss, Claude, 171
Lewis, I. M., Ecstatic Religion,
  204
Leyser, Karl J., 218, 234
Libraries, 141, 143
Liège, 250
Limburg, Duke of (Duke Walraben
  of Limburk), 167
Lindisfarne, 212
Literacy, 76, 136, 139, 145, 159; in
  Latin, 151–53
Literary representation of women,
  8, 76, 137, 149, 154–56, 199–206,
  279–80
Literature: audience for, 176;
  Christian, 199; courtly, 162;
  devotional, 145, 151; vernacular,
  7, 135–36, 151, 158–59
"The London Silkwomen of the
  Fifteenth Century," 26–38
Louis IX of France, 96

Madness. See Insanity
Male appropriation: through
  alliance with women, 274; of
  brothels, 115; of guilds, 19–20,
  23; of medical practice, 52, 65;
  of midwifery, 39; of women's
  honor, 187; of women's
  monasteries, 217, 227, 229–32
Malleus Maleficarum (Jakob
  Sprenger and Heinrich Kramer),
  56
Malnutrition, 40
Map, Walter, 230
Mären: audience of, 164;
  definition of, 163; expression of
  male dominance in, 164
Margaret, Saint, 193
Marital affection, 82–83
Marriage: alternatives to, 191, 245;
  celibacy in, 200, 247; and class,
  178–79; and concubinage,
  82–83; and guilds, 14–15;
  Pauline Code of, 176;
  prescribed, 5, 171; and
  prostitution, 96–98; regulation
  of, 172; and religious life, 5;
  rites of, 146, 151. See also
  Ideology of women's proper role

Martin V, Pope, 266, 271
Martin of Leibitz, 191, 196
Martin of Tours, Saint, 211
Mary Magdalene, Saint, 95–96
Mary of Oignies: childhood of, 246; historical record of, 244; mystical spirituality of, 247; self-mutilation of, 247. *See also* Beguines
Mascheroni, Lucia: departure of, 275; as heir to Corpus Domini, 261, 267; as leader, 272; as mother figure, 278; renunciation of vow, 275. *See also* Lay sisters; Sedazzari, Bernadina; Vegri, Caterina
Medical literature, medieval: audience for, 65–67, 71; comparison of Middle English Texts (table), 70; on gynecology, 64, 66; written by women, 72–73. *See also* Trotula
Medical practice: in England, 54; hierarchy in, 57, 63; historical record of 40–43, 49, 51, 58; licensing of, 52, 55; professionalization of, 44, 57, 76; regulation of, 52–53; in Spain, 48. *See also* Medical literature; Medical practitioners, women; Midwifery
Medical practitioners, women: competition with men, 51–52, 61, 74; in England, 50; exclusion of, 54; in Italy, 46–48; licensing of, 47; Muslims, 48; numbers of, 45–49; roles of, 44, 50
Mendicants, 245
Middle Ages, definition of, 1
Midwifery: definitions of, 58–61; licensing of, 53–55; practice of, 39–40, 44
Modesty, 67–68, 74, 88
Monasteries, numbers of (table), 213
Monasticism: decline of, 224; education and, 152; growth of, 218; political influence in, 272–74; reform of, 233; in rural areas, 217, 219–20; and spiritual suffering, 283–84
Monasticism, female: as alternative to marriage, 145, 191, 197, 218–20, 244, 280–81; church's attitude toward, 226–29; decline of, 210, 215–16, 236; growth of, 214–15; impact of reform, 225–27, 229, 238; leadership of, 220–21, 227; and prostitution, 96, 229; in rural areas, 220; vulnerability of, 222–24, 228, 232
Monasticism, male: clerical celibacy in, 238; growth of, 233; women's patronage of, 217–19, 233–35
Montpensier, Countess of, 143
Morgan Library, 149
Mother-daughter relationship, 19, 142–43, 160
Mugellano, Dino, 94
Münster, Ladislao, 46
Muscio, 66
Muslims, 48, 57

Nicholas V, Pope, 261
Norbert of Gennep, 250, 253
Norman Conquest, 216, 222

Oda of Rivreulle: childhood of, 254; as model for Mary of Oignies, 256; piety of, 256; self-mutilation of, 255
Odo of Cluny, Saint, 226
Oswald, King, 212, 227

Park, Katharine, 46
Parmesis, Bernardus, 97
Parzival (Perceval), 140, 163
Patronage: literary, 136, 144, 155; of monasticism, 3, 272, 276–77; of women's monasteries, 219, 233–35, 265–66, 270
Paul, Acts of, 203
Paul and Thecla, Acts of, 199
Pauline Code of Marriage, 176
Peter, Acts of, 202
Philip, Acts of, 205
Philip of Harvengt, account of Oda of Rivreulle, 254
Power, Eileen, 2
Premonstratensian nuns: composition of, 248–50; contemplation of, 253; expulsion of, 251; life-style of, 252; as models for Beguines, 250–52;

participation in economy, 252. *See also* Beguines; Cistercian nuns; Prémontré, order of
Prémontré, order of, 248; attitude toward female sexuality, 257; misogyny of, 250–51, 253; *See also* Premonstratensian nuns
Promiscuity, 81
Prosopography, 43, 45, 50, 264
Prostitute: life-style of, 118; rights of, 91–96, 119–20
Prostitution: acceptance of, 84–85, 98–102, 124, 126–27; canonist's treatment of, 80–85, 99; in conversion legends, 206; definition of, 79–82; economic imperatives for, 90, 101, 104–5, 121, 179; and female monasticism, 229; and guilds, 94; in London, 109–10, 123; prohibition of, 106–8; punishment of, 89, 107, 122; regulation of, 102–7, 113–20; response of church to, 97–99; and restrictive dress, 94, 104, 122; and social status, 90–92
Psalter, 141, 149

Radegund of Poitiers, Saint, 208
Rape, 22
Reformation, the, 7, 159
Repgow, Eike von, 142
Richard of Cornwall, 167
Roman law, 80
Rowland, Beryl, transcription of Middle English texts, 68–72
Rubin, Gayle, 171, 186
Rufinus, 83
Rycwer, 254

Sachsenspiegel (Eike von Repgow), 142, 158, 174
Saints' lives, 194, 210, 244–46, 254–56, 259–60
Salaberga of Laon, Saint, 208
Salernitan women, 47, 51, 58
Salvot, Michel, 59
San Barnaba, 271
Sanctity, 279
Sandwich, 112, 120
San Silvestro, 265
Santa Giustina, 271
Sant'Agostino, 271

Schönfeld, Walther, 49
Sedazzari, Bernadina: and dowry, 264–65; founder of Corpus Domini, 262, 264; as leader, 267–68; and Lucia Mascheroni, 267
Self-mutilation, 247, 255
Sex, extramarital, 85
Sexual division of labor: in medical practice, 41, 57, 61, 74; in medieval society, 168
Sexuality: control of, 107, 123, 126–27, 200, 203–4, 257; male, 8–9, 88, 101, 106; in medieval ideology, 8–9, 85–89, 99, 105; suspicion of, 86–90, 202–3, 206, 239
Single women, 119, 170, 179
Social dramas, 193
Southwark Ordinances regarding prostitution, 128–34
Southwark, regulation of prostitution in, 100–127
Spinsters, 119
Spoleto, 262
Sprenger, Jakob, and Heinrich Kramer, 56
Stereotypes of women: crusading harlot, 93; scholar abbess, 197; temptress, 101, 282
Stews, the, 109. *See also* Brothels
Stuard, Susan Mosher, 47

Taddea, 272
Talbot, C. H., and E. A. Hammond, 45
Talbot, Charles, 58
Technology, 139
Tertiaries, 240
Tertullian, 199
Teutonicus, Joannes, 88
Thecla, Acts of, 203
Thomas, Acts of, 200, 203, 205
Thomas, Saint, 92
Tithes, 92
The Tournament of Nantes (Konrad von Würzburg), 167
Trade economy, 4, 13, 286
Treatise on the Womb (Anthonius Guainerius), 62–63
Trotula, 47, 65–67, 72; texts of, 68–72
Turner, Victor, 193

Urban life, 11–13, 286

Vegri, Caterina: as author of *Le sette armi spirituali*, 279–82; childhood of, 282; as community saint, 279–80; of Corpus Domini, 262–63, 274; as daughter, 278–79; and familial obligation, 281; leadership of, 283–84; as role model, 284–85. *See also* Lay sisters; Mascheroni, Lucia; Sedazzari, Bernadina
Venice, 265
Vernacular literature. *See* Literature: vernacular
Vienna, University of, 196
Vincent of Beauvais, 148
Virginity, 204

Virgin Mary, 8, 145, 154–55, 262, 266
Virgins, veiled, 266

Weapons, and women, 184
Wedding gifts, 151, 156–57, 172–74. *See also* Marriage, rites of; Books
Wemple, Suzanne, 237
Westminster, Matthew of, 235
White Ladies, the, 96
Wickersheimer, Ernest, and Danielle Jacquart, 45
Wiesner, Merry, 21, 51, 75
Wills. *See* Inheritance
Winchester, Bishop of, 111, 125
Witchcraft, 56
Würzburg, Konrad von, 165, 167
Wycliffe, 158